# KAHN
# ON
# CODES

ALSO BY DAVID KAHN

*The Codebreakers*
*Hitler's Spies*

# KAHN
# ON
# CODES

---

## Secrets of the New Cryptology

---

## by DAVID KAHN

MACMILLAN PUBLISHING COMPANY

New York

*To Oliver and to Michael*

Macmillan Publishing Company
866 Third Avenue, New York, N.Y. 10022
Collier Macmillan Canada, Inc.


**Library of Congress Cataloging in Publication Data**

Kahn, David, 1930–
    Kahn on codes.

    Includes bibliographical references and index.
    1. Cryptography—Addresses, essays, lectures.
I. Title.
Z103.K29 1983    001.54'36    83–16213
ISBN 0–02–560640–9

10  9  8  7  6  5  4  3  2  1

Printed in the United States of America

# Contents

Z
103
.K29
1985

INTRODUCTION      vii

UNCOVERING CRYPTOLOGY'S PAST      1

*Conversations with Cryptologists*      3
*Interviews with Cryptologists*      10
*How* The Codebreakers *Was Written*      18

OVERVIEWS      23

*Lgcn Otuu Wllwgb Wl Etfown; or, "They Will Attack
     at Midway"*      25
*The Code Battle*      32

HISTORICAL AND TECHNICAL STUDIES      49

*The Grand Lines of Cryptology's Development*      51
*On the Origin of Polyalphabetic Substitution*      56
*Herbert O. Yardley: A Biographical Sketch*      62
*Yardley's "Lost" Manuscript*      72
*The Spy Who Most Affected World War II*      76
*The* ULTRA *Conference*      89
*Codebreaking in World Wars I and II: The Major Successes and
     Failures, Their Causes and Their Effects*      99
*Plaintext in the New Unabridged*      120

The Ché Guevara Cipher                                        139
Two Soviet Spy Ciphers                                        146

## THE POLITICS OF CRYPTOLOGY                                 165

American Codes and the Pentagon Papers                        167
Tapping Computers                                             170
Big Ear or Big Brother?                                       173
Cryptology Goes Public                                        186
Statement Before the House Government Information and
    Individual Rights Subcommittee                            204

## BOOK REVIEWS                                               211

The Ultra Secret                                              211
The Man Who Broke Purple                                      214
Ultra Goes to War and Piercing the Reich                      216
The American Magic                                            221

## CODES IN CONTEXT                                           225

The Defense of Osuga, 1942                                    227
Potential Enemies: The United States Views Germany
    and Japan in 1941                                         249

## THE FUTURE                                                 279

Opportunities in Cryptology for Historians                    281
Signals Intelligence in the 1980s                             292

## NOTES                                                      297

## ACKNOWLEDGMENTS                                            334

## INDEX                                                      336

# Introduction

Cryptology has gone public. A field that was once the exclusive domain of governments has become a concern of businesses and individuals. Behind their concern lie fears about thefts of proprietary information or of services, such as subscription television programs broadcast from satellites, and fears about loss of privacy, as through unauthorized inspection of personal information in computer data banks.

Companies and non-national-security agencies of government, such as health administrations, will now pay for cryptologic protection against wiretapping, interception, or improper access. Their money has attracted many private-sector individuals and companies to cryptology. This influx has led to conflicts with the government's cryptologic organization, the National Security Agency, and has raised—for the first time—political questions in the field.

The presence of many new people in cryptology and the existence of these new matters makes it seem worthwhile to assemble in this more convenient form articles that illuminate the field as a whole or explore its new situation but that appeared in publications now hard to get at. Those printed here, though published in some cases many years ago, retain, I believe, their relevance. Articles that have become outdated are excluded, such as a 1966 piece in *Scientific American* that has nothing on the data encryption standard or public-key cryptography, or a 1969 bibliography that appeared before the outpouring of books on the British solution of the German Enigma cipher machine. Also excluded are reprints of material previously published elsewhere, such as chapters of *Hitler's Spies*. The book reviews that are included comprise only those of major books or those that offer some useful ideas.

As the product of one mind, the articles overlap a little and some material repeats—such as the story of codebreaking and the Battle of Midway, or the explanation of the one-time pad. But the duplication is less than I had expected, and I have not deleted those sections because to do so would destroy the integrity of the pieces.

Articles are in general run as they originally appeared, leaving in ideas that I have later abandoned or information that new evidence has shown to be incorrect. I have given the new ideas or correct information in footnotes. Footnotes also add names and facts not given in the original articles. But slight changes in wording, elimination of such terms as "recently," and similar minor improvements in the text are not signaled. In the articles from *The Cryptogram*, I have replaced the "codenames" of members of the American Cryptogram Association, such as AB STRUSE and THE OAK, with their real names. Some of the articles have been renamed, but the source notes give the original title.

I hope that this collection, which brings together articles from periodicals as diverse as *Playboy*, *Foreign Affairs*, and *Historical Journal*, will entertain and instruct the flood of persons newly interested in cryptology. Greater knowledge of its history and its politics will, I am confident, help their advance into the future.

DAVID KAHN

*Great Neck, New York*

# UNCOVERING CRYPTOLOGY'S PAST

# Conversations with Cryptologists

Those members of the American Cryptogram Association (A.C.A.) who, like myself, learned their cryptology as isolated youngsters, by mail and by books, may have developed an attitude of awe similar to mine toward the authors of those books. They seemed to be remote, unapproachable, infallible givers of the law, the almost legendary members of a cryptologic pantheon, disembodied beings who had never done such mundane things as work for a living (cryptology couldn't be work), enjoy a steak or look at a pretty girl, who had no existence beyond that frozen in their books. For a long time I thought that this feeling was mine alone. Then in 1962 I had the pleasure of meeting the widow of Herbert O. Yardley. She told me how, when Henry E. Langen first met Yardley, he displayed all the symptoms of acute hero-worship until Yardley, removing his shoes, told Langen to take off his tight new pair and relax. From that moment on, Langen saw Yardley in a new dimension—as a human being—and the two grew to be good friends.

The story has some pertinence to this article, for it is intended to restore that missing dimension to a number of famous cryptologists. We in the U.S. know them only by their reputations, which have long spangled the cryptologic firmament. Distance lent enchantment, and so when I went to Europe on a three-week vacation in the spring of 1962 with the hope of visiting some of them, I half expected to meet

"Conversations with Cryptologists" first appeared in the November-December 1962 and the January-February 1963 issues of *The Cryptogram*.

demigods. I found human beings, whose only divinity resided in their uniform hospitality, intelligence and consideration.

It all began when I arrived at the airport bus terminal in the north of Stockholm shortly before noon on April 28. I heard my name paged, and then I recognized Kaljo Käärik, a fellow A.C.A. member, who had sent me a photograph of himself. (This meeting, like all others, had been arranged by mail.) Käärik told me that Yves Gyldén was inside the terminal. Yves Gyldén![1] The author of the only book-length study of cryptology in World War I; the writer of numerous scholarly articles on historical matters; a man whose painstaking accuracy, judicious opinions and cogent conclusions remain virtually unparalleled among published authors. In a moment, a tall gentleman moved with immense dignity into the sunlight. He was wearing a heavy brown overcoat and a black homburg, and he used an umbrella as a cane. Gyldén shook hands with me, and in his grave voice, speaking a slightly accented English, welcomed me to Sweden.

We piled into Käärik's car and drove to my hotel, the Reisen. There we chatted for a while, Gyldén telling me some stories of his work in solving codes for his country. He recites all the details of an episode in a very thorough manner, and is scrupulous in assigning credit to others. His remarks are illuminated with rather striking observations, the fruits, I believe, of broad experience mellowed by long reflection. For example, nearly everyone knows that errors made by inexperienced code clerks constitute a prime source of tips to the cryptanalyst. But who except Gyldén would have commented that experienced code clerks can be of almost as much help? He explained that the identification of the codeword for *stop* constitutes an important first step in cracking a code, for it permits the cryptanalyst to hypothesize the structure of the plaintext message. Now, inexperienced code clerks will carefully rotate the codewords for *stop* among the various homophones provided and thus make it difficult to identify the stops. But as clerks grow increasingly familiar with the code, they will find themselves remembering some of codewords for *stop*. They will use these codewords to avoid the work of turning the pages of the codebook to look up the others, and so the protection afforded by the multiplicity of equivalents is gradually eroded. "They don't use just one equivalent—they know that would be too dangerous—but they seldom use more than two," Gyldén said.

During the four days I spent in that great northern city, I conversed many times with Gyldén. A few of the talks were in his home, a spacious apartment on the fifth floor of the building numbered 130 on Valhallava-gen, a broad avenue whose apartment houses, Gyldén says, are inhabited by many retired army officers. Gyldén comes from one of Sweden's oldest non-noble families; it is listed in the Swedish version of the commoner's Social Register. His grandfather, who has a street in Stockholm named for him, was director of Stockholm's astronomical observatory; his father was head of the Royal Naval School. He himself was born in 1895 and spent most of his business life working for Astra, a Swedish pharmaceutical firm, of which he was export director at the time of his retirement. Thanks to a decade in France, he speaks French fluently, and his English is sprinkled with Gallicism—"I assisted at the conference" for "I attended the conference," *assister à* being the French for "to attend."

Gyldén says he wrote his epochal study of cryptology in World War I (published in 1931 and translated into English in 1935 as *The Contribution of the Cryptographic Bureaus in the World War*)[2] to show the doubters just what cryptanalysis could do. An unrelenting foe of the foolish and excessive secrecy that so often surrounds cryptology, he stressed that a great dissemination of information in his sphere would reduce the dangers of ignorance in cryptologic matters. He earned his first money in cryptanalysis in 1934—30 crowns for solving a smugglers' cipher. He showed me the original worksheets—neat frequency tables, clearly printed cipher alphabets—and the newspaper clippings telling of the arrest of the bootleggers by police who knew just where to wait for them. During World War II, Gyldén served as head of the section of the Swedish cryptanalytic office that solved Romance-language codes, particularly French and Italian. He told me that Rickard Sandler, author of *Chiffer* (Stockholm, 1943) was a former foreign minister of Sweden—making him perhaps the highest-ranking author of a book on cryptology[3]—who served for a while as liaison man between the Foreign Office and the Swedish cryptanalytic bureau. Gyldén donated all but a very few items of his cryptologic library to the Swedish defense department; among the remaining documents is a mimeographed copy of an unfinished textbook on cryptology in Swedish,[4] co-authored by Gyldén and Ivar Damm, a mathematician and brother of Arvid Damm, a Swedish textile engineer who designed and sold cipher machines through a firm that was the predecessor of the present Hagelin company.[5]

During my stay in Stockholm, Gyldén could not do enough for me. He took me to the royal archives to examine Swedish codes of the 1700s, was my host (with Käärik) at dinner on a tiny island in the middle of that Venice of the north, and arranged interviews for me. Thus, when I telephoned to his house to thank him on the eve of my departure and learned that he had just suffered a slight stroke, I feared that his exertions for me had brought it on. His son denied it, however, and so has he, saying it was expected because of his too intensive work in the past few years. He writes that he is home recuperating and that "the spirit is still unconquered."[6]

Not as well known as Gyldén, probably because his publications have not yet achieved the circulation that the older man's have, is Hans Rohrbach. Yet his remarkable article on "Mathematical and Mechanical Methods in Ciphering and Deciphering," published in German in 1948 in the *FIAT Review of German Science*, affords virtually the only available description of the advanced cryptologic techniques used by the German Foreign Office during World War II.[7] Rohrbach, who was awarded a doctorate in mathematics in 1932 from the University of Berlin, was drafted into the German army signal corps with cryptographic duties near the start of World War II, but was soon transferred to the German Foreign Office, where he specialized in stripping the additive from enciphered code. He is now head of the department of mathematics at the University of Mainz, one of Germany's oldest universities, and is co-editor of the *Journal für die reine und angewandte Mathematik* (Journal of Pure and Applied Mathematics), one of the world's oldest and most respected mathematical publications.

Rohrbach picked me up at 8 P.M. May 2 [1962] at the Rheinhotel Roemer-keller and drove me through the spring night to his office on the lovely campus. He is of medium height, in his 50s, with closely cropped graying hair. He had spent a year as a guest professor at the University of North Carolina about five years ago (during which time he corresponded with the former A.C.A. president Jack Levine) and so he was able to converse in English. It was a bit rusty at first, but it improved noticeably during the conversation. After his teenaged twins had gone to sleep, he brought me to his apartment, on the third floor of a building on the campus used for faculty housing. His wife served orange juice and cookies, and we spent the rest of the evening chatting about the United States. A few nights later, when Mrs. Rohrbach was away helping their newly married daughter get settled, Rohrbach and I sat together in his book-lined study, cracked a bottle of chilled Rhine wine and, sipping it from long-stemmed glasses, talked for hours about cryptology. His memory is remarkable: he recalled names, places, details and cryptanalytic techniques. He told me, with a regret that will be shared by many students of cryptology, that the fascinating list of official German technical works given in the bibliography of his article were all irrevocably lost shortly after the end of the war; his citations were made from memory. He was overwhelmingly gracious; he made long-distance telephone calls to set up appointments for me. His personality made a distinct impression on me. As far as these things can be caught in words, it seemed to me both strong and gentle. When his wife telephoned him that evening, a pleased smile spread over his features as he greeted her. Toward the end of the evening, when the pace of the conversation had slowed and the last of the wine had been consumed, Rohrbach mentioned that he had been asked whether he might like to take charge of Germany's postwar Foreign Office code and cipher (cryptanalytic) bureau. He said that he had agonized for a while over the offer, but before he could decide, the post was given to someone. I asked him then whether he had liked his cryptologic work. "Yes," he replied, "I liked it very much. . . ."

The most surprising thing about Luigi Sacco is that he has been out of cryptology since 1923. It is surprising because the third edition of his *Manuale di Crittografia*, the world's finest unclassified book on cryptology,[8] was published in 1947, and his important study of the sources of modern cryptology, *Un Primato Italiano*, first appeared in the same year. One can only wonder what his output would have been had he continued as a professional in the field until after World War II, as his successor, who is almost exactly his age, did.

If you need a cliché to describe Sacco, you might call him a lively old gaffer. He's close to 80, but he's alert, lively, with a quick sense of humor. Short and slight, with a bit of the paunch that comes with age, he has a heart-shaped face with bulging cheeks and a pointed chin. His eyes twinkle under a bald pate as his conversation bubbles along to the accompaniment of numerous smiles, gestures and interesting questions.

During most of the brilliant career that made him the first Italian army officer from a technical service to become a general (he retired with the permanent rank of lieutenant general), Sacco served as an expert in radio transmissions. His particular specialty, in which he wrote papers and gave lectures at the University of Rome, was the propagation of radio waves. He attended a number of international telecommunication conferences as Italy's representative.

My visit, May 10, with Sacco was my second; I had met him for the first time five years before, on my first visit to Europe. He spoke little English, and I no Italian, but we got along famously for four hours in French. I arrived this time at the same as before: about 5 o'clock, as the setting sun was gilding the Tiber, which flows under the window of his rather sumptuous apartment at Lungotevere Flaminio 22 in Rome. Mrs. Sacco, a plump and charming woman, set out a bottle of cognac and some cookies for us, and we began talking.

Let no one tell you that great works are always the result of premeditation. Want to know the real cause of Sacco's *Un Primato Italiano?* It is that a good friend of his was the head of the Italian library system at a time when demobilization imposed an enforced leisure upon Sacco. Whenever he needed a rare item, the friend had it shipped to a library in Rome. Sacco thus had both the opportunity and the material for a thorough study of the original documents of the cryptology of the Italian Renaissance, and so produced an important contribution to the history of the subject.

For a man whose book contains one of the more complete of the modern bibliographies, Sacco himself has a rather abbreviated selection of books on cryptology. They fill only one four-foot shelf and are largely the standard works. An outstanding exception is his fine assemblage of works dealing with the Renaissance. Many of them are copies typed by his wife. One of them served to illustrate how sharp his memory is. I had written to the archives of Venice to ask the price of a photostat of a dispatch that Sacco had cited in his book as the oldest extant cryptogram to be written with a fully developed cryptographic system. Sacco had written that the item was dated 1411, but the reply from the archives stated 1441. Since that would mean that other dispatches would have usurped the priority and since I thought that a letter direct from the archives would probably be more accurate than a book, whose copy passes through several stages of writing, typing, and typesetting, I asked Sacco about it. He promptly fetched the proper article, opened it to a reproduction of the dispatch and pointed out the 1411 date right on it. Sacco probably hadn't thought of this particular datum for half a dozen years, and the episode demonstrates how this sharp mind retains its acuity.

The only professional cryptologist I spoke to who was still active in the field is Charles Eyraud, author of *Précis de cryptographie.* I had met Eyraud also in 1957, when we talked for an hour over coffee at the Café des Deux Magots, the hangout of existentialist Jean-Paul Sartre (to whom all existence may be a cipher). This time I met Eyraud at his office in the French Navy Department, where he is employed as instructor in cryptology. When I arrived, about 2:30 P.M. on May 14, he was preparing an exercise on an old Hagelin machine. He works in a small cubicle, with a desk, two chairs and two cabinets, that overlooks a courtyard in the navy's office building 15 rue de Laborde, Paris. Book collectors will drool when they hear that piled atop one of the cabinets were almost a dozen copies, a bit dusty but otherwise apparently in mint condition, of the hard-to-find *Cours de cryptographie* by General Marcel Givierge. Also on the cabinet were several stacks of the second edition of Eyraud's own book, an expanded, reset, orange-bound tome. I tried to beg, borrow or even buy one of these exceedingly rare items, but Eyraud turned me down. It was, he said, a naval publication for official use and not for sale. (I thought of stealing one, but lacked the nerve.)

Eyraud is a small man, about five feet four inches in height, in his 60s, bald, a chain-smoker of those brownish French cigarettes. He talks like a machine gun, with wild gesticulations, and when reciting his wartime stories, with a full self-accompaniment of sound effects, I thought he was going to explode. An engineer, he got into cryptology after the fall of France almost by accident. He was out of work, and a friend offered him a job in the Vichy cryptanalytic bureau. To get the job, he had to stand on a street corner sporting a boutonniere and some prearranged items of clothing and waiting for someone to approach him with the proper password, for all the world like a spy in some movie. The melodrama did not end there either, for at one time he had frantically to burn a batch of papers on the approach of the Gestapo. But if that was just like the movies, his work was not: the cryptanalytic bureau was installed in a villa outside Lyons,[9] and until the Germans overran all of France he worked in that idyllic setting.

After the liberation, he got his present instructorship. I was pumping him about it at the end of our three-hour talk as we were walking across the courtyard to his automobile. He put me off gently: "You must not think, monsieur, that I am a very important person." A few minutes later, he dropped me at the Café de la Paix, and within seconds his car disappeared in the rush-hour traffic that swirled through the Place de l'Opéra.

# Interviews with Cryptologists

I have to begin with a disclaimer. The most frequent word that you'll be hearing from me tonight is the most odious of pronouns. But the reason is not that I want to play the great "I am." The fault lies in the topic. Lou Kruh [the organizer of the convention] asked me to talk about some of my personal experience in meeting cryptologists. And the one thing that these experiences have in common is that they all happened to me. But instead of concentrating on my person, please put yourself in my shoes and travel around with me. For, as I'll make clear at the end of this talk, I am, in a sense, just you.

As you can imagine, I began this business of interviewing cryptologists when I began researching *The Codebreakers*. I've written in *The Cryptogram* about the most important of these interviews.[1] There was, for example, Yves Gyldén, the Swedish author of *The Contribution of the Cryptographic Bureaus in the World War*. In furnishing quantities of information about the Swedish cryptanalytic effort in World War II, he gave me my first real glimpse into such an agency. There was Hans Rohrbach, author of a technical mathematically oriented article in a postwar review of German science.[2] In the interview, he filled in the names and countries that he had omitted from the article. There was Charles Eyraud, who told a little, a very little, about his cryptanalysis for Vichy France—mainly, I now believe, because he didn't have much to tell.

"Interviews with Cryptologists" was originally delivered as a speech at the annual dinner of the American Cryptogram Association, 1974; it was subsequently published in the April 1980 issue of *Cryptologia*.

But these interviews belong now to my past. I'd like to talk to you about those that belong to my present. They're the ones I have made for the book I'm now writing—on German military intelligence.[3] It covers more than just codebreaking, but that and its associated fields in radio intelligence, such as traffic analysis and evaluating the whole output, were extremely valuable to the Germans. In fact, in World War II, radio intelligence furnished their most important intelligence. Consequently, I interviewed many who were in this work for the Germans. And as you can imagine, I found these interviews more interesting than many of my others.

One of the first of the German cryptologists I met was Fritz Nebel. His name may mean nothing to you, but his achievement will: he was the inventor in World War I of the ADFGVX cipher.[4] I first met Nebel through a member of the American Cryptogram Association, Herbert Flesch. Flesch was a signal officer in the Luftwaffe and through a mutual acquaintance met Nebel, who had served in radio in World War I, had worked in business, and then had returned to radar in World War II. Nebel is a remarkable person.[5] He seems to know everybody in military communications, and since cryptology came under signals in the German armed forces, this meant he knew most of the leading personnel in that field as well. But the most amazing things about him—from my point of view, at least—are his memory and his ability to grasp what you're after. I remember that the first time I interviewed him I wanted to get some detail on what the place looked like where he worked when he got the idea for the ADFGVX. It sounds like a simple question, but somehow people don't always see what the interviewer is driving at— namely, some color. Nebel caught on at once, and instantly sketched for me the hotel in which the German army high command was then housed, showing me in which wing he had been and so on. He also gave me some very good word pictures of the people who had been in this work, and later on gave me some good hints as to where I might find some of the very hard-to-find World War I archival material.

Nebel also made one of my most productive interviews possible. It was with one of the surviving heads of perhaps the most secret agency in Nazi Germany—the Forschungsamt. This was Germany's main wire-tapping agency, which also did a great deal of important political and economic intercept and codebreaking activity. While writing *The Code-breakers*, I had sought information about it. But I had not been able to glean more than a few scraps of material. Nebel, however, had served, before World War I, in a radio unit in Münster with the man who later became a Forschungsamt department head. Nebel, who keeps up with everybody, knew or found out for me where this man lived. Then he telephoned him, giving me a warm recommendation—for Nebel and I had gotten on very well. This got me my interview: the man later told me that if Nebel had not recommended me, he would not have spoken to me.

He was Walter Seifert. The interview with him was, as I said, one of the most productive that I had. Why? Because, I believe, the elements that must be present on both sides for a successful interview were in fact present. On the interviewer's side these are knowledge of the subject and careful preparation. The more one knows, the better questions one can ask. On the interviewee's side, one element is again knowledge of the subject—in other words, his being in a position where he would know firsthand the things of interest. The other element is his emotional involvement in his work. The more interested he was, the more he will remember. Both these elements were present in Seifert. Seifert had been in radio in World War I, and during the '20s had worked in the Defense Ministry's Cipher Center. After Hitler took power, one of his associates in the Cipher Center proposed the creation of the Forschungsamt, which was accepted. Seifert joined in July 1933, a few months after the Forschungsamt came into being in April 1933. He was thus in at virtually the start of the agency's existence, eventually becoming the head of the evaluation department. This, together with his long background in the Cipher Center, with its extensive links to many people in communications intelligence, gave Seifert the first of the interviewee's necessities for a good interview: a good vantage point. And he also had the other requirement: emotional involvement. Seifert believed in the importance of communications intelligence, and he believed strongly in Hitler and became a Nazi—saying as much to me with commendable candor. Consequently, he was highly motivated in his work, and this led him to remember it clearly.

I met Seifert about 10 A.M. in his home, a tiny one-story kind of row garden apartment in Osnabrück. He was rather short, with a round head, a pug nose, a strong cigar, and a nice smile.

I set up my tape recorder and took out my list of questions. I usually begin my interviews by asking, "How did you come to this job?" I feel this question is easy and personal to get the interviewee to start talking, while also providing some important information. That's how I began with Seifert. He responded with a very to-the-point answer, not too short, not too digressive. I then pressed on, asking questions about other members of the Forschungsamt and why they had quit the Cipher Center to join it, his daily routine, the organization of the

Forschungsamt, how many intercepts a day came in, what its main successes were, both technical, as in solving a particularly difficult cipher, and political, as when an intercept enabled Germany to win a diplomatic or a military victory. He gave good answers.

Here are a series of questions and answers translated from the transcript that show the kind of information he supplied:

KAHN: Do you remember which systems you cracked—I mean American and English and French. Could you do the higher ones?

SEIFERT: Not all. There were several, but with France, Italy, and England we did crack the higher systems.

KAHN: For the English ones even to the end of the war?

SEIFERT: No, at the end, no longer.

KAHN: When did it stop?

SEIFERT: I only saw the effect. I got the decrypted reports for working up, so I cannot say exactly, and [Georg] Schröder, who was responsible for it [the cryptanalysis], is no longer alive.

KAHN: You don't know how it was with the higher American systems? How high?

SEIFERT: I don't know. I don't think that we had the highest systems. But I might add, we had the systems of small nations, Yugoslavia, Turkey, etc., and through these one broke into the others. We had a Dr. Müller, who was the main French cryptanalyst in the Defense Ministry, Helmut Müller, who didn't think much of mathematics but had a feel for the things, who said to me once, "They always begin with 'Telegram No. X,' then I know that I have the first break."

KAHN: You didn't have strategic insights into the Allied planning?

SEIFERT: No. *That* no one had.

KAHN: Was that because they weren't broken or because they weren't radioed?

SEIFERT: I don't know.

And so on. This interview lasted three hours, or until 1 P.M. By then I had covered all the points on my three pages of questions, and we were both tired. It's fatiguing to listen very attentively, and it must be just as tiring to give constantly of one's self.

I retain such good memories of this interview in part because it produced so much good information. But mainly it is because the information it yielded was some that I had long been seeking. The interview resolved a certain tension. It completed something. That's why I think back often on Seifert and my interview with him with such good feelings.[6]

Another interview that I think back on with satisfaction is that of Fritz Neeb. I heard his name first from a man who was the liaison of the German communication intelligence organization on the eastern front to General Gehlen, head of German army intelligence in the east and after the war head of the German Federal Republic's intelligence agency. This man recommended that I interview Neeb, who, like him, lived in Vienna. I telephoned Neeb, set up an appointment, and went out to his home. He too had the ingredients of a good interviewee. He had been interested in cryptology as a youth, and so when he was drafted into the German army, they sent him first into cryptography as a cipher clerk, and then later into communications intelligence. From early in the Russian campaign until its close, he served as the second in command of the communications intelligence unit of Army Group Center. The commander of this unit changed frequently, so Neeb had, despite his relatively low rank, considerable control. This insight, and his continuity in the work, together with his great interest in it, made him an ideal subject. Another factor, incidentally, was that he had never told his story before. Now, after storing up his war memories for 30 years, he could finally pour them out to an interested and knowledgeable listener. I think this charged the interview with an electricity that lifted it above the ordinary.

Neeb told me about his 24-hour routine, with its twice-daily work-ups of first the day's and then the night's results for the intelligence staff conferences. He told me about the lack of major radio deceptions on the part of the Russians. He told about his best result: the detection well in advance of a major Russian offensive, giving the numbers of the German and the Russian armies involved—numbers which proved to be absolutely accurate! He clarified for me an important point in the organization of German radio intelligence which the literature had left rather confused. I had by that time read in the German archives dozens of German communication-intelligence documents. There were monthly reports of results, individual intercepts, analyses of messages pointing to a particular conclusion. But I had never really had a clear picture of how German communications intelligence worked. Neeb's interview came at just the right time to pull all the material together. He summed it all up for me—shaped it into a whole. And so I get a good sense of satisfaction and completion whenever I think back on that interview.[7]

Curiously, I don't quite get the same feeling when I recall what was probably my most important interview. I'm not sure why, but I think it's because I didn't know as much about the subject as with the others, and I didn't know as much about the circumstances that surrounded it. So I had fewer questions in my mind. Another reason might be that I didn't anticipate it for as long as the others.

The man was Wilhelm Tranow. He was head of cryptanalysis for the German naval communications-intelligence agency, the so-called B-Dienst, for Beobachtungs-Dienst, or Observation Service. Earlier I had been unsuccessful in locating him. The people whom I had interviewed didn't know where he was. Then I interviewed the last head of the B-Dienst, Captain Max Kupfer, in Neumünster. His information was extraordinarily bad. It was full of errors, and he had forgotten a lot. I asked him where Tranow was. He's dead, he said. But in view of all Kupfer's mistakes, I thought that he might be wrong on this as well, and I asked him where Tranow had lived. Berlin, he said. So when my wife and I got to Berlin, we looked him up in the telephone book, and there he was. I telephoned, and we made an appointment for a few days later.

Now I knew from previous interviews that Tranow had been in German naval cryptanalysis since World War I. This was important for a number of reasons. Though naval cryptanalytic documents existed from that war, they didn't give the solid facts about how it all began and who was involved that a historian would want. I could get this from Tranow. Secondly, Tranow could tell about the important interwar years. What codes were attacked? How big was the unit? Who were the key figures and what happened to them? How were the results used? Thirdly, Tranow could tell about the work during World War II. This was of particular importance because this agency was probably the only unit of German intelligence that had any major effects on the war. Its solutions of British naval ciphers gave Germany great advantages during the U-boat war up until about 1943.

So it was with high hopes that we went to visit him. And he did not disappoint us. Tranow, like Nebel, was one of those men with a detailed, exact, and infallible memory of the past. He had been that way in his work. One of his colleagues said that in the '30s he could recite the movements of every capital ship of every major navy for the past three or four years—information of considerable help in cracking codes that were giving these ships their orders. And in 1970 he retained the same capacity. For example, he told us that the British had changed their naval codes in August of 1940 on the 10th of the month. The real date was the 20th. I think that that's not bad, 30 years after the event.

In the same way, he spelled out details of enemy ciphers and painted word pictures of the places he worked and of the men he worked with—all in remarkable detail. After three hours, we had completed only World War I and part of the interwar period. All of World War II was left. So Susanne and I did the only thing we could under the circumstances. We postponed our departure from Berlin for a day, and came back the next morning. It was the same thing for another three intensive hours, with Tranow providing all kinds of technical materials on the various Royal Navy ciphers, which the Germans had codenamed by cities, FRANKFURT and MUNICH being the main ones.

So the material was rich, and it was largely unknown, since the war diary of the B-Dienst does not give much technical detail. It was my most important interview, from the point of view of getting new material.[8] Yet somehow it doesn't excite me like the others. I don't find myself going back to it and re-reading it as I do, for example, Seifert's. It's a phenomenon that I really can't fully explain.

I don't want you to get the impression that every interviewee is pulsating with information that he is waiting to inundate me with, or that my brilliant interrogation technique invariably pulls out quantities of hidden data. Though I was only actually turned down twice, sometimes the interviews I do get are just busts. In one case I got to the man who headed a communications-intelligence unit facing England just before the OVERLORD invasion.[9] Here was a chance for a great deal of valuable color. But I got almost nothing, because the man had not been interested in the work and did not remember much about it. More recently, I interviewed a French general who had directed a cryptanalytic- and cryptologic-espionage unit before and during World War II.[10] Not much came out of it. In part he didn't seem to know very much, perhaps because of the compartmentalization of offices, but in part I simply was not knowledgeable enough to get more details. Again, just a few weeks ago I met a Polish cryptanalyst who, before World War II, had been one of the team of three who cracked the German cipher machine, the Enigma.[11] But he had hardening of the arteries, and his memory and his ability to speak were going, so that too proved less than valuable.

Of course, the whole business is a race with death. Sometimes I lose, and by the narrowest of margins. While I was in Freiburg, Germany, in 1969, the man who became, near the end of the war, the head of all German army communications intelligence and whom I naturally would have loved to interview,[12] died near Bonn, only four hours away. While I was in France in 1966, I read in *Le Monde* a notice of the death of Edmond Locard, a criminologist. I knew of an Edmond Locard who had written on cryptology in a criminological context, and I regretted that I had not known that he had been living while I could have talked to him. But a few years later I discovered that the real story had an even crueler twist. The man who had died was the son of the cryptologist, who was still alive when I read the obituary and whom I could therefore still have interviewed! Several years later, my wife and I passed through his home town of Lyons, and then I learned from his family how I had lost out on meeting him. But the case I regret the most is that of Andreas Figl, the great Austrian cryptanalyst who wrote *Systeme des Chiffrierens.* He had set up the Austrian military cipher bureau in 1908, had broken codes in World War I and then had done so again, as an elderly man, in World War II. The possibility that he might still be alive never even entered my head. But in 1969 I discovered that two years earlier, while I was learning German in Lindau, Germany, he was only three hours away in Salzburg—still alive and alert at the incredible age of 96. But he too had died since. That I missed the opportunity of meeting him galls me every time I think about it!

This feeling of racing against time and death comes to me more strongly in some cases than in others. Once I interviewed Luigi Sacco, the Italian cryptologist whose *Manuale di Crittografia* remains, 27 years after its publication, the best one-volume work on the technical aspects of cryptology.[13] Sacco was thus a major figure in the pantheon of cryptology. It was late one long afternoon, and for a time I stood on the terrace of his spacious apartment overlooking the Tiber. The setting sun turned that antique stream to gold, and for a few moments I was overwhelmed by the beauty, the achievement of a boyhood dream, and a sense of the evanescence of all human life.

This apprehension of this fact, this intimation of mortality, is why I interview these cryptologists. For inexorably death removes quantities of irreplaceable experience, and I seek, in these interviews, to fix a portion of that experience on paper and so preserve it against time, to make this mortality immortal. When I do this, I feel myself to be an agent of posterity, a representative of future readers. And that is why I said, at the beginning of this talk, that I am, in a sense, just you.

# How The Codebreakers
# Was Written

People always ask, How did you become interested in cryptology? and
How did you come to write so big a book?

It began when I was 13. I read a book on codes and ciphers[1] and
was hooked. I became an amateur cryptologist, making up ciphers, breaking them down, joining the American Cryptogram Association, writing
articles, collecting books. Then, in 1960, when two Americans from the
U.S. codemaking and codebreaking agency defected to Russia, I did
an article on the importance of cryptology for *The New York Times Magazine*. Next morning, when I got to work at *Newsday*, three publishers
had called to ask me to do a book. It was one of the greatest days in
my life. I finally signed with Macmillan.

The book started out as a manual on how to solve simple ciphers,
with a historical introduction. But the effects of cryptology on the affairs
of men proved so interesting and so unknown—it had never been studied
before—that I soon found I was on page 200 of the typescript of that
historical chapter and not yet out of the 1600s! I decided at first to split
the history into several chapters. Then a little later I changed the plan
of the book to a chronological one, with the methods of solution coming
in at the proper point in the development of the science. The book
grew and grew because so much of the material was new, because cryptology had played a role of high importance in World War II, and,
more basically, because cryptology involves communication, the activity

"How *The Codebreakers* Was Written" first appeared in the November 1967 issue of
*The Bucknell Alumnus*.

that makes man a social animal and so impinges upon innumerable facets of his behavior. The book took about two years part time and two and a half full time to write.

Much of the intellectual exploration that gives writing a book its excitement takes place in libraries. Most of mine took place in the New York Public Library—and I often think that without a large library like that, in which one can find the obscure journals that are referred to in footnotes and that contain valuable information, no major work of research can succeed. But running down the facts also takes legwork. I interviewed cryptologists or relatives of cryptologists in half a dozen countries under greatly varying conditions.

I spoke to General Luigi Sacco in Rome, to Dr. Hans Rohrbach in Mainz, to Charles Eyraud in Paris. In a house perched on a cliff outside Stockholm, Carl-Otto Segerdahl told some funny stories about solving German codes as all the while his six-year-old blonde daughter dashed in and out of the living room and perched on his lap. The interview with General Cesare Amè, World War II head of Italian military intelligence, took place under pressure: my date was in a hurry.

The interview with Rudolf Schauffler, one of the chiefs of the German Foreign Office cryptanalytic service, was the most depressing one I had. Elderly, not old, but broken by sickness and the ersatz food of the war years, he shuffled around his chilly apartment, barely able to put a pot of water on for tea. As rain dripped slowly from the gray sky, he ended our talk by saying, "A bridge builder can see what he has done for his countrymen, but we [German codebreakers] cannot tell whether our life was worth anything." Intimations of mortality! But as I drove back to Stuttgart from his little Black Forest village of Urach, the rain stopped, the sun came out, lighting up the hills and a distant valley, and I felt as if I had come back from the realm of the dead to the world of the living.

Most of the interviews took place in the homes of the ex-cryptanalysts. They were ordinary houses, but to me they seemed something special. Thus I was faintly surprised when I pulled up to the simple brick house at 2300 Peggy Drive in Silver Spring, Maryland, and found that it looked no different from the others on its block, that it gave off no supernatural glow, that no news photographers were clustering around. For inside lived retired Navy Captain Wesley A. Wright, a principal architect of the Japanese code solution that enabled the United States to turn the tide of war at Midway, and I had half expected that the structure itself would be literally radiating the glamour of housing a man who had helped shape the course of history!

In addition to the face-to-face interviews, I asked questions by mail. Usually a letter of a page or two would come back—though some never answered at all—but in a few cases the generosity of my informants astonished me. A retired admiral[2] wrote seven single-spaced pages, giving a colorful picture of World War I U.S. Navy cryptography. In Japan, a city editor and a professor of anthropology[3] sent essays of about 20 pages each, providing me with nearly all of my information on the Imperial Japanese Navy's cryptanalytic effort. (They each got a free copy of the book!)

A nonfiction writer's progress mostly consists of following references from one source to another. But sometimes there is a burst of excitement as fate unexpectedly leads him down a byway to a totally unsuspected treasure.

One time, I was heading down to Washington to do some research, and I stopped off at a cocktail party in New York. I hadn't really wanted to go, because I was in a hurry, but an old girlfriend was giving it and she had insisted. I chatted for a while with her current boyfriend, and it came out that I was doing research for a book on codes and ciphers. Surprised, he told me that, while a lawyer in the Defense Department, he had handled a case in the Court of Claims involving a cipher machine inventor named Hebern. He also mentioned that he had used the Patent Office files on an interference between a Hebern patent and one from I.B.M. When I got to Washington, I looked up the documents, which were unknown even to professional cryptologists—and came out with the fascinating untold story of the man who devised what is today the world's most widely used system of cipher.[4]

In another case, I was skimming through a number of *The American Historical Review* in the Great Neck Library—that being a lot easier than actually sitting down to write. I came across a review of a book published in English but in Denmark, *The Myth of Egypt and Its Hieroglyphs in European Tradition.* It sounded as if it might be valuable for my section on the decipherment of hieroglyphs, and I looked it up when I was next in the New York Public Library. Sure enough, it enabled me to recount the numerous failures that preceded Champollion's solution, these being as much a part of the story as the final success and giving my account more suspense and more depth than it would otherwise have had. But, more important, the book helped me throw light on the problem of why people associate cryptology with black magic. For, in tracing European attitudes to hieroglyphs through the centuries, the book revealed to me the existence of a mystical philosophy based on the works attributed to Hermes Trismesgistus, a legendary Egyptian priest. I discovered that this Hermetic doctrine, a kind of Christian kabbalah, had helped stain cryptology with the taint of occultism that still persists. Thus a lucky find while browsing added a new dimension to the history of cryptology.

Then there was the time I saw, in the National Archives in Washington, their mimeographed guides to German records captured in World War II being microfilmed. I picked up a set—who knew what they might have?—and in one of them I found the letter of the German postal minister to Heinrich Himmler reporting that the German post office had succeeded in solving the transatlantic radiotelephone scrambler often used by Roosevelt and Churchill!

Incidents of this kind are more than merely entertaining. They teach a lesson—and the lessons learned may often be as valuable to the writer as the material itself. These particular cases illustrate how important it is to extend one's research beyond the narrow range of the immediate subject.

Sometimes, as in these cases, this merely brings out new material. But the main advantage is in providing a perspective of the whole. I remember how, in writing about some political telegrams that played an important role in American elections in 1876, 1878, and 1880, I got the answer to "What does it all mean?" only when I departed from the articles describing the cipher solutions and looked instead into the politicians' biographies.

Another lesson I learned in writing the book was something that now seems obvious but was not when I began: to ask at the source that knows. For example, a scholarly article on Arab encyclopedias that I happened on mentioned how one of them covered a great variety of subjects. The article said nothing about cryptology. But on the chance that the author might have run across it somewhere in his researches, I wrote him. Back by return mail came an offprint from the *Journal of Semitic Studies*, which I probably would never have seen. It showed that the Arabs had practiced cryptanalysis long before the West—and provided me with the most important historical breakthrough in my whole book. Again, I knew that in World War I, the chief assistant to the famous American cryptologist Herbert O. Yardley was Dr. J. M. Manly, one of the world's great Chaucerian scholars and a member of the faculty of the University of Chicago. I asked the university library there whether they had his papers. They microfilmed for me his correspondence with Yardley, which explained the financial reasons that led Yardley to write *The American Black Chamber*, probably the most famous book in the history of cryptology. It should have been evident from the start that this kind of asking is what I should have done more often, but it wasn't until I had had good results in several cases that the lesson crystallized.

A third lesson was the importance of archival material. When I first began the book, I was sticking pretty much to published works. It was Barbara Tuchman's *The Zimmermann Telegram* that really opened up to my view the fact that unpublished documentary records also existed as sources. I realized this when, in following her references, I was checking the original Zimmermann telegram in the National Archives and saw in the files some useful additional material. The lesson was followed up when I obtained microfilms of 18th-century cryptanalyses from the British Museum. But it was really driven home when former cryptanalyst (and, later, U.S. ambassador) J. Rives Childs lent me his entire set of World War I cipher papers. I had to redo the entire chapter, so compelling was the wealth of detail. Such wealth is rarely found in, say, memoirs. Moreover, the many dates in such documents permit the historian to set up a chronology and thus to posit trends and tendencies that might otherwise escape him. Thus these sources add to both the factual and the theoretical richness of a history.

So now it's done. And so now people ask, What's next? Another book? Maybe. It's very hard to write, it's rather lonely, and every time you take a cup of coffee you feel you should be at the typewriter. Of course, when it's all over it's very satisfying. You have something to show for your work, and you know you've contributed something. So perhaps some day I'll do another. But for the moment, I'm savoring the pleasure of this one.

# OVERVIEWS

# Lgcn Otuu Wllwgh Wl Etfown;
# or, "They Will Attack at Midway"

In the embassies and consulates of almost every country in the world during the past few weeks, communications clerks have been sweating over the intricacies of new systems of code. And in the supersecret agencies that most nations maintain to break down the ciphers of others, expert cryptanalysts have been straining to crack these new systems.

This is the result of the sensational disclosures in Moscow [September 6, 1960] by the two turncoat American cryptographers, Bernon F. Mitchell and William H. Martin, that "the United States successfully reads the secret communications of more than 40 nations." For, upon hearing this, virtually every nation in the world must have taken the elementary precaution of changing their codes and ciphers.[1] They realize that history has sometimes pivoted on whether someone could make sense out of a senseless group of letters.

Deciphered Japanese messages turned the tide of the Second World War in the Pacific. American cryptanalysts, who had broken the principal Japanese naval code, provided virtually complete information on the size, course and timetable of a Japanese fleet. As a result, wrote Chief of Staff General George C. Marshall, "we were able to concentrate our limited forces to meet their naval advance on Midway when otherwise we almost certainly would have been 3,000 miles out of place."

"Lgcn Otuu Wllwgh Wl Etfown" first appeared in the November 13, 1960, issue of *The New York Times Magazine*. It was this article that led to an invitation to write a book on cryptology, which became *The Codebreakers*.

In the battle at Midway, the United States smashed the invading armada in a defeat that doomed Japan.

In another instance, England's breaking of a German diplomatic code helped push the United States into World War I. When British experts stripped code 13040 from a dispatch signed "Zimmermann," the Kaiser's foreign minister, they read of an audacious plot in which Mexico was promised her "lost territory" in Texas, New Mexico, and Arizona in return for warring on the U.S. President Wilson made this Zimmermann telegram public, and America's outrage crystallized a month later in the declaration of war that sealed Germany's fate.

In still another case, the total disintegration of the Russian cipher service during World War I led directly to the czarist army's greatest defeat—and thus paved the way for the Communists to seize power. The Russians had neglected to distribute their new wartime cipher to all units. Consequently, orders for a grand offensive had to be radioed "in clear" (ordinary language). The Germans, fully aware of the Russian plans through interceptions, devised an effective counterstrategy. In the subsequent Battle of Tannenberg, Russia lost a quarter of a million men and started the long slide into ruin and revolution.

These incidents are among the most dramatic in a science whose roots reach deep into antiquity. Ciphers are as old as writing itself:[2] the ancient Egyptians used not one but three types of cipher in their hieroglyphics.[3] The Bible, too, contains several instances of cipher. Jeremiah wrote SHESHACH for *Babel* in Chapter 25, Verse 26, by following the system (in Hebrew) of reversing the alphabet: *a* equals z, *b* equals Y, *c* equals x, etc.

This comprises an elementary form of substitution cipher, one of the two great classes of cipher. In substitution, the letters of the message are replaced by others. For example, replacing each letter by the one that follows it in the alphabet, *Friday* becomes GSJEBZ. In the other major kind of cipher, transposition, the letters are shuffled. By reversing pairs of letters, *Friday* would become RFDIYA.

Most modern ciphers are substitution systems far more advanced than the one just described. They constantly shift the equivalents for a letter according to a complex program, so that *e* might be replaced by x at one point in a message, by R at another and by v at a third. Such systems are frequently automated onto high-speed cipher machines, which produce a high-security cryptogram as fast as a message is typed out on its keyboard. These machines are currently the cryptographic rage among military, diplomatic, and commercial interests.

Though modern systems are hard to solve in themselves, governments usually give themselves an extra measure of security by changing codes before the enemy has had time to crack them. During World War I the Germans issued new editions of their front-line "Satzbuch" codes every 18 to 20 days on the assumption that it would take the French somewhat longer than that to force them.

This safeguard is not always practiced. The U.S. used its GRAY code so long that diplomats memorized many of the five-letter words that stood for common words and phrases. When, in the late 1920s, one senior consul at Shanghai was given a farewell dinner, he gave his thank-you speech entirely in GRAY—to the delight of many of the old hands, who understood him with ease.

But though regular shifts are not always made, every government changes codes on the slightest suspicion that they have been broken.[4] Even Ceylon, a relatively unsophisticated country, switched to a reserve code in 1957 when it feared a leak at its United Nations delegation. This is why it may be presumed that the Martin-Mitchell betrayal caused wholesale replacements of old codes with new. The complexity of modern systems means almost certainly that the new codes have not yet been solved, with the probable result that the United States has been plunged into a communications-intelligence blackout unparalleled in the cold war.[5]

A striking example of what this can mean to a nation came in 1940, when the English learned that the Germans were reading their invasion-defense messages. On August 20, the English changed all their codes.[6] This sudden blanking-out of an important portion of the Nazis' intelligence picture so upset them that it contributed to a decision to postpone their invasion. One postponement led to another and eventually the invasion was called off.

Voltaire branded as "charlatans" persons who claimed they could read cipher messages without the key, and the French mathematician François Viète was formally accused of being in league with the devil in 1595 after he solved Spanish diplomatic ciphers.[7] This attitude of awed incredulity still lingers. The codeword for the American decipherment of Japanese diplomatic messages in 1941 was MAGIC, and, indeed, at first glance it seems as if only sorcery can unlock the secrets of an incomprehensible farrago of letters that have no apparent pattern or clue.

In approaching such a seemingly impenetrable problem, the cryptanalyst begins with the observation that language uses some letters, letter-combinations, and words more than others. In English, for example, *e* is the most common letter, *th* the most common pair and *the* the most frequent word. If, then, a cryptogram is received with x as its most frequent letter, the cryptanalyst will try *e* for x and see whether it produces results.

More complex ciphers call for more elaborate techniques, but these still rest upon the same principle. Some of these methods are so sensitive that cryptanalysts have even solved cryptograms in languages they did not know.

Despite the efficacy of these analytical techniques, the cryptanalyst's greatest help comes from his chief foe—the enemy cipher clerks. For blunders made by them present code-crackers with their biggest breaks.

A Russian army unit repeated a message in an old cipher for the benefit of another unit that had not received the new. The enemy had solved the old cipher and thus was handed the key to the new one. The Germans used to test new ciphers by enciphering proverbs. They especially liked their version of "A bird in the hand is worth two in the bush"—and so did the French cryptanalysts, who employed it to unlock one new cipher after another.

More help comes from outside information. Suppose, for example, that the secretary of state summons the Cuban ambassador to inform him of American reduction of sugar quotas. Shortly afterward, the Cuban embassy cables a coded message to Havana. Isn't it likely that the cable will include the words "sugar," "quota," "reduce," "purchase," etc.? A cryptanalyst can jimmy open the cipher using these probable words as crowbars.

So powerful a tool is this that cryptanalysts have not been above planting messages designed to unravel knotty ciphers. One such plant played an important role in the Alfred Dreyfus case. French cryptanalysts wanted to check on the questionable solution of an Italian cryptogram that had been used to imply that the French army captain had betrayed staff secrets to the Italians. So they had a double agent feed the Italian military attaché an important-sounding message they had carefully worded to help them in their check.

The attaché fell for the trick, encoded the message verbatim and enabled the French cipher experts to verify their solution to show that the original solution had been deliberately garbled by enemies of Dreyfus to frame him.

The great number of cipher messages in modern war creates important opportunities for the cryptanalyst. Germany's tough ADFGX field cipher was first cracked through comparison of two messages with identical beginnings—a coincidence likely to occur only in heavy traffic.

Other clues come from information supplied by spies. Among the items stolen during World War II's Operation CICERO (the daring theft of documents from the British ambassador in Turkey by his valet) was some highly secret correspondence between Ankara and London. The material aided Germany's four top cryptanalysts in breaking part of Britain's diplomatic code.[8]

Today's codebreaking experts rely heavily on modern electronic computers. These can do in days what used to take months.

In 1920, when Herbert O. Yardley, chief of the American codebreaking bureau, was ordered to break Japan's diplomatic codes, it took a corps of typists from April to July just to prepare frequency tables of 10,000 syllables of Japanese telegrams, and about the same length of time to tabulate and index 10,000 code groups. Only then could Yardley begin his attack on the codes themselves. Such a delay, which could seriously handicap a nation in this fast-moving era, would not occur with computers.

These giant brains can even solve some ciphers automatically. The Nazis used such a robot cryptanalyst to break transposition ciphers, and one at the Massachusetts Institute of Technology solved one in 91 seconds. But the real strength of computers lies in their making possible the solution of highly complex ciphers by rapidly performing thousands of repetitive tasks that could not otherwise be tackled because of the manpower required.

Because of the vast national stakes involved in cryptologic operations, the National Security Agency, America's codebreaking organization, has long been the most silent of this country's intelligence services. It is not listed in the federal budget; its name deliberately masks its function; its official description—that it "performs highly specialized technical and coordinating functions relating to the national security"—describes nothing; even its recruiting pamphlet runs on for 16 pages without once mentioning "code" or "cipher."

N.S.A.'s $35,000,000, three-story, glass-and-concrete headquarters at Fort Meade, Maryland, is screened by the woods of its 950-acre reservation and is guarded by a Marine-patrolled double fence. Until recently, little more was known of this structure, built in 1957 in the form of a squared-off *A*, than that it is the third largest government building in the Washington area and boasts the "longest unobstructed straight corridor in the country"—a main hall that runs the building's full 980-foot length. Though it was generally understood that the agency's main task was to solve other countries' codes, this was never officially acknowledged.

The wall of secrecy was abruptly breached by the defection of Mitchell and Martin. These close bachelor friends, who had met in the navy in Japan, had been hired together by the N.S.A. on July 8, 1957, as "junior mathematicians" doing cryptographic analysis. They left their jobs on vacation on June 24, 1960, ostensibly to visit their West Coast homes— and turned up next in Moscow on September 6. At a press conference they announced that they had been granted Soviet citizenship and then proceeded to spill some of America's top codebreaking secrets.

N.S.A., they said, maintains a worldwide network of 2,000 radio stations to monitor the coded communications of virtually every nation in the world. These intercepts flow into the 10,000-employee headquarters, where they are cryptanalyzed in four highly specialized sections: ADVA (possibly meaning "Advanced") for high-level Soviet cipher systems and diplomatic codes; GENS ("General Soviet"?) for medium-level Soviet cipher systems and military codes; ACOM ("Asian Communist"?) for the codes of Asian Communist nations, and ALLO ("All others"?) for the codes and ciphers of U.S. allies, neutrals, and minor Communist nations.

Other divisions of N.S.A., Martin and Mitchell said, prepare systems of cryptography for American diplomats and armed forces, devise ways of "scrambling" radiotelephone conversations, study the weaknesses of cipher machines, and conduct research into new methods of cryptanalysis.

Another office works on traffic analysis—studying the senders, receivers, and frequency of radio messages to deduce such things as troop movements. Another N.S.A. section studies countermeasures, which are electronic means of confusing enemy radars, as by jamming them or sending them false signals. (The tape recorder for Soviet radar signals that Francis Gary Power's U-2 plane carried was presumably collecting information for this N.S.A. section.)

This huge operation costs the United States nearly half a billion dollars a year, the pair said. By contrast, the bill for developing the atom bomb came to $2 billion.

According to the defectors, N.S.A. operates so successfully that it has broken the codes of more than 40 nations. Asked which ones, Martin replied: "Italy, Turkey, France, Yugoslavia, the United Arab Republic,[9] Indonesia, Uruguay—that's enough to give a general picture, I guess." They refused to say whether the United States had broken Soviet codes. They credited N.S.A.'s success "primarily to the skillfulness of cryptanalysts."

This almost unbelievable ability of modern codebreakers seems to reinforce Edgar Allan Poe's bold dictum that "It may be roundly asserted that human ingenuity cannot concoct a cipher which human ingenuity cannot resolve."

Yet Poe was wrong. The unbreakable cipher exists. It is, in fact, absurdly simple. The letters of the message are transformed into numbers by any convenient scheme, and to these numbers are added a series of digits (the key) that is absolutely random and never repeats. The resulting sum constitutes a cipher that, unlike all others, cannot be broken no matter how many messages in it accumulate.

This cipher was used by Colonel Rudolf Ivanovich Abel, the highest-ranking Soviet spy ever captured in the United States. His key numbers were printed in red and black in a book so tiny he hid it in a piece of wood. Other Russian spy chiefs have used variations of the cipher, sometimes called a "one-time pad."

Since this indecipherable cipher is known, why don't all nations use it for all their messages? The answer is that the enormous volume of modern diplomatic traffic among a global network of embassies raises virtually insurmountable problems—problems that do not arise in a terse, two-way spy correspondence.

Both the punched paper tape on which the key is often prepared for machine operation, and the printed keys for manual use, must be produced in immense quantities. Then these materials must be distributed so that every embassy can communicate in cipher with every other and with its foreign office, making sure that each portion of tape is used only once. This requires a staggering amount of bookkeeping. Finally, protecting the roomsful of such material that each embassy would need presents severe security difficulties.

Consequently, most nations probably restrict this system to their most secret communications and resort to more compact and speedier ciphers for the bulk of messages. Since these ciphers, though secure, are not theoretically unbreakable, organizations like N.S.A. stay in business. And while they do, there is always the chance that a seemingly meaningless group of letters may some day spell victory or defeat in the cold war.

# The Code Battle

On June 20, 1974, a slow, unwieldy vessel filigreed with struts and derricks lumbered out to sea on a top-secret mission. She was the *Glomar Explorer*. Her secret task was to raise from the depths of the Pacific Ocean a Russian submarine that had sunk. The U.S. government wanted to obtain the submarine's missile warheads and her codes. For this, it was willing to spend $350 million of the taxpayers' money—an amount equal to giving 5 million more people Medicare coverage, sending 20,000 students to college, or buying 90 tanks, 60 bombers or a third of a nuclear-powered aircraft carrier.

Why did Washington think it was worth it?

In the spring of 1942, American codebreakers, hidden in the basement of a building in the navy yard at Pearl Harbor, broke the main Japanese naval code. Their solutions of Japanese intercepts provided virtually complete information on the size, course, and timetable of the Japanese fleet. As a result, wrote a top-ranking officer, "We were able to concentrate our limited forces to meet their naval advance on Midway when otherwise we almost certainly would have been some 3,000 miles out of place." At Midway, the United States smashed the invading armada in a battle that doomed Japan.

A year later, those same cryptanalysts cracked open a moderately long message in a subsequent edition of that same Japanese naval code. It disclosed that the mainspring of Japan's military efforts, Admiral

"The Code Battle" first appeared in the December 1975 issue of *Playboy* magazine.

Isoroku Yamamoto, would soon make an inspection trip that would bring him within range of American combat airplanes. Moreover, the message, addressed to subordinate commands, specified that Yamamoto would land at 0800 on April 18, 1943, on Ballale, one of the Solomon Islands. With this information, the Americans dispatched 18 twin-engined P-38s, which ambushed the punctual admiral in his bomber over a tropical jungle, shot it down and gave the U.S. the equivalent of a major victory.

On the other side of the world, British codebreakers, working in Quonset huts in the London exurb of Bletchley, intercepted messages of the German army high command during the precarious early hours of the Anzio landing. These revealed, just as the American forces were about to extend themselves from the beachhead, that fresh German units had been ordered into the area. General Mark Clark consolidated his forces, repulsed the German counterattack and later advanced into Rome.

On D-Day, as the Allies stormed the Normandy beaches to breach fortress Europe, the codebreakers intercepted a German message ordering a counterattack. Forewarned, General Omar Bradley took measures that helped keep the Americans from being flung back into the sea. Later, at Bastogne, codebreakers cracked a radiogram that enabled General George S. Patton, Jr., to inflict heavy losses on a redoubtable German paratroop division.

World War II had seen dozens, perhaps hundreds, of similar instances in which codebreaking had played a vital role. A former director of naval intelligence exclaimed, "It won the war!" Chief of Staff George C. Marshall declared that codebreaking was "our main basis of information regarding Hitler's intentions in Europe" and contributed "greatly to the victory and tremendously to the saving of American lives." A high official said that it shortened the war by a year. After it was all over, a congressman paid high tribute from the floor of the House: "I believe that our cryptographers . . . did as much to bring that war to a successful and early conclusion as any other group of men."

During World War II, codebreaking had become the most important means of obtaining secret information. No other source possessed to the same degree the elements of successful intelligence: volume, anticipation, and veracity. Reports based on visual observations of the enemy by patrols and on interrogations of prisoners of war were voluminous and accurate but good only for the immediate future. Spies, on the other hand, could reveal enemy plans far in advance, but suspicion permanently blighted their labors: no general would risk his men—or his career—on the radioed word of an informant whom the enemy might have paid more or put under duress. Aerial photographs yielded data as hard as could be, but they were relatively sparse, owing to their snapshot nature, and showed only what was already there or on the march. Codebreaking alone could provide the quantity and quality of intelligence necessary to sound military planning.

As the hot war congealed into the cold, the U.S. government wished to preserve the information-gathering capabilities that had proved so effective against the Axis. The trauma of Pearl Harbor, which had led to the centralization of military affairs in the Defense Department and of intelligence in the Central Intelligence Agency, eventually fathered as well a unified codebreaking agency—the Armed Forces Security Agency, established in 1949. The merits of the unified approach soon warranted expanding the role of the Defense Department's A.F.S.A. On November 4, 1952, President Harry S. Truman turned it into the National Security Agency, serving every branch of government.

N.S.A. reigns today as the supreme arbiter of all matters cryptologic in the United States. It promulgates cryptologic doctrine, establishing the rules by which, say, the State Department will encipher its dispatches. It coordinates the codebreaking agencies of the army, the navy and the air force in their specialized missions against their foreign counterparts. It issues specifications to manufacturers for components of cipher machines, which it, for security's sake, then assembles on its own premises. It analyzes foreign radar emissions, so that U.S. nuclear bombers will be able to jam or trick them in war. But, most of all, it cracks the codes of foreign governments and daily submits the solutions to U.S. officials as high as the president. This function has made it the biggest intelligence agency in the free world—bigger even than the C.I.A.—and, within the U.S. government, the most secret.

Counting the military personnel assigned to it, about 100,000 people work for N.S.A.—about five times as many as for the C.I.A. It spends several billion dollars a year. In sharp contrast to the head of the C.I.A., the N.S.A. director, normally a three-star general or admiral, never makes statements to the press[1] and rarely appears before congressional committees in public hearings.

Security is as tight if not tighter at N.S.A. than anywhere else in the government. Its headquarters—two boxy modern buildings at Fort Meade, Maryland, just visible from the Baltimore-Washington Parkway—is surrounded by three fences, two topped with barbed wire and one electrified. It is protected by U.S. marines. Inside, marines[2] escort visitors everywhere, including to the rest rooms. N.S.A. employees must meet some of the government's strictest security standards. They can be fired if the director merely finds it "to be in the interest of the United States."

All the secrecy enshrouds work sometimes far from Fort Meade. Much of it begins in lonely monitoring posts scattered about the globe, especially along the borders of the Soviet Union. There, in Quonset huts on the wind-swept Eritrean plateau in Ethiopia or in the dusty foothills of the Hindu Kush in Afghanistan,[3] far from prying eyes and the electrical interference of cities, radiomen lean forward, straining to pick up every dot and dash or every syllable of a foreign radio transmission through the static that crackles in their earphones. Their antenna fields sometimes cobweb whole mountainsides. Other monitors fly in airplanes or sail in ships as close as they dare to foreign coasts or frontiers to pick up every possible scrap of text. Sometimes their sedentary work becomes dangerous. In 1960, the Russians shot down Francis Gary Powers' U-2, which was carrying not only cameras but also "black boxes" whose magnetic tape recorded Soviet radar signals. Israeli planes strafed the U.S.S. *Liberty* as it cruised the eastern Mediterranean during the Six-Day War, its electronic ears wide open. And the U.S.S. *Pueblo* became a *cause célèbre* when the North Koreans captured it, packed with eavesdropping gear, early in 1968.

Some of the interception is automated. Satellites moving slowly above the Soviet Union receive, process and retransmit Russian radio signals. (N.S.A.'s share of the cost of lofting these squat cylindrical spies in the sky constitutes a major portion of its vast budget.) It was such a satellite with a sophisticated antenna system that reportedly eavesdropped on Kremlin leaders as they talked over the radiotelephones in their cars.

In West Berlin, in a hidden U.S. intercept post, a $3-million machine by Ampex, filling a space equivalent to two living rooms, can tape-record 2,000 channels of communication simultaneously. The tapes are burned after they are used once, because erasing them for reuse would destroy their superhigh quality. Other machines, which record everything sent on a given frequency, continue to print out periods on six-ply carbon paper when the circuit is "up" but nothing is being sent. They keep on tapping for hours, days, weeks, even months, at two minutes and 15 cents a page, just waiting for some message to come across.

In the United States, N.S.A. is reported to have monitored most cable and telex messages into and out of the country.[4] Computers scan messages for trigger words, such as "oil" and "Mideast," and have texts containing them printed out. Such economic intelligence could help the government make decisions on such matters as oil imports and grain sales, vitally affecting the cost of living. But the questionable legality of this activity is one reason that the House and Senate intelligence committees are looking into N.S.A.

Another reputed agency achievement was a spymaster's dream. The Soviet Union allegedly eavesdropped, from its embassy in Washington, on hundreds of thousands of domestic American telephone calls, including those to and from Congressmen. N.S.A. then intercepted the Soviet transmissions of the results back to Russia.[5]

Many intercepts that pour into the Fort Meade headquarters are in clear language. The communications of Soviet air force pilots with one another is an example. Analysts listen to their chatter, recognize individuals by speech peculiarities, index names and other details. From this, N.S.A. can build up a good picture of a squadron—its commander, its men, its morale, its equipment, its transfers. Many such analyses join to create a picture of the Soviet air force as a whole.

But most of the intercepts are in code, and these go to the codebreakers, a rare and peculiar breed of men. "Back-room boys," the British call them. Most of them today are mathematically inclined, in contrast to those of pre–World War II vintage, who were primarily linguists. The change reflects the worldwide shift in cryptographic systems.

They are highly intellectual, lovers of word games, puzzles and chess. Indeed, the late British chess champion C. H. O'D. Alexander was a star of the British codebreaking establishment. Once, when he was playing the Russian grandmaster David Bronshtain, he learned during conversation that Bronshtain did the same kind of work. Curiously, many of the great cryptanalysts have been fine musicians. The greatest codebreaker of World War I, the Frenchman Georges-Jean Painvin, had won a prize in cello at the Nantes conservatory. After Pearl Harbor, the Navy's codebreakers, needing more men, commandeered the band of the sunken battleship *California*. Nearly all the members proved above average and some were outstanding.

The work requires, for success, a rare and peculiar turn of mind, sometimes termed "cipher brains." It is not surprising that many cryptanalysts are magnificent eccentrics. Take, as an example, Britain's finest cryptanalyst, Dillwyn Knox, who in World War I reputedly cracked the German submarine code in his bath and in World War II helped solve the several versions of the German cipher machine Enigma. Day after day, he would try to leave his office through the cupboard. The girls there waited to see if once, just by chance, he would go out through the door. He never did. Whenever he ruled a line, he ruled his thumb in. Yet another part of his brain so illuminated the complex mechanism of the Enigma that it greatly aided Britain in staving off defeat and later in winning the war. Knox worked intuitively. A certain movement of the mechanism had been called a crab. "Where there's a crab, there's a lobster," reasoned Knox—and he found the corresponding movement.

Another of the Bletchley originals was Alan Turing. One of the greatest mathematicians of the century, he is widely known as the creator of the Turing machine, an idealization of the computer. During World War II, Turing bicycled the three miles from his rooms to Bletchley every day on a rickety contraption whose chain regularly fell off. Instead of just fixing it, Turing noted that this event occurred every so many revolutions of the pedal. He then correlated a bent gear cog with a damaged link in the chain. Only then did he attack the repair. He sometimes set his watch by making some complex preliminary calculations and then observing from a fixed point the occultation of a particular star by a certain building. He took his love of exercise to extremes, preferring to jog 14 miles across London to rushing for trains and waiting in smelly underground stations. Tall, broad-shouldered, blue-eyed, he paid not the least attention to the 100 or so girls in his department at Bletchley. Instead, he devised a telephone scrambler that baffled the Germans, who had been listening to the transatlantic conversations of Roosevelt and Churchill.[6] And he pioneered in helping develop for code-breaking purposes one of the world's first programmable computers, called the COLOSSUS. It enabled Bletchley to read many German cipher-machine messages that otherwise would never have gotten to Allied commanders in time to be of use.

But this is the era of the corporate man and of teamwork. As in science, where dozens may research a problem, whole teams of cryptanalysts may attack a foreign cipher system, and most are about as colorful as dentists or engineers. At N.S.A., codebreakers work in offices like those of an insurance company. In large rooms, each devoted to a particular world region, country or foreign-government branch, stand rows of flat-topped, gray steel desks. The cryptanalysts bend over them, scanning print-outs, testing with colored pencils solutions on square-ruled paper, flipping the pages of some reference book. They confer, stare distractedly out the windows, scribble furiously and sometimes yelp with joy. Each man is constantly scrutinizing the intercepts for some quirk, some irregularity, some pattern that constitutes the chink in the armor of the cryptogram.

During World War II, an English woman cryptanalyst sensed something odd about an Italian intercept. She quickly spotted it: The page-long cryptogram had no L's. She knew that the Italians had been transmitting fake messages in an attempt to deceive the English. She knew, too, that this particular cryptosystem precluded any letter from representing itself—in other words, an *a* in the original message could not become an A in the cryptogram, though it could become any other letter. The fact that this intercept had every letter except L therefore meant with a high degree of probability that the original message was a dummy consisting only of *l*s. On this basis, she broke into the system.

The human cryptanalyst—especially one with a cipher brain—remains even today the basis of codebreaking. Solving something still often comes down to the fitting of a half-remembered name to an incompletely solved message, and only a human being can do that. But computers help greatly. They can count torrents of letters at high speed, tirelessly compare one message with another in a search for repeated groups of letters, generate all possible solutions of a cryptogram to let the cryptanalyst find the one that's not gibberish.

Consequently, N.S.A. has assembled more computers under a single roof than probably any other institution in the world. They number in the scores, if not the hundreds. And these machines are among the fastest and most sophisticated in the world. Not content with buying the biggest and best computers it can find, N.S.A. expands and upgrades them. Some years ago, it acquired the I.B.M. STRETCH, a machine so huge that only a few other government agencies, such as the National Weather Service and the Atomic Energy Commission, had use for one. But it was not good enough for N.S.A. The agency added a portion, called the bump, that was larger than the original computer. At that time, the typical magnetic tape had only 100 bits (binary digits) to the inch. N.S.A. squeezed in 3,000—and then streamed the tape past the reading heads at 275 inches per second.

N.S.A.'s extraordinary computer capacity accounts for much of its success in the world of cryptanalysis, where success is partly a function of available computer time. Britain's present codebreaking agency, Government Communication Headquarters, at the western edge of the flower-bedecked spa of Cheltenham, is, in the view of one observer, falling farther and farther behind N.S.A. because it cannot keep up with this country's computer capability.

Although they use the most modern of marvels, the codebreakers do not disdain the most ancient of tricks: simply getting hold of the other fellow's code. This is what the C.I.A. tried to do with the Russian submarine. Maritime seizures of this kind have figured frequently in cryptologic history, and it is curious to note that the Russians were also involved in one of the most famous of these cases. Just after the start of World War I, the German light cruiser *Magdeburg* grounded in the Baltic. A few hours later, the Russians picked up the rigid body of a drowned German officer, whose arms still gripped the lead-bound codebook of the Imperial German Navy.[7] The Russians at once passed it to the British, the chief maritime power, who used it to master the German codes, first naval and then diplomatic. Later, the British sent divers down into sunken U-boats to salvage new editions of codebooks. During World War II, the land forces of both sides frequently captured cryptographic documents from the enemy.

Secret agents often steal codes outright. In August 1941, Mussolini's Military Information Service got a wax impression of a key from an Italian employee of the American embassy in Rome. The Italians made their own key and stole the military attaché's copy of the BLACK code. They could then read not only his messages but, because the code was used throughout the world, all the American military-attaché messages that they could intercept. The most valuable came from the man in Cairo. He was in close contact with the British in North Africa and daily radioed back to Washington detailed reports on British experiences, reinforcements and plans. The Italians picked these up, read them with their stolen code and used the information to foil British moves. Once, the British planned a commando-style attack on Axis airfields in the Mediterranean to reduce air strikes while they pushed a convoy through to besieged Malta. The Germans, forewarned, repelled the British attacks and forced the convoy to turn back.

But sometimes espionage backfires. In 1943, the American Office of Strategic Services (O.S.S.) rifled the offices of the Japanese military attaché in Lisbon. The Japanese detected this and changed their attaché code, depriving the Allies for more than a year of a valuable source of information.[8] So governments turn to juicier means.

An American girl working for British intelligence in Washington let herself be seduced in 1941 by an Italian, obtaining the Italian naval code, and in 1942 by a Frenchman, obtaining the French. The Russians today exert great efforts to entrap code clerks, sometimes setting 20 men on one to discover his weaknesses and exploit them. The Russians do this not only in Moscow, and one can imagine the dilemma of a young and ill-paid Syrian code clerk in an expensive Western capital when approached by a slender blonde who promises him money and herself for a few inconsequential pieces of paper. Such clerks will seldom betray an actual cipher, in whose secrecy they have been drilled, but will often pass over messages in plaintext. A comparison of these with their coded versions will, in many cases, permit a reconstruction of the cipher system and a consequent reading of future messages.

The simplest way to obtain another nation's code is to sell it one's old code machines. The United States has sold obsolete cipher machines to Turkey, for example, after carefully noting such key elements as the wiring of the code wheels. Turkey accepts this because, wanting mainly to keep her messages secret from Russia and Greece, she gets machines that will do this at a price that she can afford. She either doesn't care about American eavesdropping or talks herself into believing that some changes in the machines will prevent it. After World War II, Britain rounded up the thousands of Enigma machines that Germany had used and sold many of them to some of the emerging nations. Since she had read the machines in the '40s, she could read them in the '50s and '60s—and so could keep tabs on what that country was planning.

Does all this mean that no code secret is safe any longer? Have these three factors—the brilliance of cryptanalysts, the power of computers and the assistance of espionage—at long last validated Edgar Allan Poe's famous dictum: "It may be roundly asserted that human ingenuity cannot concoct a cipher which human ingenuity cannot resolve."

By no means. Of the hundreds or thousands of coded intercepts that flow daily into N.S.A. headquarters, perhaps only four percent are broken. The explanation for this apparent anomaly lies in the development of secret writing.

This development may be viewed as the latest in the ceaseless struggle between the makers and the breakers of codes. The makers, of course, came first. Apparently, when a culture achieves a certain level of literacy, the need for secrecy in writing reaches a critical point. Cryptography thus sprang up spontaneously and independently in the four great civilizations of antiquity and later in many other societies.

Some of the early methods were bizarre. A Persian shaved the head of a slave, tattooed onto the bald pate a message urging his son-in-law, a local governor, to revolt, waited for the hair to grow back and sent the slave off down the road. Some methods were ingenious. The ephors of Sparta wrapped a strip of leather around a wooden staff, wrote their orders down its length, took off the leather, thus jumbling the letters, and dispatched it to their general in the field. He wound it around a baton of the same diameter and read the message. And some early methods were simple. Julius Caesar replaced each letter of his message with one three places down the alphabet, so that *a* became D, *b* became E and so on.

Caesar's elementary cipher sufficed for his day, because the first code-breakers did not appear until several centuries later. It was the Arabs who discovered the principles of cryptanalysis. But their knowledge contracted as their civilization declined, and not until the Renaissance did the West rediscover cryptanalysis.

The new nation-states used it to read the messages that the foreign ambassadors in their capitals were sending to their home countries. By the 1700s, clandestine mail-opening and cipher-solving centers called black chambers existed in most of the monarchies of Europe. Often located in curtained, candlelit rooms of post offices, they employed specialists in a variety of dark arts. Some deft fellows opened letters tracelessly, usually by softening the wax seal and then passing a hot wire under it. Engravers took impressions of seals and then forged them. Batteries of secretaries took down letters dictated at high speed so that they could be returned to the mail without missing a delivery. Translators interpreted exotic tongues and cryptanalysts cracked foreign ciphers.

The codebreakers bashed away on the principle of letter frequency. In English, for example, the letter *e* is used more often than any other. So if you have a cryptogram of simple substitution—*a* becomes say, P; *b* becomes w; and so on—in which x is the most common cipher letter, you can presume that x stands for *e*. With this as a start, you can proceed rather as if you were solving a crossword puzzle. You fill in what you know and guess at the rest. The word *e?e?* might be *ever* or *even*.

Other aspects of letter frequency help. The second most frequent letter in English is *t*. Three common letters that rarely contact one another are *a*, *o*, and *i*. A high-frequency letter that follows vowels in four fifths of its appearances is *n*. The letter that most often precedes vowels is *h*. Pairs of letters have distinct frequencies as well: the most common is *th*. The experienced cryptanalyst picks out letters under their ciphertext disguises as easily as you spot friends at a masquerade party.

This principle placed a mighty weapon in the hands of the codebreakers. The codemakers soon blunted it with devices of their own. The tussle went back and forth, with cipher inventors tinkering with their systems to fill the chinks probed by the cryptanalysts, but with the codebreakers usually on top.

The cryptographer's quest for their Holy Grail, the unbreakable cipher, led at one point to a system that amateurs to this day believe to be the only one that cannot be solved: the book code.

During the American Revolution, when Benedict Arnold was negoti-

ating to betray West Point to the British, he at first encoded his messages
by means of volume I of the fifth Oxford edition of Blackstone's famed
legal classic, *Commentaries on the Laws of England.* Arnold searched for
the plaintext words in the book and then, when he found each one,
wrote down its page number, line number and word number in the
line. *General,* for example, was 35.12.8. But some words took a lot of
hunting. Arnold did not turn up *militia* until page 337. Others he could
not find at all but had to spell out, using the same system for letters.
The code proved so cumbersome and time-consuming that the conspira-
tors abandoned it after sending only a single message from each side.
Undoubtedly it was, as amateurs believe, unbreakable. But it was also
impractical.

The invention of the telegraph a few years later intensified the struggle
between the makers and the breakers of codes. But it was radio that
brought the struggle to a climax. For radio, theoretically, presents the
enemy with a copy of every message that is transmitted. How much
this helped the codebreakers first became evident in World War I.
Battle after battle was decided by the intelligence obtained from cryptanalysis. At 9:05 P.M. on April 28, 1918, for example, American monitors
intercepted a coded German message. Cryptanalysts at headquarters
quickly broke it, discovering it was an order for an attack at 1 A.M.
Half an hour before the assault, the doughboys were warned—in
time to repulse it. On the eastern front, declared a high German staff
officer, "We were always warned by the wireless messages of the Russian staff of the positions where troops were being concentrated for
any new undertaking. Only once during the whole war were we taken
by surprise."

The struggle between cryptographers and cryptanalysts reached a
climax in the 1918 work of Major Joseph O. Mauborgne of the U.S.
Army Signal Corps, himself a cryptanalyst of some expertise. Mauborgne, 36 at the time, took a couple of cryptologic ideas that were
floating around and combined them. The result was a cipher that could
never be solved.

In essence it works like this:

To begin with, you must have a key. This can be a series of letters,
numbers or electric pulses and spaces. The sequence must have two
properties (each representing one of the ideas that Mauborgne plucked
from the scientific atmosphere). It must be random. In other words,
the elements of which it is composed must have absolutely no pattern,
no structure whatsoever. And the sequence must be endless. It must
have as many elements as are in all the messages you are ever going

to send. The key must never repeat: no portions must ever be reused in one message or among several. Both sender and receiver must naturally have copies of the key. For this example, our key will comprise these numbers: 7396407718181563015169. . . .

To encipher, you first transform the letters of your plaintext message into numbers. An easy way of doing this is to let $a = 01$, $b = 02$, etc. Then the message *Attack* will become 01 20 20 01 03 11. You write these numbers under as much of your key as you need. Then you add them to the key numbers. (Using noncarrying addition will reduce errors and permit enciphering from left to right.)

$$7\,3\,9\,6\,4\,0\,7\,7\,1\,8\,1\,8$$
$$+\;0\,1\,2\,0\,2\,0\,0\,1\,0\,3\,1\,1$$
$$7\,4\,1\,6\,6\,0\,7\,8\,1\,1\,2\,9$$

The sum constitutes the cryptogram. When the recipient gets it, he writes it out above the key and subtracts. He comes up with 01 20 20 . . . which he turns into *attack*.

But no third party will be able to do that. The lack of pattern and repetition deprives him of any handholds with which he could rip open the cipher. Take the most advantageous case: the cryptanalyst has the actual plaintext of a coded intercept. He could, indeed, recover the key used for that message. But this does him no good whatsoever. Because the key is random and thus entirely unpredictable, the cryptanalyst cannot determine even the next number of the key to use in deciphering other intercepts. It lies forever beyond his ken. The same holds *a fortiori* for all the other numbers of the key in that message, and in all succeeding messages, since the key never serves twice.

What about trial and error? If the cryptanalyst runs through every possible key, won't he eventually hit upon the right one? He will. And he will also hit upon the right plaintext. But it won't do him any good. For in running through every possible key, he will also be "recovering" every possible message of the same length as the true original in every possible language. For example, with the message 67 83 99 28 01 25 27, key 59 88 79 10 06 24 07 will yield plaintext *retreat*, while key 66 89 77 27 97 22 22 yields plaintext *advance*. Other keys will yield *sideway, oranges, Fuebrer,* and *playboy*. Because the keys are patternless, nothing permits the cryptanalyst to choose one over another. All he has done through a pointless exercise is to generate a list of all possible seven-letter words in all possible languages that he might simply have taken from a shelf of dictionaries.

The system, then, is truly unbreakable. Mauborgne had achieved the dream of all cryptographers, their version of the philosophers' stone. Codemakers in other countries soon reasoned as he had, combined the concepts of randomness and endlessness and independently created the unbreakable cipher. Germany did it early in the '20s. Her Foreign Office embodied it in its classical form, which has given it its name: the one-time pad. On two sheets of paper were typed a random series of numbers—the key. Many such sheets were then bound into two identical pads, one for Berlin, one for the embassy abroad. After the cipher clerk had used a sheet to encipher a message, he tore it off and threw it away. The decoder did the same.

The Soviet Union, whose diplomatic codes had been solved by Great Britain during the trade negotiations of 1920 that led to Britain's first coming to terms with the Bolshevist regime, shifted to the one-time pad by 1930. Since then, no one has solved Russian diplomatic messages. During World War II, Russian spies, notably Richard Sorge in Japan, hermetically sealed their radioed reports to Moscow with the one-time pad. Britain's Foreign Office was using it by 1943, and thus minimized the damage done by Nazi Germany's most famous spy. This was CICERO, the Albanian valet of the British ambassador to Turkey. CICERO photographed the embassy's most secret documents and sold them—for counterfeit pounds—to the Nazis. In addition to the information itself, the texts of the cablegrams normally, in other cryptosystems, would have provided the German codebreakers with cribs to read other British diplomatic messages. But the one-time pad rendered these plaintexts utterly useless to them. And so when Hitler rejected the photographed documents as improbable, CICERO's work, a technical success, proved a substantive failure.[9]

If the one-time pad can thus confer such enormous security, why don't all nations use it for all their messages?

Because they cannot. As with the book code, practical considerations interfere.

The cipher requires that the key be used only once. Yet in network communications, especially in the haste and turmoil of war, inevitably two units will simultaneously select the same portion of key for use. This will lay those messages open to solution. Moreover, the cipher requires that every message letter have its own fresh key element. In practice, it is impossible to produce and distribute sufficient key. During World War II, the U.S. Army's European-theater headquarters transmitted, even before the Normandy invasion, 2 million five-letter code groups a day. It would therefore have consumed 10 million letters of key every

24 hours—the equivalent of a shelf of 20 average books. The production and distribution of so much material was out of the question.

The invention of the ultimate in ciphers did not, therefore, give the codemakers complete victory over the codebreakers. The cryptanalysts could still attack those ciphers that had to be used where the one-time pad could not be—and, during World War II and the postwar struggles with Communist countries, sometimes with history-making success.

One of the most important solutions of all time was that of the German Enigma machine, begun by the Poles before World War II and raised to a mass-production art by the British during actual hostilities. This solution, whose solved and translated intercepts were covernamed ULTRA, contributed enormously to the winning of three crucial battles of the war. In August 1940, ULTRA forecast hours before radar did where German bomber squadrons would appear over England. Fighter Command then concentrated its few Hurricanes and Spitfires to deny the Germans air superiority in the Battle of Britain.[10] From 1943 on, during the Battle of the Atlantic, ULTRA disclosed locations where the U-boats were refueling from their milch cows. Long-range flying boats did the rest. And ULTRA's insight into the German spy apparatus enabled Britain to control every Nazi agent on the island, thereby fooling the Germans about where the D-Day attack would come—they held an entire army, the 15th, around Calais while the real invasion securely lodged itself in Normandy.

And after that conflict was over and the iron curtain clanged down, codebreaking retained its importance. During the Korean War, cryptanalysis helped spot targets for air strikes. In Vietnam, radio intelligence was the only really valuable intelligence that the U.S. Military Assistance Command had.

In diplomatic negotiations, codebreaking likewise helped the United States, though peacetime results naturally could not match those of wartime for drama. During the Cold War, N.S.A. cracked some of the codes of more than 40 nations, among them Italy, Turkey, France, Yugoslavia, Indonesia, Uruguay, and half a dozen countries of the Near East. "I had in my desk," one former N.S.A. cryptanalyst declared, "all the deciphered communications between Cairo and its embassy in Moscow relating to the visit of the U.A.R.[11] government mission to the U.S.S.R. in 1958 for the purpose of purchasing petroleum in the Soviet Union." Henry Cabot Lodge, then United States ambassador to the United Nations, once expressed his appreciation to N.S.A. for information about the instructions sent by the Near East governments to their U.N. missions. (The presence of the United Nations in New York makes it easy for N.S.A. to intercept member nations' cablegrams.) One former high State Department official was always glad to see the man with the locked briefcase who brought around the intercepts. "I got some good clues on how to deal with various countries," he said, "and I quickly learned which ambassadors I could trust and which not." And when, every morning at 7:45, Lieutenant General Brent Scowcraft takes President Ford the latest intelligence, included are solutions from N.S.A.

How Ford feels about the work was underlined this past summer. Turkey, peeved at Congress' refusal to give her arms for possible use in Cyprus, ordered the United States to close down its four main intercept posts there. Those posts, located at places bearing such romantic names as Karamursel, had nestled close under the belly of the Soviet Union. The president declared that Congress' "reckless" action had caused "the loss of strategic intelligence data," which "in today's world is absolutely essential to our national security, even our survival."

Valuable as it is, however, codebreaking cannot supply perfect and complete intelligence. The enemy does not put everything on the air. Some plans are discussed in conference. Some orders are sent by courier. The Japanese attack on Pearl Harbor came as a surprise because no orders were given by radio.

Of the messages put on the air, not all are intercepted. U.S. monitors did not pick up the messages that might have told them that the North Koreans were going to attack in 1950 because they were targeted instead on the more promising and apparently more vital Russian transmissions. No agency has the manpower to monitor constantly every wavelength on the radio spectrum. And, finally, of the messages intercepted, not all are solved. During World War II, Germany's Army Group North intercepted 46,342 cryptograms opposite Leningrad in the 13 months beginning in May 1943. Cryptanalysts solved only 13,312, or 28.7 percent. Here, too, lack of manpower was undoubtedly a main factor. But the Russians also changed their codes before the Germans had collected the quantity of messages needed to crack them.

In addition to inherent limitations like these, advances in mathematics and electronics are today further reducing the usefulness of codebreaking.

Within the past decade, mathematicians have developed powerful new formulas for generating keys. So complex are these formulas, that, even given a cryptogram and its plaintext, the cryptanalyst would need centuries—even with all the world's computers of this and the next generation—to reconstruct them and then use the reconstruction to read the next message that comes along. In theory, the ciphers are not unbreakable, as the one-time pad is. In practice, they are. These formulas are embodied in electronic cipher machines, such as the United States' HW-28 and KW-7, which include a further security feature. Each machine has a key element of its own, making it unique. Hence, stealing one of these well-guarded machines would bare only the messages sent to and from that machine.

Moreover, the transistor and large-scale integration of circuits on quarter-inch chips, which have made it practicable to utilize these formulas in cipher machines, are becoming increasingly available to other nations of the world. This means that more and more countries are achieving absolute security for their high-level dispatches.

That is why N.S.A. fails to solve more than 95 percent of the messages it intercepts. Those it does break usually constitute the medium- or low-level traffic of major nations or the top-level traffic of the smaller countries. This is what it circulates to the officials of the State Department and the National Security Council. It continues to intercept and store the major messages of major nations—sometimes in boxcars at Fort Meade, sometimes just in cardboard boxes—in the hope that cipher clerks will err, permitting some kind of break, or that some other fortunate circumstance will arise.

The attempt to recover the Russian submarine was viewed by N.S.A. as just such a chance. In fact, it was a desperate gamble. It is doubtful that the Soviet Union is behind the United States cryptologically, and so it is unlikely that the C.I.A. would get more from the Soviet sub's cipher machine than the Russians would get from an American cipher machine. This means, in effect, little more than a few messages, many of them probably personal, sent to the submarine, and probably none from it, since the essence of its mission is to remain silent and hidden in the depths of the sea.

Why, in view of these generally mediocre results, does N.S.A. persist? Why does it bother to read the systems of these minor countries? One reason, of course, is that cryptanalysts, like other mortals, want to protect their jobs. Their motivation may be even stronger than most, since they cannot readily transfer their skills to the civilian sector. Another is that N.S.A. gives the policymakers a certain assurance that they're not missing anything. Those small countries may suddenly become important someday—witness Korea, the Congo, Vietnam. Most of the intercepts are admittedly of little interest or importance, the operation is admittedly a bit of a luxury and a waste, but the government can afford it and it does provide a margin of safety, so why not? The real question, however, is whether it is worth the billions spent on it.

The answer depends on what the money would otherwise be used for. If the government were to spend it on some more jet fighters or ICBMs, probably the N.S.A. investment is better. Intelligence is cheap and cost-effective. It can often save more than it costs. But if the government were actually to spend the money on schools and hospitals and transportation, that investment is probably better. For a nation's strength depends far less upon its secret intelligence than upon its human and material resources. No doubt a balance is best. The problem is to strike that balance, and this depends largely on the wisdom and determination of a country's leaders, and of its people.

# HISTORICAL
# AND
# TECHNICAL
# STUDIES

# The Grand Lines of Cryptology's Development

The cryptology of today differs from that of the past in three characteristics: (1) the complexity of its systems, (2) the extent of its use, and (3) the quantification or "mathematization" of its operations. Each of these is the culmination of a line of development in cryptology: the technological, the economic, and the philosophical.

Technological development deals with the advance in the applied science that is cryptology. This advance is made possible by the march of science, though the impetus for change comes from the adoption by codebreakers of some new technique that nullifies the methods used by codebreakers or vice versa. As science has moved forward, so has the substance of cryptology.

For centuries, progress in both was slow, so that ciphers based on pencil and paper dominated, and the limitations of the human brain prevented too great an increase in complexity: even polyalphabetics were shunned because they engendered so many errors that cryptograms in them often could not be deciphered by the legitimate recipients. Some progress was registered in invisible inks as knowledge of chemicals grew, so that where milk is cited in Ovid's *Art of Love*, alum is mentioned in a Renaissance work.[1]

The first great advance came with the harnessing of electricity. It permitted the invention of electrical cipher machines, such as Germany's

"The Grand Lines of Cryptology's Development" first appeared in the November 1982 issue of *Computers and Security*.

Enigma and Geheimschreiber. Later, the invention of the transistor, which led to large-scale integration of electronic circuits on chips, permitted the creation of the National Bureau of Standards' data encryption standard, an enormously complicated cipher system.

In cryptanalysis, the ability to strip lengthy additives from superenciphered code messages in time for the solutions to be used in combat, which the U.S. and German naval codebreaking agencies possessed in World War II, had to await Herman Hollerith's devising of his punched-card collating machines. Again, only after electronic tubes had been invented could the British conceive of and then build the COLOSSUS, an electronic protocomputer for solving the complex cryptograms created by the Geheimschreiber.[2] Thus cryptology has moved from the simple to the complex.

It has also continually extended the area in which it is used. This growth has followed the same simple economic law that determines the growth of other entities: it goes wherever it is needed enough to make its cost worthwhile. Because technology reduces that cost, and because the number of places in which cryptology might be needed increases as a society grows in complexity, the use of cryptology constantly expands.

When permanent embassies arose during the Renaissance, creating a voluminous governmental correspondence through a hostile territory, the consequence of a leakage of the information was great enough to compel the Italian city-states to encrypt the missives, despite the onerous burdens this imposed. Likewise, when generals drafted radio into military service, its exposure of all their messages to the enemy forced encryption of their dispatches, again despite the cost in the form of delays and drainage of manpower. In World War II, communications became so numerous that it would have been all but impossible to encrypt all of them with the cumbersome and time-consuming hand systems of World War I. But technology, in the form of cipher machines, partly automated encryption and thus made it practicable for generals to cryptographically protect nearly all their radiograms.

When individuals see the cost of encryption as greater than the potential loss from the unprotected and revealed information, they do not encrypt messages. The typical conversation of a telephone falls into this category. But when the consequence of loss of the information is high, as in discussing promising oil lands, telephone conversations are often scrambled.

Today, the volume of information that governments, businesses, and individuals store in databanks and transmit among computers is rapidly rising, while the cost of encryption, thanks to microprocessors and large-scale integration of electronic circuits, is rapidly falling. This combination of factors is driving the continued expansion of cryptography, whose use is wider now than at any other time in history.

The philosophical development, which culminated in the quantification of cryptology's operations, depends, in at least one view, on this expansion of the field.[3] For such a generalization is a necessary precursor to the secularization of cryptology, its conversion from an occult activity to a utilitarian one. The phenomenon joins cryptology to a host of other human endeavors, for secularization, or the replacement of sacred and mystical ways of thought by the more efficacious rational modes, has been called one of the four major processes of historical change. The sociologists Robert Nisbet and Robert G. Perrin say that it is "a conspicuous and enormously important trend in the history of civilization."[4] A founder of sociology, Auguste Comte, made secularization his "fundamental law of Intellectual Evolution." According to this, all human theories pass through three stages: "first, the theological or fictitious, which is provisional; secondly, the metaphysical or abstract, which is transitional; and thirdly, the positive or scientific, which alone is definitive."[5] Another great sociologist, Max Weber, regarded this general process, which he called "rationalization," as one of the master principles in history. For it shifts a people's world view from a passive to an active one.[6] Rationalization appeared most dramatically during the European Renaissance, and has distinguished Western civilization since then, but it existed before that epoch and in other places, and it has worked not only in politics but in culture generally.

Cryptology is included. It too evolved from an activity bathed in the sacred and the arcane to one contributing to the employment of power. It was, in its dim origins, suffused with mysticism; its ends were often sacred. One of its earliest uses was to get passersby to read Egyptian hieroglyphic funerary inscriptions. The scribes of some of these all-too-numerous epitaphs substituted rare signs for common ones to create a riddle that, they hoped, readers would try to puzzle out—and thereby express the words of the blessing. In antiquity and the Middle Ages, ciphers often kept magical formulas secret. The explications of the kabbalah seemed to resemble deciphering. The author of the first printed book on cryptology, Johannes Trithemius (1462–1516) seemed to intermingle cryptosystems with angel-assisted methods of long-distance instant communication. In its religious origin, cryptology resembled many other activities, such as drama and music.

Over the centuries, and especially in the Renaissance, these activities lost their theological auras and gradually came to serve secular ends. The classic example of secularization is that in which the medieval God-run universe was replaced by the modern, mechanistic one.[7] Men sought to understand the world less and less to glorify God and more and more to gain control over it for themselves. Ends became utilitarian. The same secularization took place in drama and music, in the writing of history,[8] in politics with the rise of temporal authority—and in cryptology.

The religious elements dropped away, permitting the profane uses to become relatively more numerous. Some had, of course, been present almost from the start: a letter from ancient Egypt records the intention of its author to determine the meaning of fire signals raised by the Egyptians.[9] But these secular uses had been obscured by the domination of the sacred. The shift to utilitarianism in cryptology is signalized rather dramatically: around 1466, Leon Battista Alberti apparently adapted a religious disk device, intended to generate an exhaustive list of arguments to help convert Muslims to Christianity, to create the first cipher disk, thereby inventing polyalphabetic substitution.[10] At about the same time, the rise of permanent embassies stimulated the employment of cryptology for utilitarian ends. Except for the controversies about whether Trithemius's cryptography was magical, which reverberated in learned circles for a couple of centuries, though with fading intensity, cryptology became almost entirely a technology, an applied science in the service of power.

With its nonrational elements all but stripped away, cryptology strove for yet greater rationalism. It strove to replace intuition in making and breaking cryptosystems with objective logic. This it did by using mathematics to resolve its problems.

The process was gradual, perhaps in part because much of cryptology's subject matter was seen as more philological than mathematical in nature and solution as more a question of natural (read: intuitive) ability than of statistics. So cryptology, as usual, lagged behind other applied sciences. Physics and engineering had, of course, long improved the precision and power of their analyses and predictions by quantifying as many of them as they could. By the turn of the century, Sir Francis Galton and Karl Pearson were applying mathematics, in the form of statistics, to social problems. Some historians in Göttingen had made some efforts in this direction even before that.[11] But even though cryptology's first mathematical study (that by F. J. Buck) was made at about the same time, namely, toward the end of the 1700s, and even though cryptanalysis is quintessentially statistical, cryptology did not take any steps of importance toward quantification until William F. Friedman in 1920 matched frequency distributions to reconstruct a plaintext alphabet in *The Index of Coincidence.*

World War II greatly intensified the use of mathematics in cryptology, with both Allies and Axis using mathematical tools both to break and to make ciphers. But the mathematical way of thinking has triumphed in cryptology only with the widespread advent of the computer. This epochal device permitted a much more quantified study of the subject, which made analyses both deeper and more accurate than any previously possible—as, for example, with the modeling of a cipher machine and the testing of its key-generating cycles.

Today, cryptology is almost entirely mathematized. A glance at its literature demonstrates that. This culmination of secularization has led the science into areas undreamed of not long ago. But it has shorn it of all but the last traces of mystery—and, some would say, of romance.

# On the Origin
# of Polyalphabetic
# Substitution

In an article 40 years ago, Charles J. Mendelsohn first described the evolution of the most widely used cipher system in the world, polyalphabetic substitution.[1] In its various forms, this system serves today in the computerized electronic cipher machines of the U.S. government, in the mechanically marvelous Hagelin cipher machine that almost 100 nations employ to keep their official communications secret, and in the postage-stamp-sized one-time pads of spies. During World War II, the Japanese PURPLE and the German Enigma machines, which the Allies cracked to contribute so much to their war efforts, both embodied forms of polyalphabetic substitution.[2]

Mendelsohn traced the cipher from its first appearance in a small treatise of about 1466 by Leon Battista Alberti (1404–1472),[3] one of the world's true polymaths, through its refinement by later theoreticians. But neither he nor any other scholars have looked into Alberti's source of the idea for his invention, one of the most important in the known history of cryptography.

Polyalphabetic substitution is a form of substitution cipher, one of the two great classes of ciphers, the other being transposition cipher. Transposition ciphers jumble the letters of the original message, or plaintext: *attack* may become TTAKCA. Substitution ciphers replace the letters of the original message with other letters or numbers or symbols: *attack* may become ZGGZXP. The two may be combined.

"On the Origin of Polyalphabetic Substitution" first appeared in the March 1980 issue of *Isis: Official Journal of the History of Science Society*.

All substitution ciphers employ a listing of paired plain and cipher equivalents that is called a cipher alphabet. In the example above, the cipher alphabet was $a = $ z, $b = $ y, $c = $ x, . . . , $z = $ a. Usually the cipher alphabet is written out with the plain letters above and the cipher letters below:

plain *a b c d e f g h i j k l m n o p q r s t u v w x y z*
cipher O A H M T Z X B I N U F C J P V R E K Q W D G L S Y

This juxtaposition maps the plain letters to the cipher letters and vice versa. Thus *go* = xp; hpct = *come.*

Because only a single cipher alphabet is used, this system is called monoalphabetic substitution. Its chief weakness is the fixity of its replacements. It permits solution by matching the frequency of the ciphertext letters with the known frequency of letters in the language of the plaintext. The obvious way of correcting this weakness is to give each plaintext letter more than one cipher equivalent. In the West, this technique started in the late 1300s and rapidly came into general use.[4] Though it delays cryptanalysis, it does not defeat it,[5] and because its plain-to-cipher equivalents are still fixed, the system remains monoalphabetic substitution.

The weaknesses of the monoalphabetic system disappear when the cryptographer provides additional cipher alphabets as a source of substitutes. For then not only will a given plaintext letter have several substitutes, but each ciphertext letter will stand for different plaintext letters depending upon its position in the text. The apparently capricious behavior of a cipher letter will greatly confuse the cryptanalyst. This idea first appears in Alberti's little manuscript of about 26 pages, generally called "De cifris."[6]

How did Alberti create multiple cipher alphabets? Taking two copper disks of different sizes, he inscribed the plain alphabet, including numbers for a special use, around the circumference of the larger bottom disk and wrote the cipher alphabet around the smaller, upper disk. (See Fig. 1.) Moving the inner disk from one position to another places different ciphertext letters against the plaintext letters. Each new position therefore creates a new cipher alphabet—hence "polyalphabetic" substitution.

Obviously, the two persons who want to use the system for secret correspondence must have identical disks. They must also know what successive positions are being used, or they will be as confused as a would-be cryptanalyst. So before they part they agree on a key. A simple

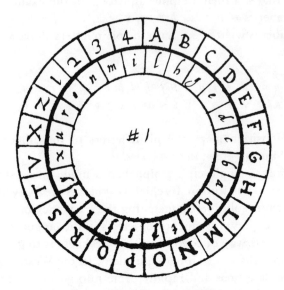

Fig. 1. Alberti's cipher disk

example is to set the disks at a prearranged position and then turn the inner one one space clockwise after enciphering each plaintext letter. The system's flexibility and strength commended it, and eventually polyalphabetic substitution in far more complex forms came to dominate cryptography.[7]

Alberti himself never said where he got the idea for his epoch-making invention. Scholars seem to have simply assumed that it evolved from his "horizon," an astrolabe he adapted for surveying, which consisted of a circle, whose circumference was graduated, over which swung a pointer.[8] It is true that both the horizon and the cipher disk are circular, have circumferences divided into sections, and have an element that rotates. But the significant feature of the cipher disk—the juxtaposition of two sequences—is lacking in the horizon. I therefore find this derivation unconvincing.

I propose another source: the mechanism devised by the medieval Catalan mystic Ramon Lull (c. 1232–1315) to combine letters, which he used to stand for philosophical concepts, in groups of three.[9] Although it cannot be proved that Lull's device inspired Alberti, there are grounds for suspecting that it did.

The device was created for purposes very different from Alberti's.

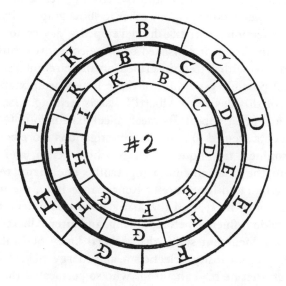

Fig. 2. Lull's disk for his "Ars magna"

Lull, at 31 converted by a series of visions to a religious way of life, determined to become a missionary to the Muslims and the Jews. To prepare for this, he spent from about 1265 to 1273 improving his Latin, learning Arabic, and reading widely. Convinced that the ultimate truth would support the Christian faith and that such truth, by comprehending all knowledge, would be acceptable to Muslims and Jews as well, he devised his *Ars inventiva veritatis,* the "art of finding truth." This took nine attributes of God, such as goodness, greatness, and power, which participated in all aspects of creation, and joined them in all possible ways to encompass all forms of existence.[10]

To facilitate the combining process, Lull employed two techniques in which scholars tend to see the germ of later scientific achievements. First, anticipating modern symbolic notation, he replaced the words for God's attributes by arbitrary letters, much as symbolic logic employs letters for sentences or elements of sentences; thus "goodness" was represented by B, "knowledge" by F, "truth" by I.[11] Lynn Thorndike has characterized this use of "brief handy designations" as the "chief contribution of Raymon Lull to modern science, or at least his chief step in the direction of scientific method."[12]

The second technique, foreshadowing the mechanisms for logic of electronic computers, automated the combining of one idea with another.[13] Working at first with pairs of concepts, Lull distributed the letters in a diagram, usually around the circumference of a circle, and drew lines from each letter to every other to show graphically all possible two-letter connections.[14] In 1289 he developed a device to combine all possible ideas in threes. It consisted of three concentric rotatable disks of graduated size with letters inscribed on the circumferences. As the disks turn, all possible groupings of three letters are juxtaposed.[15] The resemblance of this device to Alberti's disk is striking. (See Fig. 2.)

Lull's art had great appeal. Its mechanical exhaustion of all combinations of elements seemed to make its investigations more complete than other philosophical techniques, such as scholasticism, and thus better able to attain the final all-embracing truth. The many references to Lull in the letters and literature of Renaissance Italy, the many manuscripts of his work there, and the many Italian commentaries on him attest to his wide influence before, during, and after Alberti's lifetime.[16] Apparently no document states that Alberti knew of Lull.[17] Alberti's own wide-ranging curiosity, eclecticism, and energy make it highly probable, however, that he read an author who so permeated the intellectual climate of the time. The close resemblances between Alberti's and Lull's disks and the small difference between the two processes—juxtaposing letters to combine them and juxtaposing them to substitute one for another—further increase the probability that Lull's disk inspired Alberti's.[18]

As to where Lull got the idea for his disk, scholars have suggested three different possibilities. Robert Pring-Mill suspects that the volvelles of certain Arabic treatises on humoral medicine suggested the disks to Lull, who wrote on the subject. The volvelles were astrological wheels that could be revolved to show the different positions of the signs of the zodiac.[19] J. N. Hillgarth has suggested as a possible source the rotae or wheels found in the work of the encyclopedist and educator Isidore, Bishop of Seville (c. 570–636), especially those in the *De natura rerum*.[20]

Most convincing is the statement by Father Erhard Wolfram Platzeck in his comprehensive study of Lull that Lull owes the rotating disk of 1289 to the *Sefer Yezirah* (The Book of Creation), one of the pillars of the kabbalah, written between the third and sixth centuries.[21] Platzeck discusses the disk in the context of a full discussion of the possible relations between kabbalism and Lull's work. Two correspondences between Lull's art and the *Sefer Yezirah*, which describes how the cosmos was created out of the 22 letters of the Hebrew alphabet, are relevant to the disk: the use of letters to represent elements of reality, such as air, wisdom, and wealth, and the combining of the letters to form all creation. The passage on combination is particularly suggestive: "Twenty-two basal letters: they are placed together in a ring, as a wall with 231 gates. The ring may be put in rotation forwards or backwards. . . ."[22] Pring-Mill has also discerned a connection between the kabbalah and Lull, apparently through oral diffusion from kabbalistic schools existing in Catalonia during his lifetime,[23] while the existence of a translation of the *Sefer Yezirah* into Arabic,[24] which Lull could read, increases the probability that he knew of it. In addition, Blaise de Vigenère (1523–1596), a writer on cryptology, traces polyalphabetics to the *Sefer Yezirah*, though he does not mention Lull, Alberti, or disks in making the connection, whose basis he never states.[25] Mendelsohn criticizes this derivation, citing the section of the *Sefer Yezirah* quoted above. But his use of a translation that renders "ring" as "sphere" vitiates his criticism.[26]

Given the similarity in spirit between the *Sefer Yezirah* and Lull, in that both seek to seize and know the whole universe, and given the principle of combination common to both, Platzeck's derivation of the rotating disk from the Hebrew work is especially persuasive.

Whatever the inspiration for Lull's disk, it seems an excellent candidate as the source of the Alberti device that created polyalphabetic substitution. If so, Alberti's disk provides yet another example of the fate of Lull's techniques. Devised to convert the heathen to the ultimate truth, they ended by being themselves converted to secular ends.

# Herbert O. Yardley:
# A Biographical Sketch

When I was a boy, newly interested in the fascinating world of secret writing, Herbert O. Yardley's *The American Black Chamber* was my grail. Other books alluded to it; every bibliography listed it. Yet I could not find it in my school library or at the Great Neck Library, and I did not know where else to look. Finally, an advertisement in *The New York Times Book Review* led me to a company that sought out-of-print books— the Seven Bookhunters, I think. To my amazement and delight, within a few weeks the firm actually offered it to me, at the then rather steep price of $12.50, and I snatched it up.

I devoured it. It was one of the most thrilling books I had ever read. For in recounting the story of America's first codebreaking organization, which he had founded and led to one success after another, Herbert Yardley proved to be a natural storyteller.

He peopled his pages with diplomats, spies, shy codebreakers. He raced from one astonishing case to the next. He could catch the mood of an episode, indeed of the whole clandestine system, in a memorable image. The operator of a photostat machine, reproducing a letter in secret ink that can lead to a spy's execution, has a "face the color of death under the dim green lights." A schoolgirl picks her way through the Fifth Avenue crowds at dusk to a rendezvous with a German agent. in St. Patrick's Cathedral. An official whispers to Yardley, "The Spanish

This was written as an introduction to Ballantine Books's 1981 paperback reprint of *The American Black Chamber*. The editors there trimmed some portions; the complete original is given here.

code?" Moreover, his stories were revelations: Yardley was disclosing the hidden reasons of why things had happened as they did.

Yet a darkness hovered around the edges of the book. It must be part of the mystery that obscures all occult sciences. Despite the sunniness of much of the book, the darkness was never dispelled. This shadow, together with the book's readability, its disclosures, its mysteries, made it a classic of intelligence literature. Erle Stanley Gardner, the bestselling mystery writer, called *The American Black Chamber* "one of the most interesting books I have ever read."

Herbert Osborne Yardley was born April 13, 1890, in Worthington, Indiana, and grew up in that small Midwestern town—president of his high-school class, editor of the school paper, captain of the football team. His mother died when he was 16, and from his father, a railroad agent, he learned telegraphy. This gave him his first job, as a telegrapher for several railroads. Meanwhile, from the owner and card players at Monty's Place, a Worthington saloon, he learned poker, which became a lifelong passion. He came to Washington in 1913 at 23 as a $900-a-year telegrapher and code clerk for the State Department. Short, balding, witty, a marvelous raconteur, with what one acquaintance called "a dynamo of concentrated intellectual power in his head" and a way of talking that expressed utter conviction, he exercised a strong attraction upon many of those who knew him.

Yardley opened his book with an unforgettable word picture of the State Department code room in tranquil pre–World War I Washington. Codes, ciphers, their solutions, and the power that the resultant knowledge gave governments fired his imagination, and he determined to devote his life to it. With America's entry into World War I, he got his chance. He told how he was commissioned a lieutenant in military intelligence and created and organized its Cipher Bureau, its eighth section, MI-8. Though individuals had broken codes for the government since the American Revolution, no organization like this had ever existed in the United States before. MI-8 soon discovered spy letters written in invisible ink, solved German diplomatic codes and ciphers, and found specialists to read obscure German shorthand systems.

Near the end of hostilities, Yardley went to Europe and met with French, British, and American cryptologists, staying on for a tour of duty during the peace conference. Ten days after it opened, the army intelligence head was cabling Washington that "I consider the establishment of MI-8 on a peacetime basis most essential." On May 16, 1919, Yardley submitted a plan for a "permanent organization for code and

cipher investigation and attack." The need for the United States to continue to obtain the valuable intelligence it had obtained during the war
from cryptanalysis was persuasive, and three days later the army chief
of staff approved it and the acting secretary of state brown-penciled
an "O.K." on the memorandum. America had its first permanent codebreaking agency.

Yardley took a handful of people, most from MI-8, to New York,
and by July had begun the operations of an American black chamber,
officially called the Cipher Bureau. Tension was then high with Japan,
owing to that nation's expansion—in particular her receiving as man-
dates islands along the ocean route to China, Japan, and the Philippines—
and to her naval shipbuilding program, and Yardley's first major assignment was to break her codes.

In this job the Cipher Bureau succeeded. Yardley recounted how he
broke the first code in what is probably the single most dramatic passage
in the whole literature of cryptology:

> By now I had worked so long with these code telegrams that every tele-
> gram, every line, even every code word was indelibly printed in my brain.
> I could lie awake in bed and in the darkness make my investigations—
> trial and error, trial and error, over and over again.
>
> Finally one night I awakened at midnight, for I had retired early, and
> out of the darkness came the conviction that a certain series of two-letter
> code words absolutely *must* equal *Airurando* (Ireland). Then other words
> danced before me in rapid succession: *dokuritsu* (independence), *Doitsu* (Ger-
> many), *owari* (stop). At last the great discovery! My heart stood still, and
> I dared not move. Was I dreaming? Was I awake? Was I losing my mind?
> A solution? At last—and after all these months!
>
> I slipped out of bed and in my eagerness, for I knew I was awake now,
> I almost fell down the stairs. With trembling fingers I spun the dial and
> opened the safe. I grabbed my file of papers and rapidly began to make
> notes.

These soon confirmed that his vision had been correct. The solution
led, several months later, to a remarkable American diplomatic coup.
With the knowledge, gained through intercepts, of how much the Japanese negotiators at the Washington Disarmament Conference of 1921–
1922 would yield if pressed, the United States squeezed Japan to accept
less capital-ship tonnage than Japan had wished: the famous 5:5:3 ratio
among Britain, the United States, and Japan.

In the years that followed, Yardley's Cipher Bureau, which was under
the joint jurisdiction of the State and War departments, solved the codes
of 20 nations. But financial support dwindled as the 1920s proceeded

and the fear and memory of war receded. The staff shrank; some members worked only part-time. In November 1928, Herbert Hoover was elected president. He named as his secretary of state a New York lawyer with experience in government and in international affairs, Henry L. Stimson. Yardley waited until Stimson had been in office a few months, then sent him the solutions of an important series of messages. Stimson was shocked. He regarded it as a violation of the principle of trust on which he conducted both his personal affairs and the nation's foreign policy. As he said later, "Gentlemen do not read each other's mail." He withdrew all State Department funds from the Cipher Bureau. Since these constituted its major support, their loss effectively closed the office. The agency had cost the United States $329,212.49—just under a third of a million dollars for a decade of cryptanalysis.

Two days before the formal closing on October 31, 1929, the stock market crashed. Yardley, who was out of a job and had lost money in real estate in Queens, New York, where he had lived, went back to Worthington. Broke and unable to get a loan from an old MI-8 friend, University of Chicago professor John M. Manly, he decided in desperation to make some money to feed his wife and son by telling the story of his cryptologic work.

*The American Black Chamber* was published on June 1, 1931. It was an instant success. It immediately became the most famous book on cryptology published till then. Yardley's vigorous and pungent style, his narrative skill, and the total novelty of his revelations—people knew about spies, but few had heard of codes—fixed the book instantly in the popular mind. Reviews were unanimously good. It sold 17,931 copies—a remarkable figure. A British edition added 5,480 and there were French, Swedish, and Japanese translations as well as an unauthorized Chinese one.

The book catapulted Yardley to fame. He capitalized on it as much as he could. He gave lectures. He wrote articles. He tried to sell a secret ink. (During experiments for the ink, he infected the second finger of his right hand, and it had to be amputated.) And he decided to utilize the two boxes of secret documents he had taken with him when the Cipher Bureau closed to expand the central story of the book—how the solution of Japanese codes had led to the American diplomatic victory at the Washington Disarmament Conference. He had someone else write it. But the work, "Japanese Diplomatic Secrets," was never published: the government seized it [see next chapter]. Yardley then switched to a different writer and a more innocuous kind of book. This was a collection of puzzle cryptograms, each based on a brief fictional story to heighten its interest. The author was a neighbor in the coöperative apartment house he and Yardley (now back from Worthington) lived in at 95 28th Street, Jackson Heights, a neighborhood in the New York City borough of Queens. They became friendly at dances given by the coöp's club. The neighbor, Clem Koukol, was an engineer with the American Telephone & Telegraph Company, and his wife, Bee, was a mathematician with the Bell Telephone Laboratories, then located in Manhattan. Yardley, Koukol said, was always running around and played the field. He threw parties in his apartment with plenty of liquor and women. He liked Bee Koukol and would call her at one in the morning to go to a speakeasy. He and she played Russian bank, a kind of mathematical card game, night after night, with her often beating him. He loved to gamble. He would bet on how many pits there were in an orange.

One night Yardley asked Koukol to visit him at an apartment he maintained at the Hotel Holland on 42nd Street in Manhattan. They spent practically the whole night drinking gin. Yardley asked Koukol to write the puzzle book and for guidance lent him an army text on cryptology—probably Parker Hitt's excellent little *Manual for the Solution of Military Ciphers*, first published in 1916. Yardley paid him $500, and in 1932 the book, entitled *Yardleygrams* and with Yardley's name on it as author, was published. Like the unpublished "Japanese Diplomatic Secrets," it lacks the flair that *The American Black Chamber* had shown.

But so do two of Yardley's other books—or books that at least bear his name as author. Both are fiction: *The Red Sun of Nippon* and *The Blonde Countess*. Despite their rather pedestrian quality, Metro-Goldwyn-Mayer found the beautiful woman spy, the secret codes, and the infallible cryptanalyst of *The Blonde Countess* eminently suitable for its purposes. A problem was that no redblooded movie hero would settle for a dull desk job like codebreaking. But the film company fixed that up by destroying the fabric of Yardley's tale and making the hero an unwilling intellectual who wanted only to serve in the World War I trenches overseas. The result was *Rendezvous*, starring William Powell, Rosalind Russell, Binnie Barnes, and Cesar Romero. The film premiered in New York on October 25, 1935, with *The New York Times* reviewing it as a "lively and amusing melodrama." Yardley had gone to the Coast as technical advisor, but when he saw the film with the Koukols after a few drinks he was infuriated, complained loudly of what the producers had done to his story, and left before the movie was over.

In the next few years, Yardley again worked in real estate in Queens. He was not too successful, more, probably, because he was undercapitalized than because of his personality. He sliced things fine: he had the

Koukols sign affidavits that they had bought property and then would collect commissions on this.

In 1938 came a break: Generalissimo Chiang Kai-Shek, the leader of Nationalist China, hired him at about $10,000 a year to do what he had done so successfully before: solve Japanese codes and ciphers. This time he was to concentrate on the cryptosystems of the forces then invading China. He was met at Hong Kong by an interpreter, who addressed him as "advisor." They were having their first drink at their hotel, and Yardley was just about to ask him about the charms of Chinese women, when the interpreter asked him if it were true that the breasts of white women were red. Yardley, seeking to establish an aura of omniscience, at once drove with him to the police station, obtained the address of a whorehouse, and asked two French girls if they would disrobe for his friend. When they learned he was Chinese, they cried "*Le chien!,*" spat, and refused. Yardley had better luck in the port of Haiphong, where he persuaded a French manicurist to undress. The translator's curiosity was assuaged, and Yardley's good advance billing was assured.

Yardley entered China on a phony passport and with suitcases full of books on espionage and cryptology, concealed weapons, and an aircraft direction finder. Upon his arrival at Chungking, the wartime capital deep in the interior, perched on a rocky promontory overlooking the Yangtze, he was given what he was told was the home of the suddenly dispossessed mayor of the city—a 20-room, pine-floored, rat-infested house with no bathrooms. After this was destroyed by a Japanese bomb, he moved to an apartment high on the promontory; the offices occupied caves drilled into the cliffs by the government. His immediate superior, a rather stupid and chubby 35-year-old general who, Yardley said, had never smelled gunpowder and whom he nicknamed "the Donkey," headed the radio-intercept operators. The Donkey's boss was the head of the Nationalist secret service, the tough and feared Tai Li, a Chinese combination (someone said) of J. Edgar Hoover and Heinrich Himmler, about 40, gimlet-eyed, said by the U.S. military attaché to be "one of the generalissimo's most trusted officers and "a rather hard customer . . . not likely to stop at anything to achieve ends he believes to be important." Yardley, like others in Chungking, called him "the Hatchet Man." Tai presented Yardley to Chiang, who asked some intelligent questions about his work and seemed to Yardley more like a scholar than a political leader.

As a cover, Yardley disguised himself as Herbert Osborne, a trader in hides. It fooled no one in the tight-knit European community. With the help of the Hatchet Man, he soon began receiving a flow of intercepts which, with a staff of 30 young Chinese, he began attacking. Most were apparently low-level tactical army systems—two- and three-digit codes and kata kana transpositions.

But codebreaking was not his only activity in Chungking, where rain soaked everyone six months of the year, heat and dust suffocated them the other six, and Japanese bombing afflicted them at frequent intervals. He of course played poker, and sometimes drank a lot, but he mainly seemed to chase women. Everyone who knew him seemed to remark on this preoccupation. The writer Emily Hahn commented that "most of his conversation in those days was about women"; one of the assistant military attachés wrote that "sex is a major obsession with him and his conversation is filled with vulgar and bawdy references to women"; and another observed that he "has a decided weakness for women, and many Chinese women visit his apartment, but as far as is known, no foreign women." He kept a German and a Chinese mistress, though at separate times. For a young American correspondent for *Time* magazine, Theodore H. White, later famous as the best-selling author of *The Making of the President* series, he organized an oriental orgy, feeling it was necessary for him to be blooded as a man. White liked Yardley. He described him as "a balding middle-aged little fellow with the attractive and happy garrulousness of a country storekeeper. . . . He was an extremely witty man." He used to tell stories of his boyhood in Worthington and relate the adventures of his grandfather, a Union veteran and the town drunk. Others liked Yardley less, in particular Hahn, who sometimes kibitzed at the poker table while smoking a cigar. She thought he was an "an American with a loud manner of talking."

By March of 1940, Yardley reported to Tai that he had solved 19 different cryptosystems. One of his successes led to the capture of a spy. Another permitted the reading of messages dealing with troop movements in Shensi province, north and east of Chungking. He told the American military attaché that his work had been suspended until the five agencies in the Chinese government that were engaged in cryptology, with 800 or more employees, could be consolidated with himself in charge. It never happened. Weary, 40 pounds lighter than when he arrived, his foot infected from mosquito bites, lonely because of his restricted foreign contacts, unable to bring over his future second wife, Edna Ramsaier Hackenberg, a former member of the Cipher Bureau, he wanted to go home. He did so in July 1940. Back in America, he was given a contract to write memoranda on the technical details of the Japanese cryptosystems and his methods of solving them.

In May of 1941, soon after this work was completed, representatives of the Canadian government asked the U.S. Army's chief signal officer, General Joseph O. Mauborgne, to lend them someone to set up a cryptanalytic agency. Mauborgne, who was himself a cryptologist and who liked Yardley, told the Canadians: "The best man in the world for the job is Yardley." And, given Yardley's extraordinary organizational and executive ability, Mauborgne might well have been right. The Canadians interviewed Yardley, first in Washington, then in Ottawa, where, the next day, they hired him. After a trip to Washington to get his things, he returned to Ottawa on June 6, 1941, was given space on the second floor of a brand-new brick building with a wind-tunnel under it in an isolated area about three or four miles outside of Ottawa, and began setting up what was officially the Examination Unit of the Department of External Affairs. Edna Hackenberg was one of the first hired; she was followed by Gilbert Robinson, who did French; Fred Bartlett, who proved to be a natural cryptanalyst; a Japanese woman and her husband; a professor of German; a Mountie; an Englishman, who did little; a French girl; and a few others.

A radio station on the road to Ottawa, headed by an army officer, supplied the intercepts, which came as flimsies or as teletypewriter messages. Most of them were messages of German spies in South America, most enciphered in a single transposition, some in a double transposition. One message disclosed the presence of a German spy in a U.S. embassy in a Latin American country. Helped by some diplomatic texts, Mrs. Hackenberg solved a French diplomatic code and read the messages of Vichy—of considerable interest to a country with close historical and cultural ties to France.

But then Yardley blundered. He was so proud of his unit's solution of the difficult double transposition, which the British apparently had not been able to crack, that he showed off a bit. The British got wind of this work, wondered who could be that good, learned it was Yardley, became concerned about his previous breach of confidence and their cooperation with the United States, where the great codebreaker William F. Friedman, who loathed Yardley, was technical head of army cryptanalysis, and decided to withhold any further cooperation. If prolonged, this situation could have seriously damaged intelligence relations between the Dominion of Canada and the mother country. Lester Pearson, then an under secretary in the Department of External Affairs (and later a prime minister of Canada and a Nobel Peace Prize winner) whose job included dealing with Yardley, whom he seems to have liked and respected, went to Washington to straighten out the situation. But Mauborgne had retired a couple of months before, and his successor told Pearson that he would never cooperate with Canada as long as Yardley was breaking codes for her. Pearson had no choice: he replaced Yardley with an Englishman.

Yardley, angry and feeling himself unjustly treated, had his literary agent, George T. Bye, urge another of the agent's writers to intervene for him. The writer was Eleanor Roosevelt. Bye sent her a long letter, asking her to meet Yardley. But it was in vain. She sent the letter to her husband's military aide, who let it die. A few weeks later, after Pearl Harbor, Yardley heard that American secret intelligence was to be centralized under William J. Donovan, the Coordinator of Information, whose unit later evolved into the Office of Special Services. Yardley hoped to join, but the hope was forlorn. He was never again to break codes for any government.

Disappointed, he pulled up stakes in Ottawa. To Edna Hackenberg, it was like Napoleon's retreat from Moscow. They had gone up to Canada in the summer with hopes high and flags flying; they returned in the gloom of the snowy winter, cold, defeated, depressed. In Washington, Yardley opened a restaurant at 13th and H Streets, Northwest. It went bankrupt. He got a job with the wartime Office of Price Administration inspecting meat—and probably never in his life did he eat so much good meat. He refused a promotion because he wanted to keep working outside of the office, in part so he could continue to play poker during office hours. After the war, he and a professor of English, Carl Grabo, wrote a novel, *Crows are Black Everywhere*, based on his China experiences. With the $1,000 or $2,000 he received in advance, he bought a pots-and-pans business and hired salesmen. It failed. Then he got into the vacuum-cleaner business on credit, selling Filter Queens. It worked out well for a while, but eventually, it, too, went broke, and only a payment for four machines by Edna Hackenberg—now Edna Yardley—paid off the debts. Next he worked for a public-housing authority for five years and, after retiring, built houses in Silver Spring. Here he did well: a marvelous organizer, he always had the materials ready when the workmen arrived and the work that had to be done first completed when the next team of specialists arrived.

In 1954, he moved to Orlando, Florida, where he played poker incessantly in the American Legion building. Deciding to write a book on the game, he analyzed 35,000 hands, working eight to ten hours a day. The book offers rules and examples of how to win at the card game, and is spiced with some narrative passages in his inimitable style telling of how he learned and played poker in Monty's place in Worthington and of his experiences in China. It needed some rewriting, and during this time he moved back to Silver Spring, into a house on Rosenstiel Avenue that he had built. In 1957, *The Education of a Poker Player* was published by Simon and Schuster. It was an immediate success and, more than 25 years later, was still in print and selling.

A month before its actual publication, he suffered a stroke. It partly paralyzed him, but he fought it and shuffled around the house. His brain remained clear. Eight months later, he had another attack, went into a coma for eight days, and, at 12:45 P.M. on August 7, 1958, died in the house he had built on Rosenstiel Avenue. He was buried with military honors in Arlington National Cemetery.

The obituaries called him "the father of American cryptography." In the long and narrow view, that is not so. Others made and broke codes and ciphers long before Yardley appeared, and the vast cryptologic establishments of today are the lineal descendants, not of MI-8 or the Cipher Bureau, but of the Signal Corps codebreaking unit that Friedman founded and nurtured. But the world has never seen another cryptologist who fired the public's imagination as Yardley had. His books have probably recruited many who have contributed to the field, and so indirectly he may be responsible for some of its advancement. During his career, his solutions nudged world events and changed, even though only slightly, the course of history. Of few men can even that be said. It is true that the cataclysm of World War II obliterated many of these effects, and still later, he proved as mortal as other men. But in the end, Yardley beat history and death. In his books, he lives still.

# Yardley's "Lost" Manuscript

Historians have long sought the manuscript of Herbert O. Yardley's second book, "Japanese Diplomatic Secrets." It was written after the remarkable success of his *The American Black Chamber*, published in 1931, and was thought to give more details about the central episode of that book, the breaking of Japanese codes that led to the remarkable American diplomatic successes at the Washington Disarmament Conference of 1921–1922, which limited the size of the world's navies.

*The American Black Chamber*, which was translated into Japanese, had caused the Japanese to lose face by revealing that their codes had been broken. It had inflamed Japan's dislike of Americans and had rendered Japanese-American relations more difficult. So when a State Department official learned that Yardley was about to publish another book on the same subject, he urged, in a memorandum of February 12, 1933, that "every possible effort should be made to prevent the appearance of this book."

Apparently as a result of wheels set in motion by this, the U.S. attorney for the Southern District of New York wrote the attorney general in Washington four days later. He stated that the Macmillan Company, to whom Yardley had submitted his manuscript after it was declined by the Bobbs-Merrill Company (publishers of *The American Black Chamber*), had just received the Yardley manuscript and that he could arrange for the War Department or the Justice Department to read it. The next

This article first appeared in the April 1982 issue of *Cryptologia* as "Yardley's Seized Manuscript."

day, the U.S. attorney followed this with another letter saying that one of his assistant U.S. attorneys, Thomas E. Dewey (a future governor of New York and twice a Republican candidate for president), had arranged with Macmillan to get the manuscript. On February 20, U.S. marshals seized the manuscript at the Macmillan offices on the grounds that it violated a statute prohibiting agents of the United States government from appropriating secret documents. Yet no prosecution ensued against Yardley, his agent, Macmillan, or any Macmillan editors.

The manuscript vanished. Historians studying Japanese-American relations and the Washington Disarmament Conference sought in vain for it and for further details on the American cryptanalysis that had played so important a role in pressing the Japanese to reduce the size of their navy beyond what they had wanted. No solved telegrams were to be found, for example, in the State Department files, or in the papers of the secretary of state at the time of the conference, Charles Evans Hughes. Nor, apparently, could they be found elsewhere.

But the manuscript was not lost. It had remained all these years in the files, naturally enough, of the Department of Justice. In 1968, I asked the National Archives to search for it in those records, and the archivists found it in Record Group 60, Department of Justice Straight Numerical File, No. 235334.

The voluminous manuscript stuffed into manila folders indeed bore the title "Japanese Diplomatic Secrets 1921–22," with, as subtitle, "The story of the events leading up to and including the Washington conference on the Limitation of Armaments and Pacific and Far East Questions as revealed in the private diplomatic correspondence of the Japanese embassy in Washington." And the text referred to the work of Yardley's Cipher Bureau and included numerous solved Japanese dispatches. But the author was not Herbert O. Yardley. It was Marie Stuart Klooz.

The preface was dated at Sweet Briar, Virginia, on May 22, 1932. The women's college of that name in that town acknowledged that Miss Klooz had been a student there and graciously forwarded a letter about the matter to her. In a reply and subsequent telephone interview, Miss Klooz said that she had written the book at Yardley's request on the basis of papers he had. She did most of it in New York and rewrote several chapters at Sweet Briar at Bobbs-Merrill's request. She said that she thought that Yardley, who had never graduated from college, felt that he did not have the academic background needed to place this story in its proper historical context and was, in addition, "not interested in doing it himself." Miss Klooz, who had worked as a newspaper reporter and free-lance writer after graduating from Sweet Briar College in 1923, said that the contract with Yardley was made through her best friend's agent—perhaps George T. Bye, who was Yardley's agent. Apparently, she was originally to ghostwrite the book, for, she noted, "When Mr. Yardley learned that the Government opposed publication, he asked me to put my name on the title page instead of his." She said that she returned all documents to Yardley when she was finished writing. After the government seized the manuscript, "I lost interest," she said. In 1939, she "used the *published* material as the basis of my Master's thesis at Columbia University for a Degree in International Law," she wrote. But the thesis, "A Reconsideration of the Origins of the Conference on the Limitation of Armament, Washington: November 12, 1921—February 6, 1922, and the Four Power Treaty," lists, on page 251 in its bibliography, "Yardley, Herbert O. *Papers.*" She may have felt, however, that her use of them during the writing of "Japanese Diplomatic Secrets" entitled her to list them. Miss Klooz became a lawyer and worked in Washington.

"Japanese Diplomatic Secrets" is 920 typewritten pages and 19 chapters long. It is divided into seven parts: I, "Origins of the Washington Conference"; II, "Limitation of Armaments"; III, "Four Power Pacific Treaty"; IV, "Far Eastern Conference"; V, "Shantung"; VI, "Yap"; and VII, "Conclusions." It includes hundreds of what the preface says were "some five thousand messages which contained the secret instructions of the Japanese plenipotentiaries" that the Cipher Bureau solved and sent to Washington "for the information and assistance of the American delegation" during the conference. I began to list all the messages in the manuscript, but abandoned the task when it appeared that it would take more time than it was worth to a historian of cryptology. But between pages 3 and 66, I counted 39. Some of them are short enough for two to fit on a single page; others cover two or three pages. Most of the messages are to or from Tokyo and London, Washington and Paris; a few are between other such capitals as Washington and The Hague. Rarely is a message garbled. The greatest weakness, from the point of view of the historian, is that none of those examined bear either the date of solution or the date of submission to the State Department, nor—a cryptologic weakness—does the work provide any details on the code system, and it almost never gives even the name of the code used. A further weakness might be that Miss Klooz was, she wrote in the preface, "careful to reject any [telegrams] that might embarrass either the United States or Japan, and any that by the remotest chance could cause ill feeling between the two nations"—though it seems as if that damage had long since been done.

The text itself is little more than connective between the intercepts. Miss Klooz rather implied this when she stated in the preface that she "decided to edit and prepare them for publication." Nor does that text have any of the thrill, any of the racing excitement, that made *The American Black Chamber* so entrancing a book. "Japanese Diplomatic Secrets" is pedestrian. Miss Klooz was not the writer that Herbert Yardley was.

What is the importance of the manuscript? It cannot be the revelation of some dramatic and history-changing secret, for *The American Black Chamber* gave the main story back in 1931; Miss Klooz herself has conceded that "I do not think it ["Japanese Diplomatic Secrets"] has much more information than *The American Black Chamber*." Yet it does fill in gaps; it provides many more details of the information available to American policymakers before and during one of the first successful conferences to limit arms. It will be of use primarily to the historian of that conference. It does not contribute anything of importance to the history of cryptology. So it cannot be said to be worth publishing; its appeal is too limited. In the end, what the rediscovery of "Japanese Diplomatic Secrets" chiefly does is to remind the world that codebreaking, so often an instrument of war, can also serve peace.

# The Spy Who Most
# Affected World War II

Who was the man whose spying had the greatest impact on the course of World War II? Was it Richard Sorge, who told the Soviet Union that Japan would not attack it? Or his informant, Ozaki Hotsumi? Perhaps the greatest spy was Elyesa Bazna, alias CICERO, who daringly stole most-secret documents from the safe of his master, the British ambassador in Turkey. Or perhaps the accolade should fall upon the Spaniard codenamed CATO, or the German codenamed TATE, both of whose double-agentry helped deceive the Germans as to where the Allied cross-Channel invasion was coming.

Or was the spy who most affected World War II a German who has hitherto languished in virtual obscurity? This was the man who delivered documents that the Poles used to solve the German Enigma cipher machine, with all that that entailed during World War II. Though he forms the centerpiece of a French book, it uses only his codename. Neither that book nor some later ones that mention him ground their biographies in documents; none assemble all the available details; none evaluate his contribution or compare it with that of the legendary figures of espionage. This article seeks to provide, for the first time, that information and that evaluation for the man who may well have had the greatest impact of any secret agent on the greatest war of all time.

The story must begin with a stout, dynamic captain of the French army, Gustave Bertrand. Enlisting in 1914 as a private, he rose to briga-

This article is published here for the first time.

dier general. In 1915, during the ill-fated Allied attempt to open a passage to Russia at the Dardanelles, Bertrand was wounded. After the war, he was assigned to the cipher section of the general staff of French forces in Constantinople.[1]

"Cipher attracted me," he said. "I wanted to go farther. I went to the chief of the cipher service, Colonel Bassières, one of the greatest of our cryptanalysts, whom I knew, and said, 'If you need me, call me'—and they did."[2] So he served in the cipher section of various headquarters and, in 1929, in the cipher section of the army general staff. There he found that the eight cryptanalysts[3] of the section's cryptanalytic subsection, who solved for both the army and the Foreign Ministry, were "happy with the least little result."[4] Only simple systems were solved. Among them were the German army's double transposition field cipher[5] and some German codes that were superenciphered with a polyalphabetic substitution called the Universalschlüssel[6] because it served for many codes, and a British code that the French called the IBYTA, from its codeword for "full stop."[7] Yet solutions of higher systems could be the best source of information for the high command and possibly the government as a whole, Bertrand believed.[8]

"I saw that the only answer was to buy documents," he said.[9] The cryptanalysts needed the help of spies or a safecracker-photographer team. Upon Bertrand's suggestion, he was transferred to the general staff's Service de Renseignements (Intelligence Service) to set up a Section D, for Décryptement et Interceptions. It would seek to gain foreign cryptographic documents or information from individuals and to intercept and solve foreign cryptograms. Section D began operations on October 30, 1930, with Bertrand's assignment to it.[10]

For almost two years, Section D yielded nothing of great value. With the approval of his chiefs, Bertrand contacted the Polish, Czech, and British intelligence services and exchanged intercepts and direction-finding results with the first two. No cryptanalytic results seem to have been passed among any of the four, perhaps because none of any great importance had been achieved.

The Poles, like the French, had solved the German army double transposition.[11] Because this system merely scrambled the letters of the original messages, its cryptograms had the letter-frequency characteristics of the German language: an abundance of vowels and of common consonants such as *n*, *r*, *s*, and *t*, and a great variation in the frequencies of different letters. Thus, when the Poles began to intercept German army cryptograms with many rare letters, such as x, z, and Q, it was not hard to see that the Germans had introduced a new cipher, a substitution system. The almost flat frequency distribution of the letters of its cryptograms suggested that it was probably machine-generated.[12] Agent reports confirmed this. It soon became clear that the German army had put into service on July 15, 1928,[13] a cipher machine called the Enigma, which had been devised a few years earlier by a Berlin engineer, Dr. Arthur Scherbius, and offered for sale to business firms. But the army had naturally modified the commercial model for greater secrecy. (The German navy had started using the Enigma in 1926,[14] but the Poles did not detect this because, owing to lack of manpower, none of their codebreakers were working on German naval systems.)

The Enigma had a typewriter-like keyboard to input letters and a panel of illuminable letters for the output. The operator would press a key to encipher a plaintext letter; the ciphertext letter would light up on the panel. The recipient, who needed an identical cipher machine, pressed the ciphertext letter and the plaintext letter would shine on the panel. The enciphering was done by rotors. Rotors are flat cylinders of hard rubber or bakelite, about the size and shape of a hockey puck. Twenty-six electrical contacts stud the rim of each face. Each contact on one side is connected at random by wires to a contact on the other side. This means that an electric impulse entering at one point on one side will emerge at a different point on the other, thus enciphering a letter. The Enigma had three rotors side by side for the current to flow through and a half-rotor, or reflector, with contacts on only one face, to send the current back through the rotors to further complicate the encipherment. The rotors turned to vary the internal maze. Each time the operator pressed a key to encipher a letter, the right-hand, or "fast" rotor, stepped one place. When the fast rotor passed a certain point in its revolution, the middle rotor stepped one place; and the slow rotor likewise turned 1/26th of a revolution when the middle rotor passed a certain point. The rotors would eventually return to their initial position, re-creating the original wiring labyrinth, but only after more than 17,000 letters had been enciphered. The result was an extremely complicated and rather secure cipher.[15]

In their analysis of the Enigma cryptograms, the two Polish cryptanalysts, one an officer, one an engineer named Czajaner, determined that the first six letters of each message probably represented a key.[16] But they made little additional progress. A few months later, in January 1929, Polish intelligence officers surreptitiously inspected, in the Warsaw customs offices, a copy of the commercial model of the Enigma.[17] But neither the brief look the Poles got at it, nor the purchase of a commercial model a little while later,[18] helped them solve the military version. The rotor wiring was certainly different, and agent reports indicated that some kind of electrical plug arrangement had been added.[19] These differences were great enough to prevent Czajaner and his colleague from making much progress. Stymied by what appeared to be an insoluble problem, the Poles abandoned their attempt to cryptanalyze the Enigma.[20] All that remained were a few sheets of paper densely filled with writing.[21]

Then, one day in October 1932, Bertrand's efforts bore fruit. A German with access to German army cryptographic material offered the French his services. At first the offer was turned down—over Bertrand's objections—as a provocation; it seemed too good to be true. But the employee persisted, and the French arranged a rendezvous in a safe house that straddled the Dutch-German border: a person could enter the house in Germany and leave in Holland. The prospective spy brought a few samples. Though Bertrand was not allowed to attend this meeting, he had the impression this agent might hold the key to the treasure for which Bertrand had hoped since he set up Section D.[22]

The Service de Renseignements was finally persuaded that the man meant what he said and accepted him as one of their agents. They gave him, as they gave their other agents, a designation consisting of a group of letters.[23] His was HE,[24] two letters that do not seem to have borne any particular significance. In French, these are spoken /ahsh-AY/. This somewhat resembles the German word *Asche* ("ash"), which is sounded /AH-shuh/ and which became the generally used codename for the agent.

Who was this man? His name was Hans-Thilo Schmidt. He was 44 years old, having been born May 13, 1888, in Berlin, the son of Professor Dr. Rudolf Schmidt and his wife, Johanna, née Baroness von Könitz.[25] The father, 37 when Hans-Thilo was born, taught at the Charlotten school in Berlin; his dissertation was on a battle of the Thirty Years' War and, before Hans-Thilo was 8, he had published studies on two commanders of that war. Hans-Thilo was 26 when World War I began and so may have served in the German armed forces. He is said to have become—probably after the war—the owner of a chemical factory.[26] But in the depression- and inflation-ridden Germany of the 1920s, he could not turn a good enough profit. So, like many others, he sought a job with the military.

Most were unable to snare this prize, for under the Versailles Treaty the German army was limited to 100,000 men, and even many career officers had been forced out. But Schmidt was luckier than most. After World War I, his brother, Rudolf, two years older, had managed to remain in the Reichswehr. Rudolf had joined the army at age 20 as a cadet in Infantry Regiment 83. In 1913, he transferred to the Signal Corps and served mainly in this branch in World War I on both the eastern and the western fronts. In 1926, Rudolf Schmidt became the second head of the unit of the Signal Corps that handled cryptology for the army and the Defense Ministry, the Chiffrierstelle, or Cipher Center.[27] In this post he was able to give his brother a job, though not a uniformed one. Hans-Thilo became a civilian clerk who distributed cipher material and supervised its destruction when it went out of force.[28] He remained in the Chiffrierstelle after his brother left on October 1, 1929.

On December 1, 1931, a year before Adolf Hitler came to power, Hans-Thilo Schmidt was admitted to the Nazi party under membership number 738,736.[29] At the time he was married and living in the Lichterfelde section of Berlin at Lorenzstrasse 17.[30] About a year later, still in the Chiffrierstelle, he made his offer to the French.

His reason was money. A weakling, a hedonist, a dissipate, he wanted the money for his women and his high living. But perhaps there was also an unacknowledged motive for his treason. His father had attained the highest nongovernmental status a civilian could get. His mother was a noblewoman. His brother was rising in the army, Germany's most prestigious institution. He himself was a failure. Perhaps he wanted to revenge himself on his family by doing something that would undermine the society that had conferred so much upon them and that, if discovered, would destroy them.[31]

In 1933, several weeks after Hitler became chancellor, three of Hans-Thilo's Nazi colleagues in the Cipher Center left to form a new intercept, codebreaking, and telephone-tapping agency under the No. 3 man in the Third Reich, the future Luftwaffe commander and Reichsmarschall, Hermann Göring. This organization, the Forschungsamt ("Research Office"), started out as and remained the most Nazi of all the Third Reich's communications-intelligence agencies, and, enjoying as it did Goering's patronage and largesse, it soon became the richest.[32] This opportunity—and perhaps his former co-workers—beckoned Hans-Thilo Schmidt, who had the proper party credentials and whose brother's influence in the Cipher Center was diminishing as his intendancy of it receded. So in 1934, Hans-Thilo transferred to the Forschungsamt. There he evaluated the interceptions and solutions of the messages of western European nations.[33] And there he continued his treason.

He met the French 19 times during the 7 years of his activity—an average of one rendezvous every 4 months. Twelve of the meetings took place in Switzerland, 4 in Belgium, and one each in Denmark,

Czechoslovakia, and France;[34] the latter was a fête in August of 1938 to reward him for his services, at which Bertrand and another officer took him wherever he wanted to go: the Folies-Bergère, the Casino de Paris, the Moulin Rouge.[35] Present at all of the meetings except the first was Bertrand; also present was one member or another of the German section of the Service de Renseignements. A photographer went along on some missions.[36] Another person also attended. He was a legendary figure of prewar French intelligence. His codename was REX, but his original name was said to be Richard Stallmann. Before World War I he had fled his native Berlin because of cheating in gambling and cards, ending up in Paris. He became a French citizen and took as his new name "Lemoine"—no doubt as a sardonic joke, for the life he led contrasted sharply with the appellation, which means "the monk." Extremely tall, a bon vivant who loved good meals and Havana cigars rolled on the warm thighs of the factory girls, a big spender with ready money and the manner of a grand seigneur, an amusing conversationalist with a taste for risque stories, socially adept, he had set up some kind of an espionage agency, perhaps a recruiting office, for the Service de Renseignements, on the rue de Lisbonne in Paris's swanky 8th arrondissement. Lemoine may have played a role in attracting Schmidt, but this is not clear, nor is his relation to the spy, which must have been quite close since his presence was required at every meeting with Schmidt, in part to interpret if necessary, but mainly, it is stated, to ensure that the connection was made.[37] Lemoine's link to Schmidt was to last, fatefully, even after the hostilities that began in 1939 ruptured Schmidt's connection with France.

For Bertrand, the meetings began long before the actual contact with Schmidt. "Ah! Those departures from Paris, by taxi, at night, across the city, to get to the Gare du Nord or the Gare de l'Est [stations for rail lines to the north or to the east], among the neon lights and the often anxious thoughts, while I left all behind me—to find what ahead? And could ASCHE have been followed from Berlin?"[38]

The circumstances of the meetings varied. The Frenchmen arrived in Copenhagen (via England to avoid traversing German territory) to find that Schmidt, who had gone there by a complicated tourist itinerary, had wined and dined himself practically into a stupor. Scarcely presentable the next morning, he shaped up for the day's discussions and left that evening with a major assignment. Near the Czechoslovakian ski resort of Spindleruv Mlyn, Bertrand and a brother officer were astonished to see Schmidt getting off a train in full Bavarian alpinist costume, complete with Tirolean hat, suede shorts, and rucksack. He started hiking through the woods toward the Davidova Bouda hotel, a 27-room mountain chalet somewhat off the beaten track, with the Frenchmen, guns loaded, following behind. At the rendezvous, they discovered, to their pleased surprise, that the rucksack was filled with secret documents.

In Mürren, Switzerland, facing the spectacular panorama of the Alps, the spy and his spymasters, who had all arrived separately, mixed with the crowd of skiers. Later, meeting in one of their rooms seated around a table under a crystal chandelier, a czardas, heard muted from the ballroom, impelled Schmidt to prance about a little; only afterward did he unwrap his merchandise. The chief item was the German army's mobilization code, the Satzbuch E, in the blue that indicated a mobilization document and with "Geheime Kommandosache," or "top secret," stamped on it. Schmidt had extracted it from his chief's safe.

The photographer took it to the bathroom, where the clicking of his camera was less likely to be heard outside. Bertrand went with him and, lying on his belly on the floor, turned the pages for him. Meanwhile, Schmidt wrote out the answers to a questionnaire Bertrand had prepared, with Lemoine helping him with the translation. A cool riesling slaked the thirst that the work had raised and let Schmidt, who seemed obsessed with what his chief would do if he discovered the theft, relieve the tension by telling some tall stories that got some laughs while Lemoine responded with jokes. The work was complete by the middle of the night and all persons retired to their own rooms. The next morning, after an early breakfast, everyone left Mürren, and on Monday, when the chief of the Chiffrierstelle returned to work, the Satzbuch E was back in its proper place. One of the Frenchmen gave the film to the representative in Switzerland of the Service de Renseignements, who sent it by a safe route to France.[39]

Between the meetings, Schmidt passed secrets by writing to the French at various addresses in France and other countries in invisible ink between the lines of "family" letters. He sent urgent information to a cover name at general delivery, Berlin, where a French agent, alerted by a postcard, picked it up. He was paid by Reichsmarks in small- and medium-sized denominations placed in a small suitcase and deposited in the baggage room of a Berlin railroad station. The ticket was sent to him under a false name at general delivery where, using a false identity card, he was able to pick it up. A postcard to his home notified him when it was ready.[40]

The German section of the Service des Renseignements was primarily interested in the details of German rearmament, military politics,[41] and major army projects that Schmidt could supply thanks to his closeness with his brother, who by 1937 had become a major general commanding one of the new panzer divisions.[42] Rudolf discussed even the most confidential matters so freely with Hans-Thilo that the French wondered if they were being fed fake information. But when tested, the data always proved accurate.

It was Schmidt's cryptologic information, however, that was the most significant. He delivered—among others—the black code of the Abwehr, the armed forces espionage agency, cipher manuals and monthly keys for the staff and the army-wide hand ciphers, the cipher for use between military and civilian agencies, the field manuals for the German interception service, and quarterly reports of the solutions achieved by the Forschungsamt, such as, in 1936, those of 14 French codes, 3 Belgian, 3 Swiss, 2 Dutch, and 10 of other countries. But his most critical disclosures were among the first he made.[43]

He provided the French with documents on the military Enigma cipher machine. Two were official manuals. Secret Army Regulation No. 13, which was also Secret Luftwaffe Regulation No. 13, comprised the operating instructions for the machine. This made clear that the army and the air force had introduced, on June 1, 1930, a new form of military Enigma. It incorporated a new kind of plug arrangement. Called a plugboard, it was a panel of sockets, representing letters, at the front of the military machine. Short cables with jacks on their ends connected the sockets in varying ways. Each cable shifted the enciphering current from one letter to another before the current was sent through the rotors. Keys specified which pairs of sockets the cables connected. Secret Army Regulation No. 14, which was also Secret Luftwaffe Regulation No. 14 and Secret Navy Regulation No. 168, dealt with keying methods for the new machine. In addition, Schmidt furnished daily keys for September and October 1932. These included several elements: the order in which the three rotors were inserted into the machine, the positions of the geared metal rings that were attached to each rotor (except the leftmost, or slow, rotor) and that, at particular points, caused the rotor to the left to step one place, and which 6 pairs of letters (out of the 13 possible pairs) were enciphered by the plugboard. Schmidt also provided other, though less useful, Enigma material.[44]

Schmidt had contacted the French in October of 1932. At the same time, and before any of his material had reached Warsaw, the Poles had, coincidentally, begun a new assault upon the Enigma. The cryptanalyst was now a 27-year-old mathematician, Marian Rejewski (ray-YEF-ski). He had been introduced to cryptology in January 1929, when, as one of a score of German-speaking mathematics students at the University of Poznan, he had been selected for a two-night-a-week course in cryptology taught by officers of Poland's Biuro Szyfrów, or Cipher Bureau, which was seeking to expand its cadre for work on German ciphers. After attending the course for a few months, Rejewski went to Göttingen University in Germany to study advanced mathematics for a year, then returned to Poznan to teach mathematics. While doing so, he worked in an outpost of the Cipher Bureau set up in a cellar of the military command post on St. Martin's Street.[45] Mostly he and a handful of colleagues solved the Germany army double transposition.[46]

The Poznan outpost was closed in the summer of 1932, and on September 1, Rejewski and two colleagues, Jerzy Rozycki and Henryk Zygalski, began work in Warsaw as full-time employees in the Biuro Szyfrów's 4th, or German, branch, called B.S.-4.[47] Within a couple of months they solved a four-letter German naval code,[48] but before this had been fully exploited Rejewski was detached to start solving the Enigma—the same machine that had defeated the Biuro Szyfrów four years before.

In a separate office on the third floor of the north wing of the general staff building on Saxon Square, overlooking the tomb of Poland's Unknown Soldier,[49] Rejewski, after reading the few sheets of paper on the Enigma that his predecessors had left in the archives, picked up where they had left off: analyzing the six-letter keys with which each Enigma message started. Within a few weeks he extracted six chains of letters. These, and his general understanding of the machine, enabled him to set up six equations with four terms. Three of them were unknown: the wiring of the fast rotor, the combined wiring of the middle and slow rotors and the reflector, and the connections of the plug arrangement. The fourth was the wiring that led from the keyboard to the rotors. He assumed that its order was that of the letters on that keyboard: QWERT. . . .

The unknown terms in these equations were not simple terms like "$3x$," but arrays of 26 elements. The figures in them came from his quantification of the machine encipherment. Rejewski had numbered each rotor's contacts from 1 to 26 around the rim. He then subtracted the number of the output contact of each wire from that wire's input contact number. This represented by a figure the encipherment produced by that wire. The figure was one of the 26 elements in one of the arrays of unknowns; the entire array represented the encipherment that the rotor's whole wiring produced and was one of the unknowns Rejewski was seeking. If he could discover the values of the array of the fast rotor, he would know the wiring—the secret heart of the Enigma

in theory at any rate. But that approach is imperfect and laborious . . . it requires the possession of messages from two days of identical or very similar settings of the rotors; therefore, finding the wiring of the rotors would depend on luck. In addition, it requires so many trials that it is not clear whether the director of the Cipher Bureau would have had enough patience to employ several workers for a long period without certain attainment of success, or whether he would have once more discontinued work on the Enigma. Hence the conclusion is that the intelligence material furnished to us should be regarded as having been decisive to the solution of the machine."[60]

With this start, the Poles were able to master the successive complications that the Germans applied to the Enigma throughout the 1930s.[61] In 1939, just before the outbreak of war, they turned over details of the cryptanalysis and copies of Enigma machines to the French and the British. These allies, igniting their torches from the Polish flame, illuminated the darkness of combat with the light of ULTRA's Enigma intercepts—an intelligence triumph that saved so many lives during World War II.

Schmidt's own life, however, was forfeit. In November 1942, when the Germans occupied all of France after the Allies invaded North Africa, counterespionage picked up Lemoine in Saillagouse, the small town in the Pyrenees, 10 miles from neutral Spain, to which he had fled after France fell. The Germans knew of his work for the French and interrogated him thoroughly over several months. To save himself, he denounced those who had spied for France against Germany.[62] Among them was Hans-Thilo Schmidt, then still working for the Forschungsamt. He was arrested by the Gestapo. On May 8, 1943, his name was struck from the rolls of the Nazi party.[63] He was executed in July.[64] At his home were found letters of his brother, Rudolf, that, Propaganda Minister Josef Goebbels noted in his diary, "spoke very disparagingly of the Fuhrer. Now that is one of the generals of whom the Fuhrer thought especially well."[65] Rudolf Schmidt had won glory as commander of the dashing XXXIXth Panzer Corps in Russia, had risen to command the 2nd Army and, on December 25, 1941, replaced Germany's famed apostle of tank warfare, General Heinz Guderian, whom Hitler discharged as commander of the 2nd Panzer Army. Schmidt had been promoted to colonel general, the highest rank in the German army except for field marshal. But on July 10, 1943, he was ousted from his command; on September 30, he was expelled from the army. He appealed to SS leader Heinrich Himmler, but Hitler categorically prohibited any further service. He died in Kassel in 1957.[66] Lemoine, too, survived the war, dying in a French interrogation camp at Wildbad, Germany, in 1946.

What does this remarkable story mean in the dark annals of espionage? How does Hans-Thilo Schmidt compare with the other great spies of World War II? His impact exceeded theirs. Sorge and Ozaki, who correctly reported in October 1941 that Japan would move south and so would not strike the Soviet Union from behind while she was fighting Germany, may or may not have significantly influenced Josef Stalin's decision to transfer troops from the Far East to the front at Moscow; the question is far from settled.[67] CICERO revealed to the Germans Britain's diplomatic maneuvers to get Turkey into the war on the side of the Allies, thus enabling the Germans to counter some of them, but at best the German moves only delayed the Allied successes by a few months.[68] This cannot be said to be a vital matter. The two double agents, CATO and TATE, played a significant role in convincing the Germans that the Normandy landing was but a feint, thereby enabling the Allies to entrench themselves so firmly that they could not be thrown back into the sea. But their contributions, which were in any event only a part of a multifaceted deception plan, mainly reinforced the German preconceptions, and so, while they confirmed the course of history, they cannot be said to have changed it.[69]

Hans-Thilo Schmidt did. His documents enabled the Poles to achieve a solution that led to what has rightly been called "the most important sustained intelligence success in the history of human conflict."[70] The Allied reading of Germany's secret messages played a major role in the Allied victories in Africa, in Europe, in the Atlantic. Thus Schmidt's betrayals affected, in the most intimate and permanent ways, the lives of millions. For no other secret agent in World War II, or perhaps in any time, was this the case.

That is why Hans-Thilo Schmidt is the spy who most affected the Second World War.

# The ULTRA Conference

The first international conference of cryptologists took place in Germany in November 1978.[1]

The backroom boys of World War II—Allied communications intelligence experts and Axis communications security specialists—met under scholarly sponsorship to try to determine the effect of codebreaking on the war. They concentrated particularly on the Allied breaking of the German Enigma and Geheimschreiber cipher machines, whose solutions were codenamed ULTRA. The enormous Allied success in cracking these high-level German ciphers and in thereby gaining insight into top German plans and capabilities was the greatest secret of the war after the atom bomb. It also became the longest-held secret of the war: the British did not expose it until 1974, when they allowed F. W. Winterbotham's *The Ultra Secret* to be published. That revelation touched off almost frantic activity among historians of the war. Had it made their work nugatory? Would they have to rewrite the whole history of the war? What was the weight of this intelligence in the conflict as a whole?

It was to answer such questions as these that the conference was organized—and brilliantly run—by Dr. Jürgen Rohwer, Germany's leading naval historian. Rohwer is also director of the Bibliothek für Zeitgeschichte (Library for Contemporary History) in Stuttgart, and adjunct professor at the University of Stuttgart, and current head of the Arbeitskreis für Wehrforschung (Working Circle for Military Research). The

"The ULTRA Conference" first appeared in the January 1979 issue of *Cryptologia*.

extraordinary warmth of the conference owed as much to his charm
and easygoing manner as it did to the camaraderie that sprang up among
the participants. The success of the conference—participants agreed that
it was one of the most rewarding they had ever attended—owed all to
him.

The conference consisted of two parts. On 15 and 16 November, a
dozen speakers addressed 250 military and military-industrial leaders
in the municipal auditorium of Bonn on the theme "Modern Technology
and Its Consequences for the Conduct of War: The Example of Radio
Intelligence." This constituted the 45th working session of the Arbeitskreis für Wehrforschung; also participating were the Clausewitz-
Gesellschaft (Clausewitz Society) and the Deutsche Gesellschaft für Wehr-
technik (German Society for Military Technology). The speakers used
German or English, and simultaneous translation was provided. On 17
and 18 November, the Bibliothek für Zeitgeschichte and the history
department of the University of Stuttgart conducted a colloquium in
the Senate room of that university on "What Role Did Radio Intelligence
Play in the Course of the Second World War?" Sitting around a
U-shaped table, with a score of spectators at one end of the room, about
25 ex-spooks and historians grappled with the subject. The proceedings
appeared in German in 1979, and include the texts of the Bonn talks
and a transcript of the Stuttgart meeting.[2] This report will therefore
only highlight the major contributions, the most interesting of which
emerged in Stuttgart.

In the keynote address, I offered reasons for Allied superiority and
German inferiority in cryptanalysis. [These are spelled out in the following article, which is based on that talk.] Tadeusz Lisicki, who was peripherally involved in the Polish solution of the Enigma, gave for the first
time a clear and—given the nature of the audience—fairly technical
description of that feat. He said that the Poles would have solved the
Enigma even without a spy's having furnished the Enigma operating
instructions and some keys but that it would have taken them about
two years longer. He observed that the spy contributed nothing to the
fundamental problem of reconstructing the wiring of the Enigma rotors.[3]
In the next talk, Peter Calvocoressi, a wartime British evaluator, at pains
to give a true picture of the operation of the British codebreaking agency
at Bletchley Park,[4] remarked, "It is not the case that an eccentric English
codebreaker would get an idea in his bath for solving a cipher and
then would run back to his office to win the war without putting his
clothes on!" Rohwer's talk, illustrated with slides, was a masterly reconstruction of how both sides used cryptanalyzed information to help direct

their forces at sea. He warned historians particularly of the danger of thinking that all messages were solved on the day they were sent. Usually there was a delay, sometimes of days, between the interception and the solution, which meant that often these solutions were practically useless to the commands.[5]

The whole first day in Stuttgart, instead of just the morning, as scheduled, was devoted to formal presentations, and another was given on Saturday morning, rather to the disappointment of some participants, who had hoped for a more free-wheeling discussion. Some discussion did creep into the interstices between the presentations, however. For the sake of coherence and space, it seems better here to group all the presentations and then to keep together discussions and comments dealing with a single topic, though they may have been taken up at separate times.

To open the conference, Dr. Eberhard Jäckel, the administrative director of the university's Historisches Institut, posed the two questions the colloquium should address: How important was cryptology in World War II? How much must we rewrite World War II history? As a starting point for the discussion, he iterated the reasons proposed by myself for Allied superiority. No one ever alluded to them again.

In a paper read for him by Beesly, Vice Admiral (retired) Sir Norman Denning, who during the war headed the Admiralty's Operational Intelligence Centre, said that ULTRA and aerial reconnaissance provided the greater part of his intelligence. The reading of the traffic of the HYDRA key net of the naval Enigma enabled the Allies to fill in the whole picture of German naval operations, he said.

Dr. Harold Deutsch, professor emeritus at the University of Minnesota, later Johnson professor of military history at the U.S. Army Military History Institute at Carlisle Barracks, Pennsylvania, and author of numerous books on World War II, sought in a very lively talk to stimulate controversy by stating "to the absolute limit" his view on the influence of ULTRA. Perhaps ULTRA's most important contribution was its educating the higher commanders and their staffs to what was happening on the other side of the hill, he said. Churchill's support of ULTRA was his second-greatest contribution to victory, for without this support, "Bletchley Park would have been almost inconceivable." Could the war have been won without ULTRA? he asked. His answer: "In virtually all of the important encounters, ULTRA played a vital and perhaps decisive role." And, he asked rhetorically, if ULTRA was so important, why didn't it end the war sooner? His answer: "It did end sooner."

Sir Herbert Marchant, a former ambassador and Bletchley worker in the same hut of Bletchley Park as Calvocoressi, gave a nuts-and-bolts description of how the paper flowed through the hut. Colonel Donald Bussey, U.S.A. (retired), the ULTRA officer for the United States 7th Army, which landed in the south of France, told how the ULTRA intelligence came in and was used by that command. "ULTRA's greatest contribution on a day-to-day basis," he said, "was the understanding and full knowledge of German order of battle that it provided." He mentioned a remark made by the G-2, Colonel William Quinn, just after he had received an especially valuable piece of ULTRA intelligence. "You know," said Quinn, "this just isn't cricket."

Edward Thomas, a historian in the Cabinet Office helping with the official history of British intelligence,[6] told of his experiences in receiving ULTRA in his office in a former steward's bathroom aboard H.M.S. *Duke of York*. It came in by direct wire from Bletchley Park. Because naval intelligence is simpler than army and air, he said, he alone in his office could maintain all his records. "We always had good information on German submarines in the North and Polar Seas," he said.

On Saturday morning, Prof. R. V. Jones, the Royal Air Force's wartime director of scientific intelligence, spoke on ULTRA's importance in that area. He said that Churchill wanted to see the original signals, and as soon as the prime minister learned that the source was ULTRA in the case of Peenemünde, where the Germans were making their rocket trials, he accepted it quickly, in part because of ULTRA's help in enabling the British to bend the German navigational beams, misleading German bombers during the Battle of Britain, and in part because of his experiences with cryptology in World War I (when, as First Lord of the Admiralty, he received from the Russians a German naval code book that greatly helped Britain in starting its successful cryptanalytic agency, Room 40).

This concluded the set talks. The comments may be grouped under the following headings: (1) specific cases in which ULTRA played a role, (2) ULTRA's overall importance, (3) the effect of ULTRA on the war, (4) the Russians, (5) rewriting history, and (6) miscellaneous.

(1) Specific cases in which ULTRA played a role. Dr. Hans-Adolf Jacobsen, professor of history at the University of Bonn and a leading World War II historian, asked for such case histories, saying it was a fundamental point. Bussey told two stories. ULTRA-furnished knowledge that no German forces were off to the 7th Army's right flank soon after the landing in southern France let the invaders concentrate more force on a push to the north. And ULTRA revealed an impending German attack near Saverne around 31 December 1944, enabling the American command

to better its dispositions. Beesly said that when Admiral Karl Dönitz, commander in chief of the German navy and commander of U-boats, pulled his U-boats out of the North Atlantic in May 1943, he left three to emit radio messages to disguise the withdrawal. "But ULTRA told us of this so we could move our forces to the new threatened area, west of the Azores," Beesly said. Later, Jäckel asked how Bletchley Park learned that Hitler's planned 1940 invasion of Britain had been postponed. Thomas said that the first decrypts revealing preparations for the invasion dealt with the training of units for the landing. The first indication of the postponement was the abandonment of the training, as well as the release of barges and the maintenance of some elements as cover for the preparations for the invasion of Russia. A case in which ULTRA did not play a decisive role may be entered under this heading to correct published accounts. Winterbotham and others have written that ULTRA ascertained the German tactic during the Battle of Britain of sending in their bombers in waves and that this enabled Fighter Command to parcel out its pitifully few fighters most effectively. But Calvocoressi said that ULTRA intelligence tended to be late and corrupt and had too few people to interpret it in those days of 1940. When the documents are examined, it would probably be found that ULTRA did not play a decisive role in that critical battle for command of the air, he said.[7]

(2) ULTRA's overall importance. The German historians persisted on this point. They wanted a single summary assessment of ULTRA's global wartime importance. Jacobsen, for example, asked what the value of ULTRA was relative to other sources of information. Dr. Michael Salewski, author of a multivolume work on the German navy, asked how ULTRA was used in the mass. But the Americans and the Britons who had worked with ULTRA denied that answers to such questions were possible. Calvocoressi declared that "the value of ULTRA depended on the time and place [in which it was used]. It can't be quantified [over the whole war]." He criticized the "obsession" with individual cases, saying that "By talking about these particulars, one may get a false picture of the source as a whole. The main value was building up a picture from which conclusions could be drawn." Bussey remarked that ULTRA was indeed "part of a mixture, but this is to understate the importance of ULTRA in that mixture." He said that a useful analogy for ULTRA's help was the Allied radar moving-target indicator, which pierced through jamming and segregated out the moving target. Both it and ULTRA, he said, eliminated the background noise to focus on the meaningful signals. Lewin said, "Any suggestion of a structural flow in which you say ULTRA

came first [among the sources of information], this came second, and so on, distorts the picture. . . . Sometimes ULTRA was the most important, but sometimes it arrived too late." Thomas provided the most lapidary reply to the German question. "No simple answer, no generalization is possible," he said. But he noted that "ULTRA information was most sought when the enemy had the initiative, as in the case of the counterattacks."

(3) The effect of ULTRA on the war. Dr. Andreas Hillgruber, professor at the University of Cologne and perhaps the leading historian of World War II, asked rhetorically, How would the war have gone without ULTRA? He answered that the war was sped up through ULTRA and that without it, the 1944 invasion of France would have taken place later and the Russians would have gone further west. [Hillgruber seemed to imply that they would have stayed in the areas they conquered. But the Russians—like the western Allies—pulled back from such areas in the territories delimited as final occupation zones: The Russians returned three fourths of Berlin to the Allies, for example.] Dr. Gerhard Weinberg, professor of history at the University of North Carolina and first head of the American project for microfilming the seized German records, retorted with some asperity that "it is ridiculous to argue that if the Atlantic battle had been won more slowly all else would have been unchanged. If things had not gone so well in the Atlantic, the Allies would have put more resources into the Atlantic to keep on their timetable." These resources would have come from supplies intended for the Pacific—"the lesser theater. So if there had been no ULTRA in the Atlantic, the United States would perhaps have been fighting in the Philippines [in early 1945] instead of on Iwo Jima and Okinawa." Thus the Atlantic ULTRA actually helped the Pacific war, he said.

Lewin observed that "the two main decisions of the Casablanca conference do not come in any way from ULTRA." These were to give the highest priority to the Battle of the Atlantic and to destroy Germany from the air. The same goes for the invasion of North Africa, he said. "I don't think ULTRA fits in the real picture of grand strategy," he concluded. In addition, General Leo Hepp, wartime chief of staff to the German army chief signal officer, said that Allied material superiority was the crucial factor, not ULTRA. No one disputed him.

(4) The Russians. Hillgruber commented that everyone forgets the importance of the Russian front, which absorbed two thirds of the German war effort. This importance remains the same with or without the western Allies' ULTRA, he affirmed. Dr. Geoffrey Jukes, a former Bletchley worker now at the University of Canberra, who nodded his

head vigorously when Hillgruber was making this point, noted, "We don't know whether the Russians could read Enigma, and this is as big a gap as ULTRA used to be for the West." (Some evidence—nearly all of it German—indicates that the Russians could solve Enigma messages, at least at times. Some discussions at a 1943 conference of German army signal officers centered on this likelihood. In his talk in Bonn, Waldemar Werther, a wartime Luftwaffe cryptanalyst, said that the war diary of Army Group North says 11 Enigma keys have been exposed. A Russian book mentions the recovery of an Enigma from a U-boat in the Baltic in 1944.[8] Tending to corroborate this are the admittedly vaguer observations that the Russians have long been good in cryptanalysis and have also been good in subjects that go along with excellence in cryptanalysis: music, chess, and mathematics. On the other hand, their then relatively impoverished technical background suggests that they were far less likely than the Poles or the British to independently evolve electromechanical devices for automatically solving Enigma messages. Could they have used, instead of such devices, hundreds of men from their vast human reservoirs? A Finnish cryptanalyst, Erkki Pale, who during World War II had solved Russian codes, thought that such an undertaking could not be organized to succeed. Thomas said that, in his delving among the classified archives, he saw no evidence of Russian Enigma solutions. The Russians themselves have said nothing on the topic.)

Jukes raised the possibility that a Russian sympathizer at Bletchley might have told the Soviet Union of the fact of Allied success in this field out of outrage that the western Allies were not sharing this vital intelligence, in the same way as scientists at Los Alamos passed over the secret of the atom bomb. I asked whether the story was true that the British had used the famed LUCY Communist spy ring in Switzerland, headed by Rudolf Rössler, whose sources have never been revealed, as a conduit to feed disguised ULTRA information to their Soviet allies.[9] Thomas said that some ULTRA intelligence was given to the Russians in concealed form.[10] Calvocoressi said that there was no need for "mysterious people in Switzerland" because "a good deal" was sent through a special mission in Moscow headed by Edward Crankshaw, the writer. Crankshaw was disappointed that more could not be given, he said, and was finally convinced by Sir Stewart Menzies, head of the British secret service, which distributed the ULTRA material, that poor Soviet cipher security risked revealing this precious source to the Germans, Calvocoressi said. When Jukes asked whether the Allies should not have told the Russians that their ciphers were weak, Thomas replied: "There's a whole book on this subject. It will not be published." Thomas also said it was very likely that the British attacked and even solved Soviet codes and that this work was mostly done in the Mid-East [where the spheres of influence collided, especially in Iran, which was occupied jointly by Russian and British troops in August, 1941].[11]

(5) Rewriting history. Dr. Forrest Pogue, author of the standard biography of General George C. Marshall, U.S. Army chief of staff, said that to suggest that overnight all World War II history must be rewritten is to misunderstand that history is always being rewritten. The ULTRA revelations must be seen as part of this process, he said. He added that 15 to 20 years is the time lag for facts to catch up with fiction. That's how long it will take for the false story that Winston Churchill allowed Coventry to be destroyed to save the secret of ULTRA "to stop being used to keep sophomores awake in the classroom." Jacobsen said that only battle history will have to be revised; the overriding political events and global strategy would not be affected. Lewin wondered whether ULTRA might become a new form of the stab-in-the-back legend. [Promulgated in Germany after World War I, this held that the German armies did not lose honorably on the field of battle, but were betrayed on the home front by Communists and Jews.] Finally, Hepp asked whether, in a one-volume history of World War II, there belongs a chapter on radio intelligence. No, he assured himself. But there might be a chapter on intelligence in general, and radio intelligence would belong in that, he said.

(6) Miscellaneous. (a) An epigram from Werther: "The security of a cipher lies less with the cleverness of the inventor than with the stupidity of the men who are using it." (b) Karl-Otto Hoffmann, author of a three-volume history of the Luftwaffe signal corps, said that according to the Luftwaffe chief signals officer during the war, General Wolfgang Martini, usually 30 percent and sometimes up to 50 percent of Luftwaffe intelligence came from radio reconnaissance. He said that one depends more on radio reconnaissance in retreats than in advances, when one has other sources, such as prisoners of war and the population. (c) Charles von Luttichau, a historian with the U.S. Army's Center for Military History, asked whether the Germans ever thought that a single machine might be dangerous. Werther said "yes," but did not elaborate. Hepp said that he had a section to test German cipher systems. That the Enigma was provably unbreakable was never affirmed, he said, only that it could be solved. Consequently the rules for its use were constantly improved, he said. Some in the audience felt that he was placing more emphasis on Enigma solvability in 1978 than was done in 1943, when

the emphasis lay rather on the near certainty that the Enigma was not being solved. At a party at the Bibliothek für Zeitgeschichte that evening, the chief of German naval radio intelligence said that to have two machines would have cost more money and more training and would have engendered more errors and failures to get through, thus reducing the trust of the commanders in the machine and in communications. Finally, Calvocoressi noted dryly that the British, too, used but a single machine. (d) Alec Douglas, a Canadian official historian, said that more comparisons need to be made between the use of intelligence in World Wars I and II. (e) "I am surprised," Thomas said, "to see so many distinguished minds trying to fit the importance of ULTRA into the whole history of the war before we have the evidence. The cart is hurtling before the horse. I think we have 25 years' work to do in establishing the facts."

The conference ended at 12:10 P.M. Saturday with a graceful tribute by Marchant to the conference organizer. After expressing the thanks of the participants, he said that all present were glad that Beesly's Operational Intelligence Centre had not caught that German minesweeper in the Baltic on which there was working a young naval officer by the name of Rohwer.

The hard-working historians seemed oblivious during the conference to the human dramas that swirled around them but that did not touch their high purposes. How did the former enemies feel about one another? All said they held no animosities. Captain (retired) Heinz Bonatz, who during part of the war had headed the Kriegsmarine's cryptanalytic service, said he did not hate the British. "We fought against one another and now we're comrades—and historians, thank God," he said. But the British seemed a bit more reserved. "They're fine fellows—now," said Beesly. Lewin told of an odd feeling he had during the Bonn meeting. "I was talking about the deception in Normandy, and in front was a row of elderly Germans, one of whom at the end asked a question. Suddenly it shot through my head. 'I was there, and you were there, and here we are.' It was very strange."

A more poignant drama was even more suppressed. How did the German cryptographers feel as the British and American intelligence officers cited case after case in which their solutions of a machine that the Germans had said was secure cost Germany battle after battle, U-boat after U-boat, and thousands of German lives and contributed much to the defeat of their nation? Mostly the German cryptographers sat silent, for they had, after all, no comeback to this. And they denied feeling guilt or embarrassment over the proceedings.

Captain (retired) Hans Meckel, on the U-boats radio communication staff, said he feels he did his best. He said he didn't mean he never made mistakes. But he had no certain indication that the Allies had solved the machine—there were always alternative explanations for the apparent Allied foreknowledge of German moves—and so he feels he did not err about the ciphers. Hepp and Bonatz likewise both denied suffering from the situation. "I had a view and I was wrong. Now I have to correct it," said Bonatz.

But others did feel badly. The chief of staff to the U-boat commander, Admiral (retired) Eberhard Godt, not present at the conference, "suffers badly on account of this," Meckel said. And the Finnish codebreaker Pale said, "I felt depressed." Why? "Because I was on the losing side," he explained (Finland fought as a co-belligerent with Germany against Russia). He added, "It must have been very depressing for the Germans with the English firing all those cannonballs from all sides."

Indeed. For what human could not feel at least a twinge of guilt over the fact that his failure, however hard he worked at the time, helped cost his countrymen's lives? Yet the answer remains locked in the fastness of the German codemakers' hearts. And to secrets there, no one, not even the Allies' cryptanalysts, has ever been able to penetrate.

# Codebreaking
# in World Wars I and II:
# The Major Successes
# and Failures,
# Their Causes
# and Their Effects

## I

Codebreaking has played an important role in history, mainly in World Wars I and II. Its beginnings, however, may be traced back to the days of the pharaohs. A letter records the intention of a foreigner to determine the meaning of fires raised by the Egyptians.[1] (No one knows if he succeeded.) Several centuries later, in 207 B.C., the Romans intercepted a letter from Hasdrubal to his brother Hannibal, further south in Italy. It enabled the Romans to concentrate their forces at the Metaurus River to defeat the Carthaginians.[2] This was the only battle in Edward S. Creasy's *The Fifteen Decisive Battles of the World: From Marathon to Waterloo*[3] that depended upon intelligence for its victory.

For between the Metaurus and the twentieth century, signals intelligence did not help armies win any more major battles.[4] The reason was mainly lack of opportunity. Messengers were hard to capture; telegraph wires were hard to tap. All that was changed by radio.[5] The public nature of electromagnetic radiation, which makes wireless communication so easy to establish, also makes it easy to intercept. Radio turns over a copy of every message to the enemy.

This paper was originally delivered in Bonn, 15 November 1978, at the so-called ULTRA Conference. Since its publication in *The Historical Journal* in September 1980, I have made a few changes in the text, to include new information or to correct errors, and have updated the footnotes. I think its most significant contribution is its list of reasons for Allied superiority and German inferiority in World War II cryptanalysis.

Before World War I, only two nations foresaw the opportunities this would create. France, which had a successful diplomatic codebreaking unit,[6] set up army intercept posts in the northeast.[7] Austria-Hungary had picked up intercepts during the Italo-Turkish War of 1911 and had created its Dechiffrierdienst.[8] None of the other great powers seemed to expect to intercept military radio messages—although one of them, Russia, had highly effective diplomatic and police codebreaking agencies.[9] Despite this lack of foresight, however, every nation rapidly learned the value of interception soon after World War I broke out. One of the first was Germany.

## II

In the east, Germany had but one army to defend against two Russian. She had foreseen this problem and had planned to stop the northern army first, then block the southern. But at Gumbinnen, in the north, the German troops broke and ran. Russian failure to pursue saved them. Meanwhile, to the south, the other Russian army, advancing, threatened to cut off the Germans. The German operations officer, Colonel Max Hoffmann, began moving his forces to meet this more imminent threat, even though the move left the north unprotected. When the new German commander, General Paul von Hindenburg, and his chief of staff, General Erich Ludendorff, arrived to take over from the previous commander, they confirmed Hoffmann's order. But they worried. The northern Russian army, Ludendorff said, "hung like a threatening thundercloud to the northeast. [Its commander] need only have closed with us and we should have been beaten."[10]

But the Germans had, largely by chance, been forging a new and important instrument of war in the radio station of German 8th Army headquarters at Königsberg. The radio operators, having little traffic of their own to send, began listening out of curiosity to the Russian traffic.[11] Owing to Russian inefficiencies, these messages were in the clear.[12] They required only translation. And one of them early one morning lifted the burden of worry from the commanders' minds and helped them prepare one of the great military triumphs of the war. It came from the Russian northern army, and it told the Germans that that army was continuing to move at a snail's pace. Hindenburg and Ludendorff turned with easier minds to engineer the destruction of the southern army.

As they drove back, later that morning, from a conference at a corps headquarters, Hoffmann received another intercept from a signalman at a railway station. He raced after his chiefs and handed it over as his car and theirs bumped along side by side on the rutted Polish road. Everyone stopped and studied it. It proved to be nothing less than a full roundup of the situation as the southern Russian army saw it, together with the detailed objectives of each of its subordinate corps.[13] Helped by this, and by other cleartext intercepts, the Germans encircled and destroyed the Russians almost as if in a war game. The battle, called Tannenberg by the Germans, proved one of the few decisive victories of the war. Hoffmann, its architect, acknowledged the main cause of the success: "We knew all the enemy's plans. The Russians sent out their wireless in clear."[14] Tannenberg, which gave Russia its first push into ruin and revolution, was the first victory in the modern world to be made possible by signal intelligence.

But it was not the last, even for World War I's eastern front. When the Russians began enciphering their cryptograms, the Germans and the Austrians began solving them. These solutions helped the two powers win one victory after another.[15] As Hoffmann said: "We were always warned by the wireless messages of the Russian staff of the positions where troops were being concentrated for any new undertaking. Only once during the whole war were we taken by surprise on the Eastern Front by a Russian attack—it was on the Aa in the winter of 1916–17."[16] This dramatically underlines the importance of signal intelligence in the German victory in the east and all that that entailed. Indeed, it may not be too much to claim that the establishment of Communist power, perhaps the supreme fact of contemporary history, was assisted to a certain degree by the cryptanalysis of czarist secret communications.

## III

Signal intelligence often played a crucial role on other fronts, as well. After the Austrians had bloodily defeated the Italians at Caporetto, an Italian commission of inquiry reported with anguish that "the enemy had known and deciphered all our codes, even the most difficult and most secret."[17] French solution of the German military attaché code revealed that Mata Hari was a German spy[18]—and led to her execution at Vincennes one October dawn. Another French solution helped the Allies stop Germany's supreme offensives in 1918.[19] Both sides excelled at intercepting enemy field telephone conversations.[20] In 1916 the English sustained casualties in the thousands in a fierce battle to take Ovillers-la-Boiselle on the Somme. Battalions were decimated as they went over the top. When the British finally captured their objective, they found in one enemy dugout a complete transcript of one of their operations orders. A brigade major had read it in full over a field telephone despite the protest of his subordinate that the procedure was dangerous. "Hundreds of brave men perished," wrote the British signal historian, "hundreds more were maimed for life as the result of this one act of incredible foolishness."[21]

But it was the British who achieved a solution in World War I that deserves to be called the most important in history. In a sense it began on the first day of the war, when German intercepts were sent to an Admiralty official known to be interested in cryptology. He assembled four German-speaking friends, who, seated around a table, puzzled over the cryptograms. Luck, brains and perseverance brought them such success that two years later they had become a large and successful organization, called Room 40 from its location in the old building of the Admiralty.[22] Early in 1917 it read a coded message from the German foreign minister, Arthur Zimmermann, to the president of Mexico. Germany was about to begin unrestricted submarine warfare, which would almost certainly bring America into the war on the side of the Allies. To distract America, Zimmermann proposed that Mexico declare war upon the United States, and that, upon victory, she regain the territories of Texas, New Mexico, and Arizona that she had lost in the Mexican-American War of 1846. The British gave their solution of this sensational note to the Americans. When it was published on 1 March 1917, it caused a "profound sensation," and did what even the torpedoing of the *Lusitania* had not done: unified the Midwest and West with the East Coast against Germany.[23] One month later, Congress declared war. The American entry helped the Allies defeat Germany and helped bring America on to the stage of world power. No other cryptanalysis has ever had greater consequences. Neither before nor since has so much turned upon the solution of a secret message. For those few moments in time, the codebreakers held history in the palm of their hands.

## IV

Up to 1914, codebreaking had been a negligible source of intelligence. World War I demonstrated its value beyond any question. Before the war only three great powers had cryptanalytic agencies. Afterward, all did. The four major nations that had not been breaking codes before

1914—Germany, Britain, the United States and Italy—all retained their wartime agencies when peace returned.[24] Cryptology thus won widespread recognition of its importance, and so gained governmental support and a permanent organizational existence. At about the same time a technical development began that was to culminate during World War II.

This was the automation of cryptology. It took place both in codemaking and in codebreaking. The manual code and cipher systems of World War I had sagged under the heavy volume of signal traffic. Not a few cipher clerks dreamed of lightening their burden with a machine, and not a few inventors hoped to get rich by devising one. Beginning near the end of the war, a number of amateurs did devise such mechanisms.[25] Typical of these was the German Enigma machine. Devised by a Berlin engineer, Arthur Scherbius, it had a typewriter keyboard for the input and a letter plate with lights under each letter for the output. The heart of the machine consisted of three rotors. A rotor was a wired codewheel of hard rubber or bakelite about the size and shape of a hockey puck. Twenty-six electrical contacts studded the circumference of one face, twenty-six the circumference of the other. They were connected at random by wires. A letter would be represented by an electrical impulse. It would enter at a contact at one position and emerge at a contact at another position, thus enciphering the letter. The three rotors, side by side, created an electrical maze. As they turned, they changed the maze—and thereby the encipherment. The result was a rather secure cipher. The Enigma failed to sell when it was offered on the commercial market.[26] But in 1926 the German navy adopted it, becoming probably the first armed force to mechanize its cryptography. The German army followed two years later,[27] and in the 1930s the French, the British, the Italians and the Americans all adopted cipher machines. These then served in World War II.[28]

At the same time the codebreakers were automating their work. They transferred many of the repetitive processes of cryptanalysis to IBM tabulators using punched Hollerith cards. This development began taking place in the 1930s in the United States and Germany at least,[29] and probably in other countries as well. It had the effect of greatly increasing the manpower of the codebreaking agencies. In addition, other, more specialized mechanisms for codebreaking were coming into being, and during the war others emerged.[30]

These developments were still getting under way during the interwar years. That period saw many nations solving other nations' codes. But they seemed to affect the course of world events but little.[31]

## V

All that changed with the start of World War II. In discussing the cryptologic successes and failures of that conflict, three major belligerents may be eliminated. One is the Soviet Union. The public literature contains almost nothing about her codebreaking successes, and so scholars can say nothing of value about them.[32] The second is Italy. She quit in the middle of the war, and her codebreaking, though successful, seems to have played but a minor role in her campaigns. The third is Japan. She failed almost entirely to break American cryptosystems.[33] So, in her case, there is nothing to tell.

On the Axis side, this leaves Germany. She achieved a fair number of successes in communications intelligence. Some were even spectacular. She intercepted and unscrambled the transatlantic radiotelephone circuit between England and America, sometimes hearing Roosevelt and Churchill. But in general the conversations were too guarded to yield much intelligence.[34]

On the Russian front, German army communications intelligence produced much of value. Codebreaking was only one part of this. Radio direction-finding located transmitters—and thus discovered the positions of headquarters. Interception of nonencoded messages often yielded valuable information.[35] Eavesdropping on Russian field telephone conversations at Sevastopol on 21 January 1942 enabled the German 24th Infantry Division to repulse with ease some Russian counterattacks against the encircling Germans. At 10:30 A.M. on 17 February 1944 the 17th Panzer Division overheard a conversation between two posts that gave a shocking insight into Russian command procedures.[36]

ROKOT. Thirty minutes ago my patrol came out of Oktyabr and reported that no one is there. It found only our own wounded.
TOCHKA. Why was it shot into? You're dogs, bastards, traitors.
ROKOT. The battery commander fired without an order.
TOCHKA. Arrest him and shoot him with his own pistol.
ROKOT. Acknowledged.

Russian codes were broken as well. These solutions, said Army Group North in 1944, "contain operational combat reports, statements about assembly areas, command posts, loss and replacement reports, reports about chain of command and positions prepared for the attack."[37]

Success was not as great against the western Allies. But German troop units in Normandy were glad to have the warning of Allied bombings that communications intelligence was able to provide in France in 1944 and that enabled them to take cover and shift equipment.[38] And one fine piece of work did yield extraordinary results. This was the German solution of the American military attaché code.[39] Among the attachés who used it was the man in Cairo, Colonel Bonner Fellers, a perceptive and hardworking officer. In late 1941 and early 1942 he reported on the events, the nature, and the course of this new desert warfare. Sometimes he named new British forces and told of British plans—probably to show what a good job he was doing. All this he encoded and radioed to Washington.

To make sure they did not lose a word of these invaluable messages, the Germans assigned two radio posts to intercept them—one at Lauf-an-der-Pegnitz, the other often Treuenbrietzen. They forwarded the intercepts to the Chiffrierabteilung of the armed forces high command. Here the messages were rapidly broken down, evaluated, translated, encoded in a German system, and radioed to General Erwin Rommel.[40] He was eager to see them as soon as they arrived and in January 1942 used them as he chased the British back 300 miles across the desert and approached the gates of Alexandria.[41] Hitler himself expressed the hope that the attaché "continue to inform us so well over the English military planning through his badly enciphered cables."[42] But just at this time the Americans changed the code. The Germans could not read the new one.[43] And this blindness of communications intelligence was one of the factors in Montgomery's surprise at El Alamein, which Churchill called the turning of the hinge of fate.

Still, the original success and the great contributions of signals intelligence won extravagant praise from general staff officers. A head of Foreign Armies West, Colonel Ulrich Liss, called signals intelligence "the darling of all intelligence chiefs."[44] General Reinhard Gehlen, at Foreign Armies East, listed it as the most important of his sources.[45]

This was echoed by Grand Admiral Karl Dönitz. His radio interception and codebreaking service, the B-Dienst (short for Beobachtungs-Dienst, observation service), provided him, he said, with half his operational intelligence.[46] The B-Dienst cracked one British naval code after another at the start of the war. Time after time, this told his submarines where British vessels were sailing and so enabled them to lie in wait and torpedo them. On 30 August 1940, for example, the B-Dienst intercepted and solved a report that convoy SC 2, coming out of Sydney, Canada, would be at 50° 00' north latitude, 19° 50' west longitude, at noon on 6 September. U-boats sank five of the ships and Dönitz praised the B-Dienst as a "major help" in the operation.[47] In 1943 the B-Dienst intercepted 3,101,831 messages and processed many of them on its six

Hollerith tabulators.[48] These helped the B-Dienst to solve intercepts in time for the command to use them.[49]

But B-Dienst codebreaking was largely limited to the first two-thirds of the war. As the British improved their cipher security, and as the Americans, whose cipher machine the B-Dienst never cracked, flooded into the war, the B-Dienst lost its grip on one Allied system after another. When, in May 1944, Hitler asked the B-Dienst which British codes it was solving, it had to acknowledge that "The two main English systems cannot be read."[50] In the same way, the praise of general staff officers referred only to tactical and operational results. For German communications intelligence failed utterly to read Allied strategic communications.[51] Statistical probes showed that these ciphers could not be broken analytically. So the Germans concentrated their manpower on the lower-echelon messages that they could read. Eventually they gave up even intercepting the top-level messages.[52] This acknowledgement of defeat in the cryptologic war stood in stark contrast to the successes of the Allies.

## VI

The most important of those successes took place against Japan. Japan won the first battles of the war in the Pacific. She destroyed much of the U.S. fleet at Pearl Harbor, and sank the *Prince of Wales* and the *Repulse* soon thereafter. She conquered Guam, Wake, Hong Kong. She took Singapore and Malaya, the Dutch East Indies and the Solomons, the Philippines and Siam. Within six months, the Rising Sun shone on a tenth of the globe.

During this enormous expansion, Japan's navy used its main fleet code for about half of its messages. This was a superenciphered two-part code of about 45,000 groups. The U.S. navy codebreakers who were attacking it called it "JN25b"—"JN" for Japanese navy, "25" for the 25th code they had worked on, "b" for its second edition. It had come into use near the end of 1940, and by early 1942 the Americans had recovered enough codegroups to read bits and pieces of Japanese messages.[53]

By then, however, the Japanese were growing uneasy at the code's long service. They wanted to replace it. But the enormous size of their new empire, together with some administrative confusion, prevented that. They could not distribute by 1 April, nor even 1 May.[54] And so the American codebreakers continued to read Japanese naval messages.

They were reading them as Admiral Isoroku Yamamoto, commander in chief of Japan's combined fleet and her most brilliant strategist, was readying a plan to clinch Japan's victory. He would capture Midway Island. This would give him a base that would control the central Pacific and block any American approach to Japan. At the same time, his advance would lure out the remainder of the American fleet. He would fall upon it with his vastly larger force and annihilate it. This would complete the work of Pearl Harbor and would convince the enfeebled Americans to quit the war and leave Japan master of the western Pacific.

Yamamoto did not know that many of the orders he issued to his ship captains were also being read by the Americans. By the end of May, U.S. naval intelligence had been able to piece together Yamamoto's plan. And just in time. For on 1 June, as their force was advancing, the Japanese finally changed their code. But it was too late. Admiral Chester Nimitz had already summoned his aircraft carriers from the southwest Pacific and stationed them off the flank of the Japanese, where he hoped they would not be seen. And they were not—in part because the Japanese expected no major American forces in the vicinity and were not looking for them. So after the first bombing of Midway, one Japanese admiral sent below the 93 airplanes he had held on his aircraft carrier decks armed to attack ships. He ordered them armed for land bombardment. Thirteen minutes later he was dumbfounded to receive a report of enemy ships to the northwest. He cancelled his original order and had the planes rearmed with torpedoes and armor-piercing bombs. Then his Midway bombers began returning. At this most vulnerable moment, with all planes aboard and ammunition stacked in the open, the Americans attacked. The Japanese fought off the first wave, but in the next few minutes the Americans destroyed that carrier, and later the force's three others. The work of Pearl Harbor had not been completed, but avenged.

The battle of Midway marked a turning point in the Pacific War. It put the Japanese on the defensive, from which they would never recover. It knocked the keystone from the Japanese strategy, sank four irreplaceable carriers, and doomed Japan to defeat. Midway, Nimitz said later, "was essentially a victory of intelligence. In attempting surprise, the Japanese were themselves surprised."[55] The army chief of staff, General George Marshall, said that because of codebreaking "we were able to concentrate our limited forces to meet their naval advance on Midway when otherwise we would almost certainly have been some 3,000 miles out of place."[56] The solution of JN25b forged effects more crucial to the course of history than any other cryptanalysis except that of the Zimmermann telegram. For it had turned the tide of a war. It had caused a Rising Sun to start to set.

Communications intelligence contributed in two other major ways to the Allies' Pacific victory. It stepped up American submarine sinkings of the Japanese merchant fleet by one third.[57] This cutting of Japan's lifelines was, Premier Hideki Tojo said after the war, one of the major factors that defeated Japan.[58] And, secondly, it made possible in 1943 the dramatic midair assassination of Admiral Yamamoto.[59] This was the equivalent of a major victory, for it was as if Rommel or Eisenhower had been slain in full career during the war.

American cryptanalysts succeeded not only with Japanese naval but also with Japanese diplomatic cryptosystems. The most important of these was called by the Japanese the "Alphabetical Typewriter '97" (for their year of 2597) and by the Americans the PURPLE machine. It used telephone stepping switches in its enciphering mechanism—a principle entirely different from the rotor—and thus, though the Japanese had bought an Enigma in 1934, the Alphabetical Typewriter was no near cryptographic relative of the German machine.[60] U.S. army and navy codebreakers, led by William F. Friedman, one of the greatest cryptanalysts of all time, began attacking this top-level Japanese system around the beginning of 1939. In August of 1940, after 20 months of work that in other fields would be worthy of a Nobel Prize, they submitted their first completely solved PURPLE message.[61]

The PURPLE solution could not prevent the Pearl Harbor attack. Nor did it help much in the war in the Pacific, where the diplomats had little to do. It made its greatest contribution in the war in Europe. For it enabled the Allies to read the messages of Japan's ambassador and military attaché in Germany as they reported on Hitler's capabilities and plans. The Germans were loyal allies. They kept the Japanese up to date with their views. And the Japanese dispatches, dealing with the topmost levels of policy, were being intercepted and read by the Allies.[62]

On 9 October 1943 the Allies read a message of a few days earlier in which Baron Hiroshi Oshima, the Japanese ambassador, reported that he had recently visited Hitler in his East Prussia headquarters. Among many other items of interest, Hitler told him that "I am inclined to believe" that the Allies would land in the Balkans instead of moving north in Italy. About Russia, the Führer said that "we are making our stand on the Sozh but, depending on whether or not the Soviet forces resume the offensive, we may fall back to the line which we have prepared on the Dnieper. In the north, in case worse comes to worst, we can retire to a second defense line which we have prepared across the narrow strip of land adjoining Lake Peipus." He added: "I think it the best policy first to slap at the American and British forces as soon as we get a chance, and then to turn on the Soviet."[63] It is incredible to think of Roosevelt and Churchill reading these most secret thoughts of their chief enemy!

On a slightly lower level, the Allied high command was gaining valuable details of proposed German defences. Oshima and his military attaché toured the Atlantic Wall and reported on German fortifications in telegrams that the Allies also intercepted and read. These included both general information, such as that the Cherbourg defense zone was 7 kilometers deep, and very specific details of defense installations. For example, in describing the organization of strong points, the Japanese pointed out that antitank flanking fire was delivered from two or three casements equipped with 40-millimeter Skoda guns and from two or three others with 50-millimeter 60-caliber guns. The antitank ditches, in the shape of a V, were 5 meters wide at the top and 3.5 meters deep.[64] One can imagine how valuable this sort of detail would be both to planners and to the troops during the actual assault.

Thus a solution of a Japanese diplomatic cipher provided the Allies with what General Marshall called "our main basis of information regarding Hitler's intentions in Europe."[65]

## VII

Valuable as the Japanese intercepts were, however, they were intermittent. Real insight into German military operations could only come from a steady flow of German intercepts. And this the Allies had—thanks to the Poles.

Countries always want to know their neighbors' intentions, and prewar Poland was anxious about Germany. The cipher bureau of its general staff began attacking German codes and ciphers in the 1920s.[66] On 15 July 1928,[67] it noticed a new kind of cryptogram in the day's harvest of German army intercepts. Unlike the older cryptograms, which included mostly letters common in German such as E, N, D and I, the new one consisted largely of such letters as Z, X, Q and Y. This told the Poles that these were substitution cryptograms, unlike the old ones, which were transposition—the other great class of cipher. The rarity of repeated pairs and triplets of letters, together with other statistical tests, told the Poles that the new system was a machine cipher. Various bits of information suggested that it was the Enigma. But otherwise they made little progress and eventually gave up the effort.

They intensified their effort, recruiting young mathematicians and giving them courses in cryptology. But even obtaining a copy of a commercial Enigma did not help much. Then, in 1932, the French recruited as a spy a member of the Reichswehrministerium's Chiffrierstelle, Hans-Thilo Schmidt. For money, he delivered the operating instructions for the machine as well as some factual keys. The French gave these to the Poles.[68] Though this did not help the Poles with the fundamental cryptanalytic problem of ascertaining how each rotor was wired, it eliminated some problems preliminary to those determinations and thereby made it possible. By 1933 the Poles were solving Enigma messages. They built their own copies of Enigma machines to speed up the work. Then they improved on these with a cyclometer, which in effect joined two Enigmas, and then their so-called bomba, which linked six Enigmas. All of this enabled them to run through rotor combinations far faster than the Germans had thought possible, and so to solve Enigma messages.[69]

In July 1939 the Poles gave their allies, the British and the French, one copy each of their reconstructed Enigmas.[70] Now they could do what before only the Poles could—read German messages. When the war came, this ability helped the Poles and the French but little. It is an especially striking illustration of the truth that intelligence is but a secondary factor in war, which is won not in the back rooms but on the field of battle. But the Enigma solution greatly helped the British.

Their cryptanalytic agency was called the Government Code and Cypher School. It moved, about the time the war started, to a Victorian house on an estate called Bletchley Park in the town of Bletchley, about 45 miles northwest of London. Its codebreakers included some who were members of famous families—Dillwyn Knox, one of the brightest of the Bletchley contingent, had one brother who was the editor of *Punch* and another who was a famous Roman Catholic convert and translator of the Bible[71]—and many more who later became famous in their own right: chess champions, novelists, publishers, mathematicians. Bletchley also included a genius, the mathematician Alan Turing, who first expressed the fundamental concept of the electronic computer, and a mathematician, Gordon Welchman, whose stroke of genius in devising what he called the "diagonal board" enabled Britain to read more German messages faster. The place glowed white-hot with talent.[72]

The Bletchley solutions are widely known under the collective name of ULTRA. Contrary to some accounts, they did not play an important role during the battle of Britain.[73] Nor, to debunk another story, did Churchill let Coventry be destroyed because he believed that defensive measures would risk the secret of ULTRA. Critical analyses of the documents show that this is pure myth.[74]

At about this time Bletchley Park began reading the ciphers of the Abwehr, the German military espionage agency. These included both the hand ciphers of its spies, who naturally could not carry a cipher machine about with them, and the Enigma messages of its far-flung outposts, which forwarded the spy reports, often with comments about them.[75] The intercepts told the British that they had captured all the German spies in their islands and what the Abwehr thought about its spies. The British deception organization found this information very useful in persuading the Germans, before the D-Day invasion, that the Normandy landing would be a feint. And the Germans believed it with results fatal to their defense.[76]

The naval Enigma posed a more difficult problem because it was more carefully used. Bletchley was not able to penetrate it until some Enigmas had been seized from some weather trawlers and from the U-110 in mid-1941.[77] Then, on 1 February 1942, the Kriegsmarine began using an Enigma with four rotors (instead of the previous three) for U-boat communications.[78] This was not only inherently harder to solve, but, by dividing the U-boat cipher net, codenamed TRITON, from the general naval cipher net, HYDRA,[79] it reduced the volume of traffic on which the cryptanalysts could work. Bletchley was stymied. Meanwhile, the B-Dienst was reading Allied codes. Allied shipping losses reached catastrophic levels. But Bletchley's break back in, in mid-December 1942, aided the new escort carriers and very-long-range planes gradually to win preponderance.[80] Eventually, the Allies were able to pinpoint and sink the submarine fuel ships, as well as attack U-boats themselves, and so with ULTRA's help were able to win decisively this most decisive of battles.[81]

Germany was finally defeated on land, and here ULTRA provided outstanding intelligence. The Germany army had, later in the war, switched to cryptographic teletypewriters for its communications from Führer headquarters to army groups. One device, invented and produced by Siemens und Halske and called the Geheimschreiber, automatically enciphered and transmitted a message typed out on the keyboard in clear by the cipher clerk.[82] To solve its cryptograms in time to help the military commanders, the British developed purely electronic codebreaking machines. These worked much faster than the electromechanical devices (which, however, in the form of dozens of "bombes"—as the British spelled the word—continued to turn out Enigma solutions). A succession of electronic machines culminated in a remarkable mechanism about the size of three large wardrobes codenamed COLOSSUS. Its specifications were laid down by a Bletchley group headed by Cambridge mathematician Max H. A. Newman, a fellow of the Royal Society, and it was designed and built by a British Post Office research establishment team headed by engineer Thomas H. Flowers, who seems to have been chosen because in 1934 he had designed electronics into telephone exchanges for the first time in the United Kingdom. Many historians of technology regard COLOSSUS, of which two copies were built, as the first electronic computer.[83] The Germans never took the crucial step to electronics in cryptanalysis. At Bletchley the COLOSSUSES, backed by the bombes, helped the Allies keep their cryptanalyzed intelligence flowing copiously.

The completeness and continuity of this information was its chief contribution. In Normandy in 1944, for example, ULTRA was revealing routine daily Luftwaffe reports on the condition of airfields, the number and condition of anti-aircraft guns, the number of planes that could fly, unit strengths. It disclosed the location and movements of specific divisions, the subordination and transfer of units, the boundaries between units—once enabling the U.S. 7th Army to foresee and then to stop cold a German counterattack in Alsace. It gave insights into personnel losses and problems—the death in an air raid of the chief of staff and other officers of Panzer Gruppe West, the weak-kneed response of the commander of the Cherbourg garrison to Hitler's command to hold out like Gneisenau at Kolberg.[84] ULTRA seemed to reveal every single detail of enemy activity. The thousands of bits of information that it provided eased thousands of decisions for Allied commanders and helped them optimize their resources in thousands of cases. Said the U.S. 7th Army intelligence officer after one particularly good morsel arrived: "You know, this just isn't cricket!"[85] Altogether, ULTRA let the Allies advance into Germany with far more speed than otherwise.

But though this thoroughness of detail contributed more, in its accumulation, than any individual episode, nevertheless ULTRA sometimes did make spectacular contributions to victory in battle. A case in point came in Normandy. The Americans had just broken out and were pouring through Avranches. The narrow opening created a target that tempted Hitler. He directed Field Marshal Günther von Kluge, the commander in chief west, to pull at least four armored divisions out of the front and hurl them against this bottleneck to close it. Hitler's order was, however, intercepted and solved. So were von Kluge's protests. And so, finally, was Hitler's insistence. All this came to the Allied commanders, from Churchill on down, in plenty of time for them to prepare their defenses. During these preparations, the head of the U.S. 9th Tactical Air Force met with General Omar Bradley, commander of the U.S. 12th Army Group. They held their intercepts in their hands as they grinned at one another and said, "We've got them." And they had. The German attack bounced off ready American defenders.[86] Its failure ended Hitler's last hope of stopping the invasion near the beachheads. The Allies swept on through France and then Germany herself to conquer the Thousand-Year Reich.

### VIII

Given these remarkable accomplishments, the question that naturally arises is: Why were the Allies so superior in cryptology? Of the many theories that offer themselves, a couple that at first seem plausible do not in fact apply.

One is that German codebreakers were chosen for their political reliability as good Nazis instead of for their brains. This did not happen with the German cryptanalytic agencies, probably because they were not regarded as very important.[87] Secondly, and somewhat paradoxically, it is not a cause of Allied superiority that the Allies were quantum steps ahead of the Germans in cryptology. They were certainly more advanced, but the Germans knew the answer to the basic question: how to solve the Enigma. Early in the 1930s the head cryptanalyst of the Forschungsamt, Dr. Georg Schröder, said to the head evaluator: "Seifert, the whole Enigma is garbage!" And he proceeded to demonstrate a solution using alphabet slides[88] that was also known—at least later—to the Allies. Though a modification (the plugboard) vitiated this technique, the German cryptographers always claimed that the machine was not absolutely secure and continually suggested improvements—implying that they could see ways of breaking into the machine.[89] So the theory that the Allies knew how to solve the Enigma and the Germans did not is false and not a factor in the Allied cryptologic superiority.

What, then, *were* the factors? There are, of course, a variety of causes for so complex a phenomenon.[90] They may be divided into two kinds—external or general and internal or technical. There are four technical factors, all of which stemmed from purely cryptologic factors.

The first chronologically, and probably also the first in order of importance, is that the Allies knew the German machine. The Enigma was originally sold to the public. Even though it was modified for government use, and even though the several agencies of government had their own variations of it, the Allies knew its basic layout. To this must be added the information about its keys and operation provided by the spy. Cryptanalytically, this is of course an enormous head start. It is also a great psychological advantage. The Germans did not have these benefits. The British Typex and the American SIGABA machines were developed in secret. It should be stated that knowledge of a machine is not always essential for its solution. The British solved the later Geheimschreiber, and the Americans reconstructed the Japanese PURPLE machine without any such assistance—though the Americans did have the help of knowing the texts of Japanese diplomatic messages handed to the American State Department. But familiarity with the machine cannot but help.

The second technical reason is that the Germans mainly used one machine, though they supplemented it with another during the war, while the Allies, consisting of many nations, used many. This use of one machine had several effects. First of all, it meant that the Allies could concentrate more manpower on a single problem. Secondly, the greater volume of messages enciphered in that single system facilitated its solution. Thirdly, a single system increased Allied incentive, because its solution would yield a greater prize than if it were just one system among many. None of these factors operated for the Germans, and it correspondingly depressed their efforts and results.

A third cryptologic reason is that the top rotor machines of the British and Americans were far better than their German counterpart: they were never solved. The naval Enigma, the best of the German family, came with a set of eight rotors, of which four were inserted into the machine at any one time. Gears controlled their stepping. But one form of the American SIGABA (ECM, or "electric code machine," in its navy version) used no fewer than 15 rotors at a time—10 to create the electrical maze, five for moving the others in a much more irregular way than gears could. A cryptologist has said that the SIGABA was "a generation ahead" of the Enigma. It was in fact devised a decade after the Enigma, as was the Typex, and because the British did not begin equipping their army and air force, and the Americans their army and navy, with cipher machines until the late 1930s, they could utilize this more advanced mechanism without losing capital investment. The Germans, who had mechanized a decade earlier, were stuck with an older, weaker machine.[91]

Fourthly, just as the German hardware was poorer, so was their software. Two of their operating procedures proved fatal to many an Enigma cryptogram. One was the flawed keying method used by the Germans before the war and for its first year or so. It required that a three-letter keying group, such as BVI, be repeated: BVIBVI. The Germans probably did this to enable their clerks to decipher a message even if a garble affected one of the six key letters. But the repetition also created a point of entry for cryptanalysts, which the Poles and then the British quickly exploited.[92] This keying method was later changed, but by then Enigma had been cracked. The Allies, on the other hand, used far more secure keying systems which obviated this sort of attack. The other dangerous operating procedure was the repeated sending of stereotyped messages. Regulations probably prohibited that, but day after day radiomen nevertheless composed, enciphered, and transmitted identically worded messages. Often the Allies could break into a new Enigma key because an isolated outpost continued to transmit "Nothing to report" in the new key just as it had in the old. Similar cases took place on the Allied side, especially in the routine messages to and from convoys. But often the Allies padded their messages—put meaningless words or phrases at the beginning and the end to disguise routine beginnings and endings. Often, too, the Allies bisected messages—divided them in half and put the second half at the front, again to disguise stereotyped phraseology. The Germans seem not to have done this regularly.

To recapitulate these four technical reasons: Allied knowledge of the Enigma; the German use of one main machine versus the Allied use of many; a poorer German machine; and inadequate operating procedures. In addition, there were five general reasons, which flowed from external circumstances.[93]

Perhaps the most important was the fragmentation of German cryptanalysis. The Germans had a great many codebreaking agencies.[94] The Chiffrierabteilung of the armed forces high command, Pers Z of the Foreign Office, and Göring's Forschungsamt competed on the highest level. For a time the SD, the Sicherheitsdienst, the SS's intelligence arm, had its own agency. The army, the navy, and the air force each had its own unit, though there was rather more justification for that. But this multiplicity spread the available manpower, which was scarce to begin with, very thin. And it diffused the codebreaking effort. Contrast this with the concentration of effort at Bletchley Park, Britain's sole codebreaking agency, and with that in America, where the army and navy codebreaking units worked in the closest coöperation. There was some coöperation in Germany, of course. But it did not overcome the lethal effects of dispersion, which stemmed ultimately from Hitler's assigning duplicate responsibilities to his underlings so that he could retain ultimate control. The charismatic nature of his leadership enabled him to do this in many areas of government. It facilitated his rule—but it devastated his war effort, including codebreaking.[95]

Also fundamental as a reason for Allied cryptologic superiority was

Germany's aggression and the Allies' defensive posture. For intelligence is necessary to the defense, but it is only contingent to the offense.[96] Clausewitz defined the characteristic feature of the defense as "awaiting the blow."[97] An army can await a blow only if it believes that a blow is planned, and such a belief can be created only by information about the enemy. Thus intelligence is essential to the defense, and Poland, France, and England, basically in a defensive stance, cultivated it more. The offense, on the other hand, is "complete in itself," Clausewitz said.[98] An attacking army does not even have to know where the enemy force is: it can march about, imposing its will, until it meets its foe. Such an army will put more of its energy into men, tanks, planes, and guns and less into intelligence, one form of which is codebreaking. This Germany did. A number of incidents and conditions demonstrate her relative neglect of intelligence and the corresponding greater attention that the Allies paid to it.

France gained the spy who provided the Allies with vital cryptologic information in large measure because she made a great—and generally successful—effort to learn about German rearmament. The Germans, though their spies sometimes delivered useful cryptologic information, never scored a coup like France's—mainly because they never tried as hard.[99] Before the outbreak of war, Great Britain had established an Operational Intelligence Centre in the Admiralty and a Joint Intelligence Committee under the chiefs of staff. Germany never took such steps.[100]

The Allies put better men into cryptology than the Germans. Bletchley Park was an unbelievable galaxy of talent. All American recruits were given an IQ test; those who scored the highest were proposed for cryptologic work. This resulted in extraordinarily high brainpower in codebreaking units. The American army agency could have staffed a first-class university in all departments, one of its leaders said.[101] No such recruiting seems to have taken place for German codebreaking. And their agencies, despite individually bright men, did not dazzle as did the Allied units.

German training for cryptanalysis, too, was poorer than the Allies'. The only textbook the B-Dienst had was a translation of an elementary French text.[102] Cryptanalysts learned on the job. The United States, on the other hand, had developed its own textbooks and established schools and extension courses to train cryptanalysts.[103] In the same way, the Allied instructions for cipher clerks on how to set up their machines and how to encipher sometimes explained that certain procedures should not be used because they would help the enemy solve the messages.[104] The German instructions never motivated like that.[105]

Furthermore, while the Germans remained using only electromechanical devices for solving ciphers, the Allies added electronic devices. The cause of this Allied advance seems to have lain in Britain's urgent need for intelligence.[106] In 1940, with invasion still a possibility, "Bletchley foresaw that the enemy could introduce new practices which would require the [existing electromechanical] breaking machinery to be speeded up by one or two orders of magnitude at least."[107] Such high speeds had been attained in the 1930s by a Cambridge physicist, C. E. Wynn-Williams. He had devised an electronic counter to tally electron-particle events that occurred too rapidly for electromechanical counters. Many of Bletchley's staff had come from Cambridge. They thought of his electronic device when they themselves had to accelerate machinery doing similar work, and he eventually largely designed one of the precursors of COLOSSUS.[108] These electronic devices in effect multiplied the Allies' manpower and enabled them to do far more in a given amount of time. In Germany, despite a computer pioneer's 1940 proposal for an electronic cipher device, which might have suggested the use of electronics in codebreaking to the army's cryptologic authorities,[109] and despite a later B-Dienst proposal for an electronic codebreaking mechanism,[110] no agency apparently ever felt the need to build one.

All these factors suggested a widespread German disregard for codebreaking relative to the Allies, which may be attributed to German aggression and Allied emphasis on the defensive.

A third general factor was the expulsion of the Jews. The exodus or extermination of a whole people, many of them highly intelligent, cost German codebreaking—as it cost German mathematics and German physics—many useful brains.[111]

A fourth general reason was luck. Luck helped the Allies more than the Germans. It certainly played a role in the French recruiting of their important spy, and it was luck that Turing and Welchman, who had ideas that greatly helped Enigma solutions and that the Germans did not have, were Britons. But it was not as important a factor as the others.

The fifth and last reason for German inferiority is the broadest: a greater reluctance to face reality. This reluctance, combined with the lack of irrefutable evidence for enemy cryptanalysis, largely kept the naval high command from conceding during several investigations that its cipher might have been broken. The officers found it difficult to admit to themselves, to their chiefs, and to Hitler that everything they had said and done was worthless and would have to be redone. The result was disaster. Of course, the Allies, too, sometimes engaged in wishful thinking. Conferences on possible compromises of systems some-times decided, as the Germans did, that none had occurred, largely be-cause the cryptologists did not want to go through all the work of institut-ing new systems—devising, manufacturing, and distributing the new machines, training the personnel, and phasing the system into operation with the inevitable blunders that would call down the wrath of fighting admirals and generals. But conditions differed for the Allies. They were less crippled by arrogance than the Germans[112] and so more open to improvement. SIGABA's greater strength enabled the Americans to restore security in case of a compromise by simply replacing rotors; the Germans would have had to substitute a whole new system for the Enigma. Com-petition between Americans and Britons in a joint endeavour helped keep failure from being hidden for very long. Civilians headed important sections of codebreaking and intelligence agencies more frequently in Allied forces than in German;[113] because they were less concerned about their military careers than the officers and officials who headed the corre-sponding German sections, these civilians admitted unpleasant facts to their superiors more readily. For all these reasons, the Allies seem to have faced reality more. When an American cipher machine went astray in France in 1944, the American army code agency worked day and night to rewire the rotors of other machines, thus making the missing machine useless to cryptanalysts. And when the Americans got wind of the German solution to the military attaché code, they distributed a new system. So, as one American cryptologist has said, "We never kidded ourselves. The Germans and Japanese did kid themselves."[114]

These, then, are the five external conditions that helped reduce Ger-man cryptanalysis to a level inferior to Allied: the fragmentation of the German organization compared to the unity of the Allied; Germany's aggression, which led to a neglect of cryptology, contrasted with the Allied defensive posture, which emphasized intelligence; the expulsion and killing of the Jews; better Allied luck; and greater German reluctance to face reality. When these are joined to the four technical reasons, they help answer why German cryptanalysis was inferior to Allied.

## IX

What, then, does it all mean? What was the importance of codebreaking in the war?

Can the value of codebreaking be quantified? Can a historian say, for example, that it shortened the war by so many months? No. Some participants or historians have suggested figures of a year or two years, or have computed the shortening of the Battle of the Atlantic as six months.[115] But others have declined to make such estimates. They have said it was impossible and probably meaningless. As even a wartime head of the U.S. Army codebreakers said, "If you try to do that, you'd have the quartermaster claiming so many years, the air force so many, and everybody claiming some, and before you know it you'd find that the war should have been over 25 years before it began!"[116]

Moreover, in discussing the effect of codebreaking on the war, historians must never forget that it merely helped. Codebreaking and intelligence alone do not win wars. Wars are won by men and guns and will; they are won on battlefields. This helps to answer a question often asked: If the Allies had ULTRA, why didn't they win more quickly? One answer is, of course, that they did.[117] Another is that a general has to get a lot of his own men into place, supply them with guns, food, and ammunition, and then inspire them if he wants to win wars—and information about the enemy does not solve those problems.

Within the framework of intelligence, however, codebreaking became, in the course of the war, the most important form of intelligence. Its powers exceeded those of other kinds. It could provide higher-level information than prisoners of war. It could see beyond the horizons of aerial reconnaissance. It could be trusted far more than spies. In operational and tactical areas, it provided the most valuable intelligence of all. Strategically, however, it did not play a major role. The Germans never achieved solutions that would have given them those insights. And by the time ULTRA really took hold, the initiative had passed to the Allies, and there were no longer any German strategic decisions for the Allies to learn.[118]

Nevertheless, in statement after statement, high commanders on both sides testified to the value of signals intelligence in World War II. Chief of the German general staff Franz Halder called it "the most copious and the best source of intelligence."[119] Eisenhower told the administrative chief of Bletchley: "The intelligence which has emanated from you . . . has been of priceless value to me."[120] General Marshall declared that the solutions "contribute greatly to the victory and tremendously to the saving in American lives."[121]

And indeed, that was the ultimate contribution of signals intelligence. It saved lives. Not only Allied and Russian lives but, by shortening the war, German, Italian, and Japanese lives as well. Some people alive after World Wars I and II might not have been but for these solutions. That is the debt that the world owes to the codebreakers; that is the crowning human value of their triumphs.

# Plaintext in the
# New Unabridged

The new edition of Webster's Unabridged—that paragon of lexicons, that ultimate authority for puzzle-solvers, editors, and the man in the street—burst upon public attention with less than favorable notices. News stories announcing the book, published in September 1961, by the G. & C. Merriam Company under its official title of *Webster's Third New International Dictionary of the English Language Unabridged*, greeted its uncensorious inclusion of *ain't* with hoots of derision. Linguistic conservatives damned it for listing such words as *scram, soused, yakked*, and *swell* without any indication that they are colloquial. Critics sneeringly asked whether whoremistress Polly Adler and ballplayer Willie Mays, quoted to illustrate certain meanings, provided the best examples of the language used by cultivated people. The uproar reached a climax in a *New York Times* editorial suggesting that the Webster editors not throw out the printing plates of the second edition because "there is likely to be a continuing demand for it."

If there is, the public will be doing itself a disservice as far as cryptology is concerned. For, whatever faults the third edition may have, its handling of cryptology has been vastly improved over the second edition's. Scores of additional terms are defined, and—with few exceptions—these definitions are much more complete, clear, accurate, and up-to-date than those even in the 1960 printing of the second edition.

*Plaintext in the New Unabridged: An Examination of the Definitions on Cryptology in Webster's Third New International Dictionary* was published in 1963 by Crypto Press as a monograph.

*Webster's Third* marks the first time in the history of cryptology that the terms in the field have been collected and examined broadly and in quantity to see with what meanings people are actually using them, and the first time that the words of cryptology have been defined according to the best standards of modern lexicography.

Appreciation for this happy state of affairs must be chiefly tendered to Martin Joos, the dictionary's consultant in cryptology and the individual who largely wrote the definitions. Joos, professor of German and linguistics at the University of Wisconsin, has several books to his credit—*Acoustic Phonetics, Middle High German Courtly Reader,* and *Readings in Linguistics.* He was born May 11, 1907, in Fountain City, Wisconsin, earned his A.M. and his Ph.D. at the University of Wisconsin, and taught there during most of his professional career.[1] From 1942 to 1946, he served in the War Department doing "secret communications work"—to borrow the circumlocution in his biography in *Who's Who in America.* He himself cannot specify his duties because of security, but he does say: "I was taken on at an instructor's salary and ranking, to use academic terms, and finished the war in the highest civilian rank except for [William F.] Friedman himself. I was then one of a small top group called Research Consultants, a group so small that the total size of the staff was exactly one thousand times the size of this group. My 'publications' are all on the highest level of security classification, restricted each to a small number of individually numbered and registered copies, so that the whereabouts of each copy is known at every instant and nobody below the rank of Colonel ever sees a copy."[2] He was awarded a citation for Exceptional Civilian Service in 1946. His lexicographical experience consisted of work on the Thorndike-Century dictionaries and of defining the phonetics terms in the famous *American College Dictionary.* Because Webster's (in the words of Editor-in-Chief Philip B. Gove) "had confidence in Professor Joos and had convincing knowledge of his ability to define, which is an ability that does not always go with knowledge of a subject,"[3] the company asked him to undertake the work without even considering anyone else. Joos did it for them in 1956 by mail and was paid for it.

How did he go about defining the cryptological terms for *Webster's Third?* In his own words: "The G. & C. Merriam Company sent me a pretty large file (large considering that the terms are not as lavishly represented in public print as ordinary words) of 'citations' (each typically on a 3 × 5 slip, a few longer) copied from books, daily papers, weeklies, and monthlies, but not including anything from government publications. Naturally this file contained so much deadwood and redundancy that its effective size was about one third that many citations. Since they give me half a year to do the job, I first picked up more citations from current publications and from books that they had missed, and a citation or two from each of some dozens of novels; these, together with sources which I do not care to identify beyond calling them 'government publications,' enabled me to quite precisely double the effective size of their citation-file. All this material has gone back to them and is now in the citation-files in Springfield.

"Then I wrote definitions[4] for terms in the first three letters of the alphabet, following the form of the second edition. They went through that material very thoroughly and from their rewrites I was able to deduce the form appropriate to the Third New International, which I followed for the whole list (redoing the first three letters too). Six weeks after I sent that all in, they came back with queries on the terms 'bifid,' 'sequence,' 'trifid,' 'vigenère cipher,' and 'vigenère tableau.' I then rewrote each of these in at least two more versions and supplied extensive commentary to discuss." Joos submitted a total list of 501 terms. Of these, 180 are included in the dictionary.[5] The definitions are all Joos's, with only slight alterations—he estimates about three percent—to fit the book's style.

This rare concatenation of cryptological background, lexicographical experience and devoted labor resulted in the superb terminology of the third edition. Perhaps the best illustration of this excellence is the term *cryptography* itself. For many years, this word embraced the entire field of secret writing—the solution of cryptograms as well as methods of putting messages into secret forms. This was the situation in 1934, when the second edition was first published, and this broad, older definition remains one of the senses in which the word is used. But as the term *cryptanalysis*, coined at the start of the '20s by William F. Friedman,[6] gained currency outside of official publications, it tended to relegate the term *cryptography* to the narrower and less ambiguous designation of only the legitimate en- and decipherment of messages.[7] Both senses remain in active—if conflicting—use today, the broader perhaps more among the general public, the narrower among specialists. One would never guess this from the second edition's[8] terse "act or art of writing in secret characters; also, secret character, or cipher." In the third edition, both meanings are given: "*1* : secret writing : cryptic symbolization *2 a* : the art or practice of preparing or reading messages in a form intended to prevent their being read by those not privy to secrets of the form; *also* : the science of devising methods and means for this— compare CIPHER *2*, CODE *3 b* : CRYPTANALYSIS."[9]

Recently, specialists revived an old term to fill the gap in terminology, to give the whole two-sided field of secret communication a name of its own, which it never had. This is *cryptology*, which apparently fell into desuetude soon after its creation, and which, in recent years, seems to have skulked along as a kind of second-rate synonym for *cryptography*, with overtones of the occult (cryptic symbolism) and the phony (Bacon-Shakespeare) that would have no truck with honest-and-true, red-white-and-blue cryptography. The second edition, while not bothering with these nuances, set forth the basic meaning straightforwardly enough as "the study of cryptography." But the definition in the third edition takes commendable and up-to-date account of the development in the term's meaning with its "the scientific study of cryptography and cryptanalysis."[10] (Though Joos's definitions cover cryptology, his specialty is strangely listed in the front of the book as "cryptography.")

Another instance of the third edition's clarifying illumination appears under *cryptanalysis*, the third term of the triad. The second edition is vague in its definition of cryptanalysis as "decipherment of cryptograms," for *decipherment* can mean both the legitimate and the illegitimate reduction of a secret message to understandable form whereas *cryptanalysis* refers only to the latter. The third edition states plainly that cryptanalysis is "the solving of cryptograms or cryptographic systems." It also makes clear, in sense 2, that the term refers not only to a process but also to a study: "The theory of solving cryptograms or cryptographic systems: the art of devising methods for this—called also *cryptanalytics.*"

Still more good evidence of the precision and comprehensiveness of the new edition can be found in its handling of those equivocal terms, *decipher* and *code*. No hint of the sometimes contradictory subsenses of *decipher* is given in the second edition, but both are clearly stated in the third: "2 : to convert (a cryptic writing) into intelligible form : as *a* : to undo (an encipherment) by reversal of the enciphering process *b* : solve." The problem with *code* is that the public obstinately persists in using it as a synonym for *cipher*, while cryptologists restrict it to its technical meaning. No doubt a universal prescription of the technical nomenclature would end some unnecessary confusion. But, as the preface states, "accuracy . . . requires a dictionary to state meanings in which words are in fact used, not to give editorial opinion of what their meanings should be." The third edition assiduously follows this rule when faced with *code*. It first brings out *code*'s technical meaning (much more fully than the second edition, incidentally) and then gives its popular sense with a note that it is "not used technically." An admirable piece of lexicography!

code, n.

But it wasn't a code
in the technical
sense: it was a
cipher. I know--
I was there.--Joos.

According to World War II Chief of Staff George Marshall, the cracking of the famed Japanese "purple" code, for which Friedman was principally responsible, led to vital foreknowledge of Hitler's intentions in Europe and gave the U.S. Navy a priceless advantage in intelligence that led to such critical victories as Coral Sea, Midway and subsequent bold carrier strikes. Friedman himself gently declines to take so much credit. "There is no single person," he once said, "to whom the major share of credit should go. It represents an achievement of the Army cryptanalytic bureau." But the fact is that, more than any other, it was Friedman who

TIME, MAY 14, 1956    p. 33

JOOS 12 MAY '56

A building block for one of the definitions of the term "code" in *Webster's Third New International Dictionary:* a citation card clipped from *Time* magazine with a note added by the definer.

The third edition has also eliminated many of the oddities of the second. The second defines *decipherment* only as "the act of deciphering." The third has it also as "the result of deciphering." The second has the verb *encrypt* ("to encode") but no *decrypt*; but the third has both, and notes that *decrypt* emphasizes the cryptanalytic. The second has *encipher* as a verb but also as a noun, a sense in which this writer never saw it; the third has it only as a verb. The second, never realizing that keys were used to put messages into cipher, listed only the decipherment sense of *key* as "that which serves to reveal, discover or solve something unknown or difficult; as, the key to a riddle." The third provides the important encipherment sense—giving it, incidentally, virtually encyclopedic treatment, with six subsenses, three of which are entries themselves, plus five cross references. The third edition seems inferior in only one case, the definition for *cipher*, which is excessively elaborate and too complicated compared to the brevity and simplicity of the second's—though the third has redeemed itself with a cross reference to the *code* definition. Regrettably, the important distinction between the two is nowhere made explicit through a synonymy paragraph like those that explain the different connotations of words with similar denotations.

While the chief contribution of the third edition lies in the accuracy of its definitions of the most-used cryptologic terms, its host of new terms greatly enriches it. In addition to the terms previously discussed, and their run-ons, the most useful among the terms that are either new to the dictionary or have newly been given a cryptologic sense are the following: *anagram, additive, alphabet, bigram, black chamber, book code, break, cipher machine, cipher text, concealment cipher, clear, commercial code, cover text, crack, deciphering alphabet, decrypt, digram, double transposition, enciphering alphabet, fractionate, garble, indicator, jargon code, key, keying sequence, monoalphabetic substitution, null, one-part code, open, plaintext, polyalphabetic, polygraphic, running key, scrambler, security, slide, standard, substitution, subtractive, superencipherment, tableau, transposition, trigram, two-part code.* These terms enhance the dictionary's value, because each is either used popularly or is basic to cryptology.

But even Webster's Unabridged has its faults. Compared with the volume's virtues, they are minor. Still, candor and scholarship compel their mention.

Worst, of course, are the outright errors. Without a full range of citations, it is always dangerous to assail a definition as wrong, because the impression of a meaning given by just a few instances of use may be quite erroneous. Furthermore, the errors are very rare and quite minute. In no case is a definition totally wrong; most, in fact, are mostly right. Still, a dictionary of the prestige of the Merriam-Webster Unabridged ought to aim at absolute accuracy, and, in the hope of helping to attain that ideal, the reviewer will risk pointing out what he believes to be mistakes, with citations to support his views.

*Running key* is improperly defined as "an unpredictable keying sequence (as a text used as a key by prearrangement)." While the illustration is correct and thus obviates much damage, predictability does not enter into the question of whether a key is a running key. Highly predictable sequences may serve as running keys. In fact, they have done so. Successive verses of Alfred de Musset's poem *Nuit de décembre* keyed successive messages of the Duke of Orléans—a scheme that proved so predictable that the French cryptanalyst Etienne Bazeries solved one message after another.[11] A key is "running" because it consists of a long text that does not repeat over and over again; its essence lies in its aperiodicity. Joos, it should be noted, remained unconvinced, basing his defense on a very narrow construction of "unpredictable."

*Converter* is improperly defined as " *e(1)* : an electric cipher machine, esp : one adaptable to automatic operation." As a person without security clearance, like the great majority of the dictionary's users, the reviewer has heard the term *converter* used only in connection with the M-209,[12] the Army designation for the Hagelin cipher machine, which in this embodiment is mechanical and not electrical. Joos argued that "the term converter was invented specifically for the SIGABA and was promptly extended in technical use to SIGCUM and even SIGTOT, not to mention still more sophisticated machines, *all* electrical." Still, one may wonder why a definition limited only to classified devices is included in a dictionary to be used by persons with no knowledge of these devices.[13]

The definition of *specific key* is all right as far as it goes ("the key for a single cryptographic message or a small group of messages"), but it omits an important and far more common meaning. That is its designation of the variable portion of a cryptographic system as contrasted with the invariable portion usually called the *general system* (a term which is not defined). Joos defended his definition by stating that *specific key* "is a term invented to create a series of ranked terms. The term of highest rank is a cipher system. Next in rank is *period key* [which is defined in the dictionary as "the set of cryptographic key details which are kept unchanged during an agreed time" and is cross-referenced to *specific key*]. The term of bottom rank is *specific key*, which in the best practice is different for each message." All these may well be actual uses, but the use of this term to mean the variable portion of systems is too widespread to be ignored.[14]

The definition for *Bazeries cylinder* neglects to say that the disks may be assembled on the shaft in any prearranged order. This omission is critical because the secrecy of the device resides in this very variability![15]

*Nihilist cipher* leaves out the essential element of this cipher. As the definition now stands ("a substitution method replacing each letter by its row and column numbers in an alphabet square"), all that is specified is a checkerboard or a Polybius square. The cipher actually consists of the addition of a key, whose numbers are obtained from the same square, to the numbers of the plaintext; the ciphertext is the resulting sum. The Nihilist cipher is thus a polyalphabetic one, not the monoalphabetic system that is described.[16]

The *rail-fence cipher* can extend the number of lines in which the plaintext is distributed beyond two,[17] the maximum allowable in the definition ("a zigzag transposition method in which alternate letters of the plaintext are juxtaposed [as in the encipherment

$$b \, i \, {}_d g_e = \text{bigrde.}]").$$
$$\phantom{b \, i \,}r \phantom{d} e$$

If the key is 3, the cipher is still a rail-fence, as in the encipherment

$$\begin{matrix} m & & e & & s \\ & a & v & l & u \\ & & r & o & \end{matrix} = \text{mesavluro.}$$

The makers of equipment to *scramble* communications would be unhappy if they had to restrict themselves to "disarranging the frequencies of a telephonic or radio message." Many other scrambling techniques exist: splitting the stream of speech into short segments and transposing them, masking the sounds with noise, encipherment of pulse code modulation, and so forth.[18] In addition, the definition implies a restriction to audio communication, though the definition for *scrambler* extends the process to "telephone, teletype, facsimilie or television."

Finally, the definition of *cipher disk* gives that device "two movable concentric disks." Though physically both can move, cryptologically only the upper is considered to do so. The lower disk is normally regarded as fixed.[19]

Another problem is that some of the definitions are too complicated to be understood or too general to be useful. Take, for example, *Vigenère cipher*: "polyalphabetic substitution with alphabets derived from one pair of primary alphabets by sliding (as in the Vigenère tableau) for which the usual keying formula is $P + K = C$, where $P$ is the position of the plaintext letter in the plain component, $C$ that of the ciphertext letter in the cipher sequence, and $K$ that of the key letter in the normal alphabet and where positions are numbered from zero to 25 and 26 is subtracted from sums above 25." This defies comprehension by any lay reader.[20] An example of the vague definition is *Playfair cipher*: "a cipher involving a digraphic substitution from a single alphabet square which begins with the letters of a keyword and continues with the remaining letters of the alphabet less J." Because this does not explain how the cipher works, the space is virtually wasted.

This problem is linked to a larger one that pushes beyond the limits of the purely cryptologic and into the domain of the purpose and design of an unabridged dictionary for general use. The larger question is whether highly technical terms ought to be included in such a dictionary. This reviewer thinks not. First of all, the definitions of such terms are often useless to the layman, because they are either too complicated or too superficial. Secondly, it seems unlikely that a novelist or a journalist would mention, say, a Vigenère cipher without describing it, except possibly to sound erudite or mysterious, in which case only the effect is important, not the meaning.

On what basis, then, are such terms included? The stricture in the dictionary's preface—"Selection is guided by usefulness"—doesn't help much because it does not give the criterion of usefulness. Editor Gove wrote, "Our criteria for the inclusion of a technical term varies with the subject, the term and the editors available for handling it. For most of the technical entries the decision is made by a staff editor in this office on the basis of, first, usefulness, and, second, importance. However, in the case of a highly recondite and often classified subject like cryptanalysis we had to rely heavily on the opinion of our outside consultant." How, then, did Joos select his terms?

"Usable rules for inclusion or omission of headwords are extremely hard to set up," he writes, "and I have no doubt that the G. & C. Merriam Company would pay a good price for a superior rule. My practice has been to ask myself: 'Is this term at all likely to turn up in a novel about the Second World War printed within the time before the next big dictionary, say thirty years?'" Did his citations show many technical terms in novels? Joos sidestepped the question, replying instead: "Your theory of what belongs in a general dictionary would bankrupt the G. & C. Merriam Company. Technical terms do belong in a general dictionary. The citations do not have to prove, on their face, that the term has already been used in a novel without contextual explanation: that theory would also bankrupt the dictionary publishers. The definers have to guess that it may so turn up, or that it may turn up in *Time*, etc. They include, then, a small fraction of the existing technical terms. They can't sell a dictionary that includes none of them; and one that included all of them would weigh some 200 lbs. and would also be unsalable." But it hardly seems right that a dictionary of the stature—and the cost ($47.50)—of the Merriam-Webster should select its definitions on the basis of a financial criterion. The criterion should be linguistic. Furthermore, this attitude seems to contravene the oft-stated position of the editors that the dictionary is purely a history of the language.

Another reason that he included technical terms, Joos said, is that "this dictionary will be bought in several copies by the shop that I worked in; the thousands of apprentices in the art that will work there during the next generation ought to be able to get the technically authoritative definitions for those terms which *happen to be* current enough to turn up in novels at all, whether explained rightly in those novels, wrongly, or not at all." Asked whether he felt that the possibility that these apprentices would look up these terms justifies burdening a general dictionary with them, Joos answered: "I have lived among them, as I am now living among chemists and nuclear physicists and economists and so on: and all these people (yes, including the nuclear physicists!) look up technical terms in just this dictionary (they are doing it every day now in the copy we have in our University Club) to find out what the terms 'really mean,' as they say."

But why, then, were 300 terms that he had submitted kept out? Why include *Fleissner grille* (an obsolete system dating from 1889) and not *ciphony* (electronically enciphered speech, now in wide use)? Why *Wheatstone cipher* (a simple device invented before 1867) and not *Hill system* (an algebraic polygraphic cipher invented in 1929)? These seem to be on at least a par of usefulness. No doubt arguments could be advanced to support the dictionary's position, but they would probably be extremely arbitrary and ad hoc, as, to this reviewer, appear many of Joos's reasons for their exclusion.[21]

This reviewer remains unconvinced of the necessity to include highly technical terms.[22] They return too few benefits for the space they take up. The rule that should be followed is this: include only those terms that are (a) essential to understand the fundamentals of the science (as *plaintext*), or (b) likely to be used without explanation in general literature (as *substitution cipher*, whose meaning can be inferred in a general way but which deserves a definition that dispels any doubt, contrasts with *transposition cipher*, and cross-references to such terms as *monoalphabetic* and *polygraphic*.) Though dispute would probably still arise over borderline terms, this procedure would ensure substantial agreement on which terms to include—particularly as the citations would provide much objective data. The space that would be saved by cutting down on the number of technical terms (which are defined in books on the subject or in specialized glossaries[23]) could be used either to increase the supporting data on general vocabulary through a more liberal use of illustrative quotations or usage notes or synonymy paragraphs, or simply to cut the price of the book. These matters are, in a sense, extracryptologic, but they affect cryptologists to the extent that cryptologists employ the general vocabulary of English as a tool of thought.

After castigating the dictionary for including too many terms, it may sound inconsistent to charge that it ignores some. But some of the omitted terms have appeared in popular print and deserve to be recorded and defined more than some that have crept into the dictionary's narrow columns. Chief among the missing are *traffic analysis,*[24] *electronic countermeasure,*[25] *rotor,*[26] and *one-time pad.*[27] The lack is not Joos's fault but that of the editors who did not pick up the terms in their reading. Joos, in fact, wanted to include *one-time pad* but could not document one-time-pad

"That we have had much success in breaking Soviet codes -- akin to the decoding feat which played such a key role in the war against Japan -- is dubious because the Russians are notorious for their reliance on a device known as the 'one-time-pad.' This means, in effect, that each message is send [sic] in a completely different code so that even when the code is broken -- something that takes a long time at best -- the same decoding problem must be faced with the very next message recorded."

Harry Schwartz
                                    WOOLF APR 1 '65
                "Still the 'Riddle Wrapped in
"sent in by Kahn"   a Mystery'."
  Jan.18,1962                        CUMMINGS FEB 1 '62
USED F___              The New York Times Magazine-15 Mar.195_

Another citation card, this one for "one-time pad." The explanation—as so often with cryptologic terms in general writings—is partly right, mostly wrong; this cannot help the definer. The partly illegible rubber stamp at the lower left states that the term was "used for '65 addenda."

it—not a surprising situation since this reviewer, at least, knows of only two unclassified occurrences of the term before 1956, when Joos wrote his definitions.[28]

The long recital of criticisms may make it appear that this reviewer's opinion of the dictionary's cryptologic definitions is unfavorable. That is not so. It simply takes longer to explain an opposing viewpoint than to cheer a good piece of work. This reviewer wants to emphasize that most of the errors he found are minor and that they are far outweighed and outnumbered by the clear and accurate definitions. Indeed, if the dictionary's success in this microcosm indicates the quality of its definitions of technical terms in other fields, then it has performed a meritorious and valuable service indeed. The reviewer also wants to note that his views on the superabundance of technical definitions accuse the dictionary of little more than an embarrassment of riches. He feels that this may have harmed the general vocabulary, but the editors may hold a contrary opinion.

Cryptologists as cryptologists, however, have every reason to be pleased with the constellation of new definitions, produced in accordance with the best of lexicographical standards. For these contribute importantly to the clarity of thought in cryptology and so ultimately to the more rapid and precise advancement of the science. Thus, an overall review would state with pleasure that the third edition of the Merriam-Webster Unabridged has done an excellent job with its cryptologic terms. It discharges its responsibility to explain the primary terms of a science to the public so well that a browser might even grasp the basic concepts of cryptology. With minor exceptions, its definitions are in the clearest of plaintext and demand neither decipherment nor decryptment. One might say, in fact, that it ain't bad at all.

# Appendix I

## List of Cryptologic Terms in
### *Webster's Third New International Dictionary*

additive
agent cipher
agent code
albam
alphabet
alphabetical code
anagram
aperiodic
athbash *also* atbash
autoclave cipher
autokey cipher
bacon biliteral cipher
bazeries cylinder
beaufort cipher
bifid
bigram
biliteral
black chamber
book code
break
c *symbol*
caesar shift *or* caesar
  substitution
cipher
cipher *n*
cipher *vb*
cipher clerk
cipher complement
cipher disk *or* cipher
  wheel
cipher machine
cipher square

ciphertext
clear
code *n*
code *vt*
code book
code clerk
code group
code name
code wheel
code word
columnar
  transposition
commercial code
component
concealment cipher
conjugate alphabet
converter
cover text
cross-reference code
crypt
cryptanalysis
cryptanalytic
cryptanalytics
cryptanalyze
cryptic
crypto
cryptogram
cryptograph *n*
cryptograph *vt*
cryptographer
cryptographic
cryptographist

cryptography
cryptologist
cryptology
decimate
decimation
decipher *vt*
decipher *n*
deciphering alphabet
decipherment
decode *vt*
decode *n*
decoder
decrypt
decryptograph
digram
digraph
digraphic
direct
disk cipher
double-key cipher
double substitution
double transposition
encipher
encipherer
enciphering alphabet
encipherment
en clair
encode
encodement
encoder
encrypt
field code

fleissner grille
fractional substitution
fractionate
garble *vt*
garble *n*
garble table
generatrix
grille
idiomorph
idiomorphic
incoherent
indicator
interrupted key
interrupter
isomorph
jargon code
julius caesar cipher
k *symbol*
key *n*
key *vb*
keying sequence
key letter
key-sequence
key-word
mixed alphabet
monoalphabetic
  substitution
monographic
monoliteral
multiple-alphabet
  cipher

nihilist cipher
non-significant
null
one-part code
open
p *symbol*
pattern word
pentagraph
periodic key
period key
permutation table
plain component
plaintext
playfair cipher
polyalphabetic
polygraph
polygraphic
polygraphy
polyliteral
porta cipher
primary alphabet
probable word
progressive-alphabet
  cipher
rail-fence cipher
recipher *vt*
recipher *n*
reciprocal alphabet
route transposition
running key

scramble
scrambler
scytale
security
sequence
simple substitution
slide *n*
slide *vt*
specific key
square table
standard
steganogram
steganography
substitution
superencipherment
tableau
tetragraph
transposition
transposition cipher
trellis cipher
trifid
trigram
trigraph
trigraphic
two-part code
unscramble
variant
vigenère cipher
vigenère tableau
wheatstone cipher

NOTES: *n* = noun; *vb* = verb; *vt* = transitive verb; *symbol* means that the meaning of that letter when used as (cryptologic) symbol is given. No words are capitalized in the dictionary; those that usually are in writing, as *Vigenère cipher*, are marked "usu.cap." followed by the capitalized letter.

# Appendix II

## Other Views of Cryptologic Terminology

What about other unabridged dictionaries? How well do they handle cryptological terms? Only two other such dictionaries of English exist—the multivolume *New English Dictionary on Historical Principles*, published by the Oxford University Press, and the Funk & Wagnalls *New Standard Dictionary of the English Language*. Neither has been completely overhauled since its original publication (*N.E.D.* from 1884 to 1928; F. & W. in 1913), though they have been added to from time to time. Consequently, neither one can boast either the scope of the definitions in the Merriam-Webster or their up-to-date precision. The *N.E.D.*, for example, does not even include *cryptanalysis*; Funk & Wagnalls provides a fair definition in its supplement ("the scientific study and conversion into plaintext of cryptograms, ciphers, codes, and other forms of secret communication to which the key is not known"), but it does not give the modern sense of *cryptology*, which it defines only as "secret or enigmatic language; especially, cryptography." It is only fair to note Oxford is now collecting citations for a new supplement,[29] and that Funk & Wagnalls has in preparation a new college dictionary with thoroughly revised definitions.

Another famous word book, *Roget's International Thesaurus*, has just been published by the Thomas Y. Crowell Company in an updated and reset edition (the third, 1962). A cursory check showed no outright cryptologic errors in that compendium of synonyms. But the volume inexplicably omits the common verbs *encode* and *encipher* while listing instead the verbs *codify* and *code*, which are customarily used in a legal rather than a cryptologic sense, and *cipher*, customarily mathematical. Section 6 of the same Roget category (no. 612—"secrecy") offers a satisfactory collection of nouns: "cryptography, steganography, secret writing; cryptogram, cryptograph, steganogram; secret ink, invisible or sympathetic ink." *Cryptograph*, as a cipher device, should perhaps be in a new group with *cipher machine*, and *cryptology* might be added. Roget's category 486 ("Solution") somehow misses *cryptanalysis* and *cryptanalyze*. The only fault of commission, in this writer's opinion, is stylistic: this respected work unleashes a horde of polysyllabic monstrosities that may vex future readers of cryptology books when it sanctions the adjectives "cryptogrammic, cryptogrammatic(al), cryptographal, cryptographic(al), steganographic(al)." In its next edition, the thesaurus should retain only *cryptographic(al)* (and an added *cryptologic[al]*) and should remand the others back to their literary dungeon.[30]

For completeness' sake, three other noncryptologic sources of cryptologic definitions ought to be mentioned. One is the specialized dictionary whose broad field—such as communications or military affairs—subsumes cryptology. For example, *The United States Air Forces Dictionary* (Princeton, N.J.: D. Van Nostrand Co., [1956?]; Woodford Agee Helfin, editor), and the Department of the Army's *Dictionary of United States Army Terms* (Army Regulations 320-5. Washington, D.C.: Government Printing Office, 1958), both define dozens of cryptologic terms, among them *cryptocenter, ciphony, communications intelligence, electronic warfare*. A second source is bilingual dictionaries. These provide a key that permits one to delve into cryptologic literature in another language to see what an equivalent term refers to; this may illuminate the English usage. An example is the Department of the Army's Technical Manual 30-544: *Glossary of Soviet Military Terminology* (May, 1955) which, according to a study made by Howard T. Oakley, translates 138 cryptologic terms, including *one-time system* and *chief of cipher section*.

The final source is the least prolific but the most potent: the law. Congress (and perhaps Parliament) has enacted statutes that include legislative definitions of cryptologic terms. For example, Senate bill 277 of the 81st Congress (signed into law May 13, 1950, and codified as Section 798, Title 18, United State Code) states, "The terms 'code', 'cipher' and 'cryptographic system' as used herein shall be construed to include in their meanings, in addition to their usual meanings, any method of secret writing and any mechanical or electrical device or method used for the purpose of disguising or concealing the contents, significance, or meanings of communications." Anyone disclosing classified cryptographic information on the basis that these definitions are wrong risks a $10,000 fine, or ten years in prison, or both. The courts have also promulgated legal definitions. These are usually of *cipher* or *cipher dispatch* and result from decisions on whether a message was in cryptographic form to determine the liability of a telegraph company for transmitting it incorrectly. Two legal reference works index these definitions: *Words and Phrases* (St. Paul: West Publishing Co., 1952), and *Corpus Juris Secundum* (Brooklyn: American Law Book Co., 1959). Here is one such definition (from *Words and Phrases*): "A telegram reading 'selling rough at cost four cars Florida one California want none present Norfolk kicks prices . . .' held not cipher or obscure message, as a matter of law, within rule of company exempting it from liability in such messages, as both words mean unintelligible, and do not apply to messages the words of which have definite coherence and connection; a 'cipher' being ordinarily a secret or disguised written communication, unintelligible to one without a key—Western Union Telegraph Co. v. Geo. F. Fish, Inc., 128 A. 14, 16, 148 Md. 210."

# Appendix III

## Origins of "Cryptology," "Cryptography," and "Cryptanalysis"

According to the Oxford *New English Dictionary*, which sought to list the earliest occurrence in English of every word in the language, both *cryptography* and *cryptology* made their first appearance, quite appropriately, in the first English book on the subject: *Mercury, or the Secret and Swift Messenger*, published in 1641. Its author was a 27-year-old clergyman, John Wilkins, who was to become bishop of Chester and first secretary of the Royal Society. Both words appear in a Latinate form as headings for Wilkins' division of the art of secret communication into three areas: *cryptologia*, or secrecy of speech, *cryptographia*, or secrecy of writing, and *semaeologia*, or secrecy of signs and gestures. The *-ia* endings suggests that Wilkins, like many other writers of the time, borrowed the words from Latin. Whether Porta and Trithemius, who wrote in Latin and whose works Wilkins cites, used *cryptologia* and *semaeologia*, or whether he coined the terms himself, this reviewer does not know. But the term *cryptographia* appears 17 years before Wilkins' book in the title of Gustavus Selenus' *Cryptomenytices et cryptographiae* (1624), which Wilkins also cites. Interestingly, Wilkins called the field in general *cryptomenses*, for "private intimations"—a word, that, unlike the others, never achieved any currency and is not even listed in the *N.E.D.*

It took *cryptologia* only four years to Anglicize itself to *cryptology.* According to the *N.E.D.*, it makes its debut in that form in 1645 in volume 1 of *Familiar Letters,* an entertaining series of epistles written in prison to imaginary correspondents by James Howell, later England's first historiographer royal, who remarked that "cryptology, or epistolizing in a clandestin way, is very ancient."

*Cryptography* needed 17 years to assimilate itself, but it was worth the wait, for the first man to pen it enjoys a reputation as one of the greatest prose stylists in English. This is Sir Thomas Browne, the physician, part of whose solemn *Urn-Burial* was called by George Saintsbury "the longest piece perhaps of absolutely sublime rhetoric to be found in the prose literature of the world." He first used *cryptography* in chapter 3 of the *Garden of Cyrus,* his treatise on how the quincunx pervades the universe, published with *Urn-Burial* in 1658, in the ornate and glittering phrase: ". . . we might abate the Pythagoricall Musick of the Spheres, the sevenfold Pipe of Pan; and the strange Cryptography of Gaffarel in his starrie Book of Heaven." (Jacques Gaffarel [1601–1681] was a French orientalist and mystical writer.) Browne perhaps borrowed more freely from Latin and Greek than any other English-language writer; his name figures in the citations of the *N.E.D.* more often than almost any other. Many of his neologisms never took root—such as *favaginous* (honeycombed) and *digladiation* (fighting with swords)—but many have found a permanent place in the language: *medical, literary, electricity, hallucination, incontrovertible, insecurity,* and of course, *cryptography.*

For the minting of the word *cryptanalysis,* we have the report of the coiner himself. "Soon after I became interested in the field," writes William F. Friedman in a letter of March 14, 1962, "and while still at Riverbank [the Baconian cryptologic laboratories of George Fabyan at Geneva, Illinois, which Friedman left in 1920 at age 29] I recognized the inadequacy of the definitions I found in all the dictionaries I consulted. I toyed with 'cryptoanalysis' on the analogy provided by 'psychoanalysis' but decided to leave out the unnecessary vowel because I could imagine people seeing the 'toan' and pronouncing the word as cryp/tone/aly/sis. Perhaps I was wrong, because (a) many persons write the word as crypto-analysis and pronounce it that way, and (b) many find it hard to say 'cryptanálysis' and 'cryptánalyst.' " Joseph S. Galland states on page 69 of his *An Historical and Analytic Bibliography of the Literature of Cryptology* (Evanston, Ill.: 1945) that Friedman's *Elements of Cryptanalysis,* a War Department textbook published in 1923, is "the first book in any language to employ the word 'cryptanalysis.' "

# The Ché Guevara Cipher

The sheets of paper with rows of numbers on them found with Ché Guevara, the Cuban guerrilla who died in Bolivia on October 9, 1967, constitute worksheets for enciphering messages in the one-time pad cipher. The one-time pad is the only form of secret communication that is absolutely unbreakable. Invented in 1918, it has served both Allied and Communist secret agents since at least World War II. And it served Ché in this message of May 18, 1967, to Fidel Castro.

The rows of numbers fall into groups of three lines. Each line represents an element in the cipher: (1) the plaintext, or the message to be sent, (2) the key, and (3) their sum, which becomes the secret message that is transmitted.

The message to be sent is in Spanish in its original form. For the purposes of this cipher, this plaintext in letters has to be converted into numbers. The worksheets show this step already taken—the top line is the numerical plaintext. To recover the original message, the conversion alphabet has to be ascertained. Since this conversion of letters into numbers amounts to an encipherment, the discovery of the conversion alphabet amounts to the solution of a cryptogram. Barbara Harris of New York solved this and found the conversion alphabet.

In this set of messages, the conversion alphabet is:

"The Ché Guevara Cipher" was first published in 1969 as an appendix to *Ché Guevara: A Biography* by Daniel James.

The first page of the enciphering worksheets of the Ché Guevara message

```
          8 2 0 6 4 9 1 3 7 5
        ┌─────────────────────
        │ e s t a d o y
    3   │ b c f g h i j . ; ,
    7   │ k l m n ñ p q / /
    5   │ r u v w x z
```

It is formed by following the keyword ESTADOY with the letters of the alphabet that have not been used in the keyword. To convert letters into numbers, each letter in the top row is replaced by just the digit above it, while each letter in the lower rows is replaced by the digit of its row and the digit of its column. Thus $e = 8$, $t = 0$, $b = 38$, $v = 50$.

This creates a mixture of one- and two-digit "groups," but the decipherer can separate them unambiguously because he knows that any "group" beginning with 3, 5, or 7 must have two digits, and any "group" beginning with any of the other seven digits must be a singleton. Thus 9583987608 can be divided up only as 9 58 39 8 76 0 8, or *Oriente.*

This procedure shortens the messages by giving single-digit equivalents to some letters—usually the more frequent—instead of having all letters represented by two digits. Incidentally it made the solution more difficult for Miss Harris, as she was faced first of all with the problem of determining which digits formed the two-digit "groups" before she could divide up the string of numbers properly to ascertain which numbers stood for which letters.

The conversion table—known technically as a "monome-dinome table"—also contains three punctuation marks and two other signs. The sign at 73 is a letter-to-number switch, and the sign at 77 is a number-to-letter switch. In other words, instead of spelling out numbers, the encipherer writes 73 to show that numbers follow in the plaintext, then writes the actual number, repeating each digit three times for safety's sake, then writes 77, indicating that he has reverted to letter equivalents, after which he proceeds with the conversion. Thus the message "Expect 250 men." would be converted to numbers like this:

```
    e   x   pect / 2   5   o   /   m  e  n  .
    8  54  79  8 32 0 73 222 555 000 77 70 8 76 33
```

The monome-dinome table includes blank spaces in the cells at 75, 51, 53, 57, and 55. (The cells at 3, 7, and 5 in the first line cannot be used because this would destroy the division of the numerical plaintexts into one- and two-digit "groups.") These blank cells are available for special uses, if needed, or may just be "nulls," meaningless groups thrown in to leave spaces between words or at the start of the message in case of ambiguity.

To the series of digits obtained from the conversion is added the key. The key consists of a string of numbers. In the one-time pad system, these numbers are absolutely random and never repeat. The encipherer must have as many key digits as there are digits in all the messages he is ever going to send, and they must have no pattern or structure whatsoever. The key is prepared in advance, and both the sender and the receiver must have a copy of it (as well as of the conversion alphabet). The key is the second line of digits in each group of three rows.

The addition is by noncarrying arithmetic. In mathematical terms, it is performed modulo 10. This means that when, for example, 9 and 6 are added, the sum is written as 5 and not as 15, the 1 being omitted. This causes no problem on decipherment: 5 minus 9 can only leave 6. There are three reasons for this procedure: speed, capability of enciphering from left to right, localization of errors to a single digit.

The sum of the numerical plaintext and the key constitutes the cryptogram. This is the message that will be transmitted. This one begins:

| literal plaintext | | / | 5 | / | . |
|---|---|---|---|---|---|
| numerical plaintext | 53 | 73 | 555 | 77 | 33 |
| key | 09 | 42 | 791 | 67 | 22 |
| cryptogram | 52 | 15 | 246 | 34 | 55 |

| literal plaintext | | l | e | c | h | e | . | d | a | n | t | o | n |
|---|---|---|---|---|---|---|---|---|---|---|---|---|---|
| numerical plaintext | 72 | 8 | 32 | 34 | 8 | 33 | 4 | 6 | 76 | 0 | 9 | 76 | |
| key | 34 | 6 | 51 | 42 | 1 | 01 | 2 | 8 | 52 | 6 | 3 | 59 | |
| cryptogram | 06 | 4 | 83 | 76 | 9 | 34 | 6 | 4 | 28 | 6 | 2 | 25 | |

This would be divided into the five-digit groups shown on the worksheets for transmission.

The "indicativo 43339" at the lower left of sheet 1 may have been Ché Guevara's personal indicator. It may have been sent at a prearranged point in the cryptogram to let Havana know whose message was coming in and therefore which key was to be applied. Or it may have served to disguise the key indicator, which the term "hoja" ("page") followed by 025 may have been. The disguise could have been effected by adding the 43339 to the 62250 in the first row marked "ojo" and then to 025; this procedure served in other Communist spy ciphers using the one-time pad. The 025 may have referred to the page of the booklet containing the key digits; sending it as part of the cryptogram would have told the decipherer which page was used in enciphering. In the 1920s, the one-time pad consisted of an actual pad of paper each of whose sheets had a different set of random key digits and was torn off and discarded after a single use. But since World War II it has taken the form of a tiny booklet in which the key digits are printed in groups of five. Though each page is used but once, and in theory the decipherer should use successive pages on successive messages, the vagaries of communication may have made it desirable to indicate the page used.

The first six lines of the Ché Guevara message deciphered:

```
73 555 77 33 72 8 32 34 8 33 4 6 76 0 9 76 72 72 8 50 6 38 6 52 76 70
-   5   -  #      L  E  C  H  E  #  D  A  N  T  O  N  L  L  E  V  A  B  A  U  N  M

76 2 6 31 8 37 6 4 8 70 6 2 6 76 9 0 6 32 39 9 76 8 2 79 6 58 6 70 8 70
N  S  A  J  E  ;  A  D  E  M  A  S  A  N  O  T  A  C  I  O  N  E  S  P  A  R  A  M  E  M

58 39 59 6 58 8 72 39 76 30 9 58 70 8 9 58 6 72 71 52 8 72 8 4 39 37 0
R  I  Z  A  R  E  L  I  N  F  O  R  M  E  O  R  A  L  Q  U  E  L  E  D  I  ;  T

4 9 8 76 32 72 6 50 8 33 8 20 8 8 2872 70 8 6 2 6 31 8 33 73 111 77
D  O  E  N  C  L  A  V  E  #  E  S  T  E  E  S  E  L  .  M  E  N  S  A  J  E  #  -  1  -

72 8 36 6 58 9 76 4 6 76 0 9 76 1 30 58 6 76 32 39 2 32 9 37 8 20 8
L  E  G  A  R  O  N  D  A  N  T  O  N  Y  F  R  A  N  C  I  S  C  O  ;  E  S  T  E

9 2 6 38 39 6 32 6 76 0 39 4 6 4 1 4 8 31 9 4 39 76 8 58 9 8 76 72 6
O  S  A  B  I  A  C  A  N  T  I  D  A  D  Y  D  E  J  O  D  I  N  E  R  O  E  N  L  A
```

Following is part of Daniel James's translation of Ché's coded message to Fidel Castro dated May 18, 1967. The matter in brackets is James's, consisting of necessary clarification and interpretation of otherwise obscure or meaningless statements, allusions, etc. Words that are totally impossible to decipher are left as is or noted as illegible. The paragraphing is also James's, to make for easier reading. James has added a list of the pseudonyms used and the bearers' real identities, in order of appearance.

5. LECHE. DANTON carried a message; also notations to memorize the verbal report I gave him; all in key. This is the message.

—1—DANTON and FRANCISCO arrived; the latter did not know quantity and left money in La Paz; I am thinking of giving him 30 [presumably 30,000 Bolivian pesos, about $2,400] and reserving rest for when it be [necessary? word illegible]; he lacks the physical attributes and character to lead guerrillas; but that is his problem. DANTON must leave but I do not know if he will be able to given the circumstances.

—2—The farm [euphemism for the guerrilla base at Nancahuazú] was discovered and the army pursued us; we gave it the first thrashing but we are isolated.

—3—IVAN is ready to travel but TANIA is isolated here; for she came in violation of instructions and was trapped by events.

—4—We now have enough glucantine [medicine for Ché's asthma]; do not send any more.

—5—There is no news from MRIO [apparently garbling of Mario, for Mario Monje] nor do I trust them [the Party] and they have expelled the young people [members of the Party's youth arm] who side with us.

—6—I receive everything [you send] by radio but it is useless if you do not communicate it simultaneously to La Paz; we are isolated for now. . . .

Comrade Fidel Castro. From the Bolivian Oriente; where we fight to repeat old national exploits inspired by the example of the Cuban Revolution; standard-bearer of the oppressed peoples of the world; our fraternal and warm salute goes out to join with that of millions of beings who regard this date as the commencement of the final stage of [Latin] American liberation. You; your comrades and all your people; accept this testimony of our unreserved devotion to the common cause and our congratulations.

## List of Code Names

LECHE—*Fidel Castro.*

DANTON—*Jules Regis Debray,* Ché's principal liaison with Castro.

FRANCISCO, EL CHINO—the Peruvian revolutionary *Juan Pablo Chang Navarro.*

IVAN—identity unknown, but apparently Cuban and a trusted aide of Ché and Castro; in charge of La Paz communications with Havana, among other duties.

TANIA—Ché's chief undercover agent in Bolivia prior to his arrival and presumed mistress; while working for Ché she was also employed by the East German intelligence service and the Soviet KGB, and in the end betrayed Ché.

MRIO—*Mario Monje Molina,* first secretary of Bolivian Communist Party.

## Daniel James's Analysis of Ché's Message to Castro

The "message within a message," toward the end, which Ché wrote for the July 26th celebrations in Cuba, dispels the slightest doubt that Ché was anxious to lift the veil of mystery surrounding his whereabouts and to announce to the world that he was very much alive and leading the guerrilla struggle in Bolivia.

Even further, in it he says in effect that he is hoping to emulate the Cuban Revolution on a continental scale—this is "the final stage of [Latin] American liberation"—and seems to regard himself as its Simón Bolívar.

# Two Soviet Spy Ciphers

Whenever a middle-level Soviet spy wanted to put an urgent communication into his complex cipher, all he had to remember were four homely things: the nostalgic word for "snowfall," a snatch of Russian folk song, a patriotic date, and the superstition-ridden number 13. And when his chief received messages from Moscow in his unbreakable system, he deciphered them by means of numbers printed in red and black in a book so tiny he hid it in a block of wood.

The systems of cryptography used by these two Soviet spies in America are the finest and most advanced espionage ciphers ever made public. One reconstructed an elaborate multiphase system entirely from the four memorized keys. The other produced messages that would not crack under any amount of cryptanalytic battering. This was the personal cipher of Rudolf Ivanovich Abel, said to be the highest ranking Communist spy ever captured in the United States. The disclosure of the two systems at Abel's trial furnished the American public with one of the first authoritative and detailed insights into the extraordinarily high caliber of Red achievements in the black art of cryptography. American cryptanalysts had been defeated by these achievements four years earlier, when a secret message in the first system came melodramatically to light.

"Two Soviet Spy Ciphers," a paper presented at the annual convention of the American Cryptogram Association, September 3, 1960, was published that year as a monograph. It was later published in a Central Intelligence Agency journal.

Thirteen-year-old Brooklyn newsboy James Bozart dropped 50 cents in change he had received on his paper route one summer day in 1953— and found when he picked it up that one of the five nickels had split apart. Inside one of the hollowed-out halves was what appeared to be a bit of microfilm. The surprised youngster gave it to police, who turned it over to the Federal Bureau of Investigation. The F.B.I. enlarged the image on the microfilm, which had been wrapped in tissue and was five sixteenths of an inch square. The image was of a square sheet of paper with 21 rows of numbers in five-digit groups. There were 207 such groups—1,035 digits in all (Fig. 1).

```
                          207
14546 30056 64211 03919 18710 71187 71215 02906│66036 10922
11075 01238 65634 39175 37378 31013│22596 19291 17463 23551
33527 10130 01707 12366 16669 97846 76559 50062 91171 72332
10202 07849 90251 11576 46121 24666 05902 19229 56150 23521
51911 78912 32939 31966'12096 12060 89748 25362 43167 99841
70271 31154 20838 77221 58343 61164 14349 01241 26269 71578
31704 27502 51236 12982 18089 60219 22577 09454 81216 71953
20030 80779 54197 11990 23881 48834 22165 62990 86449 41742
30207 77014 31565 30902 85812 10112 03312 71320 60369 12872
12450 19081 97117 70107 06391 71114 19459 59586 80317 07522
70509 11111 36990 32060 04411 51532 91104 23162 82011 19185
50110 28876 70719 03563 28222 31671 39003 07623 93513 97175
29910 05701 '694 3 32951 97036 34592 61109 95090│24092 71008
90061 14790 15154 14655 29011 57206│77195 01256 69250 62901
39179 71229 23299 84164 45900 42227 65853 17591 60182 06315
65812 01378 14566 07719 92507 79517 99651 82155 58118 67197
30015 70667 36201 56531 56721 26306 57135 91796│51341 07796
76655 62710 33588 21532 10224 87721 95619 23191 20665 45140
66098 60... 71521 02334 01212 51110 85227 98768 11125 05321
53152 14191 12166 12715 03116 43041 74822 72759 29130 21947
15764 96851 20018 22370 11391 83520 62297
                    № 12740/622
```

Fig. 1. The message to Soviet spy Reino Hayhanen that was found on soft microfilm in a hollow nickel

The circumstances of the finding of the message must have led the F.B.I. to believe that the message was a bona fide spy cipher and to begin at once to try to break it. But despite unlimited time, despite the concentration of cryptographic brains it could bring to bear, despite the electronic computers it must have utilized for thousands of lightning-fast trials, the F.B.I. did not succeed in cracking the message.

The message was not to be read until—in an astonishing coincidence—the very man for whom it was intended defected to the West. This was Reino Hayhanen, a lieutenant colonel in the K.G.B., the overseas intelligence arm of the Soviet Union. Known to his fellow agents as VIC, Hayhanen had been working since 1952 as a spy in the United States, mostly as chief assistant to Abel. Abel, who bore the codename MARK and who held the rank of colonel in the K.G.B., was a kind of spy executive in charge of a ring that reportedly went after some of America's most vital defense secrets. Late in 1956, Abel grew to distrust Hayhanen, and eventually insisted that Hayhanen sail home to Russia for a "vacation." Hayhanen never arrived: on May 4, 1957, he walked into the American Embassy in Paris and confessed his espionage work in the United States. It was the beginning of the end for Abel, who was arrested June 21 in the Hotel Latham in Manhattan. And some time in the latter part of July or September, the F.B.I., in the person of Russian expert Michael G. Leonard, applied the cipher system and keys described to it by Hayhanen and finally read the message that had baffled the bureau so completely.

After a seven-day trial in Brooklyn's Federal District Court, in which Hayhanen was the star government witness, Abel was convicted of espionage charges October 25, 1957, by a jury that deliberated little more than three hours. Judge Mortimer W. Byers sentenced the first alien ever to stand trial for his life on spy charges in a civilian American court to 30 years in prison. Abel served part of his term in the Federal Penitentiary in Atlanta, Georgia.[1] Hayhanen's whereabouts are a mystery.

It was at Abel's trial that the two ciphers were made public. Hayhanen himself described the operation of his cipher in 40 minutes of testimony on October 16, 1957. Direct examination on the cryptographic testimony was conducted by Kevin Maroney, special attorney, Department of Justice. There was no cross-examination. Though Maroney did a masterful job in leading Hayhanen through the intricacies of the system, the cipher was so complicated that its description bored the jurors and proved dull even to an avid amateur cryptographer, largely because he could not follow it without the written program furnished the jury. Abel's system was not described in such detail; it was mentioned almost in passing.

Hayhanen began his testimony by saying that his first training in cryptography consisted of a 2½-to-3-week course in a Soviet spy school. Upon his leaving Moscow in 1952, he was assigned his own cipher system for communication with his superiors. He received messages—all consisting of groups of numbers, like the nickel one—on microfilm through "drops," clandestine meetings with other agents. He received about six or seven messages a year, a total of about 30 during the nearly five years he was in the United States. He sent about 25 messages during that time. In the summer of 1956, he said, part of the key was changed and the key derivation procedure was complicated slightly. He also said that he did not know how the nickel message, which appears to have been the first sent to him, had fallen into the hands of the newsboy.

If the vic cipher were to be given a technical name, it would be known as a "straddling bipartite monoalphabetic substitution superenciphered by modified double transposition." The four mnemonic keys were used to derive the alphabet for the substitution and the transcription order for the transpositions. Because of the cipher's complexity, the operation of the general system will be described first, and the derivation of the keys for this particular message will be given after that. And though it might seem more logical to illustrate the system by deciphering the cryptogram with which the entire episode began, it seems easier to understand a system through its encipherment. Hence this description will follow the encipherment of the Russian text, much as some Soviet cipher clerk did it in a well-guarded office of the K.G.B. on a wintry 3rd of December 1952.

Translated, the message read:

1. We congratulate you on [your] safe arrival. We confirm the receipt of your letter to the address "V repeat V" and the reading of [your] letter No. 1.
2. For organization of cover we have given instructions to transmit to you three thousand in local [currency]. Consult with us prior to investing it in any kind of business, advising the character of the business.
3. According to your request, we will transmit the formula for the preparation of soft film and the news separately, together with [your] mother's letter.
4. [It is too] early to send you the gammas.[2] Encipher short letters, but do the longer ones with insertions.[3] All the data about yourself, place of work, address, etc., must not be transmitted in one cipher message. Transmit insertions separately.
5. The package was delivered to [your] wife personally. Everything is all right with [your] family. We wish [you] success. Greetings from the comrades. No. 1, 3 December.

The Russian text was as follows:

1. Поздравляем с благополучным прибытием. Подтверждаем получение вашего письма в адрес "В" и прочтение письма №1.

2. Для организации прикрытия мы дали указание передать вам три тысячи местных. Перед тем как их вложить в какое либо дело посоветуйтесь с нами, сообщив характеристику этого дела.

3. По вашей просьбе рецептуру изготовления мягкой пленки и новостей[4] передадим отдельно вместе с письмом матери.

4. Гаммы высылать вам рано. Короткие письма шифруйте, а побольше—делайте со вставками. Все данные о себе, место работы, адрес и т.д. в одной шифровке передавать нельзя. Вставки передавайте отдельно.

5. Посылку жене передали лично. С семьей все благополучно. Желаем успеха. Привет от товарищей.

№1/03 Декабря.

The first major step in the encipherment of this text is substitution of one- and two-digit numbers for the Russian plaintext letters. For this purpose a monome-dinome table or "checkerboard" of 40 cells—ten across and four down—is set up, as illustrated below.

|   | 5 | 0 | 7 | 3 | 8 | 9 | 4 | 6 | 1 | 2 |
|---|---|---|---|---|---|---|---|---|---|---|
|   | С | Н | Е | Г | О | П | А |   |   |   |
| 6 | Б | Ж | . | К | № | Р | ф | Ч | Ы | Ю |
| 1 | В | З | , | Л | Н/Ц | Т | Х | Ш | Ь | Я |
| 2 | Д | И | П/Л | М | Н/Т | У | Ц | Щ | Э | ПВТ |

The first seven letters of the Russian word for "snowfall" (*snegopa*) are inscribed in the first row, leaving the last three cells blank. The remaining 23 letters of the modern Russian alphabet, omitting diacritical marks, are inscribed in sequence vertically in the other three rows, skipping the third and fifth columns, which, with the last cell remaining in the last column, are then filled by seven symbols. These are a period, a comma, the symbol П/Л, whose meaning is undetermined, the abbreviation №, the letter-number switch sign Н/Ц, the "message starts" sign Н/Т, and the abbreviation ПВТ for "repeat." Along the top of the checkerboard are written the ten digits in a mixed sequence determined by a process to be described later. The last three digits in the sequence, which stand over the blank cells at the end of the first row, are repeated at the left of the second, third, and fourth rows. These ten digits are known as coordinates.

Each plaintext letter in the first row of the checkerboard is enciphered by replacing it with the single coordinate above it. Each letter and symbol in the other rows is enciphered by substituting for it the coordinate at the end of its row followed by the coordinate at the top of its column. Numbers are enciphered by placing them within a pair of the letter-number switch signs and repeating them three times.

Before these substitutions are made, however, the plaintext is bisected—chopped at random into two parts—and the true start of the message is tacked onto the true end. This true start is indicated by the "message starts" sign. In this encipherment, Fig. 2, on the following pages, the sign stands seventh in the 37th line.

The sequence of coordinates resulting from the substitution—which by itself affords virtually no security—is then thoroughly jumbled by passing it through two transposition tableaux. The first tableau (Fig. 3) is a standard columnar transposition. The coordinates are written in horizontally under the keynumbers. They are taken out vertically, the column under keynumber 1 first and the others following in key order. This new sequence of digits is then inscribed into the second tableau (Fig. 4)—which, however, has a complication. This consists of a series of step-like disruption (or D) areas determined in this manner: The first D area begins in the top row under keynumber 1 and runs to the right side of that row. In each of the following rows, it begins one column to the right. When the columns are exhausted, one row is skipped and another D area is started in the following row beginning with the column under keynumber 2, and the procedure is repeated for all the rows in the tableau. (The number of rows needed is calculated by dividing the width of the tableau into the number of cipher digits; the quotient is the number of full rows, the remainder indicates the number of columns to be used in the incomplete bottom row).

The cipher digits from the first tableau are inscribed horizontally from left to right into the rows of the second tableau as far as the D areas. When all the non-D-portions of the rows have been filled, the cipher digits are written in from left to right in the D areas, starting with the top row and moving downward. Then the cipher digits are transcribed from the completed tableau in columns according to their keynumber, without any regard for the D areas. This final sequence of digits, in the standard groups of five, comprises the ciphertext. A keygroup is inserted at a prearranged point before the final message is sent. The result is that in Fig. 1.

| 9 | 69 | 20 | 63 | 69 | 61 | 19 | 20 | 12 | 23 | 61 | 25 | 4 | 13 |
|---|---|---|---|---|---|---|---|---|---|---|---|---|---|
| П | Р | И | К | Р | Ы | Т | И | Я | М | Ы | Д | А | Л |
| 20 | 29 | 63 | 4 | 10 | 4 | 0 | 20 | 7 | 9 | 7 | 69 | 7 | 25 |
| И | У | К | А | З | А | Н | И | Е | П | Е | Р | Е | Д |
| 4 | 19 | 11 | 15 | 4 | 23 | 19 | 69 | 20 | 19 | 61 | 5 | 12 | 66 |
| А | Т | Ь | В | А | М | Т | Р | И | Т | Ы | С | Я | Ч |
| 20 | 23 | 7 | 5 | 19 | 0 | 61 | 14 | 67 | 9 | 7 | 69 | 7 | 25 |
| И | М | Е | С | Т | Н | Ы | Х | . | П | Е | Р | Е | Д |
| 19 | 7 | 23 | 63 | 4 | 63 | 20 | 14 | 15 | 13 | 8 | 60 | 20 | 19 |
| Т | Е | М | К | А | К | И | Х | В | Л | О | Ж | И | Т |
| 11 | 15 | 63 | 4 | 63 | 8 | 7 | 13 | 20 | 65 | 8 | 25 | 7 | 13 |
| Ь | В | К | А | К | О | Е | Л | И | Б | О | Д | Е | Л |
| 8 | 9 | 8 | 5 | 8 | 15 | 7 | 19 | 29 | 20 | 19 | 7 | 5 | 11 |
| О | П | О | С | О | В | Е | Т | У | И | Т | Е | С | Ь |
| 5 | 0 | 4 | 23 | 20 | 17 | 5 | 8 | 8 | 65 | 26 | 20 | 15 | 14 |
| С | Н | А | М | И | , | С | О | О | Б | Щ | И | В | Х |
| 4 | 69 | 4 | 63 | 19 | 7 | 69 | 20 | 5 | 19 | 20 | 63 | 29 | 21 |
| А | Р | А | К | Т | Е | Р | И | С | Т | И | К | У | Э |
| 19 | 8 | 3 | 8 | 25 | 7 | 13 | 4 | 67 | 18 | 333 | 18 | 67 | 9 |
| Т | О | Г | О | Д | Е | Л | А | . | Н/Ц | 333 | Н/Ц | . | П |
| 8 | 15 | 4 | 16 | 7 | 20 | 9 | 69 | 8 | 5 | 11 | 65 | 7 | 69 |
| О | В | А | Ш | Е | И | П | Р | О | С | Ь | Б | Е | Р |
| 7 | 24 | 7 | 9 | 19 | 29 | 69 | 29 | 20 | 10 | 3 | 8 | 19 | 8 |
| Е | Ц | Е | П | Т | У | Р | У | И | З | Г | О | Т | О |
| 15 | 13 | 7 | 0 | 20 | 12 | 23 | 12 | 3 | 63 | 8 | 20 | 9 | 13 |
| В | Л | Е | Н | И | Я | М | Я | Г | К | О | И | П | Л |
| 7 | 0 | 63 | 20 | 20 | 0 | 8 | 15 | 8 | 5 | 19 | 7 | 20 | 9 |
| Е | Н | К | И | И | Н | О | В | О | С | Т | Е | И | П |
| 7 | 69 | 7 | 25 | 4 | 25 | 20 | 23 | 8 | 19 | 25 | 7 | 13 | 11 |
| Е | Р | Е | Д | А | Д | И | М | О | Т | Д | Е | Л | Ь |
| 0 | 8 | 15 | 23 | 7 | 5 | 19 | 7 | 5 | 9 | 20 | 5 | 11 | 23 |
| Н | О | В | М | Е | С | Т | Е | С | П | И | С | Ь | М |
| 8 | 23 | 23 | 4 | 19 | 7 | 69 | 20 | 67 | 18 | 444 | 18 | 67 | 3 |
| О | М | М | А | Т | Е | Р | И | . | Н/Ц | 444 | Н/Ц | . | Г |
| 4 | 23 | 23 | 61 | 15 | 61 | 5 | 61 | 13 | 4 | 19 | 11 | 15 | 4 |
| А | М | М | Ы | В | Ы | С | Ы | Л | А | Т | Ь | В | А |
| 23 | 69 | 4 | 0 | 8 | 67 | 63 | 8 | 19 | 8 | 19 | 63 | 20 | 7 |
| М | Р | А | Н | О | . | К | О | Р | О | Т | К | И | Е |
| 9 | 20 | 5 | 11 | 23 | 4 | 16 | 20 | 64 | 69 | 29 | 20 | 19 | 7 |
| П | И | С | Ь | М | А | Ш | И | Ф | Р | У | И | Т | Е |

Fig. 2. Substitution of the Russian text

| 17 | 4 | 9 | 8 | 65 | 8 | 13 | 11 | 16 | 7 | 19 | 20 | 69 | 7 |
|---|---|---|---|---|---|---|---|---|---|---|---|---|---|
| , | А | П | О | Б | О | Л | Ь | Ш | Е | Т | И | Р | Е |
| 25 | 7 | 13 | ·4 | 20 | 19 | 7 | 5 | 8 | 15 | 5 | 19 | 4 | 15 |
| Д | Е | Л | А | И | Т | Е | С | О | В | С | Т | А | В |
| 63 | 4 | 23 | 20 | 67 | 15 | 5 | 7 | 25 | 4 | 0 | 0 | 61 | 7 |
| К | А | М | И | . | В | С | Е | Д | А | Н | Н | Ы | Е |
| 8 | 5 | 7 | 65 | 7 | 17 | 23 | 7 | 5 | 19 | 8 | 69 | 4 | 65 |
| О | С | Е | Б | Е | , | М | Е | С | Т | О | Р | А | Б |
| 8 | 19 | 61 | 17 | 4 | 25 | 69 | 7 | 5 | 20 | 19 | 67 | 25 | 67 |
| О | Т | Ы | . | А | Д | Р | Е | С | И | Т | . | Д | . |
| 15 | 8 | 25 | 0 | 8 | 20 | 16 | 20 | 64 | 69 | 8 | 15 | 63 | 7 |
| В | О | Д | Н | О | И | Ш | И | Ф | Р | О | В | К | Е |
| 9 | 7 | 69 | 7 | 25 | 4 | 15 | 4 | 19 | 11 | 0 | 7 | 13 | 11 |
| П | Е | Р | Е | Д | А | В | А | Т | Ь | Н | Е | Л | Ь |
| 10 | 12 | 67 | 15 | 5 | 19 | 4 | 15 | 63 | 20 | 9 | 7 | 69 | 7 |
| З | Я | . | В | С | Т | А | В | К | И | П | Е | Р | Е |
| 25 | 4 | 15 | 4 | 20 | 19 | 7 | 8 | 19 | 25 | 7 | 13 | 11 | 0 |
| Д | А | В | А | И | Т | Е | О | Т | Д | Е | Л | Ь | Н |
| 8 | 67 | 18 | 555 | 18 | 67 | 9 | 8 | 5 | 61 | 13 | 63 | 29 | 60 |
| О | . | Н/Ц | 555 | Н/Ц | . | П | О | С | Ы | Л | К | У | Ж |
| 7 | 0 | 7 | 9 | 7 | 69 | 7 | 25 | 4 | 13 | 20 | 13 | 20 | 66 |
| Е | Н | Е | П | Е | Р | Е | Д | А | Л | И | Л | И | Ч |
| 0 | 8 | 67 | 5 | 5 | 7 | 23 | 11 | 7 | 20 | 15 | 5 | 7 | 65 |
| Н | О | . | С | С | Е | М | Ь | Е | И | В | С | Е | Б |
| 13 | 4 | 3 | 8 | 9 | 8 | 13 | 29 | 66 | 0 | 8 | 67 | 60 | 7 |
| Л | А | Г | О | П | О | Л | У | Ч | Н | О | . | Ж | Е |
| 13 | 4 | 7 | 23 | 29 | 5 | 9 | 7 | 14 | 4 | 67 | 9 | 69 | 20 |
| Л | А | Е | М | У | С | П | Е | Х | А | . | П | Р | И |
| 15 | 7 | 19 | 8 | 19 | 19 | 8 | 15 | 4 | 69 | 20 | 26 | 7 | 20 |
| В | Е | Т | О | Т | Т | О | В | А | Р | И | Щ | Е | И |
| 68 | 18 | 111 | 18 | 25 | 69 | 8 | 65 | 11 | 8 | 18 | 333 | 18 | 25 |
| № | Н/Ц | 111 | Н/Ц | Д | Р | О | Б | Ь | 0* | Н/Ц | 333 | Н/Ц | Д |
| 7 | 63 | 4 | 65 | 69 | 12 | 28 | 18 | 111 | 18 | 67 | 9 | 8 | 10 |
| Е | К | А | Б | Р | Я | Н/Т | Н/Ц | 111 | Н/Ц | . | П | О | З |
| 25 | 69 | 4 | 15 | 13 | 12 | 7 | 23 | 5 | 65 | 13 | 4 | 3 | 8 |
| Д | Р | А | В | Л | Я | Е | М | С | Б | Л | А | Г | О |
| 9 | 8 | 13 | 29 | 66 | 0 | 61 | 23 | 9 | 69 | 20 | 65 | 61 | 19 |
| П | О | Л | У | Ч | Н | Ы | М | П | Р | И | Б | Ы | Т |
| 20 | 7 | ·23 | 67 | 9 | 8 | 25 | 19 | 15 | 7 | 69 | 60 | 25 | 4 |
| И | Е | М | . | П | О | Д | Т | В | Е | Р | Ж | Д | А |

---

* Apparently enciphered as a letter by error.

Fig. 2 (continued)

| 7 | 23 | 9 | 8 | 13 | 29 | 66 | 7 | 0 | 20 | 7 | 15 | 4 | 16 |
|---|---|---|---|---|---|---|---|---|---|---|---|---|---|
| Е | М | П | О | Л | У | Ч | Е | Н | И | Е | В | А | Ш |

| 7 | 3 | 8 | 9 | 20 | 5 | 11 | 23 | 4 | 15 | 4 | 25 | 69 | 7 |
|---|---|---|---|---|---|---|---|---|---|---|---|---|---|
| Е | Г | О | П | И | С | Ь | М | А | В | А | Д | Р | Е |

| 5 | 17 | 17 | 15 | 22 | 15 | 17 | 17 | 20 | 9 | 69 | 8 | 66 | 19 |
|---|---|---|---|---|---|---|---|---|---|---|---|---|---|
| С | , | , | В | ПВТ | В | , | , | И | П | Р | О | Ч | Т |

| 7 | 0 | 20 | 7 | 9 | 20 | 5 | 11 | 23 | 4 | 68 | 18 | 111 | 18 |
|---|---|---|---|---|---|---|---|---|---|---|---|---|---|
| Е | Н | И | Е | П | И | С | Ь | М | А | № | Н/Ц | 111 | Н/Ц |

| 67 | 18 | 222 | 18 | 67 | 25 | 13 | 12 | 8 | 69 | 3 | 4 | 0 | 20 |
|---|---|---|---|---|---|---|---|---|---|---|---|---|---|
| . | Н/Ц | 222 | Н/Ц | . | Д | Л | Я | О | Р | Г | А | Н | И |

| 10 | 4 | 24 | 20 | 20 | 2 | 1 | 4 |
|---|---|---|---|---|---|---|---|
| 3 | А | Ц | И | И | N | U | L L S |

The key derivation converts the four easily remembered items into the complex set of keys needed for the system. One item—*snegopa*—develops the alphabet within the checkerboard. The other three—the bit of folk song, the patriotic date and the number 13—interact to generate a series of virtually random numbers that in turn yield the numerical keys for the checkerboard and the two transposition tableaux.

In the derivation of these keys two devices are used repeatedly—chain addition and conversion to sequential numbers. Chain addition produces a series of numbers of any length from a few priming digits: the first two digits of the priming series are added together modulo 10 (without tens digits) and the result placed at the end of the series; then the second and third digits are added and the sum placed at the end; and so forth, using also the newly generated digits when the priming series is exhausted, until the desired length is obtained. To illustrate: with the priming series 3 9 6 4, 3 and 9 are added to get 2 (the 1 of the 12 being dropped), which is put at the end of the series to make it 39642. Then 9 and 6 yield 5, and 6 and 4 add to 0, makes the series so far 3 9 6 4 2 5 0. Extended, it would run 3 9 6 4 2 5 0 6 7 5 6 3 2 1 . . .

Conversion to sequential numbers, or the generation of a sequential key, is an adaptation from the standard practice of deriving a numerical key from a literal one by assigning consecutive numbers to the letters of the key in their alphabetical order, numbering identical letters from left to right. The literal key BABY, for example, would generate the sequential numerical key 2 1 3 4. In the Hayhanen system a series of digits—instead of letters—is used as the breeder key, and consecutive numbers are assigned to them in their numerical order (0 is last), numbering identical digits from left to right. For example, if the breeder key is 7 1 8 1, the sequential key would be 3 1 4 2.

The derivation of the checkerboard and transposition keys for this message begins with the date—September 3, 1945—that Russia achieved

```
 9  6  0  3  3  1  8  3  6  6  4  6  9  0  4  7  5
14  8 16  2  3  1 13  4  9 10  5 11 15 17  6 12  7

 9  6  9  2  0  6  3  6  9  6  1  1  9  2  0  1  2
 2  3  6  1  2  5  4  1  3  2  0  2  9  6  3  4  1
 0  4  0  2  0  7  9  7  6  9  7  2  5  4  1  9  1
 1  1  5  4  2  3  1  9  6  9  2  0  1  9  6  1  5
 1  2  6  6  2  0  2  3  7  5  1  9  0  6  1  1  4
 6  7  9  7  6  9  7  2  5  1  9  7  2  3  6  3  4
 6  3  2  0  1  4  1  5  1  3  8  6  0  2  0  1  9
 1  1  1  5  6  3  4  6  3  8  7  1  3  2  0  6  5
 8  2  5  7  1  3  8  9  8  5  8  1  5  7  1  9  2
 9  2  0  1  9  7  5  1  1  5  0  4  2  3  2  0  1
 7  5  8  8  6  5  2  6  2  0  1  5  1  4  4  6  9
 4  6  3  1  9  7  6  9  2  0  5  1  9  2  0  6  3
 2  9  2  1  1  9  8  3  8  2  5  7  1  3  4  6  7
 1  8  3  3  3  1  8  6  7  9  8  1  5  4  1  6  7
 2  0  9  6  9  8  5  1  1  6  5  7  6  9  7  2  4
 7  9  1  9  2  9  6  9  2  9  2  0  1  0  3  8  1
 9  8  1  5  1  3  7  0  2  0  1  2  2  3  1  2  3
 6  3  8  2  0  9  1  3  7  0  6  3  2  0  2  0  0
 8  1  5  8  5  1  9  7  2  0  9  7  6  9  7  2  5
 4  2  5  2  0  2  3  8  1  9  2  5  7  1  3  1  1
 0  8  1  5  2  3  7  5  1  9  7  5  9  2  0  5  1
 1  2  3  8  2  3  2  3  4  1  9  7  6  9  2  0  6
 7  1  8  4  4  4  1  8  6  7  3  4  2  3  2  3  6
 1  1  5  6  1  5  6  1  1  3  4  1  9  1  1  1  5
 4  2  3  6  9  4  0  8  6  7  6  3  8  6  9  8  1
 9  6  3  2  0  7  9  2  0  5  1  1  2  3  4  1  6
 2  0  6  4  6  9  2  9  2  0  1  9  7  1  7  4  9
 8  6  5  8  1  3  1  1  1  6  7  1  9  2  0  6  9
 7  2  5  7  1  3  4  2  0  1  9  7  5  8  1  5  5
 1  9  4  1  5  6  3  4  2  3  2  0  6  7  1  5  5
 7  2  5  4  0  0  6  1  7  8  5  7  6  5  7  1  7
 2  3  7  5  1  9  8  6  9  4  6  5  8  1  9  6  1
 1  7  4  2  5  6  9  7  5  2  0  1  9  6  7  2  5
 6  7  1  5  8  2  5  0  8  2  0  1  6  2  0  6  4
 6  9  8  1  5  6  3  7  9  7  6  9  7  2  5  4  1
 5  4  1  9  1  1  0  7  1  3  1  1  1  0  1  2  6
 7  1  5  5  1  9  4  1  5  6  3  2  0  9  7  6  9
 7  2  5  4  1  5  4  2  0  1  9  7  8  1  9  2  5
 7  1  3  1  1  0  8  6  7  1  8  5  5  5  1  8  6
 7  9  8  5  6  1  1  3  6  3  2  9  6  0  7  0  7
 9  7  6  9  7  2  5  4  1  3  2  0  1  3  2  0  6
 6  0  8  6  7  5  5  7  2  3  1  1  7  2  0  1  5
 5  7  6  5  1  3  4  3  8  9  8  1  3  2  9  6  6
 0  8  6  7  6  0  7  1  3  4  7  2  3  2  9  5  9
 7  1  4  4  6  7  9  6  9  2  0  1  5  7  1  9  8
 1  9  1  9  8  1  5  4  6  9  2  0  2  6  7  2  0
 6  8  1  8  1  1  1  1  8  2  5  6  9  8  6  5  1
 1  8  1  8  3  3  3  1  8  2  5  7  6  3  4  6  5
 6  9  1  2  2  8  1  8  1  1  1  1  8  6  7  9  8
 1  0  2  5  6  9  4  1  5  1  3  1  2  7  2  3  5
 6  5  1  3  4  3  8  9  8  1  3  2  9  6  6  0  6
 1  2  3  9  6  9  2  0  6  5  6  1  1  9  2  0  7
 2  3  6  7  9  8  2  5  1  9  1  5  7  6  9  6  0
 2  5  4  7  2  3  9  8  1  3  2  9  6  6  7  0  2
 0  7  1  5  4  1  6  7  3  8  9  2  0  5  1  1  2
 3  4  1  5  4  2  5  6  9  7  5  1  7  1  7  1  5
 2  2  1  5  1  7  1  7  2  0  9  6  9  8  6  6  1
 9  7  0  2  0  7  9  2  0  5  1  1  2  3  4  6  8
 1  8  1  1  1  1  8  6  7  1  8  2  2  2  1  8  6
 7  2  5  1  3  1  2  8  6  9  3  4  0  2  0  1  0
 4  2  4  2  0  2  0  2  1  4
```

Fig. 3. First transposition tableau

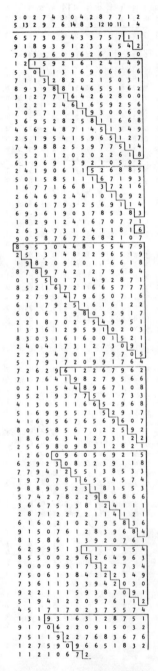

Fig. 4. Second transposition tableau, with disruption areas

victory over Japan in World War II. It is written numerically in the Continental style: 3/9/1945. Its last digit, 5, indicates the position from the end of the message of an inserted arbitrary keygroup, presumably a different one for each message. In this message it is 2 0 8 1 8. The first five digits of the date, in Line B, are subtracted from this keygroup in Line A, by modular arithmetic (without borrowing the tens digits). The result is Line C.

Line A   2 0 8 1 8
Line B   3 9 1 9 4

Line C   9 1 7 2 4

Then the first 20 letters of a line from the Russian popular song "The Lone Accordion" are divided, in Line D, into two sections of ten letters, and sequential keys are derived for each part in Line E. Under the key for the first part is written, in Line F, the subtraction result of Line C, chain-added out to ten digits. Under the key for the second part is written a standard numerical sequence, 1, 2, 3, . . . 0. The first parts of Lines E and F are added modulo 10 to yield Line G.

| Line D | Т О Л Ь К О С Л Ы Ш | Н О Н А У Л И Ц Е Г |
|---|---|---|
| Line E | 7 4 2 0 1 5 6 3 9 8 | 6 8 7 1 9 5 4 0 3 2 |
| Line G | 6 5 9 2 5 5 4 2 5 2 | |

Then each digit of Line G is located in the standard sequence of Line F and replaced by the number in Line E directly over it. The result of this substitution is Line H, which becomes the priming series for a chain addition that begins in Line K and proceeds—in rows of ten digits each—through lines L, M, N, and P.

Line H   5 9 3 8 9 9 1 8 9 8
Line J   3 7 2 4 8 9 1 5 0 6

Line K   4 2 1 7 8 0 9 7 7 2
Line L   6 3 8 5 8 9 6 4 9 8
Line M   9 1 3 3 7 5 0 3 7 7
Line N   0 4 6 0 2 5 3 0 4 7
Line P   4 0 6 2 7 8 3 4 1 1

The widths of the two transposition tableaux are found by adding respectively the eighth and ninth numbers—or perhaps the last two dissimilar numbers—in Line P to the agent's personal number, in this case 13. Since the numbers in Line P are 4 and 1, the first tableau will therefore have 17 columns and the second 14.

The sequential key derived in Line J from Line H indicates the column sequence for a vertical transcription from the block formed by Lines K through P. In other words, from under the 1 of Line J are taken the 9, 6, 0, 3, and 3 of Lines K through P. These are followed by the digits under the 2 of Line J, and so on, until 17 + 14 or 31 digits have been transcribed. These become the breeder keys for the two transposition tableaux—the 17 of Line Q for the first tableau, the 14 of Line R for the second.

Line Q    9 6 0 3 3 1 8 3 6 6 4 6 9 0 4 7 5
Line R    3 0 2 7 4 3 0 4 2 8 7 7 1 2

They are found at the top of the two tableaux, followed by the sequential keynumbers derived from them.

Finally, a sequential key is derived from Line P:

Line P    4 0 6 2 7 8 3 4 1 1
Line S    5 0 7 3 8 9 4 6 1 2

This (Line S) becomes the sequence of digits used as the coordinates for the checkerboard.

In 1956 Hayhanen's personal number was changed from 13 to 20, so that the width of the transposition tableaux was increased and their reconstruction thereby made slightly more difficult. In addition, the chain-added block was deepened by one row to increase the randomness of the digits that become the breeder keys for the transposition tableaux.

What can be said of the cryptographic merits of the VIC cipher?

First—and most important—it is secure. This was dramatically demonstrated by the F.B.I.'s failure to solve the nickel message. The system derives its great strength from the combination of two basically simple methods, monoalphabetic substitution and columnar transposition, and from the complications introduced into them.

The complication in the substitution is, of course, the straddling device in the checkerboard. Ordinary checkerboards have no unkeyed rows and so produce double-digit equivalents for all plaintext letters. The irregular alternation of coordinates of two different lengths in the VIC makes it harder for the cryptanalyst to divide the running list of numbers into the proper pairs and singletons. This division is prerequisite to a reduction to plaintext. A division entirely into pairs would straddle the correct equivalents—hence the term "straddling" in the cipher's technical description. Furthermore, the irregularity in the length of the coordinate groups would undoubtedly increase the cryptanalyst's difficulty in reconstructing the transposition tableau.

The complication in the transposition is the interruption in the inscription into the second tableau. This aims at blocking any attempts at reconstructing the first tableau. In the solution of ordinary double transposition, once the difficult job of reconstructing the second tableau is completed, the cryptanalyst can immediately attack the first tableau because he knows that its columns are found in the rows of the second. But the D areas forestall this direct attack by mixing a part of one column with a part of another. The cryptanalyst must sort out the columns before he can reconstruct the first tableau—and this sorting is a formidable task.

Second, the keying method of the vic cipher adds to its cryptanalytic resistance. The long series of calculations performed in the key derivation results in a series of virtually random numbers whose lack of pattern makes it difficult for the cryptanalyst to reconstruct the original keys and thus get clues for the solution of subsequent messages. Even more important is the key element that differs from message to message. This five-digit group, introduced at the start of the key derivation, affects the derivation so strongly that keys with different groups will bear no apparent relation to one another. Since each agent presumably had a different set of mnemonic keys, and since each message to an agent apparently included a key element that differed from message to message, no two vic-system messages of all those sent out from Moscow to secret agents all over the world would ever be keyed the same. This would greatly hinder cryptanalysts, who would have to attack each message separately.

Finally, the bisection of the message makes it harder for the cryptanalyst to find and exploit steroptyped beginnings and endings.

The vic system also has a number of operational advantages. The individual operations are easy and rapid. This reduces the chance of garbled messages. Furthermore, the ciphertext is not twice as long as the plaintext—a condition often met in high security pencil-and-paper cipher systems, such as the German World War I ADFGVX field cipher, which the vic strongly resembles. In the vic, ciphertext runs about half again as long as the plaintext. The reduction from the usual doubling is optimized by the use of single coordinates for the high-frequency letters for which the keyword is specially chosen. The key for the nickel message, *snegopa*, includes the most frequent letter in Russian (*o*, with 11 percent), four other high-frequency letters (*s, n, e, a*) and two low-frequency letters. The seven comprise about 40 percent of normal Russian text. This means that the ciphertext should average 60 percent longer than the plaintext. In the nickel message, it is actually 62 percent longer. This relative reduction means briefer communications, with the consequent lowered risk of detection.

The third and most important and unusual operational advantage of the VIC cipher is the way in which its entire encipherment may be developed from four easily memorized items.[4] The spy, of course, must know the derivation to get the three final keys, but this does not appear too difficult since each step seems to lead to the one after it in much the same way that one portion of a piano piece leads to another. No spy cipher of comparable security is known that achieves this feat of mnemonics: this speaks well for the ability of the Soviet cryptographers. To a spy, who lives in constant fear of sudden raids and searches, a cipher system that requires no betraying memoranda must be a boon indeed. Ironically, however, Hayhanen—or his superiors—did not place sufficient confidence in his wit to allow him to rely entirely on his memory for the cipher. Thus it was that when he arrived in the United States he carried microfilm notes in case he forgot the cipher that was so easy to remember!

Such was the cipher that the F.B.I. apparently failed to solve. But despite this impressive testimonial, the VIC system is not theoretically unbreakable. In fact, the technique required to solve a VIC message can be stated in a sentence: The second transposition tableau must be reconstructed in such a way that the first tableau can be assembled so that its rows yield a monoalphabetic frequency distribution; once this is done, the monoalphabetic substitution can be solved with relative ease. Whether the VIC cipher is unbreakable in practice remains unknown to the public. Once the system was known, and with a large volume of traffic, a computer might be able to run the billions of trials needed to effect a solution. But whether a single message in the VIC could have been solved while the system itself remained unknown seems highly unlikely. The weakening of frequency characteristics caused by the use of the numbers and the obliteration of repetitions resulting from the thorough transpositions leave virtually no clues for the cryptanalyst. It is therefore no surprise that neither the F.B.I. nor any other branch of the United States government managed to solve the message in the hollow nickel.

Even though the VIC cipher exhibits outstanding qualifications, it cannot be classed with Abel's system. The reason is simple: the Abel cipher is the only one known to be absolutely unbreakable. The cipher, usually called a "one-time pad" system, now appears to be a favorite among the heads of Red spy rings.

The cipher system used by Abel was never described at his trial in the detail that the VIC system was. The evidence for it consists of an F.B.I. agent's characterization of the keybook found in the block of wood as "a one-time cipher pad," plus a description of the keybook that accords with its use as a one-time pad. This keybook, apparently not much larger than a stamp, was found rolled in thin paper inside a block of wood with sandpaper around it, tossed casually into Abel's wastebasket as if it were being discarded. It consisted of about 250 pages bound together with glue. On each page a series of numbers in five-digit groups appeared; these were printed in black in one part of the booklet and in red in the other part. When Frederick E. Webb, the F.B.I. document examiner who was describing the booklet, was asked what he thought it was, he testified: "I would recognize this as a cipher pad which would be described as a one-time cipher pad."

Earlier testimony by Hayhanen cast some slight doubt on this flat statement. When asked whether Abel used the same system that he did, Hayhanen said: "MARK told me that he had the code but he was using—he was ciphering and deciphering different ways; that he was using special small books with numbers what makes ciphering and deciphering easier than by this method." This seems to imply that the booklet merely provided ready-made keys for the VIC system, to save the chief the trouble of deriving them. But three points demolish this hypothesis. (1) The special merit of the VIC system is that it eliminates just such key memoranda. (2) The final keys for the VIC system do not consist of five-digit groups. (3) Hayhanen testified that Abel asked him to decipher two or three messages Abel received between August 1954 and June 1955 but could not decipher. This suggests that the two had different cipher systems. (Hayhanen could not read the messages either, and Abel later told him that they were intended for another agent, Hayhanen testified.)

Two cipher messages that might have cleared all doubt and exposed the details of the system have, unfortunately, never been deciphered in public. One is a message of 380 five-digit groups, written on a strip of graph paper and found in Abel's room when he was seized (Fig. 4). The other is a longer message that filled each of two sheets of paper

```
03505 60476 04016 88622 36579 39249 67180 72479 66266 57127
92365 70390 04618 91915 98730 77472 67325 85535 01210 22288
99873 32256 78676 18467 21683 86588 59137 07234 10556 29355
03229 46862 90096 60275 61635 52187 54072 88348 20714 5936
79924 84435 53198 92335 92394 71287 36376 54819 19578 662
90910 93264 22572 46231 58592 35289 98190 66859 23710 2041
71142 80860 17536 17965 59087 68675 68283 08275 33139 533
75586 88949 27125 82142 42973 61195 49622 45658
```

A message enciphered in a one-time pad found in the possession of Soviet spy Rudolf Abel

with what an F.B.I. agent described as ten columns of five-digit numbers; it was found in a Kodak photographic book. There is no evidence that either of these messages, or any of the others that Abel sent and received by radio, were ever broken by American cryptanalysts.

The one-time pad system gets its name from an original form as a printed pad of keys. The random series of numbers on each leaf of the pad differs from the series on every other leaf. Each leaf is torn off and discarded after being used just once. Abel's booklet would be a modification of the pad in physical terms only. The system's operation is simplicity itself: the letters of the plaintext are replaced with numbers and then key digits are added to those numbers. If, for example, the Russian plaintext (already in numbers) began 96920 . . . , and the key were 64311 . . . , the ciphertext would begin 50231 . . .

Because the one-time pad never repeats any key and uses absolutely random, meaningless numbers as a key, messages in it cannot be broken. The reason is that no pattern can be constructed for the key. If the key were used several times within a single message, or if it were repeated in a number of messages, cryptanalysts would line up letters enciphered by the same key digit and discover what they are through the well-known principles of frequency. This is possible because the key digit would encipher a particular letter into the same ciphertext each time. Or if the key made some sense, if, for instance, it was the text of a book, cryptanalysts would use the known characteristics of language to reconstruct the key and consequently the plaintext. But the one-time pad precludes both these cryptanalytic techniques because its keys manifest neither external regularities (repetitions) nor internal ones (the statistical constants of language). No other cipher can claim this complete elimination of regularity from the key, and therefore no other cipher can boast that it is absolutely unbreakable.

Aside from its indecipherability, perhaps the most interesting fact about Abel's system is its apparent similarity to the ciphers used by two other major Soviet spies. Both Richard Sorge, head of a ring that spied on Japan from 1931 to 1941, and Alexander Foote, who worked in the spy net that operated against Germany from Switzerland from 1938 to 1941, used modified one-time pad systems. Both consisted of two steps. The first was a substitution of one- and two-digit numbers in a system much like the VIC checkerboard. (Hayhanen may have been referring to Abel's use of such a checkerboard when he said that Abel "had the code.") In the second step, a nearly random sequence of digits was added to the first set of numbers to obtain the ciphertext. The key sequence, which was grouped into fives for enciphering, came from a Swiss book of trade statistics. Sorge's radioman likewise used a book of statistics—the 1935 edition of the official *Statistisches Jahrbuch für das Deutsche Reich*—for his keys in a similar system. Because the trade statistics used as keys are not perfectly random (they may evidence partial patterns due to their tabular origin) even though they were probably used only once, the Foote and Sorge systems must be regarded as modified one-time pads.[5]

Both Sorge and Foote apparently used indicator groups that changed with each message to define the key to be used for that message. Since the VIC cipher also used a group that altered the keys for each message, it may be presumed that Abel's messages included a well-disguised indicator group that told him what part of his private keybook he should use.

The privacy of this keybook makes Abel's system the most secure of all. Its uniqueness rules out an accidental use of the same key by another agent, as well as attempts to match the tables from a common book of statistics against the ciphertext to see if a monoalphabetic distribution results. But the cipher's strength begets its main weakness. The digits of the key must be random to afford indecipherability, but because they are random, they cannot be memorized, but must be recorded somewhere. The discovery of such a keybook could cost a spy his life. A corollary weakness is that a new book must be issued when the keys of the old one are exhausted. The distribution of the new book increases the danger of discovery and exposure. Neither of these problems exists in the vic cipher.

These two Soviet spy ciphers—the vic and the Abel—seem to represent the apex of modern spy cryptography. One is absolutely mnemonic, thus providing perfect physical security. The other is absolutely unbreakable, thus providing perfect cryptographic security. Combination of these features, with the resulting improvement of the ciphers, seems impossible in theory, because the adoption of one automatically excludes the other. Yet perhaps some day an ideal cipher, combining a completely mnemonic key with absolute indecipherability, will be found—if the future of the black art stays bright.

# THE
# POLITICS
# OF
# CRYPTOLOGY

# American Codes
# and the Pentagon Papers

One of the dark charges against *The New York Times*'s publication of the Pentagon Papers is that they could give away secret American codes. The government has not raised the issue in either the *Times* or the *Washington Post* court cases, but administration officials and other commentators have said that the cryptographic loss constitutes the real damage in the matter.

They argue that, by comparing the enciphered messages, which foreign countries have intercepted and preserved, with the verbatim texts, which the *Times* has printed, these countries can reconstruct American cryptosystems. They could then use these reconstructions to read current American messages and so wreak untold havoc upon our foreign relations.

Such allegations are entirely without foundation in fact. The truth is that the publication has had absolutely no effect at all upon American cryptography.

One indication of this may be the reaction of the National Security Agency, the American codemaking and -breaking organization. At 11:45 A.M., Sunday, June 20, 1971 [a week after publication began], when on the basis of the charges one would have expected a panic-stricken flurry of activity, the Fort Meade, Maryland, headquarters seemed to be drowsing in the summer heat. The usual number of cars for a Sunday stood

This article first appeared on the Viewpoints page of *Newsday*, June 25, 1971, under the headline "Does the Enemy Care About Those Papers Because They Unlock Secret U.S. Codes?"

in the parking lot, the parking places of agency chiefs were vacant, and the only movement to be seen consisted of a lounger at the front gate staring over the sunbaked macadam.

The reason that American cryptography sustained no injury is simply that today's cipher machines are designed to withstand precisely this sort of exposure. The safety factor is built in.

Such cipher machines take the form of special-purpose computers. Their circuits, representing complex mathematical equations, generate a stream of electric impulses and spaces in a very long and almost random sequence. Applying this stream to an English plaintext message converts it into cipher form. The recipient, whose identical computer generates an identical sequence, applies his sequence to the cryptogram and reconverts it to English.

Now, if a cryptanalyst has parallel texts of the plain and the cipher messages, which he can get in various ways, he can recover the sequence used for enciphering that text. But can he deduce from that sequence the original equations, and use them to generate further streams that would translate future messages?

For many of the World War II cipher machines, the answer was usually "yes." But today even amateurs can devise equations—and commercial firms can embody them in machines—that virtually preclude this. "Virtually" means that such reconstruction would require decades, perhaps centuries, even with the help of computers. They would even then be so ambiguous that they would yield, not one certain, but dozens of *possible* solutions. The public state of the cryptographic art can thus produce ciphers that can withstand massive disclosures and that are, in all practical senses, unbreakable.

The National Security Agency stays far, far ahead of the public art. The 450 HW-28 cipher machines, costing $7,200 each, with which it replaced the State Department's older machines after the communications breakdown of the 1962 Cuban missile crisis, thus endowed the nation with cryptosystems so secure that they remain utterly undisturbed by the *Times*'s disclosures.

This central cryptographic defense is, moreover, not the only one that a foreign cryptanalyst would have to overcome. Various techniques, such as the use of varying channels of transmission and line-of-sight satellite communications, make it difficult to intercept the message in the first place.

In addition, the communications circuit no longer falls idle after a message has passed over it, as in World War II. Rather it carries a constant stream of impulses, some representing messages, but many meaningless, and all superficially identical. The dummy impulses serve partly to synchronize the cipher computers at both ends of the line, but chiefly to conceal the location of the actual messages.

Thus even though the *Times*'s messages have dates, the cryptanalyst would have to find their exact position within a 24-hour block of at least some 4,000,000 impulses. With modern cipher systems, even the most sensitive of statistical tests cannot determine this.

The charges that disclosure of plaintext messages has devastated American cryptography thus do not stand up. This is one reason the government has not made them in court. The other is that if it were to do so, it would in effect be accusing itself of not doing its job.

# Tapping Computers

Like people, computers talking to one another can be wiretapped. To protect themselves, more and more companies, such as the oil giants and banks, are putting their digital correspondence into secret form.

This has led to a demand for a common cipher—a system that would both permit intercommunication among computers and safeguard the privacy of data transmissions. The National Bureau of Standards, with the help of the National Security Agency, the government codemaking and codebreaking body, has proposed one.

The interesting thing is that while this cipher has been made just strong enough to withstand commercial attempts to break it, it has been left just weak enough to yield to government cryptanalysis.

Under the plan, all participating computers would incorporate the cipher hardware—tiny integrated-circuit chips, each mounted on an inch-long plastic wafer. For privacy, each pair of correspondents would have an individual key—a string of zeroes and ones, each string different.

The sender would use this to put outgoing messages into cipher; the recipient, to decipher incoming texts. Competitors would not be able to use their keys to unlock these messages any more than your neighbor's house key will open your front door. And even if a competitor has

"Tapping Computers" first appeared on the Op-Ed Page of *The New York Times*, April 3, 1976. One of the first to bring political issues in cryptology to the attention of the public, it helped assure that the protests of computer scientists about the proposed data encryption standard would not be ignored. But despite our objections, the D.E.S., with a 56-bit key, became a federal standard in 1978.

somehow gotten hold of the original message of a cryptogram, so many keys are to exist as to make it impractical for him to find the right one and so uncover other messages enciphered in it.

Each individual key in the cipher as proposed would have 56 zeroes and ones, or bits (short for "binary digits"). This length, two computer scientists at Stanford University say, has been craftily chosen to make it too expensive for private firms to cryptanalyze the digital messages—but not for the federal government.

Professor Martin E. Hellman and a graduate student, Whitfield Diffie, suppose that someone wanted to crack these messages by "brute force"—that is, by trying all keys possible for a particular situation. This someone could build a computer using a million of the chips. It could test a trillion keys per second. With 56 bits, the total number of possible keys is 70 quadrillion. The computer could thus exhaust all keys in 70,000 seconds, or less than 20 hours.

In large quantities, Hellman and Diffie say, the chips would cost perhaps $10 each at today's prices. To design and build a million-chip machine would come to about $20 million. If this were amortized over five years, the cost of each day's operation—in effect, the cost of each solution—would amount to about $10,000.

Who, they ask, has the money to spend on such a machine and the need for daily solutions that would justify it? Only the government. For private industry, the gains would hardly be worth the investment.

Now suppose the key length were 48 bits. The price of a machine to generate a solution a day would fall to $78,000 and the cost of each solution to $39. On the other hand, if the length were 64 bits, the price of such a machine would soar to $5 billion and of each solution to $2.5 million. This seems beyond even the bottomless pocketbooks of the intelligence agencies.

The National Security Agency and National Bureau of Standards argue that the two men's assumptions are off and that people wanting this information would find cheaper ways to get it than by breaking codes. But just because a house has windows is no reason for not locking the front door, Hellman and Diffie reply, and computer security experts at International Business Machines, at Bell Telephone Laboratories, at Sperry Univac, and at the Massachusetts Institute of Technology agree with them that 56 bits is too small. Indeed, one major New York bank has decided not to use the proposed cipher, called the "Data Encryption Standard," in part for the same reason. And the House of Representatives Government Information and Individual Rights Subcommittee is now looking into the matter [though no hearings or bill ensued.]

Hellman and Diffie urge a key length variable at the will of the user up to 768 bits, which they claim can be done at a negligible increase in cost. This would render messages insoluble forever, despite the continuing drop in computation costs.

Why should the National Security Agency be so passionately interested in the 56-bit key that it asked to attend a meeting that Hellman set up on the question and flew a man across the country for it? The N.S.A. expert declined to say. But one obvious reason is that, with a solvable cipher, N.S.A. would be able to read the increasing volumes of data that are flowing into the United States time-sharing and other computer networks from abroad.

The problem is that it would gain this information at the expense of American privacy. For it would also be able to crack domestic computer conversations as well as masses of enciphered personal files. And recent history has shown how often an agency exercises a power simply because it has it.

But perhaps the intelligence is worth it? The answer to that was given a long time ago. "For what shall it profit a man if he shall gain the whole world and lose his own soul?"

# Big Ear or
# Big Brother?

Room 6510 at the State Department is a warren of windowless offices with a special cipher lock on the door. Scrambler teletypewriters, shielded by special walls so that none of their radiation can escape, tick out a stream of material. Another door bars an inner area to all but perhaps five percent of the officials at State. This is the LDX room—long-distance Xerox. Here, the scourings of the globe's electronic environment flood in.

The environment is heavy with traffic—the *didahdidah* of Soviet Army radiograms in code or in clear; the buzzings of foreign air-defense radars; the whines of high-speed radioteletypewriter circuits carrying diplomatic dispatches; the bleeps of missile telemetry; the hums of the computer data links of multinational corporations; the plain language of ordinary radio messages; the chiming sing-song of scrambled speech. Moving on these varied channels may be Soviet orders to transfer a regiment from one post to another; Chinese Air Force pilots complaining during a practice flight about deficiencies in their equipment; Saudi Arabian diplomats reporting home from a meeting of OPEC. Tens of thousands of such messages are intercepted daily around the world and beamed to a complex at Fort Meade, Maryland, to be solved and relayed to the State Department and, simultaneously, to the White House, the Defense Department and the C.I.A.

"Big Ear or Big Brother?" first appeared in *The New York Times Magazine* of May 16, 1976.

The tall, bespectacled Air Force general sat down behind a table in the high, colonnaded Caucus Room of the Old Senate Office Building. Television focused its dazzling lights upon him and recorded his gestures. Two business-suited aides pulled up their chairs on either side of him. Before him sat the members of the Senate's Select Committee on Intelligence. A gavel banged, and the hearing began.

In appearance, the event resembled the start of thousands of Congressional hearings. What distinguished this one, October 29, 1975, was that, for the first time, the head of the largest and most secretive of all American intelligence organs had emerged from obscurity to describe some of his agency's work and respond to charges that it had invaded Americans' privacy. The big officer was Lieutenant General Lew Allen, Jr., director of the National Security Agency. N.S.A. is America's phantom ear. And sometimes it has eavesdropped on the wrong things.

In addition to sucking up and disgorging its daily load of intercepts from abroad, the N.S.A. had improperly eavesdropped on the conversations of many Americans, such as the antiwar protesters Benjamin Spock and Jane Fonda and the Rev. Ralph Abernathy, successor to Dr. Martin Luther King, Jr. At the request of the F.B.I., the Bureau of Narcotics and Dangerous Drugs and other government agencies, its vast technological capabilities had invaded the domestic field, which they were never intended to do. The committee wanted to know about an N.S.A. activity dubbed the "watch list."

Allen testified that, in the early '60s, domestic law-enforcement agencies asked the N.S.A. for information on American citizens traveling to Cuba. The assignment, he said, was reviewed by "competent external authority"—two attorneys general and a secretary of defense. All approved it, and the idea of using the N.S.A. for such purposes spread rapidly through the government. The drug bureau submitted the names of 450 Americans and 3,000 foreigners whose communications it wanted the N.S.A. to watch. The F.B.I. put in a list of more than 1,000 American and 1,700 foreign individuals and groups. The Central Intelligence Agency, the Defense Department and the Secret Service also submitted watch lists. Altogether, Allen said, some 1,650 American names were on the lists, and the N.S.A. issued about 3,900 reports on them.

But all this is over, he said; he personally abolished the watch list when he took over the agency in 1973.

The general's assurance did little to overcome the committee's overall concern—and that of many other Americans. For both prior to and since that hearing, disclosures in Congress and elsewhere have indicated a multifaceted practice of using the N.S.A. in ways that threaten American freedoms. For instance:

• The N.S.A. persuaded three major cable companies to turn over to it much of their traffic overseas. It was partly through this operation, codenamed SHAMROCK, that the N.S.A. complied with the watch list assignment. At one office, the N.S.A. man would show up between 5 A.M. and 6 A.M., pick up the foreign messages sorted out for him by company employees (who were said to have been paid $50 a week for their cooperation), microfilm them and hand them back. When messages began to move on tape, the N.S.A. got them in that form. The agency took some 150,000 messages a month, 90 percent of them in New York, and thousands of these were distributed to other government bodies. Congress got wind of SHAMROCK, however, and a year ago, after 28 years and millions of private telegrams, Secretary of Defense James R. Schlesinger had to terminate the operation.

• A previous N.S.A. director cosigned the notorious plan of White House aide Tom C. Huston to penetrate organizations considered security threats by the Nixon administration. The agency furnished Huston with several suggestions; one of them seems to have been to let the N.S.A. eavesdrop on domestic American communications. Huston conceded that the plan would use "clearly illegal" techniques. But the N.S.A. has acknowledged that it "didn't consider . . . at the time" whether its proposal was legal or not. The Huston plan was never implemented, but, said the Senate Watergate committee, the "memorandum indicates that the N.S.A., D.I.A. [Defense Intelligence Agency], C.I.A. and the military services basically supported the Huston recommendations."

• Former President Nixon acknowledged in a recent deposition to the Senate intelligence committee that he had used the N.S.A. to intercept American nonvoice communications. He said he wanted to discover the source of leaks from the staffs of the National Security Council and the Joint Chiefs of Staff.

• The agency is said to have passed reports on what prominent Americans were doing and saying abroad directly to Presidents Johnson and Nixon. Once, for example, the agency informed Johnson that a group of Texas businessmen involved in private negotiations in the Middle East had claimed a close relationship with him to improve their bargaining position.

• Two Stanford University computer scientists have recently accused the N.S.A. of promoting its own interests at the expense of the public's in a standard cipher proposed by the government for computer networks.

At issue is the key that would afford secrecy between pairs of users. The scientists accuse the N.S.A. of maneuvering to get industry to accept a key that, while too complex for rival businesses to try to solve, would be susceptible of cracking by the N.S.A.'s superior capabilities. That would permit the agency to raid the economic data flowing into the nation's computer networks, and to penetrate personal data files enciphered for security.

• In the whole area of economic intelligence, N.S.A. interception has been developing rapidly. The House intelligence committee, in its report, expressed concern over the resultant "intrusion . . . into the privacy of international communications of U.S. citizens and organizations."

At the root of Allen's appearance before the Senate intelligence committee, and of the entire congressional investigation of the N.S.A., lay the questions: Who authorized these abuses? What was there about the agency's legal basis that permitted it to invade privacy at the request of other government agencies—and with so little qualm? Was the final authority the president's—and, in that case, was he not armed with powers to play Big Brother beyond the worst imaginings of the recent past?

"[The N.S.A.'s] capability to monitor anything . . . could be turned around on the American people," said the committee's chairman, Senator Frank Church. "And no American would have any privacy left. There would be no place to hide. If a dictator ever took charge in this country, the technological capability that the intelligence community has given the government could enable it to impose total tyranny."

How essential to the nation's security *is* the National Security Agency? How can a balance be struck between the legitimate needs it serves and the freedoms it has shown itself capable of undermining? How did the whole problem originate?

Signals intelligence reaches back in America to the founding days of the Republic. But it matured only in World War I, with the widespread use of radio. During World War II, it became the nation's most important means of gathering secret information. When the Iron Curtain clanged down, the United States wanted to preserve these extraordinary capabilities. In 1952, President Truman issued a directive transforming the Armed Forces Security Agency, the interservice arm for signals intelligence, into the National Security Agency, serving all branches of government.

Therein lay the first pitfall. Unlike the C.I.A. in which all intelligence functions were centralized in 1947, the N.S.A. was not formed by act of Congress, with a legislative charter defining the limits of its mission. The cryptologic empire has only a presidential directive as its legal base. So shadowy has been the N.S.A.'s existence, however, that the text of the seven-page directive has never been made public.

This obsession with secrecy is well reflected by the agency's headquarters. At the edge of Fort Meade, just off the Washington-Baltimore Parkway, it is ringed by two chain-link fences topped by barbed wire with six strands of electrified wire between them. Marines guard the four gates. Inside lies a modern, three-story, square-A-shaped structure and, within its arms, a boxy nine-story building. From the latter, in particular, emanatès a chill impersonality, quite different from the flashiness of C.I.A. headquarters in McLean, Virginia. Topped by a frieze of antennas, the only sign of life a plume of white steam rising from the roof, the afternoon sun gleaming off its glassy facade, it stares bleakly south, toward Washington, the White House, and the centers of national power.

All around sprawl the vast macadam parking lots for the 20,000 employees who work there. They have passed some of the most rigorous security tests in the government, but they may be fired merely on a suspicion. They are enjoined from talking even to their spouses about their work. And inside the building they are physically restricted as well. The colored badge each of them wears tells the patrolling guards into which areas they may and may not go.

Their work is of two kinds. Some of them protect American communications. They devise cryptosystems. They contract for cipher machines, sometimes imposing performance standards so high and tolerances so close that suppliers quit in despair. They promulgate cryptologic doctrine to ensure that the procedures of, say, the State Department do not compromise the messages of Defense. But the main job is SIGINT— signal intelligence—listening in. To do all its work, the N.S.A. alone spends about $1 billion a year. The agency also disposes of about 80,000 servicemen and civilians around the world who serve in the cryptologic agencies of the Army, Navy and Air Force but stand under N.S.A. control, and if these agencies and other collateral costs are included, the total spent could well amount to $15 billion.

The N.S.A.'s place on the organization chart is ambiguous: It is "within but not a part of" the Defense Department. The secretary of defense merely serves as the "executive agent" of the president in carrying out the functions assigned to the agency. It is not subordinate to the C.I.A., but its director sits on the National Foreign Intelligence Board, the intelligence community's steering committee, whose chairman is the director of central intelligence—the C.I.A. chief. The N.S.A. director is always a three-star general or admiral. (The deputy director must be a career cryptologist.) The President appoints the director, rotating among the three services, which get 85 percent of its output. The seven directors before Allen held the job for an average of 3½ years each.

The agency's orders—Truman's 1952 directive—are to "obtain foreign intelligence from foreign communications or foreign electronic signals," Allen is said to have told the House intelligence committee. The agency can be remarkably successful.

"Most collection agencies give us history. The N.S.A. is giving us the present," said Lieutenant General Daniel O. Graham, a former head of the Pentagon's Defense Intelligence Agency. "Spies take too long to get information to you, [satellite] photographs as well. N.S.A. is intercepting things as they happen. N.S.A. will tell you, 'They're about to launch a missile. . . . The missile is launched.' We know in five minutes that a missile has been launched. This kind of intelligence is critical to the warning business."

During the Strategic Arms Limitation Talks (SALT) of 1972, the N.S.A. reported on the precise Soviet negotiating position and on the Russian worries. "It was absolutely critical stuff," said one high intelligence officer. The information was passed back quickly to the American diplomats, who maneuvered with it so effectively that they came home with the agreement not to build an antiballistic missile defense system. "That's the sort of thing that pays N.S.A.'s wages for a year," the officer said.

In 1973, large antennas appeared in satellite photographs of Somalia, which lies east of Ethiopia on the Indian Ocean. They looked like Soviet models. But not until the N.S.A. had learned where the antennas' signals were going to and coming from was the government certain that the Russians, who had been kicked out of Egypt, had moved their military advisers into Somalia in force and were controlling their warships in the Indian Ocean from there.

Examples like these made Allen's task a little easier when he appeared before the Senate intelligence committee. Senator Walter F. Mondale, the Minnesota liberal, told the general, "The performance of your staff and yourself before the committee is perhaps the most impressive presentation that we have had. And I consider your agency and your work to be possibly the single most important source of intelligence for this nation."

Church concurred. "We have a romantic attachment to the days of Mata Hari that dies very hard. The public has the impression that spies are the most important source of information, but that is definitely not so. The more authoritarian the government being penetrated, the less reliable the information derived from secret agents. In the Soviet Union and other Communist countries, the penetrations are likely to be short-lived and the information limited. But information obtainable through technical means constitutes the largest body of intelligence available to us, except by overt means."

And, he might have added, the most reliable. It is free of the suspicion that blights a spy's reports: Is he a double agent? Photographs from satellites also provide data as hard as can be, but, as Schlesinger once remarked, "Nobody has ever been able to photograph intentions."

On the other hand, communications intelligence is far more easily jeopardized than other forms of information gathering. If a government merely suspects that its communications are compromised, it does not have to hunt down any spies or traitors—it can simply change codes. And this will cut off information not from just one man but from a whole network. That is why the government is so hypersensitive to any public mention of the N.S.A.'s work. When President Ford refused in September 1975 to send classified material to the House intelligence committee after it made public four apparently innocuous words—"and greater communications security"—it was because of fears that the words would reveal to the Egyptians, to whom they referred, that the United States had pierced deeply enough into their communications to detect important changes. When in February 1976 he invoked executive privilege for private firms to keep them from furnishing information to a House committee looking into government interception of private telegraph and teletypewriter messages, it was also for fear of compromising N.S.A. procedures.

In doing its work, the agency doesn't just tune up its receivers and go out hunting for codes to break. It gets its assignments from other elements of the government. They tell the United States Intelligence Board [now the National Foreign Intelligence Board] what information they need that the N.S.A. can probably provide. After board approval, the director of central intelligence levies the requirements upon the N.S.A. Typical assignments might be to locate and keep track of all the divisions of the Chinese Army, to determine the range and trajectory of Soviet ICBMs, to ascertain the characteristics of radars around East Berlin. In all of these, the first step is to seek out the relevant foreign transmissions.

Some of the intercepts come from N.S.A. teams in American embassies. The team in Moscow has been spectacularly successful—at least before the Russians began flooding the building with low-intensity microwave radiation. It had picked up the conversations between Soviet leaders in their radiotelephone-equipped automobiles and other officials in the Kremlin.

More intercepts come from special satellites in space called "ferrets." Swinging silently over the broad steppes and scattered cities of the Communist world, or floating permanently above the golden deserts and strategic gulfs of the Middle East, these giant squat cylinders tape-record every electric whisper on their target frequencies. These they spew out upon command to American ground stations.

Most radio intercepts come from manned intercept posts. Some of these are airborne. The Air Force patrols the edges of the Communist bloc with radio reconnaissance airplanes, such as the supersonic SR-71, the EC-135, and the EC-121, which carries a crew of 30 and six tons of electronic equipment. These planes concentrate not on communications intelligence (COMINT) but on the second branch of signals intelligence, ELINT.

ELINT plays an important role in modern war. Suppose the Air Force were to send a bomber force against Moscow. Soviet radars would detect the force and report its range, direction and speed, enabling Soviet fighters to attack. To delay this, the Americans would have to jam the radars, or "spoof" them—i.e., emit counterfeit pulses that would indicate a false position and speed for the bombers. But to do this, the Air Force would first have to know the frequency, pulse rate, wave form and other characteristics of the Russian radars. That explains why, in fiscal 1974, according to a report of the Center for National Security Studies in Washington, the Air Force flew at least 38,000 hours of ELINT flights— better than a hundred hours a day—dissecting radar signals with oscilloscopes and other electronic means. The game is not without its risks. No nation leaves all its radar turned on all the time. So the planes sometime dart toward the country's territory. They hope the target will turn on its more secret radars. The danger, particularly at a time of international tension, is that the target will take the tease for the real thing and start World War III.

Other N.S.A.-directed posts lurk in the depths of the sea, aboard submarines in the Navy's HOLYSTONE program. This seeks, among other things, to "fingerprint" the acoustics of Soviet missile submarines. Aboard the HOLYSTONE submarine *Gato*, when it collided with a Russian sub in the Barents Sea in 1969, were eight sailors working for the N.S.A.-related Naval Security Group. The Navy also used to have nine noncombatant surface ships collecting signal intelligence. But after the *Liberty* was strafed by Israeli forces during the Six-Day War of 1967 and the

*Pueblo* was captured by the North Koreans, it decommissioned this mode.

The vast majority of the manned posts are fixed on the ground. They ring the Soviet Union and China—clusters of low huts huddling on a dusty plain or in the foothills of some remote Karakoram. In Turkey, they nestle close to the Russian underbelly. The post at the Black Sea port of Sinop—the ancient Sinope, which centuries ago colonized the shores of the Euxine—strains to hear Soviet voices. At Okinawa, the antenna field cobwebs a mountainside.

Much of the interception is done by servicemen. Earphones clamped to their heads, they hear the staccato of Russian Morse: One Soviet Army post reports the movement of half a dozen trucks to another. Other messages are in cipher. On a voice circuit, soldiers can be heard talking on maneuvers.

During moments of tension, the routine changes. Transmitters will vanish from their usual points on the dial. Station call signs will cease following their normal pattern of changes. Yet this is when information is most needed. The monitors hunch over their radio sets as they hunt up and down the frequency spectrum for their target transmitter. They can recognize him by peculiarities in sending or by the tone of his transmitter. One may sound like *dowdy-dowdow,* another like *doodeedoodee.* One may sound as if he's sending from inside a can; another may let his frequency slide up two or three kilohertz during a message.

They type out their intercepts on four-ply carbon paper and pass them back to the analysts. These men graph message routings to deduce organizational relationships. They monitor traffic volume for an upsurge that might indicate unusual activity. They extract from the message content indications of equipment capabilities, unit morale, names and characteristics of commanders. And they send the messages in cipher back to the cryptanalysts.

These are the aces, the shamans, of the communications intelligence business. They are the descendants of the ruffed divines and mathematicians who broke codes in curtained, candlelit black chambers to further the grand designs of their absolute monarchs. The N.S.A.'s modern Merlins work in large open spaces filled with rows of gray steel desks. They pore over green-striped sheets, tap on computer terminals, print letters with colored pencils in rows and columns on cross-ruled paper, sip coffee, confer. Their successes become the agency's most jealously guarded secrets.

They succeed, however, mainly with the ciphers of third-world countries and with the lower-level ciphers of major powers. Underdeveloped nations have neither the money nor the expertise to secure their messages from American—and Russian—exposure. Anyhow, they mainly want to keep things secret from their neighbors—Pakistan from India, Egypt from Israel, Chile from Argentina. So they buy commercially available cipher machines. But N.S.A. cryptanalysts, backed up by probably the largest concentration of computers under one roof in the world, some of them perhaps a generation or two ahead of any others in existence, can often beat these.

The major powers, on the other hand, use machines to generate ciphers so strong that, even given a cryptogram and its plaintext, and all the world's computers of this and the next generation, a cryptanalyst would need centuries to reconstruct the cryptosystem and use the reconstruction to read the next message. The N.S.A. in other words, cannot get the most desirable communications intelligence—the high-level messages of the Soviet Union and Communist China. (The SALT coup was partly the result of a Soviet enciphering error.) Worse, the area in which cryptanalysts may expect success is shrinking. The main reason is the declining cost of computation. This is falling by 50 percent every five years; the most obvious example is the price of pocket calculators. For the same amount of money as it spent five years ago, a nation can buy a cipher machine today with double the coding capacity. But doubling the coding capacity squares the number of trials the cryptanalyst has to make. Very quickly this work rises beyond practical limits.

So the N.S.A. asks for help. The F.B.I. burglarized embassies in Washington for it. The C.I.A. has subverted code clerks in foreign capitals: it once offered a Cuban in Montevideo $20,000. In 1966, it bugged an Egyptian code room to pick up the vibrations of the embassy's cipher machine. The N.S.A., which could not cryptanalyze this machine, though it was commercially available, analyzed the recordings, revealing the machine's settings—and hence the messages. The C.I.A.'s most spectacular assist came in 1974, when it spent $350 million in an unsuccessful secret effort to raise a Soviet submarine from the depths of the Pacific, with missiles and cipher machines intact.

In Room 6510 at the State Department, the intercepts come in on sheets of white paper bearing the heading "To Secretary of State from DIRNSA [Director, N.S.A.]." Several lines of gibberish indicating the distribution are followed by the text of the intercept, unscrambled on the spot. R.C.I. officers (for "research-communications intelligence"), one for each geographic area, insert the new material into fat loose-leaf binders and pull out the old. Once a week or so, the country directors mosey on down to Room 6510 and leaf through the file to keep current with their areas. If something urgent comes in, the R.C.I. officer calls the country director, who comes right down. Daily, an R.C.I. officer conceals the more important intercepts under black covers (the C.I.A.'s color is red) and carries them in a briefcase to the several assistant secretaries of state.

Dramatic intercepts are rare. And when they come, they seldom have much impact. Once, an intercept arrived suggesting that a coup d'état could take place in a certain country in a matter of hours. It was rushed to U. Alexis Johnson, then undersecretary of state. He read it, nodded, said, "That's interesting," and handed it back to the R.C.I. officer. There was simply nothing he could do about it.

The vast majority of the intercepts are low-level routine. At State, they deal largely with the minutiae of embassy business, such as foreign messages dealing with Soviet visa requests to foreign governments, reports of foreign ambassadors about meetings with American officials, foreign businessmen's orders. At Defense, they may include foreign ship locations, a reorganization in a Soviet military district, the transfer of a flight of Iranian jets from Teheran to Isfahan. Nearly all come from third-world countries. Usually they are of secondary interest, but sometimes their importance flares: Korea, the Congo, Cuba, Chile. And since these countries are spoken to by the major powers, their messages may carry good clues to the major powers' intentions. (This was another of the sources for the SALT intelligence.)

The quantity is enormous. In part this reflects the soaring increase in communications throughout the world. In part it marks a shift to the more voluminous peripheral sources, such as observing message routings, to compensate for the growing difficulty of cryptanalysis in areas of central interest, such as Russia and China. Unfortunately this overwhelming volume can stifle results. In late September 1973, just before the start of the Yom Kippur War, "the National Security Agency began picking up clear signs that Egypt and Syria were preparing for a major offensive," the House intelligence committee reported. "N.S.A. information indicated that [a major foreign nation] had become extremely sensitive to the prospect of war and concerned about their citizens and dependents in Egypt. N.S.A.'s warnings escaped the serious attention of most intelligence analysts responsible for the Middle East."

"The fault," the committee concluded, "may well lie in the system itself. N.S.A. intercepts of Egyptian-Syrian war preparations in this period were so voluminous—an average of hundreds of reports each week—that few analysts had time to digest more than a small portion of them. Even fewer analysts were qualified by technical training to read raw N.S.A. traffic. Costly intercepts had scant impact on estimates."

If N.S.A. failed in this major test, how does it do in its day-to-day operations?

A survey at the State Department showed that most desk officers felt that while the N.S.A. material was not especially helpful, they didn't want to give it up. It made their job a little easier. A former top State Department official was always glad to see the man with the locked briefcase. "I got some good clues on how to deal with various countries," he said, "and I quickly learned which ambassadors I could trust and which not."

At the Defense Department, most officials said they appreciated the help they got from the agency. "D.I.A. relies very heavily on N.S.A.," said Graham, "because D.I.A. puts out a warning document to American units all over the world and to Washington, and whether the warning lights are green or amber or red comes mostly from N.S.A."

For policy makers, naturally, the more information the better. But is this marginal advantage worth the billions it costs in a nation that has so many other vital human needs unfulfilled? Put that way, the question poses a false dilemma. The money for health and housing and education can—and should—come from elsewhere. It is on the vastly larger arms budget, on atomic overkill and obsolescent nuclear aircraft carriers, that the nation overspends. Intelligence is far cheaper and usually saves more than it costs. In general, with its record of some failures and some successes, and the incalculable potential value of its sleepless watch around the world, the N.S.A. is worth the money the nation spends on it.

The real question for a nation reappraising its intelligence community is not one of financial priority but of legal basis. There is no statute prohibiting the N.S.A. from activities that encroach on Americans' constitutional rights. [The Foreign Intelligence Surveillance Act of 1978 limits electronic interception for foreign intelligence purposes within the U.S.] In response to criticism, President Ford issued an executive order on intelligence that seems to forbid the N.S.A. from intercepting American communications—but also seems to leave a loophole. Even with the best of intentions, however, that cannot be an adequate approach. For what one president can order another—or even the same— president can abrogate or amend. [Ford's executive order was superseded by one by President Carter, which was in turn replaced by one by President Reagan that weakened restrictions on electronic surveillance of U.S. citizens.]

The final responsibility for all those improper activities by the N.S.A.

was, in each case, the presidents', even though it remains unclear wheth all of them were reported to the Oval Office. That alone should illustrate the hazards of an arrangement under which the powers of an intelligence service derive not from Congress but from the White House. As a basic reform, Congress should replace Truman's 1952 directive with a legislative charter for the N.S.A.

That, in fact, was the view that underlay much of the questioning of Allen before the Senate intelligence committee, and that is the substance of the recommendations on the N.S.A. contained in the committee's report on the intelligence establishment as a whole. "The committee finds," said the report, "that there is a compelling need for an N.S.A. charter to spell out limitations which will protect individual constitutional rights without impairing N.S.A.'s necessary foreign intelligence mission." The committee also made specific recommendations designed to prevent a repetition of the known abuses of the past.

The House intelligence committee, in its own report, came to the same basic conclusion, declaring that "the existence of the National Security Agency should be recognized by specific legislation," which should "define the role of N.S.A. with reference to the monitoring of communications of Americans."

There is no question that the National Security Agency, in the words of the Senate committee report, is "vital to American security." In fact, in this nuclear age, when danger-fraught situations can be best handled with knowledge about the "other side" and when many international agreements, such as SALT, are dependent on America's ability to verify Soviet compliance by its own technical means, N.S.A. intelligence, like all intelligence, can be a stabilizing factor in the world.

There is also no question that we need a new statute. No law can guarantee prevention of abuses, especially if lawlessness is condoned in the higher echelons of government, and the C.I.A.'s charter did not prevent that agency from overstepping its bounds. But a gap in the law is an invitation to abuse. An institutionalized mechanism to seek out violations and punish the guilty can best deter the sort of intrusion that so many Americans fear—and that destroys the very freedom the N.S.A. was created to protect.

# Cryptology
# Goes Public

## I

In November of 1978 a remarkable conference took place in Germany. It brought together for the first time the Allies' backroom boys of World War II and those whom they had outwitted for nearly six years—the cryptographers of the Third Reich. Together with historians, they discussed what had been the most secret part of the intelligence war. This was the Allied solution of the principal German ciphers and consequent ability to read large segments of high-level military traffic, including the very messages of Adolf Hitler to his generals.

An admiral of the Royal Navy described how his knowledge of U-boat orders enabled him to steer convoys around the wolf packs to help win the Battle of the Atlantic. An American intelligence officer told how foreknowledge of a German attack enabled the 7th Army to repel it with minimal losses. The Royal Air Force's former scientific intelligence chief recounted how ULTRA—as the Allied solutions of German messages were called—gave him the first clues to German V-weapons and enabled the Allies to bomb the research center at Peenemünde and later the launching sites in France. A historian discussed how the American solution of the Japanese diplomatic cipher machine revealed what the Japanese ambassador in Berlin was reporting to Tokyo about his

"Cryptology Goes Public" first appeared in the Fall 1979 issue of *Foreign Affairs*. The most lasting contribution of this article may be its title, which first named the phenomenon. The text was likewise the first to assemble the facts and issues, which had been reported in various journals, into a single piece.

conversations with Hitler—intercepts that became, Chief of Staff George C. Marshall said, "our chief basis of information regarding Hitler's intentions in Europe."

All of this proved too much for one of the Germans. During the war he had repeatedly assured the head of the Kriegsmarine, Grand Admiral Karl Dönitz, that the naval Enigma cipher machine was not being solved by the Allies—when, in fact, they were doing so almost solidly and often instantaneously. "If the Allies could read it all," he asked with asperity, "why didn't they win the war sooner?" An American historian answered, "They did." And no one in the high-ceilinged university senate room dissented. All agreed that ULTRA had shortened the war and saved thousands of lives. ULTRA was, one of its veterans has rightly said, "the most important sustained intelligence success in the history of human conflict."

It was typical of the traditions of cryptology that the ULTRA secret was withheld from the Germans as well as from the public for nearly 30 years after World War II ended. Governments maintain this sort of discretion for a number of practical reasons. To reveal how a cryptogram was solved would enable other countries to strengthen their cryptosystems to prevent such solutions. Even to reveal *that* a cryptogram had been solved might awaken other nations' cryptographers to the possibility that their ciphers, too, might be broken and so might impel them to change them. Disclosing the details of one's own cipher systems would obviously nullify their ability to keep communications confidential.

Finally, to admit prying into other nations' messages would embarrass a country and so burden its international relations. In only one case, apparently, did a statesman refuse to read other countries' messages not out of fear of bad publicity if caught but because he felt it was wrong. In 1929, when Henry L. Stimson became secretary of state, he ordered the closing of the combined State Department–War Department Cipher Bureau on the ground that "Gentlemen do not read each other's mail" and in the belief that mutual trust was the best road to world comity.[1] It was an act of highest international morality. But the times soon made it impossible. When he became secretary of war in World War II, Stimson was one of the grateful readers of intercepted Japanese diplomatic messages—provided by the War and Navy departments, which had kept their codebreaking groups alive in 1929.

Thus, secrecy about cryptology has been the rule at least since the science became a permanent function of state through the establishment of letter-opening black chambers in the Renaissance, as a concomitant of the rise of modern diplomacy. The Venetian Republic's Council of Ten ordained that any cryptologist who betrayed secrets could be put to death. In 1723, Britain's House of Lords asserted in a trial for treason that "it is not consistent with the public Safety, to ask the Decypherers any Questions, which may tend to discover the Art or Mystery of Decyphering." Governments still adhere to this principle as much as they can. In 1933 and again in 1950, the United States enacted laws that impose fines and jail terms for anyone revealing official cryptologic secrets. The National Security Agency (N.S.A.), responsible for U.S. cryptology, operates under the tightest possible security. The same is true of its foreign counterparts.

And secrecy has been relatively easy to maintain because cryptology has been largely a monopoly of governments. Though businessmen have sometimes used codes or ciphers to conceal their messages, they seem almost never to have intercepted and solved competitors' cryptograms.

But it is becoming increasingly difficult to keep the official lid on. With the expansion of radio communications and advances in intercept technology, cryptology has become so extensive an activity of intelligence and security that political and military events will from time to time impinge upon it and expose portions of it. The 1964 clash of the U.S.S. *Maddox* with North Vietnamese patrol boats in the Gulf of Tonkin, the attack upon the U.S.S. *Liberty* during the Six-Day War in 1967, and the capture of the U.S.S. *Pueblo* by North Korea in 1968 revealed some details about American intercept operations. Previously, in 1960, two N.S.A. employees, William H. Martin and Bernon F. Mitchell, defected to the Soviet Union and gave a press conference in Moscow about American codebreaking activities. And the 1974–75 congressional investigations into the American intelligence community revealed a good deal about the vast scope of N.S.A.'s intercept operations.

More recently, cryptology has, perhaps for the first time, become the subject of formal intergovernmental agreement. In the final stages of the negotiations of the SALT II agreements, the American side insisted that the treaty bar "the encryption or encoding of crucial missile test information," as President Carter said in his June 1979 televised address to the Congress on the treaty. Concealing information on missile tests by encryption would make it harder for the United States to ascertain Soviet missile capabilities—and vice versa.

To prevent this, the treaty provides that "neither party shall engage in deliberate denial of telemetric information, such as through the use of telemetry encryption, whenever such denial impedes verification of compliance with the provisions of the Treaty."[2] But since the treaty does allow encryption when it does not interfere with verification, the question of when encryption interferes and when it does not was looked at hard in the Senate's deliberations.

But the SALT case is relatively limited and still mainly a government problem. What is today far more interesting and significant is the degree to which new factors are causing cryptology to spill over from the governmental domain into public awareness. Major governments today are not limiting their intercept activities to official communications; they seek to draw intelligence from the communications of tens of thousands of private firms and citizens of all nationalities. The protective countermeasures of target nations necessarily include the private sector. At the same time, concerns about foreign and domestic invasions of privacy have led private firms and individuals to demand security for their stored computerized files and their electronically transmitted messages. To meet this demand, private researchers have invaded the highly technical realms of cryptology that have long been a government monopoly.

In short, what has happened to other technologies, such as atomic energy, is happening to cryptology. It is becoming a public matter, and raising a whole new set of public issues.

If one nation is intercepting communications on the territory of another, what is the proper diplomatic response to this? Should a government advise its nationals on protecting their communications from foreign exploitation when such advice might enable other nations to better protect their own communications and so deny the parent government valuable communications intelligence? May private individuals develop and publish cryptographic techniques that, because of their advanced nature, could also deprive a parent government of communications intelligence? Do First Amendment rights take precedence over the needs of national security?

We are only beginning to see the shape and scope of these and other issues raised by cryptology as it goes public. This article seeks to explore some of them.


## II

A few words about terminology may help. "Cryptology" encompasses signal security and signal intelligence. The former includes all ways of keeping secret both human messages, such as telegrams and telephone conversations, and electronic messages, such as computer-to-computer data exchanges. These ways include cryptography—varied techniques for putting the messages into secret form by code or cipher. The elements of the message—letters, electronic pulses, voice sounds—can be scrambled or replaced by other elements. The receiver, who must know the key or secret procedure used in encryption, then reverses the process to read the original message.

Signal intelligence comprises all methods of extracting information from transmissions. These methods can include identifying radars or translating telemetered data of intercontinental ballistic missiles in flight. Other methods deal largely with human communications. Among these are interception of messages in plain language; traffic analysis, which matches radio call signs to particular military or other headquarters and draws inferences from the volume of traffic on various radio circuits; and cryptanalysis, which breaks the codes or ciphers that armor messages. These three are generally grouped together as communications intelligence, or COMINT.

Nonspecialists frequently ask two questions about cryptology. Is there an unbreakable cipher? There is indeed one that is absolutely unbreakable. This is the one-time pad. It cannot be used in every situation because it requires as many random letters for its key as in all messages that will ever be sent, and this presents an insuperable distribution problem. It can serve in restricted situations, however, as in spy messages and on the Moscow-Washington hot line. There are also many ciphers that, properly used, are unbreakable in practice, since the cryptanalyst cannot assemble enough text to analyze their complexities. Because they do not have the disadvantage of the one-time pad, such systems serve in most military and diplomatic networks today.

The other question is: Have computers not made it possible to solve all ciphers? They have not. Modern cipher machines are in effect special-purpose computers themselves. Since doubling the encryption capacity appears to square the number of trials the cryptanalyst has to make, the codemaker can always stay ahead of the codebreakers.

## III

In 1975, the Rockefeller commission on Central Intelligence Agency activities revealed that the Communist countries "can monitor and record thousands of private telephone conversations." News stories later said that the Russians not only could but did monitor "millions" of domestic American telephone calls—100,000 a year in the Washington area alone. Then President Carter, at a news conference, acknowledged that "Within the last number of years, because of the radio transmission of telephone conversations, the intercept on a passive basis of these kinds of transmissions has become a common ability for nations to pursue."[3]

How did this happen? How do they do this?

Since 1950, telephone companies have increasingly sent conversations—both between people and between computers—from city to city by microwaves. These are radio waves beamed on a line of sight from a transmitter through several relay towers, usually perched atop hills about 25 miles apart, to the receiver. Communication companies like microwaves because building and maintaining towers costs less than buying land for right of way, digging a trench, and laying cable. Today about 70 percent of the toll call mileage within the United States is microwave.

But radio is easy to intercept. The intruder does not even have to reach into the microwave beam. Each relay radiates enough energy for an eavesdropper to pick up the microwave signal five to ten miles away. The antenna for this would have to be a ten-foot dish, but "The interceptor can make use of a number of innocent-appearing structures such as apartments, houses, sheds, barns or a specially outfitted van," says a study made for the White House.[4] If the interceptor can get closer to the beam, he can use smaller and less obtrusive equipment. None of this is either very difficult or very costly—around $60,000, according to the study. The real problem arises in trying to pluck a particular person's conversation out of the incredible welter of calls. And for a long time this final step seemed insuperable. There were simply too many telephone calls to check.

But the evolution of computers made individual targeting feasible. A computer can count the clicks of a telephone dial or the beedledybeeps of multifrequency pushbutton calling as they pour in torrents over the microwaves. It compares that number with a list stored in its memory. If it finds no match, it discards the call and passes to the next. But if a match exists, the system "drops" the intercept onto a tape recorder for human analysis.

The Soviet Union, acting through disguised intermediaries, has almost certainly rented houses near important microwave routes and filled them with the sophisticated electronic gear needed for interception. Senator Daniel Moynihan has said that the Russians are listening in their consulate in San Francisco, their mission to the United Nations in New York, and their apartment house in the Riverdale section of the Bronx. The two locations in New York, he states, provide "extraordinary access to telephone traffic in the whole of the New York metropolitan area, and in particular to that of the financial, commercial, and legal communities of Manhattan."

Though the aerials on the present Soviet embassy on 16th Street in Washington a few blocks north of the White House are designed for legitimate shortwave transmissions and not for interceptions, the Russians got lucky with their new embassy on Tunlaw Road, on one of the highest hills in Washington. When they were assigned the land, private telephone monitoring was unknown, and no one took into account that the site bestrides some important microwave beams. A primary telephone trunk group for the eastern seaboard runs close by on the relay between microwave towers in Arlington, Virginia, and Gambrills, Maryland. A Defense Department digitized voice circuit from the Pentagon to Western Union's Tenley Tower on Wisconsin Avenue passes almost directly over the site.

Late in 1977, the Soviet Union added another new and important mode of interception when it installed big antennas in Cuba to monitor communications sent by satellite. These comprise telephone calls, telegrams and computer data moving between the United States and 55 other nations. The messages are directed upward to one of several satellites hovering 22,300 miles above the Atlantic; the satellite then retransmits them back down toward a receiving station on the ground, usually on the other side of the ocean. But the downward beam spreads widely, and even from outside its fairly large "footprint" on the surface of the earth it is easy to pick up its signals, though the cost of a steerable 30-meter dish for such interception has been estimated at $1.5 million.[5]

All this seems an extraordinary effort to gain information that on its face does not seem very important. Why does the Soviet Union do it?

One reason is that codebreaking no longer yields the quantities of central information it once did. The transistor and large-scale integration of electronic circuits, which made pocket calculators so cheap, have placed excellent cipher machines within the price range of more countries than ever before. This means fewer codebreaking results, and this reduction has driven the Soviet Union, as well as the United States, to gather information from the unencrypted, plain language messages—both human and computer—that pass over telephone circuits.[6] Though plain language intercepts seldom provide the insight that cryptanalyzed ones do, they have their strengths. "Anyone listening in to a senator's telephone conversations for two weeks would own him," says one senatorial aide with tongue only halfway in cheek.

Another reason for the shift to telephone eavesdropping is that it can provide quantities of a kind of information that is becoming more and more important: economic intelligence. Information that might warn of dollar or energy crises is becoming as critical as military and diplomatic information. The Soviet Union, for example, is reported to have used its intercepts of American grain dealers' telephone conversations to advantage in its big grain purchase. Monitoring the data flowing by microwave and satellite in domestic and international time-sharing computer networks could reveal financial transactions of giant multinationals, once the trivia of airline, hotel and rental-car reservations are screened out.

The United States, too, is seeking economic intelligence through interception. In its leaked 1976 report, the House intelligence committee said that American signals intelligence "in this area has rapidly developed since 1972, particularly in reaction to the Arab oil embargo" and the Soviet grain deal success. Recently it was reported that intercepts of oil-producing nations' messages warned the U.S. government of their intention to raise oil prices.

Almost certainly, too, the United States eavesdrops extensively on communications within the Soviet Union. Monitors at the embassy on Tchaikovsky Street in Moscow are known to have listened in on the limousine radiotelephones of Soviet leaders, even though they apparently got only scraps of intelligence (including, according to a columnist, views on the ability of a favorite masseuse). It seems likely that such activities are targeted as extensively as possible on other Soviet internal communications, particularly those of a sort that would be between private citizens in America. (In the 1950s the C.I.A. did manage to tap the military telephone lines used by Soviet forces in East Germany, through a tunnel under the East Berlin boundary, but this was probably a one-time success after its discovery by the Russians.) No doubt the Western powers get fewer intercepts from East European countries and the Soviet Union than those powers obtain in the West, but because information is harder to come by in the closed Communist societies, the West's intercepts are more valuable.

## IV

As these new techniques become known, the two superpowers are taking steps to close them off. And these steps have generated some of the new controversy and discussion. What are they?

The Soviet Union has flooded the American embassy with non-signal-carrying microwaves, apparently to jam the American eavesdropping devices. But microwaves pose a health hazard, for this is the same radiation that at higher intensities cooks food in microwave ovens. Although there was a brief scare, American officials have since emphasized that they have no evidence that the radiation has yet been responsible for any illnesses.

But that is not a solution in the United States, as much for environmental as for technical reasons. Nor is a proposal by Moynihan, who grew incensed about the apparent double standard applied against interceptions. "We are standing around in the Rose Garden pinning medals on one another for having discovered that the F.B.I. is tapping somebody's telephone," he said, but nobody is doing anything about the Soviet intrusions. He introduced a bill that calls upon the President to declare persona non grata any individual with diplomatic immunity who is "willfully engaging in electronic surveillance on behalf of a foreign power."

One problem with this idea is that the Russians might retaliate in the same way against American eavesdropping, which would probably hurt the United States more than the Soviet loss of intelligence would hurt them. Another is that expelling a foreign eavesdropper might cause more loss than gain. For the United States has apparently learned about Soviet eavesdropping mainly by "piggybacking," or intercepting Soviet transmissions of their urgent American intercepts back to Russia for analysis. To reveal details officially might compromise the source.

Probably for these reasons, the executive branch has rejected the Moynihan proposal. Carter has said that "I would not interpret this use by the Soviet Union or by other embassies to be an act of aggression."[7] What then is the United States doing to deprive the Soviet Union of this intelligence?

It is undertaking a multimillion-dollar program to protect American domestic communications. On February 15, 1979, the White House issued a three-page, single-spaced National Telecommunications Protection Policy directive. It divides messages into three categories and specifies different safeguards for each.

"Government classified information relating to national defense and foreign relations"—military and diplomatic messages—will come, as before, under the control of the National Security Agency, the government's cryptologic body. It has already transferred many sensitive telephone circuits from microwaves to buried cable, and is expanding the Electronic Secure Voice Network. This uses telephone scramblers—

each about the size of two file drawers—to render conversations unintelligible to eavesdroppers.

The other two categories will be handled by a new Special Project Office in the Commerce Department's National Telecommunications and Information Administration. Associate Administrator Donald Jansky has an annual budget of $2 million and 20 experts for the job, the main part of which he expects will last five years. His teams have already spoken to almost a dozen telecommunication common carriers on how to protect messages in the second category: "unclassified information transmitted by and between government agencies and contractors that would be useful to an adversary." Some companies are looking into such matters as the practicability of bulk encryption to scramble all messages transmitted over a particular microwave link. The teams will also survey the needs of government agencies and will recommend particular cipher systems to them.

The third category consists of "nongovernmental information that would be useful to an adversary." Examples that Jansky gives include the strategy to be used by American firms in negotiations against foreign competitors, changes in the prime interest rate, crop forecasts, the availability of critical materials, and developments in advanced technologies. The White House directive requires that such information "be identified and the private sector informed of the problem and encouraged to take appropriate measures." Jansky's office is not chartered either to analyze the problems of particular firms or to recommend specific ciphers. But it will draw up guidelines for evaluating types of protection systems that the firms will probably buy.[8]

The entire program comes under a National Security Council subcommittee that will settle jurisdictional disputes between Commerce and N.S.A.[9] It marks the first time that any government has ever dispensed advice on codes and ciphers to the public. This has helped bring cryptology out of the closet. So has the question of cost. Jansky predicts that for the carriers and private firms this will reach "probably in the billions."[10]

## V

The new program is linked to the rising debate on cryptology in another way as well. One of the cipher systems that it will recommend to some government bodies and contractors lies right in the crossfire of the argument over whether foreign code-cracking intelligence is more important than protecting citizens' privacy by giving them good ciphers. The cipher is known as the D.E.S., or Data Encryption Standard. As bank cash-dispensing machines grew in number, bank officers became concerned that the wires between these machines and the central office computer could be tapped to gain information and then used to "tickle" a money machine to make it disgorge its average cash holdings of $20,000. So the International Business Machines Corporation devised a cipher to encrypt the identifications, amounts and account numbers passing over these wires. Modern semiconductor techniques enabled it to be extremely complex and yet embodied on an integrated-circuit ceramic "chip" the size of a thumbnail: it is the tiniest known "cipher machine" ever produced.

In 1973, the National Bureau of Standards, responding to the increasing public concern about data privacy—such as the confidentiality of individuals' Internal Revenue Service files—solicited for a standard cipher. Government agencies would have to use it when encrypting personal files, and private firms would have to use it when communicating with these agencies in secret mode. By far the best system submitted was I.B.M.'s.

It was, in fact, so good that a miniature debate seems to have broken out in secret between the two halves of the National Security Agency, which was advising the Bureau of Standards. The codebreaking side wanted to make sure that the cipher was weak enough for N.S.A. to solve it when used by foreign nations and companies. The codemaking side wanted any cipher it was certifying for use by Americans to be truly good. The upshot was a bureaucratic compromise. Part of the cipher—the "S-boxes" that performed a substitution—was strengthened. Another part—the key that varied from one pair of users to another— was weakened. In this form the government proposed its adoption as the Data Encryption Standard for non-national security messages and files and for interfacing with the private sector.

At once a storm of controversy broke.[11] Computer scientists and mathematicians clamored that the D.E.S. was still too weak. They charged at technical conferences and in the press that N.S.A. had secretly pressured the standards bureau to weaken the cipher so it could solve it more easily. N.S.A., they contended, had no right unilaterally to decide a question of such importance to so many people. They also said it was possible that I.B.M. and the code agency had built a "trap-door" into the cipher that it alone could spring to reach a solution, and argued that lengthening the key was necessary to afford proper protection to personal records. The bureau replied that the cipher was strong enough and that lengthening the key would increase the cost of encipherment unacceptably. So vociferous did this first national debate on cryptology become that the standards bureau set up two workshops on the D.E.S. These vented some of the criticism but otherwise nothing changed. As of July 15, 1977, the D.E.S. became the official government civilian cipher.[12]

Later the Senate intelligence committee staff investigated the matter. It issued a report saying that no one had exercised any improper influence on anyone else and noting that the N.S.A. had recommended the cipher for use by the Federal Reserve Board.[13] For the present, the furor has abated. D.E.S. chips are now being manufactured by a dozen firms, and it is a sign of the new interest in secret communications that the D.E.S. bids fair to become what no other cipher ever has been: profitable in sales to business.[14] The American Banking Association has endorsed it, and it will therefore protect many financial messages in the coming era of electronic funds transfers. (The protection of the security of such transfers is, of course, a matter of grave private concern. But there is also the possibility that hostile elements or terrorists, if they could break into the system, might introduce spurious messages designed to throw the whole financial system into chaos.)

But in five or ten years advances in computer technology will so greatly reduce the time needed to crack the D.E.S.—a time now measured in years, even with the fastest computers—that the cipher will have to be strengthened. The debate will resume. It will again bring into confrontation the needs of national security through codebreaking and those of individual liberties through codemaking.

## VI

Another great debate in cryptology continues to simmer. Should free inquiry be allowed in the field, or are its implications for national security so great and so sensitive that research should be controlled by the government?

For a long time this issue did not really exist. The only cryptologists outside N.S.A., with its squadrons of brilliant dedicated mathematicians and engineers backed by banks of the biggest and fastest computers, were a few hundred hobbyists who solved pencil-and-paper cryptogram puzzles. The spread of computers and of data communications began changing that. Whereas stealing a paper file required physical access to it, stealing data that was stored and transmitted electronically could be done by copying it at a remote terminal. Computer crime, wiretapping and terrorism made this threat real. One defense was encryption, and computer scientists in many firms and universities began studying it; the D.E.S. is a product of this interest. Very rapidly the quantity and quality of information on cryptology being circulated outside of government channels exceeded by far what it had ever been before.

The expansion was accelerated by two Stanford University scientists' development of public-key cryptography, the most revolutionary new concept in the field since polyalphabetic substitution emerged in the Renaissance.[15] Unlike standard cryptosystems, such as the D.E.S., in which the same key serves both to encrypt a message and to decrypt it, public-key cryptography employs one key to encrypt and another to decrypt. The two keys are mathematically related to one another, and each user possesses a pair. Each makes one key public. The other he keeps secret. Suppose user A wants to communicate secretly with user B. He looks up B's public key and encrypts his message to B in it. B applies his private key to decrypt the message. Thus anyone can send B a secret message, but only he can read it. This asymmetry can eliminate one of the most vexatious problems in practical cryptography: distributing keys to a correspondent before secret communication can be started with him. And a twist makes possible what has never been possible before with electronic messages: unforgeable signatures.

The seeming impossibility of these schemes, their boldness, and their elegance have attracted numbers of first-rate mathematicians to cryptology. There is now, for the first time, an informal network of scientists who can do sophisticated mathematical cryptology and who bounce ideas off one another in the way that advances a study rapidly and rationally.

Suddenly the nation is faced with a problem it has never had before—an information explosion in cryptology. N.S.A. worries that any mention of codebreaking might make other nations change their codes, losing intelligence and forcing the agency to redo much of its work. This happens far less often than the agency likes to think. In 1941, for example, Japan did not change its principal diplomatic cipher despite an unequivocal report that the United States had broken it. Nor did the German Navy alter its systems in World War II, despite much suspicion. Several of the countries named by the defectors Martin and Mitchell in 1960 as having had their codes broken by N.S.A. did not change them thereafter. But more cautious nations do replace their cryptosystems upon suspicion of solution, and N.S.A. fears that all the new activity in cryptology may not only dry up the flow of foreign intelligence but also inadvertently expose principles used in American ciphers. All of this has caused it to ask whether the right of unrestricted inquiry is worth the national security losses. The issue has surfaced in three recent episodes.

One dealt with inventors of cryptographic systems. Dr. George I. Davida, a bright and articulate professor of electrical engineering and computer science at the University of Wisconsin, had applied for a patent for a cipher device using advanced mathematical techniques. The law requires that, if competent government authority deems that disclosure of an invention "would be detrimental to the national security," the commissioner of patents "shall withhold the grant of a patent." On the advice of N.S.A., the commissioner ordered that Davida's invention be kept secret. The university's Milwaukee chancellor protested that the secrecy order had "a chilling effect on academic freedom." The N.S.A. director argued, on the other hand, that the decision to seek a patent implied a profit motive, not academic freedom. "If the individual had elected to publish in academic journals there would have been no question of a secrecy order," he said. But this dodged the fundamental issue of whether publication of Davida's work would have impaired the government's cryptologic operations.

While this matter was working its way through the government and university bureaucracies, the commissioner of patents imposed another secrecy order. This was against a "phaserphone" voice scrambler invented by four West Coast men originally for use with citizen's band radios; it would let C.B. and telephone users who had it chat without being overheard by others. The four estimated that the device could sell for $100 and could have a large commercial market. The leader, Carl R. Nicolai of Seattle, angrily charged that the secrecy order "appears part of a general plan by the N.S.A. to limit the privacy of the American people. They've been bugging people's telephones for years and now someone comes along with a device that makes this a little harder to do and they oppose this under the guise of national security." (The 1974–75 investigations revealed that N.S.A. had in fact listened to the conversations of 1,650 Americans and had intercepted millions of private telegrams up to the mid-1970s.)

The storm of publicity led to a quick about-face by N.S.A. It lifted the secrecy orders on both applications. But the agency's vacillation suggested that it had not resolved within itself the issue of freedom versus security that the incidents had raised.

The third episode began when an eccentric N.S.A. employee, J. A. Meyer, wrote on his own a letter to the Institute of Electrical and Electronics Engineers, one of the largest professional societies in the world, which was holding a session on cryptology as part of a symposium in Ithaca, New York. Meyer warned the I.E.E.E. that the session and articles on cryptology that it had published might violate the government's

International Traffic in Arms Regulations.[16] These implement the law authorizing the president "to control the import and export of defense articles and defense services." On the U.S. Munitions List that enumerates these articles, which include guns, ammunition, and warships, are, in Category XIII(b), "speech scramblers, privacy devices, cryptographic devices," and ancillary equipment.

To export a warplane or a cipher machine, the exporter must apply for a license, which the State Department grants or denies after consultation with the Defense Department. (It is easy to evade these controls for cipher devices, some manufacturers note. They ship the mechanisms to the foreign country's Washington embassy, which then sends them home by diplomatic pouch.) But the regulations also require a license to export "technical data" touching these "implements of war." "Technical data" is defined very broadly. It covers "any unclassified information that can be used . . . in the design, production . . . [or] operation" of any Munitions List items as well as "any technology which advances the military applicability." At the same time, the regulations in effect define "export" very broadly. Before publishing something in a periodical with subscribers outside of the country, the writer must seek government approval, the regulations say. They declare that "an export occurs whenever technical data . . . is disclosed to foreign nationals in the United States (including plant visits and participation in briefing and symposia)." This seems to mean that every time someone publishes a paper or gives a talk at a conference on cryptology or on any of the other items on the Munitions List without government approval, he is breaking the law. These regulations seem never to have been tested in court.

When Meyer's letter reached the I.E.E.E., officials cravenly urged authors of papers on cryptology to clear them with the government. As a consequence, some of the speakers conferred with their universities' lawyers, and the Massachusetts Institute of Technology suspended distribution of a monograph on public-key cryptography. There was a flurry of news stories. But in the end, all the papers were read—though one tenured professor read papers by two of his graduate students to protect them—and the mailings resumed.

For a while, many people thought that N.S.A. was behind the Meyer move. But the Senate intelligence committee cleared the agency of this charge. What has not been clarified is the threat of government crippling of research posed by the arms regulations. The then director of the N.S.A., Vice Admiral Bobby Inman, a tall, boyish, brown-eyed intelligence specialist, sought first to calm the waters. "I am striving," he said, "to open up a dialogue" between the agency and industry and academia. He did so by talking to private researchers, giving interviews to the press, making a speech in public. No other director has ever thus come out officially from behind N.S.A.'s triple barbed-wire electrified fence at its Fort Meade, Maryland, headquarters; Inman said he did so out of concern that a bad press might harm recruitment.

Inman's substantive proposals on cryptologic research flowed from his "deep convictions that the national security missions entrusted to the agency are in peril." He considered imposing restrictions "on domestic dissemination of nongovernmental technical information relating to cryptology," though he would have limited this to "a central core of critical cryptologic information that is likely to have a discernible adverse impact on the national security." It was rumored that he sought a law for cryptology analogous to the Atomic Energy Act, which places under government control not just government-generated secrets but "all data" concerning atomic weapons and "special nuclear material." Present laws on cryptology deal only with government secrets.[17]

On the export problem, such a law would presumably have provided a stronger basis for action than the purely administrative International Traffic in Arms Regulations. And, as a possible step in this direction, N.S.A. sought to have cryptology included among the "critical technologies" whose export would be controlled under a House bill introduced by the administration (H.R. 4034).[18] [It was not enacted.]

But George Davida, his erstwhile opponent in the patent secrecy dispute, sees many problems in this approach. Who can foresee where the critical areas are? Microprocessors—which put practically an entire computer on a single chip—may confer greater cryptologic ability on a country than all the seminar papers ever given. Yet they are not cryptologic in themselves. Mathematicians working with no thought of cryptology may find that their work touches upon it directly. Complexity theory, which deals with how hard some problems are to solve, is a current example. "How are you going to clamp down on complexity theory?" Davida asks. "And to turn a complexity theorem into encryption is trivial. If Inman is trying to monitor everything, he'll find it very hard. In universities, where we have to keep up with new developments in computing science for our livelihoods, we find it hard."

Nor are the problems confined to the United States. They are as universal as science. Several nations, among them France and West Germany, have passed laws requiring that stored or transmitted personal data be encrypted where necessary.[19] Work is under way to create effective protocols. Though cryptologic activity seems not as great among mathematicians and computer scientists abroad as in the United States, interest is growing. Individuals and firms who ten years ago would not have given a passing thought to cryptology are now devoting substantial portions of their time to it. The problems of transborder data flows, which some governments are trying to restrict for fear that too much of their national "information capital" may fly to nations powerful in data processing, include encryption; the study committees of industry and government have not yet grappled with them.

Among these questions is the variability of practice among governments in dealing with encrypted information coming into their territories by cable or radio. Some countries impose no restrictions; others require knowing the cryptosystem used.[20] Some countries insist upon this for domestic communications as well. For most nations, the new public awareness of cryptology has not yet become a major concern of their governments. Even in Britain, where the most public work is being done, persons studying cryptology have not gotten the feeling that the government cryptologic agency is trying to discourage the activity. But there seems little doubt that such concerns will eventually emerge.

## VII

Davida and Inman, at odds on a number of points, agreed on others: cryptology is no longer a government monopoly; the debate is just beginning; it will be political; it will attract many participants. Davida thinks that the question of government regulation in the field is a matter that "each person must decide for himself." Inman said that the question has to be "fully examined by the executive branch, the Congress, and the interested segments of the public."

But the examination itself may raise more difficulties than it settles. Is it paradoxical to seek public resolution of a matter that deals in secrets? Will it be done by legislation or executive order—or not at all? How can one balance the conflicting demands of national security and individual freedom?

And the problems are almost impossible to predict. Will the experts in the National Security Agency (who are reported to have invented their own type of public-key cryptography some years ago), be able to stay a step ahead of the inventors, or will their closed work system eventually be matched (as it may have been in that case) and even surpassed by the open interactive community of bright scientists who refuse the restrictions and nonrecognitions of work in a clandestine agency?

Will the study of cryptology become an epidemic that even all the government's resources will be unable to stem?

So cryptology, in 1945 a nation's most closely held secret, has gone public. But not even the procedures or forums for coming to grips with the new problems have been settled on. Their evolving substance will be harder still to resolve.

# Statement Before the House Government Information and Individual Rights Subcommittee

Gentlemen:

I thank you for the opportunity to participate in the democratic process. I hope that my ideas will help.

Perhaps I should begin by listing some of the credentials that, I believe, have led to the invitation to appear here. Cryptology has been a hobby of mine since I was 13. As an outgrowth of this interest, I wrote a history of cryptology, entitled *The Codebreakers*, published in 1967, which kind people have called the classic on the subject. I have since written frequently on cryptology, including for such publications as *The New York Times Magazine* and *Foreign Affairs*, and am a co-editor of the new scholarly journal *Cryptologia*. I am a past president of the New York Cipher Society and of the American Cryptogram Association. I have also written on wider aspects of intelligence, which helps put cryptology into perspective, most notably in my 1978 book, *Hitler's Spies: German Military Intelligence in World War II*. I work as an editor for the Long Island daily *Newsday* and hold a Ph.D. in history from Oxford. I am married, have two sons, and was raised and live in Great Neck, New York.

The committee has asked for my "view of the confrontation between

Statement of David Kahn, given at 9:30 A.M., Thursday, March 20, 1980, printed in U.S., Congress, House of Representatives, Committee on Government Operations, *The Government's Classification of Private Ideas*, Hearings, 96th Congress, 2nd Session (Washington, 1981), 411–415.

public cryptography and national security interests exemplified by the imposition of secrecy orders on independent researchers."

May I first of all propose a terminological clarification? It is to use "nongovernmental cryptology" instead of "public cryptography." "Public cryptography" risks confusion with a new concept in the field, "public-key cryptography." But, more important, the word "public" may be construed as governmental, as in "public corporation," when actually the opposite—private individuals—is meant. "Nongovernmental" avoids this problem. The term "cryptography" is used today to mean only "making codes and ciphers," while "cryptology" encompasses both making and breaking them. I feel that you would do better to avoid a term that might elicit obfuscatory answers from officials or that might tend to limit the inquiry.

May I secondly observe that the imposition of secrecy orders forms part of a broader issue and cannot really be discussed without it? This issue is the government's attempt to abate or even to suppress nongovernmental research on cryptology. It applies to more people than secrecy orders, and it raises problems more fundamental than those thrown up by secrecy orders. I believe, therefore, that it is the real issue with which you must someday grapple, and so, with your permission, I shall address it.

Why is the government concerned about outside work on cryptology? Basically, it fears that as scientists publish ever better cryptosystems, foreign countries will adopt these and the United States will lose valuable information it now gets from cracking the present, weaker codes of these countries. So it is taking measures to prevent such a loss.

This situation is new. It has never existed before. How did it come about?

The esoteric field of secret codes was, for centuries, a government monopoly. Nation-states made—and still make—codes to protect their instructions to their ambassadors and their generals, and they break the codes of other nations to learn the plans of other commanders in chief. But in the past few years this monopoly began crumbling under the onslaught of a variety of social and technological factors.

The growing concern of many individuals about the privacy of information about them in the hands of government and business has led security experts to consider cryptography as one method of protecting these files from unauthorized access. Fear of terrorism and industrial espionage has caused many business executives to scramble their telephone talk. The approach of electronic banking and the office of the future, whose electronic networks are far more vulnerable to remote-access interception and disruption than today's paper flow, has created worries about communication security. Revelations that the Soviet Union is eavesdropping on American business's telephone calls (including computer-to-computer data exchanges), most of which move over easily intercepted microwave radio links, has raised a debate about how best to protect them. At the same time, the decreasing cost of electronic components, which has made hand calculators so ubiquitous, has for the first time made good cryptosystems cheap enough to serve in these many applications.

All this has generated a broad, economically motivated interest in cryptology outside the government for the first time in history. Mathematical and engineering journals, which used to ignore the subject, now frequently publish articles on it. No computer conference is complete these days without its session on cryptology. Once the only people outside the government interested in ciphers were hobbyists, who solved cryptogram puzzles for fun. Today a net of mathematicians and computer scientists trade high-powered ideas on new cryptosystems and how they can best be used. More than a score of small firms are developing and selling cryptosystems; I.B.M. and A.T.&T. have teams working on cryptographic problems. International bank transactions are now routinely encrypted, which they never really were before. Dozens of firms among the Fortune 500 are now guarding their messages by cipher systems for the first time.

All this activity has caused the National Security Agency, the nation's codemaking and codebreaking organization, to grow anxious about the possible reduction in American intelligence as a consequence of improved foreign codemaking. The foreign governments in question are not, of course, the major powers, such as the Soviet Union or France, whose high-level codes have long been unbreakable, but the developing nations. Their codes, now often solvable, will eventually become unbreakable. N.S.A. wants to delay this as much as possible. It might seem that the messages of these nations do not contain anything worthwhile. But further reflection will show that most of the post–World War II hotspots have been in just such countries: the nations of the Mideast, Korea, the Congo, Cuba, Vietnam, Iran, Afghanistan. So their messages are worth reading.

Eager to preserve national security, the N.S.A. has sought to slow down public work in cryptology. At its direction, the Patent Office placed under secrecy orders two applications for patents for cipher devices (after heavy adverse publicity, the orders were withdrawn). One of N.S.A.'s employees sought to intimidate researchers in the field by citing the federal International Traffic in Arms Regulations (I.T.A.R.), which require a license to export "technical data" on, among other things such as guns and warships, "cryptographic devices." "Technical data" includes "unclassified information" and "exporting" includes publishing in a periodical with subscribers outside of the country or talking at a symposium in the U.S. with foreign nationals present. Though the N.S.A. employee pulled his stunt on his own, the agency never repudiated his effort. Moreover, it brought the I.T.A.R. to the attention of many cryptologists who never knew they existed and made many of them think twice before publishing their work. Perhaps feeling that the administratively based I.T.A.R. were not strong enough to proceed under, N.S.A. sought to have inserted in a bill a provision that all cryptologic information be subject to export controls. This effort, too, failed. The N.S.A. director, Vice Admiral Bobby Inman, greatly concerned about the new activity in cryptology, broke the agency's rule of silence and spoke out publicly on the need for restraint. He said he is considering restrictions on "domestic dissemination of nongovernmental technical information relating to cryptology." In addition, he is visiting leading nongovernmental cryptologists in universities and research laboratories in a soft sell to get them to lay off. In at least one case, he has succeeded.

Is all this not merely a case of a bureaucracy's simply trying to protect its job or to conserve the power its vastly superior knowledge of the field gives it? No. For though the N.S.A. is indeed trying to do both these things, so are the cryptologists in business and academe. Thoughts of tenure and raises and fame are not far from their minds when they analyze ciphers or write about them. So this argument cuts both ways and may not fairly be used against the N.S.A.

Instead the issue is whether what the N.S.A. is trying to do is the best for the country. Should the government suppress cryptology on national security grounds?

The question should not be answered by a knee-jerk negative. It deserves consideration. For without security, there is no freedom. Moreover, the nation has responded to the same question in another area with an affirmative—if legislation is any evidence. The Atomic Energy Act places under government control not just government-generated information about atomic weapons and "special nuclear material" but "all data" concerning them. This was the basis for the action against *The Progressive*'s publication of publicly available material on an atomic bomb. (The I.T.A.R. provide another broad weapon for control in many areas, though its publication provisions seem not to have been tested in court.)

Some people might argue that codes differ fundamentally from atomic bombs: No code has ever killed anyone. The N.S.A. would retort that the difference is more apparent than real. Good codes are a form of weapon. By enabling a nation or a terrorist group to keep their plans secret longer, they reduce the time available to the United States to take countermeasures—and so in effect do kill people.

There are weaknesses in this response. It could turn almost every activity of a free society into a weapon that could be used against it. Every news story, every campaign speech about President Carter's mistakes and weaknesses could be seen as helping the enemy. The development of microprocessors, which are revolutionizing our lives but which, by conferring great computing power upon a nation, also expand its cryptologic capabilities, may be viewed as a boon to American rivals. Nevertheless, the N.S.A. argument has validity in some cases, as with atom bombs. How are these cases to be determined?

The test should be whether the activity in question benefits the nation at home more than it harms it abroad. The argument seems to hold with nuclear recipes. Why should it not also apply to cryptology? Do any benefits accrue to the nation from the unrestricted development and publication of studies on codes and ciphers? Four do.

One is that work in cryptology can help improve the nation's own cryptologic effort. Two of the most important concepts in American codes and ciphers were developed by amateurs. One was an inventor, Edward Hebern of California, and the other was better known as a President of the United States: Thomas Jefferson. It may be that the time of individual innovation is over in cryptology as it is largely in science. But still, two computer scientists recently independently invented a revolutionary new concept, the one I mentioned before, public-key cryptography. Though cryptologists in N.S.A. and/or its British counterpart had devised this earlier, its reinvention by two individuals demonstrates that nongovernmental workers can yet do important work. Such results help America more than other nations because America is more advanced. A negative instance may help show the importance of outside input. In 1940, Nazi Germany ordered all books on cryptology withdrawn from circulation. No one would claim that this was one of the main causes of Germany's catastrophic defeat in the war of the cryptologists, whose loss so harmed Germany on the fields of battle. But this censorship could not have helped Germany.

Another benefit to the nation is that work in cryptology can produce results of importance in allied fields, such as communications, mathematics, and computer science. During World War II, for example, Claude

Shannon got some of the ideas for information theory, one of the most seminal ideas of our time, while working on cryptologic problems. Here, too, such results help America more than other nations. The rich grow richer not only financially, but scientifically.

A further benefit is continuing protection of information that needs protection. As computer scientist and cryptologist Martin Hellman of Stanford University has pointed out, the United States is the most computerized nation on earth and so has the most to lose from hostile penetration of its data networks and data banks. Cryptosystems do not retain their integrity forever: they grow increasingly vulnerable as the speeds of computation increase and costs decrease. New systems must therefore be constantly developed. Cannot the N.S.A. provide these new systems? Many people do not trust it, in view of its history of intercepting private American telephone calls and its apparent tampering with a cryptosystem approved for nonnational security use, as for transmission or storage of social security records (the National Bureau of Standard's Data Encryption Standard). Private initiative in cryptology is therefore needed to assure people that their data is truly protected. Is their personal peace of mind worth a decline in national security? To ask this question is to ask whether democracy is worth its costs. Most Americans will say yes.

A final benefit is that refusing to restrict cryptologic studies erects yet another rampart against the chipping away of American liberties. Is this rampart, again, worth the danger to national security? Yes, because the danger is not as acute as the N.S.A. wishes people to see it. N.S.A. wants people to think that publication of cryptologic material would slam shut its window into Third World countries. In fact such publication has little effect. The nations that need this information most cannot utilize it. They have no way of embodying it in machines and they do not have the personnel to properly use this high-technology equipment even when it is available, as salesmen for cipher-machine firms will attest. They have many needs to fill before they spend money on cipher machines. And publication of a cipher will not automatically cause them to abandon their old system, for few men are as intransigent in their beliefs as cryptographers are about the unbreakability of the ciphers they have invented or introduced. The national security dangers are not so great as to dismantle individual freedom.

For all of these reasons, then, no limitation should be placed on the study of cryptology. And beyond them all lies something more fundamental that, in the end, will probably prevent any restrictions anyway. It is called the First Amendment.

I thank you.

# BOOK REVIEWS

From *The New York Times Book Review* (December 29, 1974), 5. I think it fair to say that this review helped make *The Ultra Secret* a bestseller. The print order before publication was for 5,000 copies; it eventually sold 100,000.

## THE ULTRA SECRET

*by F. W. Winterbotham*

Harper & Row, 199 pp., $8.95.

This book reveals the greatest secret of World War II after the atom bomb. It is a must for World War II and intelligence buffs. But it has to be read with caution.

*The Ultra Secret* tells how the British and the Americans exploited the information they obtained from cracking German messages enciphered with a cipher machine named the Enigma. So valuable was this intelligence that it was given a special security classification, ULTRA, which the intelligence itself came to be called. The author, an R.A.F. officer, was put in charge of distributing ULTRA under tight security to Churchill and to commands around the world. Winterbotham therefore saw much of the output and in this book has correlated it with the events of the war.

The stories he tells are revelations.

During the Battle of Britain, ULTRA told the R.A.F. Fighter Command well in advance of radar detection how many bombers would be thrown against England and when.[1] This enabled the British to parcel out their few fighters so that some would always be available to attack an oncoming wave. These tactics denied the Germans command of the air over England and consequently any possibility of invasion.

During the campaigns in North Africa, ULTRA kept General B. L. Montgomery informed fairly exactly of General Erwin Rommel's order of battle and, in some cases, of his plans. It also enabled the British to know when supply ships would sail from Italy—and to sink them, thus eventually starving Rommel of vital fuel. Another intercept led to the Battle of Cape Matapan, which turned the Mediterranean from an Italian to a British lake.

The tide of the Battle of the Atlantic turned when ULTRA dug deep into the naval Enigma in 1943 and revealed where the U-boats met their milch-cow supply submarines. Throughout the tough fighting in Normandy, ULTRA delivered masses of intercepts from Hitler's messages on down, often within hours of their dispatch. This, "probably ULTRA's greatest triumph," Winterbotham says, led to "the destruction of a large part of the German Army in the west."

Dozens of such stories crowd *The Ultra Secret*, which is filled as well with sketches of the famous as Winterbotham, this bringer of good and bad tidings, saw them (Churchill was always polite). This makes exciting reading, and it constantly provides fresh insights into some of the best-known episodes of the war, for even the official historians did not have access to ULTRA intercepts. The new material makes the book essential to the historiography of World War II.

But all is not exactly as Winterbotham tells it. He exaggerates the importance of ULTRA, calling it "decisive" and writing as though it alone won the war.

Everyone now agrees that ULTRA was of supreme importance, and that without it the war would have lasted longer. Even General Mark Clark, criticized here for not exploiting ULTRA properly during the Italian campaign, acknowledges that the reading of some Hitler signals saved his neck during the Anzio landings. But neither Marshal of the Royal Air Force Sir John Slessor, who wrote the foreword, nor Vice Admiral Sir Norman Denning, who was in charge of the Admiralty's U-boat tracking room, would say, in answer to my questions, that without ULTRA, Britain would have lost the battles of Britain and the Atlantic.

Winterbotham, however, seems often to suggest that merely cracking the Enigma sufficed to win the war. Of course it did not: otherwise things would have been a lot easier. But though Winterbotham himself sometimes gives cases where knowledge of German signals could not affect a battle, usually for lack of men or guns, cases where no messages were intercepted, and also cases where a change of plan falsified ULTRA information, his attitude of ULTRA-won-all negates them.

This tone is the basic flaw of the book, the reason the general reader needs to salt its information with knowledge of how wars are won. It is why the book is not history but merely a contribution to it. One that has to be checked, at that.

Winterbotham has written from memory 30 years after the events, using messages in the German archives to refresh his recollection of intercepts where he could, so it is not surprising that errors stipple the text. The American solutions of the Japanese diplomatic and naval cryptosystems had nothing to do with the breaking of Enigma. Winter-botham's attributing the original Enigma solution to information from a Polish employee of the cipher machine factory cheats the Poles of credit for one of the great cipher solutions of history. The facts are these:

On July 15, 1928, Polish cryptanalysts noticed a decided change in the letter frequencies of German army cryptograms, which they were intercepting. The Poles quickly concluded that the Germans had begun using the Enigma, which was invented and publicly sold early in the 1920s. Purchase of one of the commercial models showed that the Reichswehr had altered it for secrecy.

In 1932, the Polish Biuro Szyfrów (cipher bureau) got additional man-power in the form of three young mathematicians, Henryk Zygalski, Marian Rejewski and Jerzy Rozycki. They had achieved a partial solution in their office, hidden in the forest of Pyry outside Warsaw, when Po-land's French allies furnished some key Enigma documents.[2] Major Gus-tave Bertrand of French cryptographic espionage had obtained them from a Reichswehr cipher unit employee, Hans-Thilo Schmidt, who wanted money. (Bertrand has told this story in his book, *Enigma*.) With this help, the Poles completed their solution, and on July 26, 1939, pre-sented two reconstructions of the machine to the French and two to the English.[3]

These enabled the British codebreaking unit at Bletchley, a small town 50 miles northwest of London, to solve the later variations of the machine and other machines used for different branches of the German armed forces. Security forbade Winterbotham from recounting these details, but he properly and generously credits the achievement. To generate up-to-the-minute solutions for these other machines, incidentally, the Bletchley geniuses evolved perhaps the first modern electronic computer, which they nicknamed the COLOSSUS.

Why has this story remained under tight wraps so long? It seems that after World War II, Britain gathered up as many of the tens of thousands of Enigmas as she could find and later sold them to some of the emerging nations. Presumably if she could read Enigma messages in 1940, she could do so in 1950. Only recently have these countries replaced their Enigmas with new cryptosystems.

From *Army* magazine (April, 1978), 73.

THE MAN WHO BROKE PURPLE: THE LIFE OF COLONEL
WILLIAM F. FRIEDMAN, WHO DECIPHERED THE JAPANESE
CODE IN WORLD WAR II

*by Ronald Clark*

Little, Brown & Co., 271 pp., $8.95.

One approaches this book with anticipation. By an experienced biographer of scientists, whose work includes well-received lives of Albert Einstein and Bertrand Russell, it deals with a fascinating subject: William F. Friedman (1891–1969), America's top cryptologist. He led the team that in 1940 solved the main Japanese cipher machine, which the Americans codenamed PURPLE (following the ORANGE and RED machines).

Ronald Clark provides many new details about Friedman. He pens a good portrait of an intellectually brilliant, psychologically insecure man—jealous of his prerogatives, insisting on being addressed as "Mr.," always in coat and tie. He tells how one day Friedman and three subordinates solved, between 11:12 A.M. and 2:43 P.M. (with 50 minutes out for lunch), a cryptogram enciphered on a new machine touted as unbreakable.

He describes Friedman's anguish over the fact that his great PURPLE solution did not prevent—and, in my opinion, could not have prevented—Pearl Harbor. He reveals secret Friedman missions to England in 1957 and 1958, apparently to restore cooperation with Britain in reading other NATO countries' cryptosystems.

He reports the despicable needling of Friedman by security officers of the National Security Agency. And he discloses Friedman's despondency and possible suicidal tendencies. The author attributes these to an inner conflict between Friedman's morality and the impropriety of reading other people's mail—a false ascription, in my view, because thousands of other people did not succumb to it. (The causes of Friedman's neuroses were, I believe, of classical psychological origin.) All of this is set down in a style that is usually fluent and interesting.

On the other hand, none of the fundamental elements of the book are new. It cannot be said that Clark expands or changes in any significant way the known outlines of Friedman's life. Aside from a standard printed source that provides much of this outline and that he never cites, the author also used Friedman's annotations on his collection of cryptologic books, his private correspondence (which, however, has nothing on his official work), and interviews with his widow.

He seems not to have sought to have material declassified, nor to have interviewed more than one or two of Friedman's former associates. This has entailed the central failure of the book. Clark's account of the solution of the PURPLE machine, the heart of his story, adds nothing—either in new material or as a fresh dramatic retelling—to what has already been printed.

The reader hungers for more details of what that pulse-pounding struggle against Oriental secrecy was like, how it felt to work in a team with Friedman, what his contribution was compared to those of other army and navy cryptanalysts, and the sense of gathering doom that must have permeated the work. All this belongs in a popular history, and the story surely merits it. But author Clark gives us none of it.

There are other failures as well. Potentially one of the most important areas of the book deals with the enormously valuable post–Pearl Harbor effects of the PURPLE solution.

General George C. Marshall said in 1944 that "our main basis of information regarding [Adolf] Hitler's intentions in Europe is obtained from [Ambassador] Baron Oshima's messages from Berlin reporting his interviews with Hitler and other officials to the Japanese government." Yet Clark gives us not one new piece of data about this.

The thinness of his research has compelled him to pad the book with a number of twice-told tales that have nothing to do with Friedman, such as the shooting down of Admiral Yamamoto. Numerous errors of detail further show that Clark has not taken the trouble to acquaint himself sufficiently with the science about which he is writing.

It is not the case that the frequency counts of substitution ciphers reveal the language of the underlying plaintext. The Japanese J-19 system was not a machine. The World War I German ADFGVX cipher was never betrayed by a message sent in the clear. Codes are not ciphers. And so on.

In the end, the anticipation sours to disappointment. The overwhelming impression that I get from this book is one of perfunctoriness. It is as if Clark set himself a deadline and refused to change it. One can write news stories like that, but not books. The result is that he has cheated a man who deserves a far finer monument.

From *The New Republic* (March 17, 1979), 28–31.

ULTRA GOES TO WAR

*by Ronald Lewin*

McGraw-Hill, 398 pp., $12.95.

PIERCING THE REICH: THE PENETRATION OF NAZI
GERMANY BY AMERICAN SECRET AGENTS DURING WORLD
WAR II

*by Joseph E. Persico*

Viking, 376 pp., $14.95.

To read these two books together is to take a short course in military
intelligence. Lewin's book tells about the Allied breaking of German
ciphers—called ULTRA from its supersecret nature—and its effect on
World War II. This feat has rightly been called "the most important
sustained intelligence success in the history of human conflict." Persico's
work relates how the Office of Strategic Services, the predecessor of
the C.I.A., sent spies into Hitler's Germany. The dedication of the spymasters and the bravery of the agents is unquestioned. But the results
were almost trivial, practically not worth the effort.

The pattern laid down then persists today. Spy reports stand second
to technological data—communications intelligence and satellite photography—in the secret information presented to policymakers: the technological material is usually harder, cheaper, fresher, more voluminous,
and more trustworthy than spy reports. Men believe pictures and intercepts. They doubt spy reports. They fear that the agent may only report
accurately just to lure his recipient into a trap. This shortcoming has
led intelligence agencies to use spies mainly to suggest targets for the
other means of collecting intelligence.

In a sense, the eclipse of the spy—the replacement of man by machine—constitutes the Industrial Revolution of intelligence. The process
really began in the great watershed of World War I. The only thing
strange about it is that it took so long to be recognized. Perhaps the
chief causes of *this* cultural lag were the novels of Eric Ambler, Ian
Fleming and John LeCarré.

Like their books, Persico's is a good read. He spins an exciting tale.
A good example is his story of the O.S.S.'s DUPONT mission. Headed
by a tall, good-looking California former dentist, Lieutenant Commander
John Taylor, the four members of the group—the three others were

anti-Nazi Austrians—parachuted in October 1944 onto the marshy eastern shore of the Neusiedlersee, a shallow lake southeast of Vienna. "The
untimely call of marsh birds sounded in the night. The members of
the DUPONT team were sounding their prearranged rendezvous signal."
But as they were burying their parachutes, the airplane that had dropped
them made a second run, trying to drop supplies that had gotten stuck
in the bomb bay. This alerted the Germans: "Searchlights stabbed the
darkness and red-orange bursts of antiaircraft fire illuminated the sky.
. . . DUPONT's arrival on enemy soil had been announced with fireworks
and flashing lights." Meanwhile, "the parachutes bearing their radios
were floating down onto the calm surface of the Neusiedlersee."

The team spent much of its time moving from one town to the next
to avoid arrest. Taylor observed signs of construction of a major defensive line, but without his radio he was unable to report it. An attempt
to send a sympathizer to another O.S.S. team failed. The Austrian members sought contacts to get shelter and help. These brought only temporary assistance. And finally a gamble failed: a potential contact betrayed
two members of the team to the Gestapo. They were arrested, and soon
afterward Taylor and the other man were seized after a savage struggle
in the hayloft where they were hiding, and were sent to the Mauthausen
death camp. Taylor survived to testify at Nuremberg.

Persico has pieced his story together from excellent sources: mainly
documents from the O.S.S. files and some of his 86 interviews. (Had
he footnoted his facts, his work would have been a much better source
for historians.) He has fleshed out his fast-paced tales with details of
the technical side of espionage—the forged documents, the "legends"
invented for the agents, the communications techniques, the problem
of recruitment. And he has given admirable sketches of the often colorful
spies and spymasters, many of whom later became prominent in the
C.I.A. and in other sectors of American and European life.

What came out of all the effort he vividly describes? What great secrets
of the Reich did the O.S.S. spies discover?

Very few. Their reports dealt with the observable minutiae of military
movements and installations. The HAMMER group reported from Berlin
that the Klingenberg power plant was operating and that one railroad
marshalling yard had 26 freight and 18 passenger trains. The GREENUP
team reported the departure of trains for Italy via the Brenner Pass—
enabling the U.S. 15th Air Force to destroy virtually an entire convoy.
Another agent reported the movement of a German army headquarters
and the location of ammunition dumps; his intelligence too "put bombers
into the skies." But none of these dealt with high matters of state; none

revealed any of Hitler's top secrets. Though one anti-Nazi in the German Foreign Office came to the O.S.S. on his own with helpful intelligence, the O.S.S. never recruited and never inserted the classic kind of spy, the agent-in-place.

If the informational level of the reports was low, so was their volume. At the end of 1944, the O.S.S. had a total of three agents inside Germany. All told, it inserted only 200. The most fecund team sent back 52 messages. In the end, O.S.S. spies contributed no vital intelligence to the Allied war effort. Perhaps nothing demonstrates this better than the report—not mentioned by Persico—that the head of O.S.S. passed to President Roosevelt during the frightening Hitler onslaught that became the Battle of the Bulge. It was an analysis of stories in Swiss newspapers.

The origins of American spying needed recording, and Persico has done a fine job with it. The trouble is, it didn't matter.

What did matter was Allied codebreaking. Four years ago, Group Captain Frederick W. Winterbotham stripped the veil from this longest-kept and second-greatest secret of World War II (after the atom bomb). But his book, *The Ultra Secret*, epochal though it was, was largely a memoir, with all the limitations of that genre, and it incorporated several serious mistakes. Now Ronald Lewin, a British military historian with several books and a major prize to his credit, corrects and completes the story in this fascinating work. Michael Howard, Chichele professor of the history of war at Oxford, is right when he says that this is "perhaps the most important book to have appeared on the Second World War since Chester Wilmot wrote *The Struggle for Europe* a quarter of a century ago."

*Ultra Goes to War* recounts the story of the work of the 10,000 British codebreakers and assistants and details the effect of their output on the war. Housed mostly at Bletchley Park, an ugly Victorian estate surrounded by temporary wartime structures in the exurb of Bletchley, about 50 miles northwest of London and equidistant from Oxford and Cambridge, they formed a galaxy of genius that in its breadth and brilliance has probably never been equaled before or since. Chess grandmasters, mathematicians of renown, novelists, poets, classicists, physicists, publishers and other businessmen, editors, soldiers and Wrens [members of the Women's Royal Naval Service, a wartime auxiliary] worked around the clock to solve cryptograms in Germany's top ciphers, translate and evaluate the results, and pour them out in a stream of hundreds of messages a day to high commanders in the field, to the chiefs of staff, to Churchill. The intercepts included the orders of and reports to Hitler himself. What a contrast in insight and in volume to the meager results of the spies! And what a difference they made to the conduct of the war!

In one of his most dramatic episodes, Lewin tells of the impact of ULTRA upon the battles in the Normandy hedgerows. At the end of July 1944, a massive British offensive that was to shatter the German front and clear the way for an American breakout had thrown the Germans into disarray. On August 2, the breakout began, with the Americans streaming through the narrow Avranches gap. The next day, Hitler radioed his western front commander that

> the armored divisions which have up to now been employed on that front [the one facing the British] must be released and moved complete to the left wing [opposite the Americans]. The enemy's armored forces . . . will be annihilated by an attack which these armored formations—numbering at least four—will make.

The Allies intercepted this order and made their preparations. Lewin tells how the American commander and his air corps chief stood with their ULTRA intercepts in their hands and grinned at one another and said, "We've got them!" And they had. When the German counterattack was launched on August 7, the Americans checked it before the sun stood at its zenith. It was, Lewin writes, "a model example of ULTRA's power to guide a brilliant commander all the way to victory by supplying precise foreknowledge of the enemy's intentions." During World War II, and even World War I, only technological means furnished information fast enough and with enough certainty to make possible victories like that. No spy ever has.

In addition to serving as an ideal case history for technological intelligence, Lewin's book may also serve as a model of how to write about intelligence in general. For unlike so many writers on this subject, who all too often seek to show how secret information alone has won victories, Lewin repeatedly emphasizes that not intelligence but men, weapons, and willpower win them. This imparts a verisimilitude, a balance to his book that makes it much more truthful and much more useful.

*Ultra Goes to War* also corrects for a wide audience two major canards that Winterbotham inadvertently originated and others have broadcast. One is that Churchill deliberately sacrificed Coventry by not warning the city of a German air raid he had learned of through ULTRA because to do so would risk exposing that priceless secret. Lewin cites documents and interviews to show that this is "a monstrous distortion." The other falsehood is that a spy in the German Enigma cipher-machine factory betrayed the secret of the device. This deprives of their rightful credit three young Polish mathematicians who in the 1930s cryptanalyzed the Enigma. Lewin restores to them the honor of having made one of Poland's great contributions to mankind.

His book has, however, a few flaws of its own. All are minor. He follows Winterbotham in ascribing a central role to ULTRA in the Royal Air Force's defeat of the Luftwaffe in the Battle of Britain. But people who were working on Luftwaffe intercepts at the time have said recently that this is an exaggeration and that, when the documents are examined, ULTRA's role will probably be found to be distinctly minimal and inferior to that of radar. Lewin is sometimes harsh on the American cryptanalytic organization, though its solution of the Japanese PURPLE cipher machine was never equaled by the British. U.S. Army Chief of Staff General George C. Marshall called the intercepted PURPLE messages of the Japanese ambassador in Berlin "our chief basis of information regarding Hitler's intentions in Europe." Lewin omits all this. He skimps the critical role ULTRA played in sending ships and planes directly to where U-boats were to sink them, though Churchill called the Battle of the Atlantic "the dominating factor all through the war." The book all too rarely cites the specific source of a fact, thus unnecessarily diminishing its value as the work of reference it is sure to become.

The greatest disappointment in *Ultra Goes to War* is in the writing. The style is workmanlike and clear, but it is flat. At the moments of great victory, when the human mind triumphs over the Gordian intricacies of a cipher, or the Allies satisfyingly rout the forces of evil, the soul cries out for a thundering climax, for a crash of cymbals and a blare of trumpets, to set the seal on a magnificent achievement. Lewin doesn't provide it, and the reader will feel the lack.

This is regrettable. But it is, after all, not essential. Michael Howard declared that "all historians must now read what Lewin has to say before putting pen to paper." He is again right. *Ultra Goes to War* will long remain fundamental in the historiography of intelligence and of World War II.

As submitted to the *Chicago Sun-Times*, which published a slightly trimmed version on February 28, 1982.

## THE AMERICAN MAGIC: CODES, CIPHERS AND THE DEFEAT OF JAPAN

*By Ronald Lewin*

Farrar, Straus & Giroux, 332 pp., $14.95.

Ronald Lewin, author of the justly acclaimed *Ultra Goes to War*, the story of how the British solution of German ciphers helped defeat Hitler, has here written its American counterpart: the tale of how U.S. code-breaking helped beat Japan. Alas, it in no way matches the excellence of the previous book.

MAGIC was the cover name given to the American solutions of Japanese messages. (Sometimes the solutions were also called ULTRA, though this was primarily applied to British readings of German messages.) MAGIC played a critical role in the war in the Pacific. The Battle of Midway, which halted Japan's offensive and put that nation on the defensive, was made possible in large measure because U.S. Navy crypt-analysts had cracked the Japanese naval code JN-25b. Admiral Isoroku Yamamoto, the imperial navy's commander and Japan's most charismatic leader, met his death as a consequence of information revealed by code-breaking.

The island empire was starved of food and supplies by American submarines, who often knew where Japanese convoys were in the vast wastes of the Pacific because American codebreakers had found out. Solutions of Japanese army messages helped American commanders in winning their victories on the dozens of landings and land battles in their island-hopping campaigns. And, towards the end of the war, code-breaking revealed the frantic efforts of Japan's diplomats to keep Russia neutral and to persuade their government to sue for peace.

If much of this—except for the material on the Japanese army—produces an effect of déjà vu, it is because the stories are indeed thrice told. Unlike ULTRA, which was revealed only in 1974, the effects of crypt-analytic success in the Pacific have long been known. The author might have overcome this problem with a strong narrative drive steadied at various points by analysis, with a greater use of color, by telling about the thoughts and feelings of the cryptanalysts (available through interviews), and by going more deeply into individual episodes. But these opportunities have not been grasped.

The fundamental flaw of the book, however, is that it never comes to grips with its subject. Everything is hazy, in soft focus. We do not get the feeling of an author in control of his material. We get no vivid picture of the personalities and their interplay, of what the cryptanalysts did all day, how Japan's codes were broken, how many codes were solved, how many messages a day were read, how the solutions were turned into finished intelligence, how important an intelligence source code-breaking was compared to others—all of the information that would have shown that the author understands codebreaking, has viewed it as a whole, and has set it into the context of the war.

The dominant impression is of undigested sources thrown together and of an undisciplined pen churning out enough words to make a book. The author seems to be writing off his photocopies. In his text he constantly cites documents, which not only reinforces the sense that he is being run by them but also destroys all dramatic tension. His chapter on the messages of the Japanese diplomats in Berlin is unrelated to what his own subtitle calls "the defeat of Japan." Whole sections have nothing to do with codes but deal instead with noncryptologic personalities and strategies.

The haziness is intensified by the inexcusable slackness of the writing. It is the windiest this reader has seen for a long time. Needless phrases, gratuitous and pointless comments, adjectives, rhetorical questions, strained and unilluminating metaphors are everywhere. And the writing is careless. "It is a curious fact that the British probably learned . . ." is just a short example. Lewin always wrongly uses "less" before numbers instead of "fewer." He repeats quotations, one three times. A couple of chapter titles are, if not offensive, thoughtless. Small errors fleck the work. Clausewitz is misquoted. Some names are wrong. And a remark that the Japanese PURPLE cipher machine could encipher scientific language as well as diplomatic is inane, for it makes as much sense to say that a typewriter could tap out both.

The remark also reveals that Lewin has not learned the technicalities of a technical subject, and this, with the consequent failure to dominate his subject, is perhaps one reason that the book is so disappointing. Another is that Lewin, knowledgeable though he is about the campaigns in Africa and western Europe and the China-Burma-India theater, seems at a loss in the largely naval war run by Americans. A third may stem from the book's most curious feature: after telling about some major feat of cryptanalysts that led to an Allied victory, Lewin scants the military outcome. For example, after a chapter devoted to the codebreaking that resulted in the triumph of Midway, he says of that crucial battle only that "Here it is enough to say that the Japanese stretched their bow to its uttermost limit, and it cracked." Again, of the shooting down of Yamamoto by American airplanes, perhaps the single most spectacular result engendered by cryptanalysis, he says little more than "The rest is history." This strange technique cheats the reader of the denouement for which he hungers.

But has this book no redeeming virtues? Can it not at least serve as a useful compendium of the codebreaking of the Pacific war? It does bring together in a single volume the outlines of that achievement. But this, its sole merit, is nullified by its inadequacies.

# CODES IN CONTEXT

# The Defense
# of Osuga,
# 1942

Much has been written about military intelligence, and much of it is rubbish. Many writers fictionalize, hoping that no one will be able to check their work in the gloom of fake identities and destroyed documents. Many concentrate on spies, neglecting the other, often more important sources of information and omitting the vital function of evaluation. They regale the reader with tales of the spies' great coups, but almost never say what effect—if any—these had on the course of wars or battles.

Indeed, in the whole vast literature of military history, there is, to my knowledge, no study of the workings of all facets of intelligence in a single operation. Scholars, of course, have mentioned the role of intelligence in battles, and have sometimes even acknowledged its essential contribution, as at Tannenberg and Midway. But no one has taken a battle, traced the various strands of information used in it to their sources, seen how they were woven together into a picture of the enemy and his intentions, and judged how they helped or did not help in winning that battle.

This article attempts such an analysis. At the suggestion of Dr. Earl F. Ziemke, it utilizes as a case history the German defense against the

"The Defense of Osuga, 1942" first appeared in the Winter 1981 issue of *Aerospace Historian*. Its unique contribution is mentioned in the second paragraph.

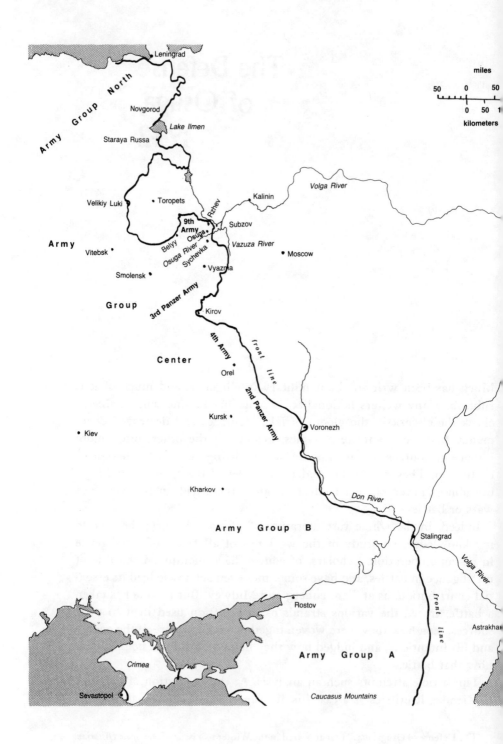

miles

50   0   50

0   50   1

kilometers

Leningrad

Army Group North

Novgorod

Lake Ilmen

Staraya Russa

Volga River

Kalinin

Velikiy Luki

Toropets

Rzhev

Subzov

Army

9th Army

Osuga

Vazuza River

Moscow

Vitebsk

Belyy

Osuga River

Sychevka

Osuga

Smolensk

Vyazma

Group

3rd Panzer Army

Kirov

Center

4th Army

Orel

front line

2nd Panzer Army

Kursk

Voronezh

Kiev

Kharkov

Don River

Army Group B

Stalingrad

Volga River

Rostov

Astrakha

Crimea

Army Group A

front line

Sevastopol

Caucasus Mountains

major Russian attacks on the 9th Army salient of Army Group Center in November 1942. There were several reasons for this choice: documentation was relatively complete, the tactical situation was easy to understand, the methods and organizations for acquiring enemy information were by then well developed in the German army, and the outcome was clear-cut. The case also affords an excellent instance for showing how radio intelligence contributed to that victory and how it fit into the overall pattern of intelligence, supplementing other sources and being itself supplemented by them. Here, then, is a study of military intelligence in action that seeks to close a major gap in military historiography.

## I

When the Russian front stabilized early in 1942, the remnants of the advance on Moscow still bulged toward that city, only 112 miles away. This bulge presented a good springboard from which the Germans could try again to capture the capital. Consequently, in the summer of 1942, the Russians had struck hard at it.[1]

They merely dented it, however, and left a kind of bulge on the bulge. This was a trapezoid thrusting northward. Its base, trending southeast, formed part of the general front. Its body stuck out like a fat thumb on a palm-up right hand. This thumb was formed by one of Army Group Center's four armies, the 9th. On the eastern face of the thumb, the 102nd Infantry Division held a narrow portion of the front. It defended this as, toward the end of summer, the Russian attacks began to die slowly away.

During these days, Adolf Hitler and the German high command were concentrating upon their drives farther to the south—on the Caucasus and on Stalingrad. Except in areas under attack, as in the 9th Army sector, the question of what the Russians would do next probably did not much concern them. They were dictating to the Russians, and any thoughts of the Russians dictating to them remained inchoate and secondary. But when they viewed the 9th Army trapezoid as they surveyed the thick paired blue and red squiggles that marked their own and the enemy's lines on their large tan situation maps, various possibilities arose vaguely in their minds.

One was for the Russians merely to contain the salient and use the forces that had assaulted it at other points on the front. Another was to feint against it, to trick the Germans into holding troops there while a main Russian offensive came elsewhere. A third was to renew the attacks. And a fourth was to strike heavily both at the salient and else-where.

Of these possibilities, the first two and the last seemed least likely. Most probable seemed a resumption of the attacks. Both the situation—the salient still threatened Moscow—and experience—the Russians had already tried to eliminate it—argued for it. But one of the most successful weapons of warfare is surprise, and surprise consists precisely in doing what the enemy regards as unlikely. Thus the other possibilities stayed alive.

Such considerations owed everything to military imagination and nothing to military intelligence. One task of German intelligence was to draw the attention of the generals to the enemy and to help them crystallize their unformed impressions of his possible course of action. This it did by furnishing new information about the foe that would point to one Russian course of action as more probable than the others.

For the eastern front as a whole, this job fell to a branch of the Army General Staff called Foreign Armies East. The head of this 200-man unit was Lieutenant Colonel Reinhard Gehlen, a brilliant, slender, ener-getic officer. To Foreign Armies East pulsed streams of information about enemy activities from every source. Around 8 A.M. and 8 P.M., intelligence officers at the army groups submitted their evaluations and reports, which they had in turn distilled from similar reports of lower commands. High-level aerial reconnaissance, radio intelligence, and espi-onage units reported to it. It translated captured documents and interro-gated prisoners for strategic information. Twice a day it assembled all this material into an enemy situation report, which Gehlen brought in writing to the morning and evening situation conferences of the army chief of staff. There the stiff and correct gray-clad officers, with the eagle-borne swastika on their right breasts and the double carmine stripe indicating membership in the general staff on their trousers, dis-cussed what these enemy activities meant and how they had to take them into account in their own plans.

On 29 August, Foreign Armies East, taking a long-range view, pre-dicted that the Russians would have considerable offensive potential in the winter. Where would they use it? Most probably against Army Group Center, to eliminate the threat to Moscow and to gain a success where the configuration of the front would not overtax the tactical capa-bilities of the lower commanders.[2] As of 13 September, however, the intelligence branch had not yet discovered any signs of such an attack. It viewed the Russian rail traffic observed by the Germans northwest of the 9th Army trapezoid as mainly bringing up replacements of men and materials for the still-continuing summer battles.[3] Indeed, two days later, Foreign Armies East, foreseeing an enemy offensive against Army Group B, which had driven a salient to Stalingrad, and assuming that the Russians did not have enough strength to carry out two offensives at once, declared that the troops for this southern attack would have to come from the front opposite Army Group Center.[4] But then, on 17 September, Foreign Armies East began to reverse itself. It hinted that something bigger than local attacks might be up in the 9th Army area. Though it could not tell whether or not the observed rail traffic exceeded that needed for simple replacement, it had planted the seed of this possibility.[5]

Toward the end of the month, the Germans saw the Russian rail traffic radiate from originally only northeast of the trapezoid to towns opposite its eastern and western faces as well. None of the latter traffic advanced toward the German front opposite the western face of the trapezoid—toward the palm facing the thumb.[6] What did this mean to Chief of the General Staff Franz Halder? He read all this as indicating that the Russians were reinforcing and restocking their units around the trapezoid.[7]

Soon the Germans observed the Russians pulling troops out of the front south of the trapezoid and making heavy rail movements elsewhere along the front. Halder advanced a step in his estimate of the situation. The Russian forces assembling around the 9th Army were battle forces.[8] He did not yet venture to predict a Russian attack, perhaps because of a counterindication. The Russians appeared to be shifting to a defensive posture around Rzhev, a port on the Volga with major road and rail connections that formed the northeast cornerstone of the 9th Army block and that had been the unsuccessful target of the Russian summer attacks.[9] They redistributed their artillery in depth and reduced their offensive activity. On the other hand, an unusual Russian operation suggested that they had not lost interest in the trapezoid. On 24 September, 300 to 400 Russian paratroopers dropped into the salient.[10] They sought to sabotage the important rail line that ran north and south just behind the eastern face of the trapezoid, bringing supplies into Rzhev. One of its stations, before which the 102nd Infantry Division was committed, was a village called Osuga. On 1 October, Russian long-range artillery succeeded in destroying the rails and a water tower there and in temporarily interrupting the trains.[11] All these obscure and contradictory glimpses of enemy activity kept the Germans from forming any clear picture of Russian intentions.

But the movements of Russian troops continued. The Germans observed a concentration around Toropets, a town between the 9th army thumb and the palm of the other German forces. Presumably they were there for an attack. But where? Hitler thought that they would strike south to deepen the cleft between the thumb and the palm. The danger of this split might compel the Germans to pull out forces from the south, where they were fighting for Stalingrad. Hitler's military experts held views different from his. The head of the Armed Forces Operations Staff, General Alfred Jodl, thought that the Toropets forces would form one prong of two—the other coming from the east—designed to amputate the thumb.[12] Gehlen's Foreign Armies East steered a middle course. It concluded in the middle of October that the pattern of movements foreshadowed a major winter operation, probably against the middle and the left wing of Army Group Center.[13] On the left was the 9th Army.

## II

Formed for the Russian campaign, the 9th Army had acquitted itself well during the advance toward Moscow. It had lost some luster during the retreats of the winter of 1941 and 1942, but it remained a tough and resilient fighting force. Its commander was the dynamic Colonel General Walter Model, 51, almost a caricature of the Prussian officer with his monocle and his laconicism. But his men revered him. When he took command in a difficult situation in January 1942, his officers had asked him what he had brought to carry out the operations he was proposing. "Myself!" he replied—and burst out laughing. A Nazi in thought, he represented the new type of commander: the favorite of Hitler who specialized in stubborn defense.[14] Model was a good if not a great general, for he performed well one of a general's essential functions—to make a decision and to stick resolutely to it despite the constant, well founded, and conflicting importunings of subordinates to change it.

To supply the information he needed to reach his decisions and to expand these decisions into the detailed orders of troop movements, supply, signals, and the like that they entailed, he had a staff. Regulations prescribed its organization, which was essentially the same at the different levels of German army command.[15] At its head (except at the division level) was the chief of staff, the commander's main assistant, able to issue orders for him in his absence. Model's chief of staff was Major General Hans Krebs, 44, once an assistant military attaché in Moscow and destined to become Hitler's last chief of the general staff. Under him the staff had six sections, each indicated by a roman numeral, with subsections marked by an appended small letter. The I a, or first general staff officer, was the operations officer. He planned and supervised the carrying-out of German operations. This was a responsible and interesting post, the goal of all young general staff officers.

Intelligence was handled by the I c, or third general staff officer. (The I b post, for supply, existed as such only in homeland or peacetime units; at the front, a quartermaster dealt with supply.) Like the I a, the I c was normally a member of the general staff, a corps of about 1,000 highly intelligent, hardworking officers who had been trained at the War Academy and were the pick of the army. Because of shortages in general staff officers, however, the I cs at nearly all divisions and many corps were reserve officers.[16] At all other levels, the I c was younger and less experienced than his superior, the I a.[17]

The I c of the 9th Army was Colonel Georg Buntrock, 37, a small, wiry infantryman, in the general staff since 1938, who had come from a divisional I a post in the Crimea.[18] To get to his next real goal, I a of a corps, which had been promised him, he had to learn intelligence. He had never handled this work before and, in fact, had abhorred it. "I saw in the I c service only the heavy responsible toil, the queer resigned work far from troop life and battle, in the midst of which I had been up to now."[19] But his eyes began to open during an "interesting and gripping" three weeks at Foreign Armies East, in which "I was surprised to observe and experience how this branch succeeded in unveiling the hidden image of the enemy situation."[20] Before taking up his new duties he worked for 10 days with his predecessor at the 9th Army, an old friend, who had set up a well running I c apparatus. On 30 July 1942, Buntrock became I c of the 9th Army in its headquarters at Sychevka, a small town with a large freight yard on the railroad to Rzhev near the southeastern corner of the trapezoid. "It took some time before the nature of the I c service opened up to me in all its ramifications and possibilities. But then it enthralled me."[21] He saw the post's independence and value; he mastered the characteristics and usage of the various organs of reconnaissance and the evaluation of their output; he became fascinated at discovering the enemy mentality and tactical development and the personalities of the enemy commanders. So when Model later refused to part with Buntrock for the corps job, Buntrock discovered that he was glad to stay in intelligence.[22]

His intelligence staff was tiny: two adjutants, two interpreters, two Luftwaffe liaison officers, and a handful of clerks, typists, and draftsmen. (Six other officers handled his nonintelligence duties, such as censorship, counterespionage, and troop entertainment.)[23]

He obtained the information he needed to make intelligence estimates for the 9th Army from sources identical to those used by Foreign Armies East. A great deal of the information, and the most basic, stemmed ultimately from the front-line troops' reports of enemy activity. This could range from full-scale attacks through harassing fire and patrols down to simple digging at the front and movements of truck and troop columns in the rear. More came from the divisional interrogations of enemy prisoners and deserters. These reports formed the meat and potatoes of Buntrock's estimates. Spicing them were the more exotic forms of intelligence: army-level aerial reconnaissance, radio intelligence, espionage, and observation of enemy artillery.[24] He assembled all this into his twice-daily reports—written, oral, and graphic—to Model and Krebs and to the Army Group Center I c.

What situation faced Buntrock in that fall of 1942? The 9th Army did not have the overall view of the situation that the Führer headquarters did and, in the manner of subordinate echelons everywhere, it felt that its sector was particularly endangered. The preparations that Foreign Armies East had so cautiously weighed in the balance of the entire war with Russia were seen at the 9th Army as clearly directed against it. Eventually, however, the views of the topmost echelon coalesced into a congruence with those of the 9th Army. On 29 October, Buntrock drew up a comprehensive report that summarized the past weeks of observation and teletyped it at 7:30 P.M. to the army group headquarters in Smolensk.[25] It agreed in essence with the Foreign Armies East analysis of two weeks earlier. The enemy would mount a major offensive against the 9th Army, striking both the east and the west faces of the trapezoid. Buntrock did not have to spell out the probable objective of the attack, because he could assume that the army group's general staff officers, trained in the same school as he, would see it as he had. This objective was to break into the trapezoid from both sides, encircle the troops in it, annihiliate the 9th Army, crack open the front, destroy Army Group Center, and seal this victory by advancing in triumph to recapture Smolensk.[26]

But this recognition did not end Buntrock's work. On the contrary, it merely started it. For he now had to ascertain in detail where and when the Russians would attack. Only with this knowledge could Model properly dispose his reserves and choose a time neither too early nor too late to raise his troops to a pitch of watchfulness. Buntrock began to refine his determinations.

Though he could not yet specify a date for the attack, he could give a nondate: not within the next day or so. Buntrock believed that the

Russians would synchronize their blows and that, while they had completed their preparations in the east, they had not done so in the west.[27] An increase of transport to Toropets and from there to the Russian front at the west of the trapezoid, spotted by German air reconnaissance the day after the next, tended to confirm Buntrock's views.[28]

At the same time, the question of "Where?" began to clarify itself: on the eastern face of the trapezoid, which was held by the XXXIXth Panzer Corps. The 9th Army usually had four to six corps distributed around its defense perimeter. Of these, the XXXIXth Panzer Corps, which had been in the forefront of the great German advance into Russia in 1941, had only recently been transferred to it.[29] The corps commander was General Hans-Jürgen von Arnim, who half a year later would win notoriety in North Africa when he surrendered the last of the German forces on that continent.

In these days, as October turned to November, something unusual attracted the attention of the Germans to the corps' northern wing. The Russians sought to camouflage their activity with smokescreens,[30] but air reconnaissance spotted a battalion-strong column marching toward the part of the front opposite the XXXIXth's northern wing.[31] Though Russian traffic had declined somewhat, it remained noteworthy.[32] Then, on 3 November, the Germans detected a further strengthening of this sector. Probably through prisoners of war taken during the three previous days by raiding parties, the Germans learned that Russian Artillery Regiment 1165, last observed on 20 August at Rzhev, had arrived at Kudrino, a village opposite the northern wing of the corps.[33] On this wing stood the 102nd Infantry Division.

## III

The 102nd Infantry Division was better than its relatively high number perhaps suggested. It had been put together in September 1940 out of regiments from three active divisions and thus was virtually the equivalent of an active division itself. It had fought in the Russian campaign from the start and had more than a year's battle experience.[34] The Russians, a captured document showed, rated it as especially high grade.[35] With its commander on leave, its 2,477 combat troops[36] were commanded by the artillery officer, a colonel. Its Ic was a reserve captain, Dr. Friedrich Lange.[37] To assist him he had two adjutants and two translators, mainly used for interrogating prisoners. Because the division had lain in its position for several months, he knew the terrain fairly well.

This was flat, open farm land. The uncultivated fields were speckled with bushes; here and there grew scraggly woods of mixed deciduous and coniferous trees. To the north stood a few low hills. Innumerable little Russian villages, including Osuga, dotted the area. Each had its single street with houses lining both sides. They seldom lay more than half a mile from one another. Through this terrain the division's front lines ran north and south. Cutting them diagonally to the northeast flowed the Osuga River, a meandering stream, some 75 feet wide, that was soon joined by the similar Vazuza River. The two then spilled into the Volga.

On the steep left bank of the Osuga the 102nd had erected its field headquarters—a few long wooden bunkers with earthen roofs topped with sheet metal. The division commander had one, his staff another. Here they lived and worked. Toward the front, the troops had gradually built up a system of field fortifications.[38] From them and from the hills, they could look over into the enemy territory between the two rivers and see the Russian troops eating, moving, and digging; sometimes they could hear them as well.

The increase in Russian strength opposite the 102nd that the army Ic had noted on 3 November in the form of the new artillery regiment manifested itself more directly to the division two days later. The Russians had been harassing the division by day and by night with long-range fire, some of it on Osuga.[39] On 5 November it included for the first time shells of all calibers and salvos of 16 rounds, which suggested the arrival of a "Stalin organ," or rocket gun. That afternoon, aerial reconnaissance confirmed the presence of two new Russian battery positions before the division. This fit with the growth in artillery just north of the corps detected over the past weeks by an artillery observation battalion.[40] Such battalions located and ranged enemy guns by a line of visual observation posts that spotted their muzzle flashes and a line of microphones that picked up their muzzle roars. Though the Russians sought to confuse these posts by rapid staggered firing and by frequently changing their firing pits, Observation Battalion (Panzer) 116 ascertained that the number of the guns along a road to the north of the corps had recently doubled.[41]

This indication of a gathering of enemy forces was but one of many all over the Army Group Center front early in November. Everywhere Russian movements quickened. Long-absent armor appeared before the 9th Army. Several hundred men marched toward the front before the 102nd Division and its neighbor to the south, the 5th Panzer Division.[42] A Russian reconnaissance and raiding party attacked the 5th's lines. And from all along the army group front, prisoners and deserters reported that the Russians intended to attack on 7 November, Red Army Day. Gehlen, concerned at Foreign Armies East with the overall situation, wondered whether this would be the great offensive everyone was waiting for, or just a series of local attacks.[43]

This question was more academic at the lower echelons, which would have to fight much the same way against either. There the physical evidence for an early attack continued to mount.

During the night of 5–6 November, the 102nd threw back a probing Russian attack, supported—as if to show that it was serious—by three or five tanks. On 6 November, a division at Rzhev saw 800 to 1,000 men coming up to the front opposite. Air reconnaissance spotted considerable train traffic leading to the fronts around Rzhev and on the east of the trapezoid. Heavy artillery and grenade fire harassed the northern sector of the XXXIXth Panzer Corps. Movement grew lively in front of the same sector: before the 102nd, 600 to 700 men marched toward the front in company-sized groups. A Soviet radio message intercepted at the division hinted at an attack. The meaning of all this, however, was interpreted variously by different German intelligence officers, depending on their different perspectives. Buntrock, at 9th Army, thought it all amounted merely to further preparations.[44] Lange, at the 102nd, regarded it as readying for an immediate attack, but he was not panicked into thinking it would be a major offensive, for he wrote, "On the basis of the observations up to now, there appears to be insufficient enemy forces for an undertaking with an operational semistrategical goal."[45]

The next day was Saturday, 7 November, Red Army Day. Despite the deserter statements, little seemed to be happening. Artillery harassed the north wing of the XXXIXth.[46] Before the 102nd, where trench traffic was normal and movements in the rear slight, the most unusual Ic event of the day was a Russian smokescreening of a shifting of two antitank guns in a gully.[47] Later, a 43-year-old Red Army soldier, Private Kurganov, deserted to the Germans. One of Lange's interpreters, Boris Pudkewitz, interrogated him. A shoemaker from Kursk, Kurganov had received 45 days of training to become a machinegunner. He confirmed the location of his unit, the fourth company of the second battalion of Rifle Regiment 426, which the 102nd knew. Its assignment was defense, but Kurganov said that a Russian attack was planned toward Rzhev and Sychevka. He did not, however, know the date.[48]

Night fell without any attack. But 20 minutes before midnight, a barrage crashed thunderously down upon the 102nd. For more than two hours, the Russians bombarded the division with guns of all calibers from all directions. The Red Army Day attack was at hand! The German artillery returned fire against the gully between two villages where earlier a babble of voices had created the impression of a large assembly of men.[49] The men in the trenches gripped their rifles, ducked when shells screamed in, and peered over the parapets of their field fortifications to see the enemy.

No infantry advanced. The barrage died out. Still the Germans waited anxiously. Who knew what the Russians might be up to? But as day broke, sunny and bright, with no further sign of enemy activity, tension ebbed. Red Army Day had come and gone without the predicted attacks. The Russians had thrown the Germans off balance. They had raised anticipations—and then had not fulfilled them. This anticlimax led the Germans to some frustration, some fatigue, and possibly a slight loss of confidence in intelligence and command. But these effects at best were minor, and the Germans renewed their efforts to foresee the real attack.

A great tense calm settled over the front. The unresolved questions of the time and place of the major Russian offensive hung in the electric air like a cloud of ions. But the respite gave the German command time to digest a comprehensive appreciation of the situation before Army Group Center that Gehlen had issued on 6 November. This supplemented his regular daily main report—which, on that same day, had included an arresting dispatch from Germany's star spy against the Soviet Union, codenamed MAX.

Under this signature MAX's reports became famous among dozens of intelligence officers. His true identity was known to very few. He was Fritz Kauders, a tubby, half-Jewish, Viennese ex-journalist in his mid-30s.[50] He operated out of Sofia, where he seemed to spend the days in cafes meeting people and the nights dining well and chasing women. But his villa on broad Patriarkh Evtimiy Boulevard in the heart of town housed not only himself but a squad of radiomen. They picked up faint messages from deep within Russia, which Kauders rewrote, annotated, and then passed back to the radiomen for re-enciphering and transmission to Berlin.[51] There, the Abwehr, the German armed forces espionage agency headed by Admiral Wilhelm Canaris, forwarded them after a cursory evaluation to Foreign Armies East.

Much was obscure about MAX. How had he been selected for the job? Why had Canaris himself approved his appointment, and then forbidden the Sofia Abwehr unit from mingling at all in his affairs?[52] Most mysterious of all were his sources. Some Abwehr members whispered that he got his information from the Japanese, who still had representatives within Russia.[53] Another theory was that his sources, originally cultivated by White Russians, lay among elements eager to topple the Communist regime.[54] Yet they seemed to include people at the very center of power, for they reached into the Kremlin itself. And they seemed—at least to the Abwehr, to Gehlen, and to some high commanders at the front—to be utterly credible and unimpeachable. Foreign Armies East often gave him its imprimatur by distributing his dispatches as appendices to its daily situation reports.[55]

The message Gehlen attached to his report of 6 November was dated two days earlier. Reported MAX: "On 4 November war council in Moscow presided over by Stalin. Present: 12 marshals and generals. In this war council the following principles were set down: a) Careful advance in all operations, to avoid heavy losses; . . . f) Carrying out all planned offensive undertakings, if possible before 15 November, insofar as the weather situation permits. Mainly: from Grozny [out of the Caucusus] . . . in the Don area at Voronezh; at Rzhev; south of Lake Ilmen and Leningrad. The troops for the front will be taken out of the reserves. (The area around Toropets seems to be meant with the term 'south of Lake Ilmen')."[56]

This spy report, apparently exposing the basic Russian strategy approved by Stalin himself, tallied with Gehlen's views. It further supported his comprehensive appreciation of 6 November. This sought to answer, in the framework of the entire eastern front, where and when the major Russian offensive against Army Group Center would come.

"Before the German east front," began Gehlen, "the point of main effort of the coming Russian operations looms with increasing distinctness in the area of Army Group Center." Gehlen then backtracked and wondered about the forces that the Russians had been assembling further south, at Stalingrad, around the tip of Army Group B, which had conducted one of the two German summer offensives. Would the attack there be larger, or would it be limited by an insufficiency of forces, which would prevent the Russians from seeking a decision in two places at once? This, Gehlen hedged, was "still unclear." His next consideration, however, in effect iterated his first sentence. "The enemy's attack preparations in the south are not so far advanced that one must reckon with a major operation here in the near future simultaneously with the expected offensive against Army Group Center." He backed this up with presumed Russian reasons for their choice of Army Group Center for an imminent decisive operation: the political and military need for a quick big success, "which the enemy believes he can obtain better at Army Group Center than at Army Group B"; the greater advantages for assembly and jumping-off points offered by the front at Army Group Center; the possibility of destroying Army Group Center and cutting off German forces to the north contrasted with the greater difficulties and lesser exploitation possibilities of the southern operation. He portrayed the likely enemy onslaught in all its awesome sweep: "simultaneous enveloping attacks . . . to dislodge and destroy the north-eastward-jutting block of Army Group Center." Among the attacks would be a punch to the southwest through the eastern face of the 9th Army trapezoid. He concluded by explaining the apparent inconsistency of the Russian forces seemingly not sufficing for so gigantic an offensive. More forces were probably there than he had detected; others could be brought up rapidly; the Russians had often set goals too distant for the forces they used.[57]

All this could not have surprised the high command, nor shifted its thinking. For it but amplified what Gehlen had said as far back as 29 August and had been repeating in his daily reports, and the high command had come to adopt his view of the enemy situation as its own.

Could they, however, have been the victims of a massive Russian deception? Could the various indications of attack preparations that the Germans had seen all have been fakes, designed to fool the Germans into thinking that the attack would come at one point while it would really strike with surprise at another?

In practical terms, no. To preclude betrayal by deserters or prisoners, the Russians would have had to convince riflemen at the deception point that they were going to attack and riflemen at the real point that they were not. They could do this by sending supplies to the one and withholding them from the other. But on the one hand they did not have so much—nor does any army[58]—that they could squander them like this, and on the other, the attacking troops truly needed guns and ammunition. Could the dozens of trains that the Germans observed have been running empty? The Russians desperately needed them to actually carry men and supplies. The same need would keep them from emplacing hundreds of guns in woods and firing them merely for show. Moreover, if all these observations involved deception, where would the "real" attack come?

It would require some preparation, and these measures would almost certainly leak out on a front as engaged as the Russian. More to the point, the Army Group Center bulge legitimately tempted the Russians with an "attackable" front and a rich prize. All this argued against deception. Gehlen might have erred in assessing the operation against Army Group Center as larger than the one to the south, as this assumed knowledge of Russia's total strength. But in deciding in general where these operations would come, he almost certainly had not fallen for a gigantic hoax.

## IV

The high command had more time to consider this during the vast calm that had gradually come over the Army Group Center front early in November, becoming especially marked from about 8 November.[59] The reason was mud.[60] Twice a year—during the spring thaw and during the autumn rains—the unpaved Russian roads turned into quagmires. Axle-deep, the thick, clinging mud drastically slowed all movement, German as well as Russian. This "mud period" lasted about four weeks, until the ground dried or froze. In 1942 the rains began in mid-October.[61] A week after they had started, prisoners were telling Germans that the mud period had somewhat immobilized the Russians.[62] The frost that set in,[63] at first at night, and then during the day as well, was for many weeks not hard enough to solidify the ground[64] to support tanks. Mud continued to hinder operations. The calm persisted.

Particularly on the 9th Army perimeter, scouting and raiding virtually ceased. The Russians thinned out their front lines,[65] in part to reduce the number of deserters and potential prisoners, in part apparently to deceive the Germans as to where their strength lay. The older, defensive units, such as the deserter Kurganov's, generally remained in their front-line position to prevent clues seeping out from any insertion of strike forces. These assembled deep in the rear. Forces nearer the front were forbidden to leave during daylight the houses in which they were quartered. No bivouac fires were permitted. Secret police sought to keep soldiers from talking with the civilian population. In some strips, civilians were evacuated. Nearly all Russian radios fell silent. The few that did transmit did so under strict discipline. Strong fighter and antiaircraft forces sought to deny Russian areas to German aerial surveillance. Opposite the 102nd Infantry Division, enemy troop movements appeared from their regularity to constitute not reinforcements but merely reliefs.[66]

Did all this quiet mean that the Russians had abandoned their attack intentions? No, for the Germans could detect the continued, half-concealed quiverings of the Russian war machine through the veil thrown over it.

Energetic aerial reconnaissance in the early morning hours—usually with the Focke-Wulf FW-189, a twin-engine plane carrying a pilot, gunner, and observer—often spotted small units as they scurried into their daylight shelters. The frequency and extent of these discoveries suggested a major movement, carried out at night. Aerial reconnaissance also observed heavy rail and truck traffic, including night convoys with headlights on. This traffic presumably was bringing up still more supplies.[67] MAX disclosed the shipment of 110 tanks and other armored vehicles from Moscow to the forces that would attack Rzhev. Later he reported that the equivalent of two divisions of men, who had just arrived in Moscow from the Urals, were being transported to three towns around the northern and eastern fronts of the 9th Army trapezoid to serve as future replacements.[68] Artillery continued to pour in before the 102nd: 22 new batteries in the first ten days of November.[69] Lange thought that the proportion of artillery to infantry was too great. Either, he postulated, the enemy was using dummy guns or, as deserters to the 5th Panzer Division to his right reported, infantry replacements as well as a whole new division were to come up. This, he said, would give the enemy picture "a thoroughly offensive nature."[70]

Despite the Russian radio silence, a few units transmitted,[71] either in error or with special permission, or because they were beyond the silent zone. These beepings tickled the alert ears of German radio intercept operators, basis of the extensive radio intelligence organization. This organization consisted of intercept and direction-finder nets, each with an evaluation center that fed results to a particular command. The 9th Army, for example, had a short-range radio reconnaissance company as the 11th company of its signal regiment. The company had set its three direction-finding teams in a convex arc beneath the western leg of the trapezoid; they took fixes on the location of Russian transmitting stations. Its intercept platoon was in a small village in the same area, not far from the company command post.[72] Army Group Center had a larger agency, quartered in the former secret police building at Smolensk,[73] while a still more comprehensive one served Foreign Armies East.[74] The proliferation of the radio intelligence units reflected the German army's recognition that they produced results more valuable than any other agency of military intelligence.[75]

It was this organization that ethereally detected the presence of five new Russian army staffs. Three lay around Moscow, two—more ominously—northeast of Rzhev.[76] Experience had shown that such staffs, which served at first mainly to house, train, and forward units, could also become battle commands. Radio intelligence also ascertained that motorized formations had been brought up opposite the 9th Army's western front,[77] and it contributed to German knowledge of three air corps headquartered in towns to the east of the Army Group Center bulge.[78]

On 13 November, the XXXIXth Panzer Corps drew a map that graphically exposed the enemy's intentions in its sector.[79] The map located enemy divisions opposite the corps, giving the boundaries between one division and another. Most held fronts of moderate extent, but in two places divisions were packed into a tightly compressed area. One was opposite the southern end of the eastern leg of the trapezoid; the other was opposite the 102nd Infantry Division. Because in war superiority in manpower at the point of attack is regarded as one of the preconditions for victory, it seemed reasonable that the Russians would attack where their troops were massed.

This and similar evidence pointed to specific locations on the eastern, northern, and western faces of the trapezoid as targets for the attack. Lack of transports or scouting in other areas pointed away from those areas. Suddenly, in one of those quiet places, off the northwest corner, a deserter reported the presence of a panzer corps. Radio reconnaissance hints about an assembly of forces, and espionage suggestions about the bringing up of forces apparently confirmed the original report, and the Germans considered the possibility of an attack there as well. Next day, however, they somehow determined—perhaps by special interrogation of prisoners—that the Russians had collected these forces for fear of a German attack, and that they had been dispersed.[80] But German fears had been aroused, and for the next few days, in their attempts to read the cloudy portents of the future, they anxiously scanned every item of intelligence about this corner. These included a deserter's "unbelievable" report about six more divisions behind the lines, "inconclusive" radio reconnaissance showing two armored brigades from another area now communicating with the Russian army command there, and increased scouting and raiding.[81] But when Buntrock saw no solid indications of attack preparations, he dismissed the raiding as a deception,[82] and the northwest corner faded from German concern.

At about this time, the quiet around the 9th Army declined to a stillness.[83] Enemy activity all but disappeared from German view. At the 102nd, day followed clear day. The air was calm and hazy. The temperature hovered in the low 20s.[84] The ground and the roads were hardening. In their lines, the Germans built up their field fortifications, stood watch, lined up for meals, and kept an eye on the enemy. Nothing special was occurring; the attack did not seem imminent. The days grew shorter; the orange sun cast its shadows longer and longer across the stubbled fields.

In the world outside, historic events were taking place. The British attack on the German-Italian forces at El Alamein late in October had developed into a rout for the unbeatable Rommel. At the other end of North Africa, the Americans had landed. The Germans occupied Vichy France. On Guadalcanal, the U.S. Marines advanced. At Auschwitz, five new crematoria had begun to smoke.[85] Gehlen, watching the Russian buildup in the south, reassured his superiors that though an attack could be expected there soon, "the available enemy forces may be too weak for far-reaching operations."[86] The army talked more, however, about Hitler's recent replacement of Halder as chief of staff with the relatively junior Kurt Zeitzler and about his pullback of his headquarters from near Vinnitsa in the Ukraine to his compound in East Prussia.[87] The Army High Command, with Foreign Armies East, moved back into the wooden huts of its nearby lakeside encampment. Hitler himself soon left for Munich,[88] where, on the 19th anniversary of his beer hall putsch, he shouted at his party comrades: "On this very day, which represents for us the memory of the worst collapse of our movement, a collapse that for many then appeared to mean the end of the party, I can only say: For us National Socialists this memory must betoken an enormous strengthening, a strengthening to defy every danger, never to waver, never to weaken. . . ."[89] Then, with Eva Braun, he departed for two weeks of relaxation in Berchtesgaden.

The men of the 102nd barely heard these tintinnabulations of the great world. It was all too distant to affect them. What mattered was when the attack would come, and that on the 17th low clouds ended the succession of bright days, and snow fell.[90] The mud period had ended.

## V

The next day, 18 November, the ten days of calm ended as well. The Russians shattered the stillness with a peppery harassing fire onto the wings of the 102nd. The fire included rocket guns. For the first time, the division observed skiers and sledge parties in winter clothing.[91] It heard the enemy digging and hammering. Though all this could not be said to reconfirm that the attack would be directed against the division, it did nothing to repeal that likelihood. And, at a higher level, the first good possible answer to the vexing question of "When?" finally came in.

It had been transmitted by the Abwehr post in Rumania, that unwilling ally of Germany. From circles around the Swedish legation in Bucharest, the German spy agency had heard that the Russians would soon open an attack with all available forces in the Rzhev area aiming toward Smolensk.[92] Foreign Armies East and the various I cs were already aware of this. But the next two items were new. The assault would be commanded by Marshal Georgi K. Zhukov, whose assignment had been approved only five days earlier by Stalin himself. And the dispatch specified, for the first time among all the German intelligence reports, a date for the attack: 27 or 28 November. But all this came probably at fourth or fifth hand from a place far from where the decision was made and far from where the attack would come. The source could have had his own reason to deceive the Nazis. The report required confirmation.[93]

On the 19th, a Thursday, the Russians loosed the attack far to the south[94] against Army Group B that Gehlen had foreseen, had regarded as secondary to that expected against Army Group Center, and had only the day before predicted would have a limited goal.[95] The intelligence officers within Army Group Center and its subordinate commands asked themselves anew when their turn would come. Answers came in with increasing frequency. But they differed.

After the Russians had lost 26 men in feeling out the 102nd's left wing with raiding parties against Hill 207.3 on Friday, 20 November, the division brought in a Russian who had sought to avoid capture by playing dead. Under interrogation, he said that an attack was planned for the last days in November or the first in December.[96] An earlier date came in the same day from a radio station in Russian territory feeding information to a commissar who had deserted to the Germans on the 9th Army's western front: at least in this sector, the attack would be made at 6 A.M. on 25 November, the source said.[97] The differing reports left the precise date undetermined.

The location, on the other hand, was repeatedly reconfirmed. The raids against Hill 207.3, which lay athwart the front line, had pointed yet again to the 102nd as one of the targets of the enemy attack.[98] So did many other indications. Traffic grew livelier between the Osuga and Vazuza Rivers.[99] The Russians again reconnoitered in strength against the 102nd's left.[100] German airplanes spotted signs of heavy troop occupancy of the woods before the center and the north wing of the XXXIXth Panzer Corps.[101] The regular German ten-day artillery check showed that Russian guns had become denser before the corps since the 10th.[102]

Not every item fitted neatly into this pattern. A deserter who arrived in the middle section of the 102nd stated that he belonged to Rifle Regiment 521. But this was an element of Rifle Division 133, whereas up to this time Rifle Division 88 had stood for weeks opposite the 102nd. Had the Russians shifted their troops? Deserters, prisoners, and captured papers almost daily had reasserted the presence of the 88th. Lange thought that the deserter simply had slipped away from his own division to the neighboring 88th before crossing over.[103] Another contradictory fact came to the attention of Buntrock at 9th Army. Radio intelligence stated that the Russian VIth Panzer Corps had withdrawn from opposite the trapezoid's eastern face. Buntrock acknowledged that this would weaken the Russian blow, but could neither refute the fact nor explain it.[104]

The German preparations for defense continued. Model flew in his light plane almost daily to the fronts,[105] where on a caterpillar-tracked motorbike he inspected fortifications, viewed the enemy, discussed the situation with officers, and showed himself to the troops.[106] The number of Russian deserters, who clearly wanted to avoid dying in the assault, swelled. They were questioned about the attack date. One said the 25th, another the 22nd, still another the 26th, which he had heard at a conference. But Buntrock said on Saturday, the 21st, that he could not yet see any preparations active and tense enough for those dates.[107]

This picture began changing the next morning and intensified the next day. Enemy movements quickened. Supply traffic increased. Ski units appeared. Infantrymen received snow clothing. Artillery massed. The number of deserters rose during the night to a flood. And now they agreed overwhelmingly that the attack was set for Wednesday, 25 November.[108]

At 10 A.M. Monday, the 9th Army teletyped its subordinate corps: "According to deserter statements Russian attacks will begin on the 25th or 26th of November. Greater defense readiness is to be secured everywhere. Reserves including those of the higher commands are to be held ready for the most rapid commitment. . . ."[109] Early in the evening, enemy radio traffic suddenly leaped into life. The listening Germans sensed that the armored formations had arrived. The intercepts enabled them to determine the presence of a whole Russian army headquarters in the west that they had previously merely suspected.[110] During the night many Russian scouts felt out the center and the northern wing of the XXXIXth.[111] In the 102nd's sector, a raiding party struck at Hill 207.3. Prisoners told of 250 tanks as well as artillery and mortars assembled opposite the division.[112] As the morning of Tuesday, 24 November, dawned, German soldiers could see movements that spelled a strengthening of the enemy's front troops. With binoculars, German officers scrutinized the new bridges across the Vazuza capable of carrying tanks.[113] The XXXIXth's artillery observation post detected eight new enemy guns firing, several of them rocket guns.[114]

Tuesday, on the basis of all these indications, Buntrock finally concluded that the enemy attack was imminent.[115]

The Army High Command freed its own and Army Group Center's reserves. Model ordered German artillery to harass the enemy's suspected points of assembly. His chief of staff, Krebs, passed to the corps some clues to Russian tactics that German press monitors had extracted from a recent article in *Izvestia:* the Red Army owed the success of its offensive in the south to short but strong artillery preparation, to attack in the dawn's earliest light, and to far-set goals.[116] At 6:20 P.M. Tuesday, the 24th, the XXXIXth alerted its divisions by teletyping them an abbreviated version of a warning it had received that morning from the 9th Army. This stated that the attacks would begin on the 25th or the 26th and called for increased readiness.[117] Finally, at 8:40 P.M., the corps ordered the 102nd: "From the 25th to the 26th positions are to be fully occupied between 4 A.M. and full daylight."[118] In this order, which put the German troops in a posture of readiness well before the attack, culminated the work of the Ics. A finishing touch was put to it when the corps forwarded the *Izvestia* summary to its divisions.[119]

Midnight came, and with it Wednesday, 25 November. The troops tried to sleep. At 3:45 A.M., a quarter of an hour before they were to take up their positions, they were surprised by a sudden Russian attack in battalion strength just where the Osuga River cut the 102nd's front line.[120] Was it a last-minute probe for a weak spot? An attempt to throw the Germans off balance? A real attack made with nothing to lose and the hope of perhaps wedging an entry? A mistake? The Germans did not know and seemed to care less. They threw it back with little difficulty. Along the rest of the line, the troops, now in position, tensed. At 5:55 the first shells of what soon developed into a barrage fell upon them. The false alarm of Red Army Day had started this way, too, but now the indications for an attack were much more certain. The Germans steadied. For an hour and a half the bombardment lasted, and when it lifted, at 7:30 A.M., the brown masses of Russian infantry emerged from their assembly places in the woods. Tanks, 25 thundering, spitting monsters, rolled forward to support them. Wave after wave of Russians advanced against the 102nd Infantry Division.

The Germans were ready. Standing in their trenches, they fired over their parapets into the enemy masses sweeping forward over the barren fields. Their machine guns raked the Russians. Antitank guns cracked flatly; field guns roared. And the Russians fell. A handful reached the German lines and were captured. Others charged forward. But at 9:40

they paused to catch their breath. When they renewed their attacks, this time in a light snowfall, the men of the 102nd again drove them back. The end of the day found the Germans firmly in possession of their lines.[121] They had repulsed, right at "the presumed point of main effort,"[122] "on the very day"[123] that they had expected it, the strongest onslaughts of the "anticipated"[124] Soviet winter offensive.

## VI

The German success that day was followed by others as the Russians flung their mighty forces for weeks against the great block of the 9th Army. Here and there they broke in, but they bounced off the 102nd, which successfully protected Osuga and the rail line. And, in general, the 9th Army had held, had preserved the integrity of Army Group Center, and had persisted in its irritating jut toward Moscow. The Russian plans shattered upon that trapezoid. Superb operational intelligence, which had forewarned the troops and their commanders with precision of enemy intentions, had contributed in no small degree to that defensive victory.[125]

But that success was, like all others in Hitler's Reich, only temporary. Eventually the 9th Army had to withdraw.[126] The situation would compel it. The Russian offensive in the south that Foreign Armies East had seen as secondary and limited[127] had bitten off the German salient and had encircled and destroyed a German army. It had done so at a city of rubble and doom and glory whose name has become immortal. Stalingrad.

# Potential Enemies:
# The United States Views
# Germany and Japan
# in 1941

How important was intelligence in assessing the plans and capabilities of the potential enemies of the United States before December 1941?

This paper concludes that intelligence played a distinctly subordinate role. Nonintelligence factors contributed far more to forming American plans. Against Germany, these factors were geography and events. Since they accurately depicted the real world, they guided American leaders effectively. Against Japan, the factors were racial prejudice and a presumption of rationalism. Since they did not present the reality of Japan, they harmed American planning. Yet, insignificant though it was, intelligence was gathered, analyzed, and presented to America's leaders, who considered it in making their decisions.

In examining prebelligerency American intelligence, this paper will discuss (i) the nonintelligence factors that shaped American expectations; (ii) the sources of American intelligence; (iii) the machinery for evaluating it; (iv) the specific intelligence available on the plans and capabilities of Nazi Germany and the use made of it in U.S. planning; (v) the same for Japan; (vi) the reasons that American intelligence failed to achieve significant results against Japan, which would have enabled it to overcome the prejudices that blinded American leaders about Japan's intentions and so perhaps to foresee the Pearl Harbor attack, and gained less specific information about German strength and intentions than it might have.

This paper was prepared for the conference on Potential Enemies at Harvard University, 11–13 July 1980, under the chairmanship of Professor Ernest May.

The paper focuses on Germany and Japan because Italy was relegated in the minds of American planners to being merely the follower of Germany.

I

The potential for America's conflict with her two World War II enemies was created decades before 1941. The rise of Japan, with her defeat of China in 1895 and of Russia in 1905, clashed with America's new interests in the Far East in the form of the 1898 annexation of the Philippines. Germany's expansionism alarmed the U.S. at the end of the 19th century, and the U-boat threat to American trade routes led in 1917 to hostilities. These preconditions intensified American concern about later events, beginning in Asia with the occupation of Manchuria in 1931 and in Europe with the accession of Hitler in 1933. There followed the militarization of both countries, the aggression against Ethiopia, the suppression of liberties in Italy, Germany, and Japan, the takeover of the Rhineland, the German and Italian help to Francisco Franco, Japan's attack upon China, Germany's invasion of post-Munich Czechoslovakia, the discrimination against Jews, the spying against the United States (revealed in a series of sensational cases), the onslaught against Poland, the fall of France, the takeover of Indochina. All these demonstrated a greed and an antidemocratic tendency that suggested that the United States might some day be the target, if not the victim, of the aggressors.

What about the Soviet Union? It was committed, at least in theory, to overthrowing the capitalist system. Its agents were constantly being exposed. It occupied part of Poland, attacked Finland, and absorbed the Baltic states. Many Americans hated and feared it. But many other Americans, though vexed by its inflammatory propaganda and overwhelmingly sympathetic to little Finland,[1] appeared less concerned about its intentions. Its internal problems, such as the purges of the late 1930s, distracted and sapped it, while its territorial aggressions—as against the Baltic states—seemed confined to its traditional sphere of influence. Moreover, the Soviet Union was neither a neighbor nor a world trader nor a colonial power, so conflicts over territory or markets or strategic outposts could hardly arise. Ideology was the only possible cause, and that was an exceedingly improbable one. Furthermore, any war between the United States and the U.S.S.R. would have to be fought across either Europe or Japan, both of which possibilities were highly unlikely. Perhaps as a consequence of these considerations, the Army, though strongly anticommunist, never formulated a war plan against the Soviet Union.[2] When Secretary of State Cordell Hull remarked at a meeting in September of 1940 that Russia could not be trusted, Secretary of War Henry L. Stimson agreed but observed that "her interests in the Pacific ran parallel with ours [meaning against her old rival Japan] and that probably she could be trusted to go along as far as her interests went and that was all we need ask."[3] Public opinion polls in December 1938 and January 1939 found that, if a war broke out between Germany and Russia, 83 to 86 percent of the respondents would rather see Russia win. In July 1941, after this war had actually started, though 47 percent thought that Germany would win and only 22 percent thought that Russia would, 72 percent wanted to see Russia win and only 4 percent Germany.[4] And on 1 October 1941 the United States agreed to supply material for the Soviet war effort. So the United States had not only never considered the Soviet Union a potential military enemy, but had actually moved to help her against what was regarded as a much more threatening enemy, Germany.

It was what Germany and Japan did that made them appear as dangers to Americans and America's leaders. Japan's aggressions in China, including the rape of Nanking and the bombing of the *Panay*, angered many Americans, and Roosevelt responded by imposing economic sanctions on Japan. As Japan continued her menacing activities in an area where the United States had many possessions and interests, such as the Philippines and, with its rubber, the Netherlands East Indies, tension rose between the two nations. The United States increased its pressure upon Japan, culminating in such demands as that Japan withdraw from China and support the Nationalist government there. These would have required Japan to reverse its whole course of foreign policy; they were, consequently, unacceptable to it. The United States, on the other hand, would not acquiesce in Japan's aggression. The two moved on a collision course.

But geography made the danger from Germany appear more imminent than that from Japan. Germany was closer. Early in 1941, Roosevelt explained the geographical aspect of the German threat in a fireside chat. Declaring that the Nazi threat extended to Dakar, the Azores, and the Cape Verdes, he noted that these "are only seven hours' distance from Brazil by bomber or troop-carrying planes. . . . Control or occupation by Nazi forces of any of the islands of the Atlantic would jeopardize the immediate safety of portions of North and South America, and of the island possessions of the United States, and, therefore, the ultimate safety of the continental United States itself."[5]

Intensifying concern about German proximity was the unstable, anti-

Yankee nature of the governments of Latin America. "Quislings would be found to subvert the governments in our republics," Roosevelt said, "and the Nazis would back their fifth columns with invasion, if necessary."[6] Still other nonintelligence factors led the United States to regard Germany as a more immediately probable enemy. Trade with Europe averaged a quarter more than with Asia and so more could be lost through German aggression than through Japanese.[7] Germany was opposed by the western democracies, including particularly Britain, with whom the United States had the closest possible cultural and economic ties. Hitler's anti-Semitic program created anti-German pressures by American Jews. And while diplomatic conversations with Japan gave at least the impression of checking aggression, Germany raged uncontrolled.

What strengthened the belief that Germany was a more immediate threat than Japan was America's conviction that Japan would not attack her. This feeling arose from two preconceptions in the American worldview: rationalism and racism.

American policymakers expected that the Japanese would act in a logical and reasonable way, which to them meant Occidental laws of thought. This presumption of rationality precluded one nation's attacking another whose population was double that of the aggressor and whose industrial output was nine times as great.[8] But the Japanese looked at the world differently. The United States, in their view, had consistently opposed Japan's interests, particularly the establishment of the Greater East Asia Co-Prosperity Sphere. American embargoes and demands, such as for Japan to withdraw from China, had grown increasingly obnoxious to the empire. In October 1941, the government that had been conciliatory toward the United States fell. The new and more aggressive government, under General Hideki Tojo as premier, concluded that submission to American demands would forfeit the power, the authority, and eventually the very existence of the empire. Diplomatic means were evidently not sufficient to secure Japan's ends. Yet war with the United States seemed to entail defeat. No matter, the government felt. The war had to be fought. Japan might lose if she went to war, but she would lose if she did not, the thinking went, so the war was necessary. The Japanese hoped that the destruction of America's Pacific Fleet, together with a ring of impregnable defenses around the island empire, would deprive the United States of the will and ability to dictate to Japan, which would then wax fat upon her conquests and prosper as the mistress of Asia. But even if defeat were foregone, one leader said, the nation would have to fight since Japan's existence was at stake. Tojo himself said that "at some point during a man's lifetime he might find it necessary to jump, with his eyes closed, from the veranda of Kujimizu-dera [a Buddhist temple on a Kyoto height] into the ravine below."[9] This samurai willingness to lead the nation to defeat, to, in effect, commit national hara-kiri, was incompatible with Western ways of thinking. And so the leaders of America failed to envision the possibility that Japan would attack her.[10]

The disbelief in a Japanese attack was reinforced by America's racial prejudice: its belief in the superiority of the white race. This led many Americans to underrate Japanese abilities. Racism asserted that neither the people nor the products of Japan were a match for those of the United States. Americans looked upon the Japanese as buck-toothed, bespectacled little yellow men, forever photographing things with their omnipresent cameras so that they could copy them. Such opinions were held not only by common bigots but by opinion makers as well. Attachés submitted reports denigrating the Japanese on racist grounds; the Office of Naval Intelligence issued one doing the same; the military press—the U.S. Naval Institute *Proceedings, Our Navy, Aero Digest, Aviation*—carried articles with similar comments; books incorporated racism as a fundament of their arguments.[11] A book by the widely known writer on naval subjects, Fletcher Pratt—his 1939 *Sea Power and Today's War*—differed only in compressing more aspects into less space than most of them. Pratt, like the others, sought to justify his prejudices by basing them on "facts":

> Every observer concurs in the opinion that the Japanese are daring but incompetent aviators; hardly any two agree on the reason. Four main theories have been advanced, explaining it on a) medical, b) religious, c) psychological, and d) educational grounds.
>
> According to the first postulate the Japanese as a race have defects of the tubes of the inner ear, just as they are generally myopic. This gives them a defective sense of balance, the one physical sense in which an aviator is not permitted to be deficient.
>
> The second explanation places the blame on Bushido and the Japanese code that the individual life is valueless. Therefore, when the plane gets into a spin or some other trouble, they are apt to fold their hands across their stomachs and die cheerfully for the glory of the Empire, where Westerners, with a keener sense of personal existence, make every effort to get the plane out of trouble, or bail out at the last minute. This explanation has been advanced by several aviation instructors who have been in Japan.
>
> The psychological theory points out that the Japanese, even more than the Germans, are a people of combination. "Nothing is much stupider than one Japanese, and nothing much brighter than two." But the aviator is

peculiarly alone, and the Japanese, poor individualists, are thus poor aviators.

Finally, the educational explanation points out that Japanese children receive fewer mechanical toys and less mechanical training than those of any other race.[12]

In the same vein, Pratt criticized what happened "as soon as Japan began to build her own warships instead of buying tailor-made vessels abroad." One top-heavy vessel capsized on her sea trials. When a cruiser with welded joints fired a salvo, she sprang her seams. Since riveting the joints would have given the ship excessive top hamper and insufficient freeboard, a turret had to be removed to reduce weight. "The whole story is typical," wrote Pratt with ill-disguised scorn. Even in copying the Japanese were inept, he said. For their patrol flying boat, commissions sent abroad reported on the best of the foreign seaplanes. "Japanese builders accordingly copied the Short hull, attached to it a pair of German-type wings and mounted a homemade copy of the Pratt & Whitney motor atop. They are still wondering why the combination did not give them world-record performance."[13]

Another writer, Captain W. D. Puleston, a former director of the Office of Naval Intelligence, was not so blatant in his book, *The Armed Forces of the Pacific: A Comparison of the Military and Naval Power of the United States and Japan*, published by Yale in 1941. Still, he wrote that "Japan has been energetic in her efforts to create naval aviation, but she is usually a phase behind. She cannot match in numbers the planes carried on American carriers, and what is equally important, her personnel cannot send planes aloft or take them aboard as rapidly as American personnel."[14] These remarks were in no way exceptional. They paralleled others in the military and general press.[15]

Thus rationalism and racism implied that Japan would not and could not seriously menace the United States. The consequent lack of concern, together with the closer and more voracious German threat, contributed, after the fall of France, to a basic realignment of American military policy.[16] In the 1930s and into 1940, when the United States, with a tiny army and a one-ocean navy, was not strong enough to win a war against both Germany and Japan, U.S. strategy had, in the words of the army's war plans chief, to "provide for a main effort on one front and a strict defensive on the other."[17] Because England and France were expected to contain Germany, the United States planned to make its main effort against Japan, leaving its Atlantic front on the defensive. France's collapse undermined the foundation of this policy. So, as the chief of naval operations, Admiral Harold L. Stark, and the army chief of staff, General George C. Marshall, put it: "If Japan be defeated and

Germany remains undefeated, decision will still not have been reached."[18] They drew the logical conclusion and promulgated what became the Allies's overall wartime strategy—to defeat Germany first—in the Joint Army and Navy Basic War Plan, Rainbow No. 5, of 26 May 1941: "Since Germany is the predominant member of the Axis Powers, the Atlantic and European area is considered to be the decisive theater. . . . If Japan does enter the war, the military strategy in the Far East will be defensive."[19]

And indeed, Germany did threaten America more. Policymakers had inferred from the succession of events in Europe that Germany would not refrain from aggression against the United States, and they were to be proved correct: Germany declared war on the United States four days after Pearl Harbor. Policymakers had inferred from geography that Germany was more dangerous than Japan, and they were right.

In making these decisions, military intelligence about Germany and Japan played no role whatsoever. Such matters as whether Germany had 100 divisions or 300 and whether Japan had 10 carriers or 20 were not even raised when policymakers examined the basic issues of strategy. When, on 13 June 1940, President Franklin D. Roosevelt put several questions to his army and navy intelligence chiefs, not one dealt with Axis plans, and only one with Axis strength.[20] When, in December 1940, the head of war plans asked the head of military intelligence "to prepare an Estimate of the Situation for use in formulation of Joint Army and Navy Basic War Plan Rainbow 5," the only question specifically on enemy countries concerned "the effect on Germany and Italy of steadily augmented air operations, combined with economic starvation through blockade."[21] When, at the same time, Marshall discussed, in a memo to Stark, keeping the fleet in the Pacific until a major offensive began against the Axis in the Atlantic instead of moving the fleet at once to the Atlantic, he did not mention German or Japanese forces or plans and, indeed, did not seem to be thinking of them at all.[22] And when, in October 1941, the War Plans Division prepared a strategic estimate, it likewise based it largely on geography and the military-political situation in discussing possible Axis moves and possible American actions.[23] The omission of intelligence from all these discussions of high policy shows how subsidiary it was to the nonintelligence factors.

## II

Still, intelligence did participate, though insignificantly, in the thinking of American leaders. What did it consist of?

Of the sources of information, six seem the most important:

1. diplomatic reports;
2. information from friendly nations;
3. military attaché reports (technically a subspecies of the diplomatic reports, but distinct enough in practice to merit a separate category);
4. radio intelligence;
5. the press, in all forms—newspapers, magazines, books, radio, and newsreels;
6. private individuals.

The list omits spies. For the United States had, in the years before World War II, no centrally run secret agents in foreign countries—only a few who assisted attachés.[24] The chief reasons appear to have been insufficient funds from Congress, a belief that setting up spy rings would not produce information worth the effort (compared, say, to what more attachés could provide) or worth the damage to relations in case of exposure, and a lingering sense of rectitude (though this was more rationale than reason, for it would not have stopped the creation of spy nets if they were thought needed any more than it blocked intercepting other nations' messages or the violations of citizens' rights during, say, the Palmer anti-Red raids of 1919 and 1920).[25] But, given the lack of success that most spy networks had during World War II, the American deficiency may not have been a very great lack.

To look at the six existing sources in turn:

The diplomatic dispatches maintained a practice that had continued unbroken since even before the United States had constituted itself a nation. In addition to conducting negotiations, diplomats resident in foreign countries reported on what was going on around them. They got their information by personal observation, by reading the newspapers (or translations of them made by their staffs), by talking with officials and private citizens of the host countries, and by exchanging information with other members of the diplomatic corps.

The top American representatives in the Axis countries were usually highly experienced diplomats or, if not, were otherwise highly qualified: they were not political hacks. Several—and this was sometimes more important than anything else—had personal ties to the president. Joseph C. Grew, a professional diplomat who had gone to Groton and Harvard with Roosevelt and once worked on the Harvard *Crimson* with him, had served as undersecretary of state and had been in Japan since 1932.[26] William Phillips had served in Europe, England, and China and as assistant secretary and undersecretary of state; he had been in Italy since

1937.[27] William E. Dodd, a Jeffersonian liberal and a professor of history at Chicago who had received his doctorate in Germany, served in Berlin from 1933 to 1938,[28] when he was replaced by Hugh Wilson, a quiet, pleasant, observant man who had been in the foreign service for 27 years and had been attached to the Berlin embassy twice before.[29] When Wilson was recalled by Roosevelt to protest the anti-Semitic orgy of November 1938, the embassy was headed by the chargé d'affaires, Alexander C. Kirk, a wealthy man of penetrating, original mind whom Roosevelt had as a guest aboard the presidential yacht and whom he once urged to stay on in a "Dear Alex" letter.[30] The quality of all these men was high.

Though they normally handled the high-level contacts, they were not the only persons in the embassies to probe and report. Subordinate officials—the first, second and third secretaries, the counselors—also did so. In addition, consuls in other cities of the host nations submitted information on activities in their areas of interest to the United States.

Not all of the information on Germany, Japan and Italy came from the American diplomats there, however. Much came from the American emissaries to countries that feared that they might some day become objects of Axis aggression. The officials of these countries were highly motivated to gain information about the Axis nations and often scored remarkable successes. Poland, for example, cracked the German Enigma cipher machine,[31] and France built up a fairly accurate picture of German rearmament.[32] Especially after war broke out, the statesmen of these enemies of the Axis gave portions of this information to American officials. Mostly these items came through the American representatives abroad. Chief recipients of them were the ambassadors in Paris and in London. In France, William C. Bullitt, a brilliant, charming, financially independent sophisticate who had served as the first American ambassador to the Soviet Union, attained extremely intimate relations with the statesmen of his host nation. In Britain, Joseph P. Kennedy, an long-time supporter of Roosevelt whom the British correctly regarded as defeatist, received less information than Bullitt.[33] Sometimes the information about the Axis was passed to American officials by foreign diplomats in Washington.[34] Much of it was, of course, calculated to win American support. Some attempts were less subtle than others. The chief of U.S. army intelligence noted in February 1941 that the British, who had been pressing for the dispatch of four America cruisers to defend Singapore, had reported almost simultaneously in Washington and from Tokyo, Vichy, and London the imminence of a Japanese attack. "It is difficult to believe that all of this pressure . . . is coincidental," he minuted. "It all looks very like concerted British pressure on us to commit ourselves in the Far East. . . ."[35]

Some information came directly to American leaders from the leaders of the nations fighting the Axis. Winston Churchill and Roosevelt began corresponding when Churchill was still first lord of the Admiralty and continued when he became prime minister.[36] At the Atlantic Conference of August 1941, when the two met, the British chiefs of staff passed assessments of Germany to the American joint chiefs and discussed strategy with them.[37]

The main sources of American information about the Axis nations' military capabilities, so helpful in determining intentions, were the military and naval attachés, their assistants and their air specialists in those countries. They formed part of a tradition reaching back, in the United States, to the 1880s.[38] They constituted part of the staff of, and had their offices in, the U.S. embassies in Berlin, Tokyo, and Rome. Like the other diplomats, they gathered their information from newspapers, from official publications such as training manuals, from talking with officers of the host armed forces, observing equipment and troops at parades and maneuvers, and touring army camps and naval vessels, and exchanging tidbits with other attachés.[39] Sometimes, attachés were attached to host country army units for extended periods. In August 1937, for example, Captain Merritt B. Booth was assigned for ten days to Japan's 38th Infantry Regiment at Nara. Discussing a 6.5-millimeter automatic rifle, Model 11 (1932), he wrote, "I fired 120 rounds and hit all targets many times. I noted also that excellent results were being obtained by all engaged in this exercise."[40] Later in the year, he was attached for three and a half months to the 27th Infantry Regiment at Asahigawa on Hokkaido. During the first part of that period he "observed and participated in infantry battalion and regimental field exercises and maneuvers, machine gun training, range firing of the rifle, light machine gun and heavy machine gun, combat firing of the above weapons, and a maneuver of the medical bridge." He also took part in the annual fall maneuvers of the 7th Division.[41] In his long and detailed report, Booth also submitted drawings from Japanese manuals of a light machine gun and the Japanese infantry rapid-fire gun.[42] Another observer, attached to a different unit, took many photographs of Japanese weapons, both standing alone and being served, and submitted them in his report.[43] Reports like these often ran to 90 pages.

Observation sometimes provided not just this static intelligence but also current operational information. Booth wrote that he "not only counted troops of war organization marching to the station to depart for China, but also witnessed final inspection of organizations by the divisional commander preparatory to the departure."[44] Indeed, observation was, another officer wrote, "the principal means of garnering information on organization and to a large extent on tactics and material."[45] The reason, he said, was "the mania for secrecy which prevails in the Japanese army."[46] Of course, even without this mania, Japan, like other countries, did not give foreign observers their real secrets. An American signal corps lieutenant, attached to Japan's communications school, wrote that he was told candidly by its commanding general that, because of the secrecy surrounding research being done there, the American "would be asked to remain away from a portion—this later proved to be a major slice indeed—of the school's activities."[47] He noted about codes and ciphers that "I was able neither to attend classes nor to get any of the students or other officers to discuss, in general terms, the type of codes and ciphers used nor their methods of using them."[48] In general, the attachés got only the data that their hosts wanted them to have: none seemed to have any secret sources inside the governments.

Despite this limitation, the attachés in Japan and Germany gathered a great deal of information, which they analyzed very carefully, sometimes generating extremely useful and accurate conclusions. All this they poured into Washington in many voluminous reports. In 1940, for example, a package arrived in Washington from Tokyo about every two weeks.[49] The one that came in on 18 June included, in addition to administrative papers such as requests for home leave, a report on the national defense budget, population statistics for 1940, an estimate of men reaching military age, and a report on field operations in China. The next package, which arrived on 8 July included biographical sketches of seven lieutenant generals, discussions of air transport of troops and supplies, of parachute training, of field operations in China, of military and industrial installations in Tokyo, and still more.[50] The material from Germany comprised similar topics and was even more voluminous.[51] In both cases, however, volume and importance declined as war approached and arrived. In 1939, for example, the one-line listing of items from Japan required eight pages; in 1940, five. The cause was probably tightening restrictions on movement. In the spring of 1941, for instance, Germany limited foreign attachés to 50 gallons of gasoline a month and refused to let them travel outside of greater Berlin.[52] This forced the attachés to obtain a greater proportion of their information from controlled publications and propaganda handouts—a far skimpier source than observation. Still, the attachés provided more military information about America's probable enemies than any other source.

Second to them was radio intelligence. This consisted of radio direction-finding, radio fingerprinting, traffic analysis, and cryptanalysis.[53]

In radio direction-finding, a radio receiver, hearing a transmission, swings its antenna until it hears the signal most loudly. This tells the direction from which the signal is being emitted. Another receiver does the same thing. A central post, to which these bearings have been reported, draws them on a map. The point where the lines cross marks the position of the transmitter. If it is aboard ship and moving, successive fixes can plot the vessel's course and speed. In radio fingerprinting, an experienced intercept operator recognizes a radio transmitter and its operator through their characteristics, which are as identifiable as handwriting, even though the transmitter's frequency, call sign and location vary. Traffic analysis deduces the lines of command of military or naval forces by ascertaining which radios talk to which. And since military operations are usually accompanied by an increase in communications, traffic analysis can infer the imminence and direction of such operations by watching the volume and routing of traffic. These three techniques together can often approximate the where and when of a planned movement.

But they do so by inference. Cryptanalysis, on the other hand, produces its information much more directly: it provides the actual words of the information targets. This is intelligence of the very highest quality, and it is, moreover, often very fast, providing intercepts to leaders sometimes as quickly as the legitimate recipients are getting the messages. Like the other elements of radio intelligence, cryptanalysis can attain a volume great enough to generate a relatively full and continuous picture. Because the work is done at home behind locked doors, it risks disclosure less than spying and so reduces the likelihood of international tension. And finally—a factor not to be neglected—because the work then required little equipment besides a radio receiver, pencil and paper, it was cheap. For all these reasons, intelligence officers and policymakers like radio intelligence.

Radio intelligence came into permanent existence in the United States, as in other countries, in World War I. By the 1930s, the Navy's unit was headquartered in the wooden temporary World War I Navy Building that disfigured the Mall in Washington. It was called OP-20-G, the OP for the Office of the Chief of Naval Operations, the 20 for the 20th division, the Office of Naval Communications, and the G for Communications Security Section; this latter both protected the Navy's own communications and analyzed those of other navies. It consisted of some 700 officers and men, many of them in its nine intercept posts, others in its Mid-Pacific Strategic Direction-Finder Net, whose monitor posts curved in a gigantic arc from the Philippines through Guam, Samoa, Midway and Hawaii to Dutch Harbor, Alaska. In addition, small communications intelligence units were located in Hawaii and the Philippines.

The Army concentrated its work in a branch of the Signal Corps called the Signal Intelligence Service (S.I.S.). Headquartered in the Munitions Building, the next-door counterpart to the Navy Building, it consisted of about 330 officers and men there and in eight intercept posts scattered around the continental United States and overseas. Its technical head was one of the greatest cryptanalysts of all time, William F. Friedman, a rather uptight man given to bow ties, then in his late 40s.

The Navy utilized direction-finding, radio fingerprinting and traffic analysis more than the Army because it had more occasion to do so; compared to, say, the French Army, the U.S. Army's Signal Intelligence Service had little opportunity to overhear the maneuvers of nearby hostile forces. The U.S. Navy listened mainly to Japanese naval communications, and even without cryptanalysis its other techniques of radio intelligence told it a great deal about the Japanese Navy. Washington's weekly communication intelligence reports named the battleships and aircraft carriers, listed the numbers of cruisers, destroyers and auxiliaries, and specified their locations and command organizations. On 25 November 1941, for example, the report noted with loupelike precision the presence of a single destroyer of the Third Fleet near Maizuru, a port on the Sea of Japan. But radio intelligence was not omniscient. The same report conceded that "The composition of the Fifth Fleet is still unknown."[54] Hawaii issued daily communication intelligence reports that concentrated more on activity than organization: "The entire fleet traffic level is still high which leads to the conclusion that organizational arrangements or other preparations are still not complete," it noted on the same day, November 25.[55]

OP-20-G was attacking the cryptosystems of the Japanese, Italian and German navies, but had made hardly any progress with Italian and German and little more with Japanese, on which it concentrated. It was reading about 10 percent of Imperial Navy traffic, but most of this was in minor cryptosystems such as those used for weather reports; it read the main fleet code only spottily and the flag officers' code not at all.[56] In part this stemmed from a lack of intercepts, in part from a lack of cryptanalysts.

In the same way, S.I.S. was trying to solve, in the late 1930s, the cryptosystems of the armies of Germany, Italy, and Japan. Even by the time of Pearl Harbor, no Japanese army codes could be read, chiefly because of a paucity of material.[57] Little effort had been expended against Italy; consequently, results were almost nil. Likewise, S.I.S. did not work much on German military messages, many of them enciphered in the Enigma, because the British had these "under control" and the Americans believed that the British would supply any vital information obtained from their solutions that might help the Americans.[58] S.I.S. began working on the big German diplomatic code in 1938. The Federal Bureau of Investigation photographed a new code that a German businessman, acting as a courier, was bringing to South America. This alone did not permit S.I.S. to read messages in it, for a numerical sequence was added to the codenumbers to disguise them. Only when a lazy code clerk in Buenos Aires repeated portions of the sequence—in violation of regulations—could S.I.S. break in.[59] Later in 1938, with the threat from Japan growing and that from Germany still contained by England and France, the S.I.S. concentrated its limited manpower on Japanese diplomatic messages, and kept it there as negotiations intensified.

These were in several quite different cryptosystems. The most secret was a machine cipher, which the Americans called PURPLE.[60] An S.I.S. team headed by Friedman, with considerable help from OP-20-G, reconstructed the PURPLE machine in August 1940 after 18 months of arduous, brain-cracking work. Thereafter, the Americans read top Japanese diplomatic messages almost as fast as (and sometimes even faster than) the Japanese diplomats themselves. Messages in other systems, in particular one called J-19, sometimes took longer to read than PURPLE. In part this was a characteristic of the cryptosystems—PURPLE was harder to break in the first place, but once solved was easier to keep up with—and in part it was because the cryptanalysts set messages in secondary systems aside until those in higher-level systems were read.

The cryptanalytic results were copious: 50 to 75 messages a day in the fall of 1941. Some of these, such as the diplomatic notes, were in English; others were in Japanese and required translation. The top officers of the Army and Navy Far Eastern intelligence sections selected the important intercepts and brought them in locked briefcases to Roosevelt, the secretaries of state, war, and navy, the chief of staff, the chief of naval operations, and the heads of the Army and Navy war plans and intelligence divisions. The messenger officers waited while these leaders read them, and then took them back and burned them.

These intercepts were known collectively as MAGIC. Those who received MAGIC were, in Secretary of State Hull's words, "intensely interested" in it. When the Army suspended deliveries to the White House, partly because of a security breach, partly because it felt these diplomatic matters should go to the president through the State Department, Roosevelt requested MAGIC. The Navy war plans chief thought that MAGIC, which was then largely diplomatic, affected his estimates by about 15 percent. The Army intelligence chief regarded it as the most reliable and authentic information that the War Department was receiving on Japanese intentions and activities.[61]

Like all sources, however, MAGIC had limitations. It could not provide more information than the Japanese transmitted to their diplomats—and they did not tell their envoys everything. It could not provide information from areas to which it had no access—and it had not penetrated Japanese military and naval communications. MAGIC's amazing capabilities tended to lull its recipients into thinking they were learning everything the Japanese were plotting. But MAGIC was not omniscient.

Nor was a source that lay at the opposite end of the secrecy spectrum from MAGIC. This was the press.

The American correspondents in Germany during the prewar years of Hitler's power were among the best the American press had. Their names are famous: William L. Shirer of the Columbia Broadcasting System, Louis Lochner and Richard C. Hottelet of the Associated Press, Joseph C. Harsch of the *Christian Science Monitor*, Edgar Ansel Mowrer of the *Chicago Daily News*, Otto Tolischus of *The New York Times*, Karl von Wiegand of the Hearst papers. They were experienced reporters; virtually all spoke German, had spent several years in Germany (Lochner, for instance, had been there since 1924), and knew German history and culture.[62] Three won Pulitzer Prizes for their dispatches from Berlin: Mowrer in 1933, Lochner in 1939, Tolischus in 1940. Martha Dodd, the attractive young daughter of the American ambassador, felt that the newspapermen were "on a pretty high level." "On the whole," she wrote, "the stories that came from Germany . . . presented a pretty accurate picture of what was happening there. . . . The newspapermen I knew were amazingly conscientious, had excellent sources, both German, foreign, and diplomatic, and knew Germany and the developments better than most people."[63]

This contrasted sharply with the situation in Japan. The correspondents in Tokyo were mostly young and relatively inexperienced newcomers—a great many had been there only since around 1937. None knew Japanese; few had much previous knowledge of Japan. Even the experienced men, such as Tolischus, transferred there from Berlin, and Wilfred Fleisher of the *New York Herald Tribune*, had little background in Japan and few contacts there. All were dealing with an oriental mentality, quite foreign to their western outlook. These handicaps reduced the quantity and quality of copy coming out of Japan[64] as compared with that out of Berlin. This difference, together with Germany's closer social and cultural ties to the United States, meant that Germany got more and better coverage in the American press. *The New York Times Index* for 1938 gives 20 columns to Germany and 6 to Japan. And the stories out of Germany show an insight that those from Japan do not. The correspondents in Germany often filed, for example, on the bitter rivalry between the army, once the most powerful institution in the country, and the paramilitary SS, rapidly coming to run the German police state.[65] The correspondents in Japan, though they occasionally reported on the factional struggles within the Japanese government, more often sent stories suggesting aggression and intransigence.[66]

A final source of information came from private individuals. The most famous such personality is Charles A. Lindbergh, who visited Germany three times in the 1930s. More obscure, and deservedly so, is Dr. E. M. Sebree of Los Angeles. Billing himself as a lecturer and teacher of mental science, he wrote the War Department in 1935 that later that year Japan would attack Hawaii and California. This information he "obtained metaphysically," he said. The War Department expressed its appreciation of his "patriotic interest in our National Defense."[67]

### III

Such, then, were the main sources that furnished information to the United States government. To whom did it go? And what did these recipients do with it?

It did not all go to all the same places. Some material, such as that in newspapers, went to everybody. Some filtered through evaluating agencies on its way to policymakers. Some, such as MAGIC, went to only a few top individuals. They received this material raw, and it was they who analyzed and judged it.

Among the evaluating agencies was the bureaucracy of the State Department. Probably all of the innumerable reports from the foreign service officers were read by somebody or other, but few got to the desk of Secretary of State Cordell Hull, fewer to Roosevelt's, and almost certainly fewer still to their memories. What little effect the dispatches had is shown by the attitude of William Phillips, at the time undersecretary of state, when he visited Ambassador Dodd in Germany in 1935. After a morning conference with embassy specialists, including the military attaché, who told him that "Germany is one vast military camp," and the commercial attaché, who said that "In two years Germany will be manufacturing oil and gas enough out of soft coal for a long war," Phillips was "amazed and distressed." Dodd noted that "all this information has been going to the Department for two whole years. But no high official can master all the reports as they pile up there."[68] Though the reports were filed by subject in the State Department's useful decimal file, no mechanism existed to assemble the various files—economic, political, military—into a current whole for analysis. Nor do the reports seem to have been reviewed periodically in an attempt to determine any trends.

This operation, in which the general bureaucracy served as the organ for evaluating information, differed from that in the armed services, both of which had specialized agencies to analyze information. The army's Military Intelligence Division (M.I.D.), a headquarters unit that dated in various forms to 1885, was headed by the assistant chief of staff, G-2, Brigadier General Sherman Miles. The son of a former commanding general of the army, Nelson Miles, he had had extensive experience abroad, having served as an attaché in Russia, Turkey and London, and with commissions or embassies in Austria, Yugoslavia and Czechoslovakia; he had served in the Military Intelligence Division from 1919 to 1921 and, in addition to holding various field posts, had served four years with the War Plans Division. He had headed the Military Intelligence Division since 1 May 1940. In 1941, that body had 856 people in Washington.[69] Its opposite number, the Office of Naval Intelligence (O.N.I.), founded in 1882, was designated OP-16, the 16th division of the Office of the Chief of Naval Operations. It had 600 people in Washington and had been headed since 15 October 1941, by Rear Admiral Theodore S. Wilkinson. He was bright—he had graduated first in the class of 1909 from the U.S. Naval Academy—and he had served abroad at the limitation of arms conferences in Geneva in 1933 and London in 1934. But his previous assignments—office work on shore and the command of ships at sea—had never included an intelligence post.[70] The work of both M.I.D. and O.N.I. included counterintelligence,[71] and the evaluating sections for Germany and for Japan in each were rather small. The Far Eastern section of M.I.D., for example, consisted of 11 officers, only three of them assigned to Japan.[72]

The sources that they most used seemed to be the attaché reports, news stories, and—for the highest officials only—MAGIC. The officers in each section read this incoming material, rejected what they considered were false reports, determined the possible core of truth in the sometimes contradictory or exaggerated data, judged how much weight to give to the remaining facts and opinions on such bases as the motives of the sources and their congruence with other data, and from all this inferred the probable strength and intentions of other countries. They issued these conclusions in both periodic and special reports. Since the officers who drafted these were usually low-ranking officers who did not have access to MAGIC,[73] and since the ultimate sources of their information did not differ all that much from those exploited by the American correspondents, the reports often resembled a weekly summary in *The New York Times*—except that they were not as well written. As with the news stories, the intelligence reports sometimes included predictions of foreign moves. But mostly they just summarized the situation.

Two other intelligence agencies were getting their work under way at the time of Pearl Harbor. Since cooperation between M.I.D. and O.N.I. was spotty,[74] the Joint Army-Navy Board, the father of the Joint Chiefs of Staff, brought them together formally by establishing a Joint Intelligence Committee as "an agency responsible to the Joint Board." This was in October 1941, but the board first met formally on 3 December.[75] It had issued no reports by the time the United States entered the war. The second agency was created when William J. Donovan, a Columbia Law School fellow student of Roosevelt's, a World War I hero, and a prominent Republican politician who had run for governor of New York (losing, in 1932, to Herbert Lehman), proposed a unified intelligence agency to Roosevelt after making two trips to Europe to gather information for him. Roosevelt accepted the idea, and, on 11 July 1941, named Donovan coordinator of information. He was "to collect and analyze all information and data which may bear upon national security; . . . and to make such information and data available to the President and to such departments and officials of the Government as the President may determine."[76] After the United States entered the war, his organization evolved into the Office of Strategic Services.

## IV

Throughout the years and months preceding the German declaration of war on the United States, information poured into Washington about Germany. It ranged from the details that serve to make up a picture of the whole to judgments about Germany's next moves.

The details covered an amazing range. The military attaché for many years was Major Truman Smith, an observant, lively, intelligent Germanophile.[77] He wrote a powerful but undisciplined prose, and his main message was that Hitler wanted peace.[78] In technical matters, he was rather more accurate. Often he succeeded in providing remarkably precise figures on the strength of the Germany army. In July 1939, just before the outbreak of the war, he counted the number of German army formations almost exactly. He was one under on the number of infantry divisions, one under on the number of panzer divisions, one over on the number of motorized infantry divisions, and right on target on the number of mountain and light divisions and on the single cavalry brigade.[79] On the other hand, he greatly overestimated the number of available reserve formations. He figured on 123; in fact, only 103 were available.[80] He hated the press, which painted what he thought was a false picture: "Hitler looking around for new nations to conquer" and "marching gray-clad armies and a succession of German conquests in Eastern Europe."[81] But it was more prescient than he was. On the level of particulars, it reported during the prewar years a great variety of useful details: the creation of the XIVth Corps, with headquarters probably at Würzburg, a new steel helmet, new weapons, the 1938 shakeup in the high commands (this even before the official announcement).[82] Moreover, it provided a flood of information about Germany's politics, economics, labor conditions, racial measures, and foreign relations—the context of the military activities The diplomats, too, poured out quantities of information on the same subjects.

Everybody paid a great deal of attention to the age's new wonder weapon, the airplane. The American attachés had been following its growth as a military weapon in Germany since before the Luftwaffe's existence was formally disclosed in 1936. In November 1934, an attaché calculated, on the basis of figures for civilian airplanes and for pilots' tests, that Germany had 1,200 training airplanes and about 1,000 combat planes. This was close to the actual 1,300 trainers but considerably overestimated the actual 670 combat planes.[83] As Germany's rearmament progressed, security tightened, and Smith and his air assistant cleverly called for help in breaching the secrecy upon the man who was possibly the most famous individual in the world: Charles A. Lindbergh.[84]

Lindbergh consented, and paid the first of three annual inspection visits to Germany in July 1936. He visited aircraft factories and Luftwaffe airfields, examined planes and flew them, talked with pilots and high air officials, including German air force chief Hermann Göring. In 1936, the leader of an elite fighter unit gave him what proved to be accurate information about the speed, armament, and ceiling of the Messerschmidt Me-109, which later became Germany's basic single-seater fighter; in 1937, he examined one and watched it fly at the Rechlin testing field.[85] Before he left that year, he and Smith prepared a "General Estimate" of Germany's air power. It was an apocalyptic document. "Germany is once more a world power in the air," it began. It spoke of the "astounding growth of German air power," of this rise's being "one of the most important world events of our time," of the "remarkable" German advance in aeronautics, of how the United States could be "doomed to . . . inferiority." It asserted that "technically Germany has outdistanced France in practically all fields" and, at the end, warned that "Germany should obtain technical parity with the U.S.A. by 1941 or 1942."[86] A few months later, Lindbergh wrote a memorandum for Ambassador Kennedy in London about his trip. "Germany is probably the strongest air power in Europe," he declared. At a Henschel factory near Berlin, where Dornier Do-17s were in production, he noted, "There were twenty wings and twenty fuselages in the final assembly hangar. These were moving through on tracks and made one complete round of the hangar during the process of assembly, so that as the plane left its assembly jig the jig was back at the beginning of the line, ready for a new fuselage." This memorandum went to Roosevelt, who sent it on 10 February 1938 to Marshall and Stark.[87] Lindbergh also reported on his impressions orally to General H. H. "Hap" Arnold, chief of staff of the Army Air Corps, to naval officers, to the secretary of war and to F.D.R. himself.[88]

In France in October of 1938, Lindbergh was told by French authorities that Germany could build 24,000 planes a year (compared to the French production of 540) and already had 6,000 modern planes. In Germany a few weeks later, he again visited factories and this time did not merely view the Me-109 but actually flew it. It "handled beautifully," he said.[89] Perhaps it was from Lindbergh that Arnold got the frightening information that he gave Congress early in 1939: Germany had approximately 1,700 planes capable of flying from the west coast of Africa to the east coast of South America.[90]

Roosevelt's concern about German aviation was heightened by other sources. In January 1938, a French visitor told him that German planes could fly over France with impunity; in October, Bullitt, his trusted ambassador in France, said that the Germans would be able to bomb Paris at will. When war broke out in Europe, Bullitt cabled, "There is an enormous danger that the German air force will be able to win this war for Germany before the planes can begin to come out of our plants in quantity."[91]

Paralleling this were the frequent warnings against underestimating Germany. Truman Smith wrote that American leadership in the air "must . . . not lead to an underestimate of what Germany will achieve in the future."[92] Undersecretary of State Sumner Welles said during his 1940 trip to Europe that the two most experienced members of the diplomatic corps in Berlin believe "that the Allied governments grossly underestimate Germany's military strength."[93] A few months later, the American naval attaché declared that "Germany as a fighting nation is tremendously powerful. Under no circumstances should she be underestimated."[94] Yet the problem was not underestimating Germany. On the contrary: everybody was overestimating her.

The naval attaché estimated airplane production in February 1940 at 1,800 to 2,000 planes a month maximum.[95] The actual figure for all of 1940 averaged under 900 a month.[96] The French premier said Germany had ten times as many planes as France; the actual figures around then were France, 3,289, Germany, 4,665.[97] The Military Intelligence Division issued on 11 July 1941, after the German attack on the Soviet Union, a strategic estimate of the situation that set the number of planes for the Luftwaffe at 11,000,[98] a figure which in September it specified referred to "front-line combat airplanes."[99] In fact, on 5 July 1941, the Luftwaffe had only 3,094 fighters and bombers.[100] The Coordinator of Information attained almost Wagnerian proportions in his overestimations. On 12 December 1941, using figures no doubt worked up previously, he credited the Germans with 29,000 planes.[101] Yet on the Eastern Front, outside of Africa the only combat area, the German army chief of staff counted on that very day 950 fighters and bombers.[102] The Coordinator estimated, also on 12 December, that Germany had 30,000 tanks at the start of the invasion of Russia.[103] There were 3,332.[104] He guessed that the Reich was producing 1,000 to 17,000 tanks a month, or 12,000 to 204,000 a year. In fact, in all of 1941 Germany built only 3,256.[105] All this was the other side of racism. America despised the little yellow men of Japan, but she glorified the blue-eyed blonds of Germany.[106]

American estimates of the ground troops were closer to the mark. Though the Coordinator's estimates of casualties in Russia doubled the actual number, his figure of 9,000,000 men in the Germany armed forces in June of 1941[107] stood only a quarter higher than the actual 7,234,000.[108] Comparisons of the estimated with the actual figures of the number of German army divisions are difficult to make for two reasons. First, the published German documents list only divisions at the fronts whereas the American estimates include divisions at home. And second, with a gross disregard for the needs of historians, M.I.D. failed to issue its estimates on the same day that the German army general staff's organization section tabulated units. But a rough index of accuracy may be attained by comparing American estimates and German listings close in time and by choosing easily matched portions of the force total. On 11 July 1941, M.I.D. estimated 60 German army divisions in the west;[109] on 27 June, there were 49.[110] On 1 December 1941, O.N.I., no doubt getting its information from M.I.D., counted 27 divisions in Holland, Belgium and France;[111] on 2 January 1942, there were 29.[112] The overestimation followed by an underestimation depicts no pattern. But M.I.D. did have solid information on German strength in an area of importance. When M.I.D. stated in August of 1941 that Germany had twenty armored divisions in Europe and one in Libya,[113] its figures were exact.[114]

When it came to Hitler's intentions toward the United States, few people ventured to prophesy. The military and the naval attaché reports in the latter part of 1941 do not mention the possibility of war.[115] Nor do the diplomatic reports.[116] When Churchill and his advisors met Roosevelt and his at the Atlantic conference, no one even mentioned that Hitler might declare war on America.[117] And all were then correct in not doing so. Hitler had just invaded Russia. For the next several months, he would be "thoroughly occupied in beating Russia," as Secretary of War Stimson put it,[118] "immersed in the conflict with the U.S.S.R.," as M.I.D. put it.[119] While engaged in that struggle, he would not want to clash with the United States, their thinking seemed to run.

And indeed, he apparently did avoid problems. He restrained his admirals, who wanted to let their U-boats sink American ships bringing supplies to Britain.[120] Even Churchill sensed, in August, that Hitler's current naval policy gave little prospect of an incident that might bring America into the war.[121] Three did occur—those of the American destroyers *Greer*, *Reuben James*, and *Kearny*[122]—but Roosevelt, blocked by isolationists, did not use them as an excuse for war.[123] Fears persisted about German subversion in Latin America, but these were groundless: Hitler had talked about "a new Germany" in Brazil but had taken no concrete action to realize this either there or in other Latin American countries.[124] On the other hand, German spying in the United States— exposed in the summer of 1941 by 29 headline-making arrests—implied at least preparation for some hostile action or other.[125]

A "Brief Periodic Estimate of the World Situation," issued by M.I.D. on 5 September 1941, made, in an almost offhand manner, the only reference to Germany's possibly warring on the United States that the intelligence documents seem to contain: "It is estimated that Germany has large submarine forces in hand, which she will use with the utmost caution in the North Atlantic until she is ready to run the risk of provoking the United States or until hostilities with America begin."[126] In its conclusions, however, the report does not mention war with the

United States.[127] This suggests that the remark about hostilities was unimportant and was perhaps only a case of M.I.D.'s protecting itself with a throwaway prediction in case war did come.

In October, the Army's War Plans Division issued a "War Department Strategic Estimate." Examining Germany's possible lines of action, it declared that Germany "will not be in a position to attempt major offensive operations in the Western Hemisphere for at least a year, and then only if she acquires large numbers of British ships, both commercial and war vessels. The effect of U.S. active participation in the war would probably cause Germany to accelerate her operations in the Russian theater in order to bring about the defeat of the Russians before our fighting capacity reaches decisive proportions. Further, the early defeat of Russia would release much-needed manpower for employment in German industry to match U.S. expanding war industries."[128]

All of these views were speculation. None of them cite any hard evidence about Hitler's intentions toward America. None of them imply that they obtained information about whether Hitler planned to fight America from codebreaking or an attaché's honorable spying or the secret agents of a friendly power. And this for a very good reason: Astonishing though it may be, Hitler had no plans on how he would conduct a war against the United States. The Japanese attack on Pearl Harbor was as much of a surprise to him as it was to the Americans, and his notification to his armed forces high command that he was about to declare war on the United States exposed the embarrassing lack of even a contingency plan for hostilities with that country.[129]

His decision was unpremeditated and partially irrational, precipitated by the Pearl Harbor attack.[130] There was therefore no way in which any intelligence agency could have obtained any foreknowledge of it. The United States's first solid information of Hitler's intention came from a MAGIC intercept of a Japanese message from Berlin to Tokyo on 8 December.[131] A warning was flashed to American defense commands, but the United States did nothing else until, on 11 December, Hitler had the Reichstag declare war. The Congress replied with a similar declaration that same day, and the potential enemies became real ones.

## V

If with Germany the question of strength, or capabilities, attracted more interest than that of intentions, which seemed to be rather taken for granted, with Japan it was just the reverse. Diplomats, correspondents, intelligence evaluators, and policymakers focused, not on the forces available to Japan as they had concentrated, for example, on the Luftwaffe, but on where the Japanese might strike next. Perhaps the reasons for this were in part that it was easier to gain information on Germany than on Japan, in part that Germany seemed to have no real options until after she had beaten Russia, while Japan had many, all in a region in which the United States had possessions and interests.

Japan's options—assuming she intended to exercise them—seemed to require no military intelligence to ascertain. They seemed set by geography, economics, and politics. She could expand only in one of four directions: north, south, east, and west.

Each of these moves had its champions within the imperial government. They urged their positions in debates in the cabinet. To the west, where Japan was fighting China, Japan might concentrate an effort in Yunnan province, to cut the Burma Road that brought supplies to Chiang Kai-Shek and so to complete the conquest of China. To the north, Russia, a traditional enemy, writhed in mortal battle against Japan's ally, Germany. Japan might advance against Siberia to help defeat the Soviet Union and abolish forever the Soviet rivalry in the Far East. To the south lay Malaya and the Netherlands East Indies, with their riches of oil and rubber, and other countries with the markets Japan needed for economic dominance in Asia. To the east rolled only the empty Pacific; much farther east, America growled and muttered. But despite these disincentives to go east, increasing American pressure finally led Japanese leaders to conclude that they had to make war upon the United States to attain their objectives. On 25 November, a task force of carriers and escort vessels sailed from the remote Kurile Islands north of Japan to initiate a war of conquest or death at Pearl Harbor.[132]

Throughout 1941, American intelligence officers and the policymakers they served tried with growing urgency to determine what Japan would do. The determination of which of the four geographical options Japan would choose[133] would be made on the basis of current intelligence. But these reports would be refracted through an American world view before reaching American consciousnesses, and Americans' presumption of rationality and their racism prevented current details from being assembled into a pattern that might indicate what was happening in Japan. The possibility that one nation would attack another so much more powerful that the war might well end in national suicide was so alien, so distant to American leaders' thought-processes that it seems never to have entered their occidental minds. And even if a struggle were to take place on a basis of material equality, as in a naval battle, Americans believed that they were so much better than Japanese that the United States would win. Thus rationality and racism implied that Japan would not move east to war upon the United States. Many writers, including Pratt and Puleston, drew this conclusion from their presumptions.

"The Japanese, brave, self-confident and ingenious, are the most willing of all nations to stake their chances of success on some tactical or technical trick," wrote Pratt. "But even they would hardly engage the United States Fleet in anything but a battle of desperation; the material superiority is too great. . . . Japan dares provoke or enter no war in which the United States Fleet will be engaged on the opposite side."[134] Puleston concurred. " . . . a sober estimate of the situation could convince leaders in Japan that they could not reasonably hope to defeat the United States, whose population, resources and military position are superior to their own. There are no economic reasons that could justify the Japanese Government in accepting the hazards of war with the United States." Then he became more specific. "The greatest danger from Japan, a surprise attack on the unguarded Pacific Fleet, lying at anchor in San Pedro Harbor [California], under peacetime conditions, has already been averted. The Pacific Fleet is at one of the strongest bases in the world—Pearl Harbor—practically on a war footing and under a war regime. There will be no American Port Arthur." Other writers expressed the same opinion: "there is no danger of Japan attacking Hawaii in any force so long as it harbors the battle fleet" and a "Japanese attack upon Hawaii is a strategical impossibility."[135]

American intelligence officers shared this view. Though they acknowledged that an attack on Pearl Harbor was not impossible, they dismissed it as improbable. And it was from within this framework that they scrutinized the latest details of the intelligence picture.

This included information on the land forces of Japan. Throughout the fall of 1941, the Military Intelligence Division was refining its figures on the Japanese army. By 5 December, Army intelligence chief Sherman Miles was reporting to Marshall that Japan had 62 active divisions, 22 independent and 5 cavalry brigades, 13 tank regiments and 15 depot divisions in Japan and Manchuria as well as garrison and railway guard units. He listed their locations: 30 divisions in Manchuria, 8 in north China, 10 in central China, and so on.[136] His figures were over the true numbers. At the time of Pearl Harbor, Japan had only 48 active infantry divisions, 13 depot divisions, and 24 independent mixed brigades.[137] In estimating combat aircraft production, military intelligence underestimated the Japanese. It figured 200 planes a month; the actual rate was 426.[138]

Of far greater interest than the army was the Japanese navy, for it offered the possibility of predicting where Japan would strike: the island empire would need her naval forces for any move, and American radio intelligence might be able to track them.

And indeed, the United States had, for much of 1941, good radio intelligence on the composition and movements of Japan's naval units. It was admittedly not complete: the coded orders of the major commands remained sealed to Americans. But its basic excellence, combined with a fluke in history, paradoxically led OP-20-G and the outpost units into a fatal misapprehension.

In July, the Japanese, taking advantage of Vichy France's weakness, occupied French Indochina. The naval preparations for this grab were clearly indicated in the radio traffic. During it, however, not only were no messages heard from the aircraft carriers but none were sent to them either. Naval communications intelligence reasoned that the carriers were standing by in home waters as a covering force in case of counterattack and that communications to and from them were not heard because they were transmitted on short-range, low-powered transmissions that died away before reaching American intercept receivers. A similar blank of carrier communications had obtained in a similar tactical situation in February. American intelligence had drawn the same conclusions then and had been proven right. Events soon confirmed the July assessment as well. When, early in December, the carriers again vanished from the radio picture while observers and other intelligence told of ships moving south, the February and July situations seemed to be recurring. OP-20-G and the Hawaiian radio intelligence unit thought the carriers were again in home waters. But the carriers were not in home waters—they were in the vacant wastes of the central Pacific, heading east, under radio silence.[139] Moreover, not only did they send no messages, they received only one, to confirm that the attack was to be carried out. This consisted of an open-language code phrase ("Climb Mount Niitaka") used just that once: its meaning was impossible to determine.

As the U.S. Navy gathered radio intelligence and made its false deductions from it, the diplomats sought clues to Japanese intentions. They found nothing concrete. On 17 November, Grew cabled Hull, "Recent reports from our consuls at Taihoku and at Harbin point to Japanese troop concentrations in both Taiwan and Manchuria, and all other available indications are that since the general mobilization of July last, troop dispositions have been made to enable new operations to be carried out on the shortest possible notice in either Siberia or the southwest Pacific or both."[140] This was a fancy way of saying that he didn't know whether Japan would move north or south.

Nor did specific information come from MAGIC. To a degree, in fact, MAGIC may have obscured the likelihood of an attack on Pearl Harbor. Its numerous intercepts of Japanese diplomatic messages told of espionage interest in Latin America, of observations of Soviet submarines and minesweepers at Vladivostok, of attention to Thailand and Burma.[141] What American policymakers read of this must have fragmented their attention, rendering it more difficult to conceive of a Pearl Harbor attack. In the same way, military intercepts revealing that Japanese agents were reporting on the arrival, presence, and departure of warships in major American ports presented a misleading picture. For they pointed away from Pearl Harbor. The number of ship-movement messages translated between 1 August and 6 December dealing with Pearl Harbor totaled 20; those dealing with the Panama Canal totaled 23, and those with the Philippines, 59.[142]

The intercepts of dispatches to the Japanese ambassadors in Washington likewise yielded no specific clues to a Pearl Harbor attack. For they were never told about it and remained ignorant of their government's intentions. So MAGIC could not foretell where Japan would move. What it could and did do was provide a constantly increasing sense of urgency, an indication of the constantly rising tension. Intercepts made clearer and clearer that Japan was going to rupture relations with, and perhaps even go to war with, the United States. On 22 November, Tokyo told its ambassadors in Washington that after the 29th, "things are automatically going to happen." On 30 November, a dispatch to Berlin ordered the ambassador to "say very secretly to them [Hitler and Foreign Minister Joachim von Ribbentrop] that there is extreme danger that war may suddenly break out between the Anglo-Saxon nations and Japan through some clash of arms and add that the time of breaking out of this war might come quicker than anyone dreams."[143] There followed a rash of messages about destroying codes,[144] and on the evening of 6 December the first 13 parts of a 14-part note rupturing negotiations. Roosevelt read it in his lamplit office in the presence of a MAGIC courier and his aide Harry Hopkins and said, in effect, "This means war."[145] But knowing that war is coming does not mean that one knows where or when it is coming.

The lack of information[146] about where the Japanese would strike was reflected in M.I.D.'s estimates. On 2 November, Miles submitted a report that listed the alternatives that Japan could take without stating which he thought was the most likely. On 5 December he repeated the list, merely adding that "The most probable line of action for Japan is the occupation of Thailand."[147]

Two days later, airplanes from the Japanese carrier force attacked Pearl Harbor, to the utter consternation and astonishment of everybody in the United States and the Territory of Hawaii. Surprise was complete.

## VI

How had it happened? Why did intelligence fail? Why did it not achieve the significant results that would have enabled it to overwhelm the prejudices that ruled American leaders, or the extra precision that might have given it more accurate details about the size of the Luftwaffe or the moment of Hitler's declaration of war?

The failure lay not in analysis but in collection. American intelligence had simply not gotten any hard information at all about Japan's planned attack. Japan's superb security had kept U.S. intelligence from picking up even one solid datum about her intentions toward Pearl Harbor. American intelligence officers and policymakers could do no more than infer—or, better, guess—Japan's plans, but in attempting this, their racism, their presumption of Japanese rationalism, and the carrier movements of February and July deceived them. Only more data, such as knowledge of the existence of a serious plan of attack or of the location of the carriers, could have overcome their prejudices and the invalid patterns of the past.[148] Presumably such data could have been generated if the principal Japanese naval codes had been broken, or if spies had been recruited or inserted within the Japanese cabinet or admirality, or if high-altitude, long-range planes could have flown almost invisible aerial reconnaissance of the Japanese fleet. Likewise, against Germany, more data could have been gained from, say, a spy in the right Luftwaffe office. If some or all of these things had been done, intelligence might have succeeded against Japan, or done better against Germany. So why were they not done?

The fundamental reason is economic. It was exacerbated by a sociological factor.

The United States had, for two decades, greatly restricted its appropriations for the military, including intelligence, particularly strategic intelligence. This limited what intelligence could do. There was no money to set up intercept posts close to Japan to pick up the many Japanese naval messages needed to solve the main codes, to hire the cryptanalysts and translators that would be required, or to provide the additional aircraft that would have made it possible to fly 24-hour aerial reconnaissance around the Hawaiian Islands. Yet a primary function of intelligence is to optimize resources. It could perhaps prevent constructing unnecessary warships or fortifying the wrong outposts or losing men and installations and ships through a surprise attack. It would therefore save money and lives. In other words, it is cost-effective. All this seems self-evident. So why did America's leaders not give intelligence a larger share than they did of the admittedly small military appropriations?[149]

Mainly because experience had not taught them the importance of intelligence. What seems self-evident now was not self-evident then. In 1939 or 1941, intelligence did not have the public support that it enjoys today and that seems so natural. People certainly acknowledged the usefulness of strategic intelligence, of knowing whether and when and where another country might attack. But this was essentially lip service. Americans did not have a gut sense of the importance of intelligence, because nothing had ever demonstrated its value to them. It seemed, for many, something that was nice to have but was not essential. America's Army and Navy were the finest without it. So the nation was unwilling to spend much money for it. Pearl Harbor began changing that. It taught Americans in the most brutal way the need for intelligence. After World War II, the Cold War, with its fears of Soviet subversion and expansion, intensified leaders' pressures for information about the world. But in the 1930s, Germany, Japan, and Italy did not seem as ominous to America as the Soviet Union did in the 1950s: Americans had not yet lived through dictators' attacks on other nations; the three countries were less powerful, more dispersed and less in contact with American zones of influence than the postwar Soviet Union; they were more distant in the sense that rockets and atom bombs had not then made destruction of America's homes a possibility; capitalistic fascism did not inspire the dread among many establishment figures that communism did. The public of the 1930s therefore lacked the feeling for the importance of intelligence that the public of today has, and so a much smaller proportion of the tiny defense budget went to intelligence then than now. This precluded the gathering of much information.

The widespread disregard for intelligence had an important sociological repercussion. It permitted the generals and admirals to downgrade the intelligence function, which they viewed as a threat to their power. The Army general staff, Dwight D. Eisenhower has written, treated intelligence as a "stepchild." "For example, the number of general officers within the War Department was so limited by peacetime law that one of the principal divisions had to be headed by a colonel. Almost without exception the G-2 [intelligence] division got the colonel."[150] The reason for this lay in the antagonism of line officers to intelligence, as to every new specialty that technology created. For if a specialty became important, its officers would be able to compete for higher posts, giving the officers in the older branches difficulties they otherwise would not have had. Such hostility was nothing new: in European armies of the 17th and 18th centuries, infantry and cavalry officers had bitterly opposed granting officers' commissions to artillerymen. American commanders feared the same thing as others: if intelligence could win wars, no one would need generals. So they fought the threat of intelligence by giving its head a lower rank than the other assistant chiefs of staff, by keeping the number and importance of courses in it at the staff colleges low, and by assigning poorer quality officers to it—Eisenhower slightingly called the attachés "estimable, socially acceptable gentlemen."[151] The officers in control justified this with an assumed morality: spying was dishonorable; consequently, they, as officers and gentlemen, could not engage in anything tainted by this unclean endeavor. This was only a rationale, a mask for the officers' struggle for power.[152] But this sociological conflict no doubt contributed to the reluctance to get spies in Japan and Germany as well as to the denigration of all intelligence, with the consequence deleterious results for the United States.

The general neglect of intelligence, and the officers' antagonism to it, ultimately helped block America's gaining information that might have warned of the Pearl Harbor attack. These conditions perhaps prevented sharpening the German intelligence picture as well, but they were not as harmful there because geography and events—the two nonintelligence factors—accurately indicated German intentions.

In the end, American intelligence against its two potential enemies may be assessed like this: Its role was secondary to the nonintelligence factors. Like them, it was generally right about Germany, wrong about Japan. The success was not its alone. But neither was the failure.

# THE FUTURE

THE FUTURES

# Opportunities in Cryptology for Historians

The study of government intelligence operations is one of man's most fascinating. But somehow historians have neglected it. One reason may simply be that scholars have not seen its research opportunities. This article seeks to correct that problem by indicating some fruitful areas of study in one sector of intelligence operations: cryptology. This sector, always one of the most trustworthy forms of secret intelligence, is today one of the most important. The American codemaking and codebreaking organization, the National Security Agency, employs more men and spends more money than the Central Intelligence Agency. The subject is thus relevant. Yet, despite a few scholarly studies, vast periods and whole kingdoms have been touched on only superficially.

Most of the previous works have dealt with the organization of the agencies that intercepted and solved communications—the black chambers. Such studies constitute a necessary first step. But no one has gone on to investigate the most critical and important aspect of cryptology: how the information it produced served kings and ministers in their policymaking. Nor has anyone written the intriguing technical chapter of how the experts opened letters without a trace, counterfeited seals, or developed secret inks.

I indicate below some of the main areas of research needed. Where

"Opportunities in Cryptology for Historians" first appeared as "Cryptology and History: Secret Writings for Historians" in the fall 1972 issue of *The Maryland Historian*, except for the portion dealing with World War II material.

I know them, I cite studies that can serve as a starting point for deeper investigation or name archives in which cryptologic documents can be found. Many of these have come to my attention since the publication of *The Codebreakers;* I have generally not included references already cited in that work. Study of these new documents in conjunction with the political archives should show how cryptology has played a role in the decision-making process. There should be more than one good dissertation cached below. It should be easier to get a publisher for it than for many others since it would pioneer in a field of history which has contemporary importance and interest and also promises to return a modest profit in both dollars and fame.

Though Venetian ambassadors complained of British interception of the dispatches under Henry VIII, the first British systematic surveillance of foreign communications began under Elizabeth with Sir Francis Walsingham. The most famous case in which his decipherer Thomas Phelippes was involved was the one that sent Mary, Queen of Scots, to her death.[1]

Later, John Wallis, the great mathematician, solved cryptograms for the crown. One series, he said in asking for a raise, upset Louis XIV's plans for Poland. This episode, in its cryptanalytic effects, has never been studied. Wallis has left a number of manuscript volumes with his solutions, two of them only recently acquired by Oxford's Bodleian Library.[2] Through a chain beginning with Wallis's grandson, there grew up in England the Private Office for opening mail with its appended Decypherers. One Decypherer rose through his cryptanalytic ability to become bishop of Bath and Wells when Bath was at its fashionable height in the 18th century; he and two sons, likewise Decypherers, were buried in Westminster Abbey. They left extremely voluminous records—the collection of French intercepts alone runs some 2,000 pages.[3] The impact of these solutions on policy has never been explored.

The first permanently employed French cryptanalyst, Antoine Rossignol, who served under Louis XIII and Louis XIV, has left echoes of his fabulous deeds in the chronicles of the time. One says that a besieged town capitulated when a general sent back to it an intercepted message for help that Rossignol had solved, for example. He was important enough to be mentioned in the major memoirs of his day, such as those by Saint-Simon, and to have been celebrated in verse. But no one has dug into the unprinted records of the time to substantiate these stories, to seek out others, to create a picture of his work and its effects, or to flesh out the man himself. Some clues can come from memoirs;[4] others can come from the fine work by Eugène Vaillé, *Le Cabinet noir.*[5] Most of the information can probably be found in the archives of the Ministry of Foreign Affairs, totally unexplored, even by Vaillé, for this purpose. Much in the great series *Correspondance Politique* seems to consist of intercepts of foreign messages. For example, the volume *Angleterre 47* includes messages strictly between Englishmen, such as between the ambassador to France and the king of England. From the handwriting, they appear to be documents of the time and not later copies from English archives. Comparison of them with other political documents should help clarify the role of secret intelligence in the policymaking of the *Ancien Régime*.

Vienna's efficient black chamber has formed the subject of a number of studies.[6] But none have investigated how, for example, Kaunitz or Metternich used the intelligence that it produced, even though a portion of the *Intercepta* have survived, despite periodic destruction.

Within Germany, Saxony had a black chamber for a brief period under August III.[7] Hanover lent some of her experts to England after the crowns united in 1714 and so engaged in black chamber activity.[8] Prussia had to send cryptograms to John Wallis for solution around 1700, and my cursory inspection of her archives catalogues showed no evidence of any black chamber activity. But it nevertheless seems unlikely that in the 1700s no such activity existed here while it did in nearly every other court in Europe. Moreover, black chambers did exist in Prussia in the early 1800s.[9] Bavaria may likewise repay investigation. Sweden used ciphers and perhaps solved them as well, though I know of no references to such activity.[10]

Venice was the first Italian city to begin reading other government's messages soon after ambassadors began to report regularly, with the start of permanent diplomacy in the Renaissance. She was followed by Florence, Milan, less systematically the Vatican, and perhaps other city-states. Their cryptanalytic activities left traces in their archives, most richly in Florence.[11] Perhaps the researcher will be lucky enough to find the lost manuscript by one of the West's first great cryptanalysts, Giovanni Soro of Venice!

The Russian Revolution threw up some material about Czarist black chambers, and the many works on the secret police should provide more handholds.[12] In addition to the archives in the Soviet Union, whose catalogues (if any) I cannot read, the Hoover Institution on War, Revolution and Peace in Stanford, California, may have some good material.

Though many studies of Spain's Renaissance cryptology exist, I know of only two discussions of cryptanalysis and of nothing dealing with a systematic interception.[13] Moreover, the reaction of Philip II to François Viète's solution of one of his ciphers—that Viète accomplished it through black magic—further suggests lack of a black chamber. But perhaps one grew up there later. The archives are at least extensive and relatively complete.

The Moslems developed an exceptional theoretical knowledge of cryptanalysis.[14] This knowledge bespeaks a fair practical experience with interception and cryptanalysis, though some scholars have written that they doubt it. The various Moslem archives remain relatively unexplored and thus might bring exceptional rewards to the investigator. China had a well-developed postal system, and at least one reference suggests a black chamber operation.[15] Though the American postal service grew up in the heyday of black chambers, and though the papers of the Continental Congress contain several volumes of intercepted letters, no black chamber developed here. Why? The question has never been studied.

Cryptology has things to say to others than political historians. It can offer topics to the historians of technology as well. Invisible inks have been known since at least the time of Pliny the Elder, and have served intelligence purposes since the Renaissance. Besides their appearance in standard works such as Giovanni Battista Porta's *Natural Magic*, they turn up in unexpected places.[16] Spies used them extensively in World War I when they first became quite "specific," or detectable only with a narrow range of reagents. In World War II they served less often—being supplanted by the microdot—but attained considerable sophistication, some requiring biological means to be made visible. Although *The Codebreakers* offers some starting references, no one has ever really studied their development.

A curious field, totally unexplored, deals with techniques for clandestinely opening letters, sometimes called "perlustration." Specialists in this field worked in the black chambers.[17] On letters closed with wax seals, they sometimes simply passed a hot knife or wire through the seal and opened it. When they feared a seal might break, they took an impression of the wax seal to make a mold of their own with which they could reproduce the original—this being faster, cheaper and more accurate than the rival technique of engraving a counterfeit. The literature records at least three formulas for this procedure.[18] As envelopes came into use, an expert in the Czarist black chamber invented a device for extracting letters from them. This was a flexible stick, like a knitting needle, slit halfway down its length. He inserted it at the corner of the envelope, caught the letter in the slit, furled it tightly around the stick, and pulled them both gently out at the corner.[19] A study of how these gentlemen worked should make fascinating reading, with reverberations to the present: they were the wiretappers of their day.

An examination of the cryptographic systems existing before and after the telegraph came into use suggests that it worked effects as profound in the field of secret communications as it did in communications in general. Thus it seems to have exterminated the nomenclator as the basic system of secret communication and to have engendered in its place the full-fledged code for the high-level military and diplomatic communications and the field cipher for low-level military communications. But no one has looked into the transition period itself to see whether any documents in fact support this thesis and to show how the change actually took place. Probably the best place to look would be in the archives of the major armies' engineer corps, which were originally entrusted with signal duties, and in the correspondence sections of the foreign ministries.[20]

The mechanization of cryptography began in the 1920s with the founding of a number of firms to develop, produce, and market cipher machines. The best-known inventors were Edward H. Hebern in California, whose few remaining documents and machines I now have, Arvid Damm of Sweden, whose firm's archives were absorbed by his successor, Boris C. W. Hagelin and his firm, Crypto AG, which possesses a remarkable collection of cipher machines in its museum, and Arthur Scherbius, whose Enigma became the chief Wehrmacht cipher machine in World War II but whose firm and its archives seem to have disappeared in the German collapse. At the same time, some larger companies, including the International Business Machines Corporation and the International Telephone and Telegraph Company, engaged in research in the same field. Germany's Standard Elektric Lorenz and Siemens und Halske firms both developed machines in the 1930s. All should have some remains of this work in their archives. France bought the Hagelin machine, but from what I have seen of patents there, the French seem not to have done much in this field. England's work has been shrouded in the deepest secrecy.[21] Japan's activities, which culminated in the PURPLE machine solved by the United States before Pearl Harbor, have been discussed from the administrative and espionage aspects,[22] but the technical evolution still awaits its scholar.

\* \* \*

Since this article was first published, the disclosure that the Allies were solving the major German cipher machine, the Enigma, has flooded American and British archives with the documents created during this work. This disclosure has also touched off the delivery to American archives of the results of American solution of Japanese cryptograms, and to both American and British archives some World War I records.

The documents are mainly of two kinds: the texts of the intercepted and solved Axis messages, and studies of cryptology, many of them of the effects of the Allied cryptanalyses on the war. The volume is immense, but this ore contains so many valuable nuggets that it is well worth sifting. In addition, some other items have come to light that seem worth mentioning.

The new British World War I documents are mainly those of Room 40, the Admiralty's codebreaking organization, which dealt not only with naval but with diplomatic intercepts. Patrick Beesly successfully urged the British authorities to release many of the records of Room 40—they were reluctant to do so though the documents were more than 60 years old!—to the Public Record Office in Kew, outside London. He used a number of them in his excellent work *Room 40: British Naval Intelligence 1914–18* (London, 1982), listing some in his bibliography, such as ADM 137/3956–62 and ADM 137/4057–4189. But though he inspected those relevant to the main intelligence stories of the war—Jutland, the *Lusitania*, the Zimmerman telegram, the U-boat war—certainly further study of intercepts would yield details of many other episodes that Beesly could only paint with a broad brush. Examples of these might be the Luxburg telegrams, which played a role in Argentina's breaking relations with Germany, and individual case histories of the use of cryptanalysis in actions against U-boats. Examination of the documents will surely suggest other areas of investigation.

Some papers of Malcolm Hay of Seaton, chief of M.I.1b, the British army's codebreaking unit in World War I, are in the library of Aberdeen University in Scotland. They cannot yield the full-blown picture that the formal archives of an agency can, but they can provide useful detail. It is possible that the Public Record Office has the M.I.1b archives, perhaps open to researchers, which may help some historian to balance the stories of French and American military codebreaking with British ones. The records of the codebreaking units of the British Expeditionary Forces and its subordinate armies must be studied as well to complete this picture.

Still waiting to be exploited are three remarkable sources that can fill with extraordinary detail the well-known outlines of the achievements of French military cryptanalysis in World War I. Two of them are from the pen of General Marcel Givierge, head of the French army headquarters cryptologic section. One is his massive study of that body, its predecessors and successors, and its superordinate, subordinate, and parallel units from 1889 to 1921. This "Étude Historique sur la Section du Chiffre" appears to have been written off the documents, since phrases such as "Next we find a sheaf of papers that . . ." sometimes occur. Its value is all the greater since the documents, according to my skimming of the inventories at the French military archives at the Château de Vincennes, no longer seem to exist. (For example, one inventory describes the documents for the Section du Chiffre, archival number 5 N 292–328, as mainly mimeographed extracts of press intercepts; there is nothing about codebreaking. The documents may well have been destroyed in the defeat of 1940. Only at the army level do some intercept documents survive, as 19 N 1187-90, VII^e Armée, Rapports des postes spéciaux d'écoutes, décembre 1915-avril 1917.) The minuteness with which the "Étude Historique" scrutinizes events may be imagined from its length: more than 2,000 typescript pages. It is accompanied by an extremely detailed index.

Givierge's other manuscript consists of his memoir, "Au Service du Chiffre: 18 ans de souvenirs, 1907–1925." Apparently based on the "Étude Historique," and naturally overlapping somewhat, it is much more personal, with sometimes biting comments. It runs about 1,000 typescript pages. Both works await their researchers in the Département des Manuscrits of the Bibliothèque Nationale in Paris.

The third French source consists of the papers of the greatest cryptanalyst of World War I, Georges-Jean Painvin, solver of the German ADFGVX field cipher. These apparently comprise of intercepts, worksheets, memoranda, and correspondence, and would provide technical details additional to those given by Givierge. An amateur bookbinder, Painvin bound them into about eight leather volumes. They stand in the French army's Musée du Chiffre in the fort of Kremlin-Bicêtre in the Paris suburb of that name.

Most of the records of the German army in World War I were destroyed in an Allied air raid in 1944. However, some communications intelligence papers survive in the archives of the Württemberg, Bavarian, and Saxon contingents in Stuttgart, Munich, and Dresden, respectively. Some army papers are also found here and there in the German naval archives. Those archives, which have survived relatively completely, also hold a considerable quantity of naval cryptologic material that may shed some light on German intelligence in the U-boat war and the battle of Jutland, among other episodes. Sample volumes are PG 77146 and 77147, "Tagesmeldungen der E[ntzifferungs]-Stelle West," PG 78146–52, "Beobachtungen des engl. FT [Funktelegraphie]-Verkehrs, 13.4.1915–30.6.1918," and PG 90610, "E. Stelle, E. Wesen, 5.5.1916–13.3.1918."

Though the intelligence records of Germany's ally, Austria-Hungary, were burned at the end of the war, one of the leading intelligence officers,

Colonel Max Ronge, has deposited his papers in the Kriegsarchiv in Vienna. Their heart consists of three volumes of memoirs, in the old German *kursiv* handwriting, dealing with communications intelligence against Russia, communications intelligence against Italy, and telephone-eavesdropping and translation services. These are supplemented by numerous memoranda and contemporary documents. The whole will amplify the studies of Austro-Hungarian intelligence now in print.

For World War II, the outlines of the achievements of the various cryptanalytic agencies has become known through these books: Ronald Lewin, *Ultra Goes to War* (New York, 1978) and *The American Magic* (New York, 1982); Patrick Beesly, *Very Special Intelligence* (London, 1977); Ralph Bennett, *Ultra in the West* (New York, 1979); Jürgen Rohwer and Eberhard Jäckel, eds., *Die Funkaufklärung und ihre Rolle im 2. Weltkrieg* (Stuttgart, 1979); Jürgen Rohwer, *The Critical Convoy Battles of March 1943* (London, 1977); F. H. Hinsley, et al., *British Intelligence in the Second World War* (London, 1979-); John Costello, *The Pacific War* (New York, 1981); Clay Blair, *Silent Victory* (Philadelphia, 1975); and David Kahn, *The Codebreakers* (New York, 1967) and *Hitler's Spies* (New York, 1978). But the volume of material pouring into the archives is so great that plenty of opportunity exists for scholars to investigate the role of solved intercepts in individual episodes of the war.

The Public Record Office documents consist of messages sent from Bletchley Park, the British codebreaking center, to Allied commands. These are generally called the ULTRA signals from the codename for their security level. Bennett estimates that 45,000 were sent to western and Mediterranean commands between January 1944 and May 1945. He says that he utilized all of operational importance for his book, which is subtitled *The Normandy Campaign of 1944-45*, but this leaves plenty of work for historians who want to study the African, Italian, southern France, or air campaigns in terms of ULTRA. The documents he used are in the massive series DEFE 3. The P.R.O. seems not to have yet published any catalogue of its ULTRA holdings.

The National Archives, on the other hand, is constantly issuing updated lists of the new material on cryptology being passed to it by the National Security Agency. These form the new Record Group 457. The documents fall into two categories: translated Japanese and German intercepts, and reports on various aspects of communications intelligence.

The latter include such mouthwatering papers as "Radio Intelligence in World War II Tactical Operations in the Pacific Ocean Areas" (January 1943, 688 pages); reports by ULTRA representatives on their work and its effects; "A Brief History of the Signal Intelligence Service" by William F. Friedman (June 1942, 18 pages); "The Role of Communications Intelligence in Submarine Warfare in the Pacific" (1945, 8 volumes totalling 2,442 pages); "Operational History of the 849th Signal Intelligence Service," Mediterranean Theater of Operations (210 pages); and "Use and Dissemination of Ultra in the Southwest Pacific Area, 1943–1945" (195 pages).

But these are mostly secondary sources, valuable for hints as to subjects and for background. The historian will need to investigate the primary material: the actual intercepts.

And here the volume is amazing. The Japanese army intercepts alone total more than 130,000 pages. In a largely naval war, they are probably mainly of tactical interest, serving for studies showing how codebreaking helped win land battles in the advance across the Pacific. The solutions of naval intercepts, together with their evaluations in such forms as summaries of ship locations, total over 150,000 pages—and when to this is added the intercepts dealing with Japanese water transport for just from April 1943 to June 1944, the number of pages soars to almost 200,000. These cannot help but make clear the intelligence background of the Pacific war, to explain how codebreaking helped cause things to happen as they did—or how (and why) it did not do so in certain cases. The water transport intercepts should provide case after case of how American submarines won one of the most important victories in the Pacific: the sinking of the Japanese merchant fleet, due in considerable measure to U.S. knowledge of the marus' estimation of forthcoming positions. Clay Blair has done much of this; more can be done. For the study of a war at sea, these naval documents are invaluable.

The intercepts that are the most interesting, because they deal with the highest levels of policy, are those of Japanese diplomatic messages. They are called "MAGIC Summaries," after the U.S. codename for Japanese intercepts. The messages from Berlin, enciphered in the PURPLE machine that the United States solved in 1940, include reports of conversations with high Nazi officials and the Japanese diplomats' own views of these personalities, of conditions in Germany and of the German war effort. Badly needed for the more than 11,000 pages is an index. Alexander S. Cochran, Jr.'s *The MAGIC Diplomatic Summaries: A Chronological Finding Aid* (New York, 1982), is utterly inadequate, with its lack of an index, its numerous errors, and its failure to identify persons, places, and abbreviations.

One of the most important messages ever intercepted by the United States during World War II, I have been told, was a message of the Japanese military attaché in Berlin reporting on his inspection of the defenses of the Atlantic Wall in 1943. This was picked up by a monitoring post in Asmara, Ethiopia, and, decrypted, provided General Dwight D. Eisenhower, then planning the cross-Channel invasion, with immensely helpful details of German defenses. MAGIC Summary No. 631 of 17 December 1943 contains the available portions of this report; earlier intercepts contain the reports on the same subject of the ambassador, a general who had formerly been a military attaché. To match these reports with Allied assault planning might undergird the views of the significance of this intercept.

Among the other MAGIC summaries are reports of conversations of Adolf Hitler with the Japanese ambassador that seem not to exist in the German documents and thus are new finds for the history of World War II. Probably the most fruitful areas deal with Japanese-Russian relations, the tentative peace efforts between the Soviet Union and Germany, and, near the end of the war, the attempts of Japanese diplomats to make peace. All of these are mentioned from time to time in the MAGIC summaries. Anthony Cave Brown touches upon the peace efforts of the summer of 1945 in his *Bodyguard of Lies* (New York, 1975), at 812, but a more intensive study, perhaps correlated with the American decision to drop the atomic bomb, will certainly repay the historian.

What about Axis codebreaking? For Germany, though my book *Hitler's Spies* outlines the main accomplishments, additional details, particularly of the army and the navy efforts, may be dredged from the documents, nearly all of them now available. Moreover, the National Security Agency possesses a series of reports, written just after the end of World War II, dealing with the German communications intelligence agencies. These so-called TICOM reports are not yet declassified but, based as they are on interrogations made while memories were fresh, should be useful. The Japanese seemed to have little success in communications intelligence, so a study here should bear but little fruit. I do not know where the records of Italian communications intelligence are, or if they survived. The question is complicated by Italy's midwar surrender.

Two other questions need investigation. One, which may throw light on the origins of the Cold War, concerns the amount of cryptologic information that the Allies sent to the Soviet Union. Hinsley discusses this matter, but a more exhaustive study would be useful. The other, which deals with the so-called special relationship between the United States and Great Britain, concerns American solution of British codes and British solution of American. This is a highly sensitive subject, but evidence of such solutions appears here and there in the literature and in the records, and a study of it might well throw new light on their relations, particularly on British pressure on the United States to enter both World Wars I and II.

# Signals Intelligence
## in the 1980s

Signals intelligence is comprised of two branches. One is communications intelligence, which involves interception of people-to-people communications, direction-finding, traffic analysis (which studies volumes of communications to see what may be going on, say, on the right flank as compared to the left flank) and finally, of course, codebreaking or cryptanalysis, which consists of attempting to break the actual code armor of a message to read what's inside. The other element of signals intelligence is electronic intelligence, which deals with radars and information concerning radar locations, capabilities, wavelengths, frequencies, and other operating characteristics of the radars so that our bombers, if they fly into the Soviet Union, for example, can spoof or in some other way nullify those radars.

You are familiar with the historical importance of codebreaking. Some information came out shortly after World War II, when we all heard about how we broke some Japanese codes before Pearl Harbor, which didn't help very much, and broke others later that did help very much before the Battle of Midway, in the midair assassination of Admiral Yamamoto, and in the successful American submarine blockade of Japan, which very largely brought the Japanese empire to its knees. More recently there have been the revelations about ULTRA, by Group Captain Winterbotham and by others, about how important Britain's codebreak-

"Signals Intelligence in the 1980s" is the edited transcript of a talk presented before a symposium of the Consortium for the Study of Intelligence, Washington, D.C., on October 30, 1981.

ing of German cipher machines was in winning the war. Generals on both sides acknowledged that codebreaking was their most important form of operational, strategic, and tactical intelligence. There is a very good quote to that effect by General Franz Halder, who for a long time was chief of the German general staff, and there are well-known quotes by Generals Marshall and Eisenhower, all to the same effect.

But in 1978, President Carter said somewhat the opposite: "Recently, however, I have been concerned that the trend that was established about 15 years ago to get intelligence from electronic means might have been overemphasized, sometimes to the detriment of the assessment of the intelligence derived, and also the intelligence derived through normal political channels"—although he added, "not secret intelligence."[1]

Nevertheless, SIGINT remains an extremely valuable commodity to the United States, and presumably to other nations. As I see it, it has a number of advantages over other sources—and I'm thinking in particular of aerial photography, which is almost the only other secret source that we have in peacetime.

The most important, as I see it, is that it can give you warning in advance of other sources, and in particular, before photo intelligence. Photo intelligence can only show you what's there or what someone is building so he can put something there. Signal intelligence can very often give you his plans for putting something in long before anything is actually done. So it gives you an extra step in time or an extra beat, moves you ahead, as it were, of the events, which the visual forms of intelligence cannot do. SIGINT is also particularly trustworthy. Spies may feed you information, good information, in any number of instances. But the question always remains: Is this guy setting us up for some other situation in which he is going to feed us false stuff and make us fall into a trap?

Of course, it's possible to create hoaxes in SIGINT, such as fake signal nets. But this seems to be more amenable to detection, partly because of the greater variety of information, the greater spectrum of material, and the greater volume of material that comes in, and partially because it seems to take much more effort to create a successful SIGINT hoax than it does just to turn a double agent around. Historically, there have been relatively few radio intelligence hoaxes. The few that I know about were Soviet hoaxes on the Eastern front during World War II. All seem to have been detected.

So, to repeat, radio intelligence or communications intelligence has the double advantage of speed and trustworthiness. As a former director of the Defense Intelligence Agency[2] said to me, "Spies take too long to get information to you. Photographs do as well. N.S.A. [National Security Agency] is intercepting things as they happen. N.S.A. will tell you, 'They are about to launch a missile. The missile is launched.' We know in five minutes that a missile has been launched. And this kind of intelligence," he said, "is crucial to the warning business." That is true. The stuff comes in at the speed of light.

Moreover, although I don't know of any studies that have been specifically done on this subject, I have the feeling, and intelligence people tell me, that communications intelligence is cheaper than other forms of intelligence. Essentially, all you need is one person sitting down with a radio to pick up the information and another working to break the code. Of course, with the advent of computers and with the use of satellites, this may have changed, but the feeling that I have is that communications intelligence is still cheaper, man for man, or datum for datum, whichever way you want to do it.

Finally, another advantage is that when SIGINT activities are discovered there seem to be fewer international repercussions than when spies are caught on the territory of a country. Nobody goes around making a big fuss if it is somehow disclosed that their codes are broken. They simply change the codes, and they don't go around crying "foul" or saying that people shouldn't be doing this. Immanuel Kant, in his book, *Perpetual Peace*, stated that spying is a kind of a crime against the international order because if discovered, it causes international difficulties.[3] But this doesn't seem to happen with SIGINT.

There are also disadvantages to communications intelligence. One of the greatest is that it seems to engender a feeling of overconfidence. When they get the transcript of a telephone wiretap, many policymakers seem to have the feeling that they're getting a full picture of the situation. Well, of course, they're not. And this may lead them into dangerous misconceptions to which they might not be subject with other forms of intelligence. Signals intelligence is also more easily lost than other forms of intelligence. As I mentioned briefly, if a country discovers that its codes are being read, all it has to do is change its codes. It doesn't have to go around hunting for a human mole.

Finally, [aerial photography expert] Amrom Katz touched on perhaps another disadvantage when he said, "Nothing convinces like a photograph." When you're dealing with signals material that is full of inferences or that comes in in bits and pieces, or when you realize that you are depending essentially on little peepings in the earphones of listeners, you may have less confidence in the result than you would be if you had an aerial photograph spread in front of you.

As we head into the '80s, I see two problems for SIGINT. We have heard about the window of vulnerability. When it comes to codebreaking and cryptanalysis, we have a closing window of accessibility. By this I mean that the countries whose codes we can now read, which are essentially Third World countries, are gradually depriving us of this ability. That is the first problem. One reason for it is the spread of technology to Third World nations. Microprocessors are giving everybody the ability to make extremely good cryptosystems. The other reason is the ability of codemakers to stay ahead of codebreakers. This has been quantified in a rough rule of thumb: If you double the capacity of a code, you square the work that the codebreaker has to do. In other words, you have a cipher machine with 5 key wheels, and it takes someone, say, 8 hours to solve a message in that system. You double the machine to 10 wheels, and instead of now working 16 hours, the cryptanalyst has to work 64 hours to solve a message in the system. The point is today that cipher machines and other forms of cryptography have become so complicated and so far advanced that anybody who has the money, the technological knowledge and the skilled manpower can make his messages unbreakable to anybody else. As the knowledge of cryptology spreads, the number of countries whose codes the major nations can break is shrinking, and so fewer and fewer nations' messages are being read.

The second problem is that we are losing precision in the information that we are getting from signals intelligence. If you are reading the actual text of a coded message, you are getting very good information; you are getting it, as it were, from the horse's mouth. If, however, you can't get this kind of material, you have to move out to the periphery and deal increasingly in such matters as traffic analysis and direction finding, and you have to have much more volume to get information of lesser quality. So, though you expand your organization, you are not able to get quite as much information as you were before.

Well, then, what should we do? What should be the direction for codebreaking in the 1980s? No question, number one, we are going to have to concentrate on Third World nations. We can't break the codes of the major powers these days, and we have to work on these other countries. This may be a blessing in disguise because, when you look back at the hot spots over the world in the postwar era, you'll find they have all been at one time or another in the Third World countries—Korea, Cuba, the Congo, Vietnam, Iran, and things like that. We are also gathering more and more economic data. In a world that is increasingly interdependent, a world where everybody can be inconvenienced by an oil embargo, to say nothing of an oil shutdown, where we are selling grain to the Soviet Union, where we are concerned about strategic minerals, economic data comes increasingly to the fore as an intelligence target.

Another area, of course, is terrorism. Within the United States, anti-terrorist SIGINT can't be done by the National Security Agency but has to be done by the attorney general. But internationally, terrorists are a legitimate target for the National Security Agency. Then there is missile telemetry. It is of increasing importance that we listen to Soviet missiles to find out whatever we can of their characteristics, and it is to be hoped that whatever arms limitation treaty is finally ratified will retain the language in the SALT II treaty that prohibits the encryption of telemetry data.

A quite different area should involve the rest of the intelligence community in attempts to help SIGINT by stealing foreign signals intelligence material in the form of codes and keys and plaintexts. When it's not possible to break codes, we have to get them in some other way. And I think that very likely this is going to be an increasing effort on the part of the human intelligence collectors. These keys will enable us to unlock doors into a treasure of interesting material. The *Glomar Explorer* was just one aspect of that.

Finally, we need a greater proportion of analysts to collection people. There has been talk about the "all-source glut" and there has certainly been a glut of information derived from SIGINT, but the take is no good unless it is analyzed. And I think that in the future we are going to see an increasing emphasis on analysis, and that that's going to be one of the best ways we can increase the value of signals intelligence.

# NOTES

NOTES

# Conversations with Cryptologists

1. Pronounced "yule-DEHN."
2. *Chifferbyråernas insatser i världskriget till lands* (Stockholm, 1931); trans. Military Intelligence Division (Washington, 1935; reprinted Laguna Beach, Calif., 1978.) I believe that his chief source for much of the information on French cryptology was Edmond Locard, who had served in the French army's Bureau de Chiffre in World War I and had collaborated with Gyldén on a bibliography of cryptology.
3. In a ministerial sense. Socially, he is outranked by Duke August II of Braunschweig-Lüneberg, author of *Cryptomenytices et Cryptographiae libri IX* (Lüneberg, 1624).
4. *Kryptografins Grunddrag* (c. 1918), 165 pp.
5. The Hagelin company is now Crypto AG (Aktiengesellschaft, or stock company) of Steinhausen, Zug, Switzerland, a branch of the giant Siemens Corporation, German electrical-products manufacturers.
6. Gyldén died in 1963.
7. "Mathematische und maschinelle Verfahren beim chiffrieren und dechiffrieren," *FIAT Review of German Science 1939–1946: Applied Mathematics*, Part I (Wiesbaden, 1948) 233–257. English translation by Bradford Hardie as "Mathematical and Mechanical Methods in Cryptography," *Cryptologia*, 2 (January 1978), 20–37, (April 1978), 101–121.
8. The declassification of William F. Friedman's *Military Cryptanalysis* and advances in computer science have invalidated the superlative. But it was true at the time, and the work remains outstanding.
9. I doubt if this was the Château de Fouzes, codenamed CADIX, used by the Poles and the French to read German Enigma messages until the Germans occupied all of France in November 1942. CADIX was near Uzès, in the south of France near Avignon, and would hardly be characterized as "outside Lyons," which was 125 miles away. I do not know to which bureau or villa he refers.

# Interviews with Cryptologists

1. Reprinted as preceding article.
2. See citation in notes to preceding article.
3. Published in 1978 by the Macmillan Publishing Company as *Hitler's Spies: German Military Intelligence in World War II*.
4. The major German field cipher, an ingenious combination in which a checkerboard substitution (using the letters A, D, F, G, V, and X as coordinates of the 6 × 6 square) was followed by a columnar transposition. Details of the system, and its solution, by France's Georges-Jean Painvin, in David Kahn, *The Codebreakers: The Story of Secret Writing* (New York, 1967), 339–347.
5. Nebel died in 1977 at 86.
6. Seifert's information was used in the section on the Forschungsamt in *Hitler's Spies*, 178–184.
7. Neeb's information appears in *Hitler's Spies*, pp. 200–201.
8. Tranow's information was used throughout Chapter 14 of *Hitler's Spies*, "The Codebreaker Who Helped the U-Boats," 213–222.
9. Captain Horst Wiebe.
10. Gustave Bertrand.
11. Henryk Zygalski. He did not make the initial break but participated in the cryptanalysis of the Enigma in the 1930s as the Germans kept complicating the system.

12. General Fritz Boetzel.

13. See comment in notes to preceding chapter.

## How *The Codebreakers* Was Written

1. Fletcher Pratt's *Secret and Urgent,* in the 1942 Blue Ribbon reprint edition of the 1939 original.

2. Vice Admiral W. W. Smith, U.S.N., Ret., who had dealt with codes and ciphers as a junior naval officer and had written an excellent exposition of the solution of the Playfair cipher for the English edition of André Langie's *De la cryptographie* (1923).

3. Shiro Takagi, the editor, and Naotsune Watanabe, the professor.

4. Edward H. Hebern. But the rotor system that he invented is no longer "the world's most widely used."

## Lgcn Otuu Wllwgh Wl Etfown

1. This turns out not to have been so. Certainly, keys were changed in some countries, and completely new systems put into place in a few. But information I gained after I wrote this article makes me now doubt that there was a wholesale replacement of cryptosystems or that communications clerks were "sweating over the intricacies of new systems of code."

2. Not quite. Writing always precedes secret writing.

3. In fact, only one basic form was used, but in it, normal hieroglyphs could be replaced by others in a variety of ways.

4. Fortunately for cryptanalysts, this is not so. The costs—in development, production, training, mix-ups, and embarrassment—are too high. Nazi Germany's navy, for example, did not replace the Enigma cipher machine despite many suspicions that it had been broken.

5. This seems unlikely, though the Martin-Mitchell revelations did cause a loss of cryptanalytic intelligence.

6. Only naval codes.

7. He was informally accused of practicing black magic.

8. This is in error. The British messages were in the one-time pad and could not be broken.

9. The United Arab Republic was a union of Egypt and Syria that began in 1958 and ended when Syria withdrew in 1961, though Egypt retained the U.A.R. designation until 1971.

## The Code Battle

1. Vice Admiral Bobby R. Inman, director from 1977 to 1981, breached this tradition.

2. No longer. Now ordinary General Services Administration security personnel fulfill this function.

3. The United States has been forced out of both these posts.

4. Congressional hearings later confirmed this.

5. Later information suggests that the implication of U.S. reading of Soviet transmissions was not true.

6. He did not devise this system, but helped test its security. The scrambler, which masked vocoder voice sounds with never-repeated random noise, was developed by Bell Telephone Laboratories. Bell called it Project X; the Signal Corps called it SIGSALY. For details of the system, see Robert Price, "Further Notes and Anecdotes on Spread-Spectrum Origins," and William R. Bennett, "Secret Telephony as a Historical Example of Spread-Spectrum Communication," both *IEEE Transactions on Communications*, 31 (January 1983), 85–97 and 98–104.

7. This romantic story, which first appeared in *The World Crisis* (New York, 1923), a history of World War I by Winston Churchill, who at the time the code arrived from the Russians was First Lord of the Admiralty, appears on the latest evidence to be false. According to Patrick Beesly, *Room 40* (London, 1982), 5, the codebook, now in Britain's Public Record Office, "shows no sign of immersion." He quotes a Russian source that says the book was found in its "customary place in the charthouse." But whatever the details, the book did arrive at the Admiralty and gave the British their start in reading German messages.

8. The O.S.S. sought to minimize this, according to Anthony Cave Brown's biography of O.S.S. director William J. Donovan, *Wild Bill Donovan: The Last Hero* (New York, 1982), 306–307. Cave Brown cites a contemporaneous document of Donovan's saying that the episode had not reduced Japanese use of the cipher. This allegation conflicts with that of Chief of Staff George C. Marshall in a letter to Thomas E. Dewey (cited in David Kahn, *The Codebreakers* [New York, 1967], at 607); additional research may resolve the differences.

9. Evidence I came across after writing this article suggests that Hitler did not reject the CICERO documents. But their value was limited. They did not help in any way to defend against the Normandy invasion, as some writers have suggested. At best, they helped the Germans stave off British demands upon neutral Turkey for a few months.

10. ULTRA's assistance was not uniform but was concentrated during the later battles.

11. United Arab Republic.

# The Grand Lines of Cryptology's Development

Not referenced are historical statements found in generally available reference works on the history of cryptology.

1. *John Baptista Porta's Natural Magick* [reprint of 1658 edition] (New York, 1957), bk. 16.

2. Brian Randell, "The Colossus," in *A History of Computing in the Twentieth Century*, ed. N. Metropolis et al. (New York, 1980), 47–92.

3. Peter E. Glasner, *The Sociology of Secularisation: A Critique of a Concept* (London, 1977), 42.

4. Robert Nisbet and Robert G. Perrin, *The Social Bond*, 2d ed. (New York, 1977), 213.

5. Auguste Comte, *System of Positive Policy* [reprint of London, 1876, edition] (New York, 1966), 3:23.

6. Nisbet and Perrin, 115.

7. Arnold E. Leon, *Secularization: Science Without God?* (London, 1967), 13.

8. Herbert Butterfield, *The Origins of History*, ed. Adam Watson (New York, 1981), 198–220.

9. Georges Dossin, "Signaux lumineux aux pays de Mari," *Revue d'Assyriologie et d'Archéologie Orientale,* 35 (1938) 174–186.

10. David Kahn, "On the Origin of Polyalphabetic Substitution," *Isis: Official Journal of the History of Science Society,* 71 (March 1980), 122–127. Reprinted as next chapter in this volume.

11. Konrad H. Jarausch, "Quantitative History in International Perspective: Some Introductory Considerations," paper of January 1982.

# On the Origin of Polyalphabetic Substitution

I thank Cecil Grayson, Serena Professor of Italian Studies in the University of Oxford, and Robert D. F. Pring-Mill, Lecturer in Spanish in the University of Oxford, for their comments on the thesis set forth here.

1. Charles J. Mendelsohn, "Blaise de Vigenère and the 'Chiffre Carré,'" *Proceedings of the American Philosophical Society,* 82 (1940), 103–129.

2. David Kahn, *The Codebreakers: The Story of Secret Writing* (New York, 1967), 18–24, 427–433, 398–400, 606, 655; F. W. Winterbotham, *The Ultra Secret* (New York, 1974); Ronald Lewin, *Ultra Goes to War* (New York, 1978).

3. Jacob Burckhardt, *The Civilization of the Renaissance in Italy,* trans. S. G. C. Middlemore (1929; reprinted ed. New York, 1958), 148–150; Joan Gadol, *Léon Battista Alberti: Universal Man of the Early Renaissance* (Chicago, 1969).

4. Aloys Meister, *Die Anfänge der modernen diplomatischen Geheimschrift: Beiträge zur Geschichte der italienischen Kryptographie des XV. Jahrbunderts* (Paderborn, 1902), 41 and passim.

5. J. P. Devos and H. Seligman, eds. *L'art de deschiffrer: traité de déchiffrement du XVII siècle de la Secrétairerie d'État et de guerre espagnole* (Louvain, 1967), esp. 43–89.

6. An early copy (no holographs seem to exist) is reprinted in Aloys Meister, *Die Geheimschrift im Dienste der päpstlichen Kurie: von ibren Anfängen bis zum Ende des XVI. Jahrbunderts* (Paderborn, 1906), 125–141. Portions in English, with discussion, appear in Kahn, 125–129. For a list of the known manuscripts with their locations see Charles J. Mendelsohn, "Bibliographical Note on the 'De Cifris' of Leone Battista Alberti," *Isis* 32 (1947), 48–51. For discussion of the origins of its linguistic analysis, see Cecil Grayson, "Léon Battista Alberti and the Beginnings of Italian Grammar," *Proceedings of the British Academy, 1963,* 49 (1964), 291–311, on 302–303.

7. Kahn, 150–151, 153–154, 191.

8. Gadol, 171–174, 208.

9. The device is reproduced widely, e.g., in Frances Yates, *The Art of Memory* (London, 1966), 183, where I first saw it. See also Robert D. F. Pring-Mill, "Ramon Lull," *Dictionary of Scientific Biography,* (New York, 1970–1980), 7:549.

10. Pring-Mill, 547–551. See also R. D. F. Pring-Mill, "The Analogical Structure of the Lullian Art," in *Islamic Philosophy and the Classical Tradition: Festschrift for Richard Walzer* (Oxford, 1972), 315–326 at 315.

11. Pring-Mill, 549; J. N. Hillgarth, *Ramon Lull and Lullism in Fourteenth-Century France* (Oxford, 1971), 8, 315; see also Erhard Wolfram Platzeck, *Raimund Lull: sein Leben—seine Werke—die Grundlagen seines Denkens (Prinzipienlehre)* (Düsseldorf, 1962–1964), 1:265–266.

12. Lynn Thorndike, *A History of Magic and Experimental Science* (New York, 1923–1958), 4:27.

13. Pring-Mill, 549; Martin Gardner, *Logic Machines and Diagrams* (New York, 1958), 9–14, 19.

14. Pring-Mill, 548; Platzeck, 1:321.

15. Pring-Mill, "Analogical Structure," 318; Pring-Mill, 549; and Platzeck, 1:332 and 321, in which the first I should be an F.

16. M. Batllori, "Le Lullisme de la Renaissance et du Baroque: Padoue et Rome," *Xième Congrès International de Philosophie, Actes* (Amsterdam, 1953), 13:7–12 at 10–11; Miguel Batllori, "Relíques manuscrites del Lul-lisme Italià," *Analecta Sacra Tarraconensia*, 11 (1935), 129–141; Hillgarth, 137–138, 281; Paul Oskar Kristeller, *Iter Italicum: A Finding List of Uncatalogued or Incompletely Catalogued Humanistic Manuscripts of the Renaissance in Italian and Other Libraries* (London, 1965–1967), 1:165, 278, 292, 302, 303, 307, 308, 312, 317, 345, 370, 427; 2:19, 107, 140, 141.

17. Discussions of Alberti's sources do not mention Lull, e.g., Gadol; L. Zoubov, "Léon Battista Alberti et les auteurs du Moyen Age," *Medieval and Renaissance Studies*, 4 (1958), 245–266; Paul-Henri Michel, *La Pensée de L. B. Alberti* (Paris, 1930); Franco Borsi, *Léon Battista Alberti*, trans. Rudolf G. Carpini (New York, 1977); George Sarton, *The Appreciation of Ancient and Medieval Science during the Renaissance (1450–1600)* (Philadelphia, 1955).

18. A difference between Lull's disk and Alberti's lies in the sequence of letters. Lull's is alphabetical (though with gaps). Alberti, however, specified that his disk's letters be "not in regular order, . . . but scattered at random." This greatly improves the cipher. Alberti may well have got the idea for mixing the sequence, not from current cryptographic practice, which rarely did it, but, as Gadol also thinks (207), from the movable type of the printing press, which Alberti mentions at the beginning of his treatise.

19. Pring-Mill, 548, and letter, May 5, 1972.

20. Hillgarth, 19. The *rotae* are illustrated in Isidore de Seville, *Traité de la nature*, ed. Jacques Fontaine (Bordeaux, 1960), 190 and 190-bis, 212 and 212-bis, and Harry Bober, "An Illustrated Medieval School-Book of Bede's 'De Natura Rerum,' " *The Journal of the Walters Art Gallery*, 19–20 (1956–1957), 65–97, at 91.

21. Platzeck, 1:327–332. On the *Sefer Yezirah*, see Gershom G. Scholem, *On the Kabbalah and Its Symbolism*, trans. Ralph Manheim (New York, 1969), 166–169.

22. The *Book of Formation (Sepher Yezirah) by Rabbi Akiba ben Joseph*, trans. Knut Stenring (1923, reprinted New York, 1970), Ch. II, Sec. 4. See Platzeck, 1:330, 332.

23. Pring-Mill, 547.

24. Lazarus Goldschmidt, trans. and ed., *Das Buch der Schöpfung* (Frankfurt, 1894), 30.

25. Blaise de Vigenère, *Traicté des chiffres* (Paris, 1587), 23r, 36r.

26. Mendelsohn, 122–123.

# Herbert O. Yardley: A Biographical Sketch

The sources for the biography of Yardley, in addition to those cited in David Kahn, *The Codebreakers* (New York, 1967), include:

interviews with Edna Yardley 10 February 1969 and in the fall of 1979
an interview with Grover Batts (who roomed for several years with the Yardleys), 29 March 1981
the notes of Louis Kruh's interview with Clem Koukol, 25 April 1979, and a letter of Koukol to Kruh, 26 May 1976
a memorandum of Yardley, 5 January 1942
Yardley's personnel file in National Archives, Record Group 165, Military Intelligence Division File 10039-299 (Box 2594A)
National Archives, Record Group 59, Office of the Counselor, Boxes 202 and 212
Library of Congress, Papers of Leland Harrison, Boxes 24 and 115
copy of *The American Black Chamber* annotated by former colleagues of Yardley, in the William F. Friedman Collection at the George C. Marshall Library, Lexington, Virginia
Herbert O. Yardley, *The Chinese Black Chamber* (Boston, 1983)

## The Spy Who Most Affected World War II

1. Gustave Bertrand, *Enigma, ou la plus grande énigme de la guerre 1939–1945* (Paris, 1973), 12.

2. Bertrand, interview, 12 July 1974.

3. L[ouis]. Ribadeau Dumas, "Essai d'Historique du Chiffre de l'Armée de Terre: 4e Partie (1919–1939)," *Bulletin de l'A.R.C.* [Association des Réservistes du Chiffre], nouvelle série, no. 3 (1975), 19–34 at 23.

4. Bertrand, 18.

5. Bertrand, 37.

6. Ribadeau Dumas, 30.

7. Bertrand, interview.

8. Bertrand, 18.

9. Bertrand, interview.

10. Ibid.; Bertrand, 18; Henri Navarre et al., *Le Service de Renseignements 1871–1944* (Paris, 1978), 69–70.

11. Jozef Garlinski, *The Enigma War* (New York, 1979), 18, though Garlinski's statement that from 1926 the Poles could no longer solve this system is in error.

12. Wladyslaw Kozaczuk, "Enigma Solved: How the German machine cipher was broken and how it was read by the Allies in World War II," manuscript translation by Christopher Kasparek of *W Kregu Enigmy* (Warsaw, 1979), 15, 22.

13. [Marian Rejewski], "Enigma, 1930–1940: Metodi i historia rozwiazania niemieckiego szyfru maszynowego (w zarysie)" ("Enigma, 1930–1940: The Method and History of Solving the German Machine Cipher [an outline],") unpublished manuscript, translated in part by Alfred Piechowiak, at §1. This document is a carbon copy of a typescript. According to Alfred Piechowiak, it was given to his father, a Polish intelligence officer, during World War II, to hold. Alfred Piechowiak mentioned it to me when we met in Oxford, allowed me to make a photocopy of it, and translated part of it for me. Later, Tadeusz Lisicki identified the corrections on it as in Rejewski's handwriting. It is probable that it served Rejewski in the writing of his later memoir on breaking the Enigma.

14. Ibid., §1.

15. The best descriptions of the machine and its keying are in Gordon Welchman, *The Hut Six Story: Breaking the Enigma Codes* (New York, 1982), 38–52, and C. A. Deavours and James Reeds, "The Enigma—Part I: Historical Perspective," *Cryptologia*, 1 (October, 1977), 381–391, with excellent close-ups of the machine's elements.

16. "Enigma, 1930–1940," §2; S. A. Mayer, "The breaking up of the German ciphering machine Enigma," unpublished manuscript, 31 May 1974, at 1.

17. Garlinski, 2–3.

18. "Enigma, 1930–1940," §2.

19. Ibid.

20. Ibid.; Marian Rejewski, "How Polish Mathematicians Deciphered the Enigma," trans. Joan Stepenske, *Annals of the History of Computing*, 3 (July 1981), 213–234 at 213.

21. Rejewski, 213.

22. Bertrand, 21, 23.

23. Navarre, 56, 57, 58, for example.

24. Ibid., 54, 70. This seems more likely than Bertrand's statement, at 24, that the agent chose his ominous codename of "ash" himself.

25. Berlin Document Center, file of Hans-Thilo Schmidt, Party Membership Number 738,736. For parents: letter of Militärarchiv, 20 May 1983, enclosing copy of service record of Hans-Thilo's brother, Rudolf, from its Sammlung Krug, MSg 109/2373. Father's books are *Die Schlacht bei Wittstock, Ein Kalvinist als kaiserlicher Feldmarschall im Dreissigjährigen Krieg,* and *Otto Christof von Sparr.* Biographical details from British Museum, *Catalogue of*

*Printed Books,* vol. 215, cols. 415–416, and Library of Congress, *National Union Catalog, Pre-1956 Imprints,* vol. 257, p. 558. How do we know that ASCHE was Hans-Thilo Schmidt? There are several ways: One comes from Gert Buchheit, "Verrat deutscher Geheimcodes," *Politische Welt,* 10 (1967), 10–14, which, despite some errors, reported that "Thilo Schmidt" delivered to the French, among other items, details about the Enigma. Buchheit does not give his source. Another way is my telephone interview on 12 July 1974 with Walther Seifert, head of evaluation in the Forschungsamt and thus Schmidt's boss, in which the full name was revealed for the first time, to the best of my knowledge. The conversation took place in the middle of my interview with Gustave Bertrand, who had run Schmidt, at the Hotel de la Tour de l'Esquillon at Théoule-sur-Mer, of which Bertrand was mayor, near Cannes in southern France. In his book, *Enigma,* Bertrand had written that ASCHE had worked from 1934 as an evaluator in the Forschungsamt. I asked Bertrand what had eventually happened to him, and he told me that ASCHE had been arrested and executed during the war. I excused myself and rang Seifert, whom I had twice interviewed, at his home in Osnabrück to ask him if he knew of anyone in his branch to whom this had happened. He named Schmidt, thus proving that Schmidt and ASCHE were one and the same. I had hoped Bertrand would be impressed enough to give me more information, but whether he was or not, he did not verify the correctness of the name. In a letter of 7 August 1974 Seifert typed out the name and added the information that Schmidt was a member of the Nazi party. At my request, the Berlin Document Center, which houses Nazi party files, searched for such a name and found it. This provided documentary proof of the man's existence as well as such data as his party number, date of membership, date of birth, and home addresses. I published the name in a review of Frederick W. Winterbotham's *The Ultra Secret* in the *New York Times Book Review* for 30 December 1974, and sent the review to Bertrand. He replied with a furious letter of 6 January 1975 that inadvertently confirmed from his side that Hans-Thilo Schmidt was ASCHE, for in it he declared that "I will not hide from you that I am very angry at the indiscretion that you have committed in unveiling the name of the employee of the Cipher Center, which I had always carefully concealed, since his brother and his wife (as well as his children) are still living. . . ." (The brother had in fact died in 1957.) Finally, indirect confirmation comes from the mention in the Goebbels diary of the arrest for treason of the brother of Colonel-General Schmidt (Josef Goebbels, *The Goebbels Diaries, 1942–1943,* ed. and trans. Louis P. Lochner [Garden City, N.Y., 1948], 369, entry for 10 May 1943). References to Hans-Thilo Schmidt in the works of Navarre, of Paul Paillole, *Services Spéciaux 1935–1945* (Paris, 1975), and of others are all subsequent to these publications and so cannot be taken as independent verifications of Schmidt as ASCHE.

26. Gert Buchheit, *Spionage in zwei Weltkriegen* (Landshut, 1975), 95. This expands on the *Politische Welt* article and, like it, is based in part on the article by F. S. [Franz Seubert], "Die Asse des französischen Nachrichtendienstes vor und während des Krieges 1939–1945," *Die Nachhut* (15 November 1967), 8–11. All three contain many errors.

27. Militärarchiv, letter; National Archives, Record Group 165, Military Intelligence Division, G-2 Report No. 17,316 of June 7, 1940, from military attaché, Berlin; Hugo Kettler (wartime head of what was then the Cipher Branch), interview, 30 August 1967.

28. Buchheit, 95.

29. Berlin Document Center.

30. Ibid.

31. Navarre, 55.

32. David Kahn, *Hitler's Spies: German Military Intelligence in World War II* (New York, 1978), 178–179, 181, 575.

33. Bertrand, 29.

34. Bertrand, 25.

35. Bertrand, 29.

36. Bertrand, 25, 29; Navarre, 55.

37. Bertrand, 35; Buchheit, 93–94; Paillole, 64; Michel Garder, *La Guerre secrète des Services Spéciaux 1935–1945* (Paris, 1967), 84.

38. Bertrand, 24.

39. Ibid., 25–28, 24. For the Davidova Bouda hotel: *Fodor's Guide to Czechoslovakia*.

40. Navarre, 55.

41. Ibid., 54, 55.

42. Militärarchiv, letter.

43. Bertrand, 30, 34–35.

44. Bertrand, 32; "Enigma 1930–1940," §4.

45. Christopher Kasparek and Richard A. Woytak, "In Memoriam Marian Rejewski," and Richard A. Woytak, "A Conversation with Marian Rejewski," trans. Christopher Kasparek, both *Cryptologia*, 6 (January 1982), 19–25 and 50–60 at 20, 51.

46. Henryk Zygalski, interview, 29 July 1974.

47. Woytak, 52.

48. Kozaczuk, 19–21; Woytak, 52.

49. Zygalski; Kasparek; and Woytak, 20.

50. Rejewski, 213–234.

51. C. A. Deavours, telephone interview, 20 May 1983.

52. Bertrand, 37. The date of "1931" given on this page is a typographical error, since Bertrand twice (21, 23) says the first contact with Schmidt took place in October 1932; moreover, he later wrote Rejewski that the "1931" should have been "1932" (Woytak, 54).

53. Bertrand, 37.

54. Woytak, 54.

55. "Enigma 1930–1940," §4.

56. Rejewski, 221. In the quotations of Rejewski that follow, I have used what I consider the best elements of the Stepenske translation and the better but unpublished translation of Kasparek, appended to Kozaczuk. In addition, I have changed the technical terms to correspond with current usage, such as replacing "drum connections" with "rotor wirings."

57. Ibid.

58. Ibid.

59. Bertrand, 61. L[ouis]. Ribadeau Dumas, "Le Décryptement de l'Enigma," *Bulletin de l'A.R.C.*, nouvelle série, 7 (1979), 32–40, states, at 35, that Bertrand did not give his documents to the army's Section du Chiffre as a consequence of security and personal motives. It seems incredible to me that Bertrand's superiors would permit documents to be given to the Poles and not to another section of the French general staff, but whether or not this was the case, the cryptanalysts of Bertrand's own Section D certainly saw the documents, yet even so they did not solve the Enigma.

60. Rejewski, 221. In this translation, the verb is given as "has been," which implies that the other approach was not known at the time. In the translation by Kasparek the verb is "was," which makes the anti-Schmidt case stronger and so is used here. Would the Poles have been able to solve the Enigma without Schmidt's documents? Opinion is divided on this point. A Polish engineer peripherally involved in the Enigma reconstruction believes that Rejewski would have solved the Enigma in two years even without the Schmidt documents, since they did not bear directly on the critical question of the rotor wiring (Tadeusz Lisicki, "Die Leistung des polnischen Entzifferungsdienstes bei der Lösung des Verfahrens der deutschen 'Enigma'-Funkschlüsselmaschine," in Jürgen Rohwer and Eberhard Jäckel, eds., *Die Funkaufklärung und ihre Rolle im 2. Weltkrieg* [Stuttgart, 1979], 166–186 at 184). But an American mathematician who has analyzed in depth Rejewski's solution believes that the documents made the solution possible. For they eliminated one of the unknowns (Deavours, telephone interview). Rejewski himself said different things at different times. In "Enigma 1930–1940," Rejewski wrote: "In principle the problem was solvable and no doubt would have been solved if the attention of cryptolo-

gists working on the Enigma cipher was not channeled in another direction [he apparently refers to the 1929 attempt]." But in a later article, he wrote (see his quotation in the text of this article) (a) that he did not know whether the equations in four unknowns were solvable and (b) that, even if they were, a solution depended upon a fortuitous combination of circumstances. Only in the opinion that such a solution would have required a great deal of time—"a number of years," he wrote in "Enigma 1930–1940"—was he consistent. In any event, any answer to whether Rejewski would have solved the Enigma without Schmidt's documents would be hypothetical and thus impossible of proof.

61. These complications would almost certainly have defeated a cryptanalyst who had not previously broken the machine. When Rejewski cracked the machine, the Germans were changing the rotor positions every three months; on 1 February 1936, they began changing them every month; from 1 October 1936, they changed them daily. Also, on 1 October 1936 they raised the number of plugboard connections. On 2 November 1937 they replaced the old reflector with a new one. On 15 September 1938 they changed their original vulnerable key procedure. On 15 December 1938 they put two extra rotors into service, forcing the cryptanalysts to determine which three of the five were in use each time and greatly multiplying the number of trials they had to make. Twice in 1939 the number of plugboard connections was increased. These complications deprived the cryptanalysts of the conditions necessary for a first solution—even with Schmidt's documents— and so made it impossible. Their effect is shown in the experience of Britain's brilliant cryptanalyst, Alfred Dillwyn Knox. He began work on the Enigma problem in 1936 and made some progress, in the form of the so-called method of batons. But he never solved the machine (Penelope Fitzgerald, *The Knox Brothers* [London, 1977], 203; Kozaczuk, 96; Woytak, 56–57; C. A. Deavours, "La Méthode des Batons," *Cryptologia* 4 [October 1980], 240–247).

62. Bertrand, 250–253; Navarre, 56.

63. Berlin Document Center. Schmidt's Nazi Party file contains no details of why he was expelled from the party. And the surviving records of neither the Volksgerichthof— the post-1933 court that dealt with some treason cases, now in the Bundesarchiv in Koblenz—nor of the Reichsgericht—the older court that dealt with treason, now in the Zentrales Staatsarchiv in Potsdam—contain any dossier on Schmidt. The question arises, Why did the Germans not realize, once they had caught Schmidt, that the Allies might have been reading Enigma messages? One possibility is that neither Lemoine nor Schmidt told them about the thefts of the Enigma documents. Another is that the Germans were told but believed that complications added since 1932 had preserved the system's security. In any event, Schmidt's capture did not lead to Germany's replacement of the Enigma by another system.

64. Bertrand, 252; Navarre, 56. Buchheit, 101, errs in saying that Schmidt committed suicide in 1941.

65. Goebbels, 369, entry for 10 May 1943.

66. Albert Seaton, *The Russo-German War 1941–45* (London, 1971), 119, 232, 360; Zentralnachweisstelle des Bundesarchivs, letter, 19 October 1982; Militärarchiv, letter.

67. The evidence of Sorge's influence is conflicting. John Erickson, *The Road to Stalingrad: Stalin's War with Germany* (New York, 1975), 238–239, says of Sorge's report that Japan would move south against the British and the Americans, that "this was information which Stalin both received and acted upon, to draw off divisions from the Far East command and rush them to the defense of Moscow." But Erickson offers no support for his view of Stalin's reasoning, and others, by their silence, suggest that Sorge was not all that important: Seaton, in his solid book, does not mention the spy, nor does Marshal Georgii Zhukov in his memoirs. Personally, I wonder whether Stalin would have risked a stab in the back from Russia's traditional enemy in the Pacific on the word of a professional liar. More probable was that he was moved mainly by urgent necessity combined with the observed lack of any activity on the part of Japan's Manchurian forces. The

question of how important Sorge's information was in Stalin's decisions has not been definitively answered.

68. Kahn, 340–346.

69. Sefton Delmer, *The Counterfeit Spy* (New York, 1971); Gunter Peis, *The Mirror of Deception* (London, 1976); John Masterman, *The Double-Cross System in the War of 1939 to 1945* (New Haven, 1972). For German preconceptions: Kahn, 488–489.

70. W. P. B. [William P. Bundy], in *Foreign Affairs*, 57 (Winter 1978/79), 415. F. H. Hinsley et al., *British Intelligence in the Second World War: Its Influence on Strategy and Operations* (London, 1979– ), 1:494, says that the Polish solution merely saved the British seven months in solving the Enigma. I believe that this is wrong and that without the head start provided by the Poles the British probably would not have broken through the more complicated Enigma system of 1939 at all.

# The ULTRA Conference

1. This means public conference. Obviously, cryptanalysts of allied nations—such as Britain and the United States—had met in secret before this.

2. The proceedings appeared in German in 1979 as *Die Funkaufklärung und ihre Rolle im Zweiten Weltkrieg*, Jürgen Rohwer and Eberhard Jäckel, eds. (Stuttgart, 1979). The U.S. Naval Institute Press, which had been considering whether to publish an English translation, decided not to.

3. But this has been questioned. See note 60 to preceding article.

4. He has since published a book on this: *Top Secret Ultra* (London and New York, 1980).

5. Jürgen Rohwer, " 'Special Intelligence' und die Geleitzugsteuerung im Herbst 1941," *Marine Rundschau*, 75 (November 1978), 711–719.

6. Since published as F. H. Hinsley with E. E. Thomas, C. F. G. Ransom and R. C. Knight, *British Intelligence in the Second World War: Its Influence on Strategy and Operations* (London, 1979– ).

7. This is not quite so. Hinsley et al. say at 1:179, 182 that although signals intelligence at first came in too late to help during the Battle of Britain, later it improved and contributed to the effectiveness of Fighter Command during the crucial aerial battles of August and September 1940.

8. *Krasnoznamennyĭ baltiĭskiĭ flot v zaversbayushchiĭ period velikoĭ otechestvennoĭ voĭny, 1944– 1945* (Moscow, 1975), 234.

9. This hypothesis is said to be false in Hinsley et al., 2:60.

10. Some details in ibid., 58–66, 70, 109–110.

11. Some details in ibid., 1:52, 53, 199.

# Codebreaking in World Wars I and II

1. Georges Dossin, "Signaux lumineux au pays de Mari," *Revue d'Assyriologie et d'Archéologie Orientale*, 35 (1938), 174–86.

2. Livy 27. xliii. 1–8.

3. (1851).

4. David Kahn, *The Codebreakers: The Story of Secret Writing* (New York, 1967), passim. Henceforth cited as Kahn.

5. Ibid., 298–9.

6. Christopher Andrew, "Déchiffrement et diplomatie: le cabinet noir du Quai d'Orsay sous la Troisième République," *Relations Internationales*, 3 (1976), 37–64; Marcel Givierge, "Etude historique sur la Section du Chiffre," Epoques 1–4, N.A.F. 24353, Département des Manuscrits, Bibliothèque Nationale, Paris.

7. François Cartier, "Le service d'écoute pendant la guerre," *Radio-Electricité*, 4 (1923), 453–60, 491–8 at 498.

8. Maximilian Ronge, *Kriegs- und Industrie-spionage* (Zurich, 1930), 58–60; August von Urbanski, "Wie unsere Chiffren-Gruppe entstand" (Oktober 1924), Nachlass B-58, Kriegsarchiv, Vienna. See also Harald Hubatschke, "Die amtliche Organisation der geheimen Briefüberwachung und des diplomatischen Chiffrendienstes in Osterreich," *Mitteilungen des Instituts für Osterreichische Geschichtsforschung*, 83 (1975), 352–413 at 412–13.

9. Russia (1923–, U.S.S.R.), Kommissia po izdaniu dokumentov epokhi imperializma, *Die Internationalen Beziehungen im Zeitalter des Imperialismus: Dokumente aus den Archiven der Zarischen und der Provisorischen Regierung*, ed. M. N. Pokrowski, German ed. Otto Hoetzsch (Berlin, 1931–42), passim, shows that Russia intercepted and solved diplomatic messages of England, France, Germany, Austria, Italy, Bulgaria, Turkey, Persia, and Greece before World War I. For police codebreaking, Richard J. Johnson, "*Zagranichaia Agentura:* The Tsarist Political Police in Europe," *Journal of Contemporary History*, 7 (1972), 221–42; Kahn, 618–21.

10. Erich Ludendorff, *Ludendorff's own story* (New York, 1919), 1:57–58.

11. Major [Kunibert] Randewig, "Die deutsche Funkaufklärung in der Schlacht bei Tannenberg," *F-Flagge* (magazine of German army signal troops) (1936), 135–8, 154–7 at 135.

12. Arthur Schuetz (pseud. Tristan Busch), *Secret service unmasked*, trans. Anthony V. Ireland (London, [1948]), 58; Nicholas N. Golovine, *The Russian campaign of 1914*, trans. A. G. S. Muntz (Fort Leavenworth, 1933), 171–2; Germany, Reichsarchiv, *Der Weltkrieg: 1914 bis 1918*, 2 (Berlin, 1925), 351.

13. Max Hoffmann, *War Diaries and Other Papers*, trans. Eric Sutton (London, 1929), 2:267.

14. Ibid., 1:41, 18.

15. Ronge, passim; Yves Gyldén, *The Contribution of the Cryptographic Bureaus in the World War*, trans. Military Intelligence Division (Washington, 1935), 60–77.

16. Max Hoffmann, *The War of Lost Opportunities* (London, 1924), 132.

17. Odoardo Marchetti, *Il servizio informazione dell'esercito italiano nella grande guerra* (Roma, 1937), 181.

18. Intercepts dated 14, 21, and 27 December 1916, 5 N 83, Service Historique, Etat-major de l'Armée de terre, Château de Vincennes; Givierge, "Etude historique sur la Section du Chiffre," Epoque 15, 98–9; Sam Wagenaar, *Mata Hari*, adaptation de Jacques Haubart (Paris, 1965), 198–203.

19. "Conference de M. Georges Jean Painvin," *Bulletin de l'A.R.C.* (Amicale des Reservistes du Chiffre), new series, 8 (1961), 5–47, at 17–45; Kahn, 339–47.

20. Henri Morin, *Service secret: À l'écoute devant Verdun*, ed. Pierre Andrieu (Paris, 1959), passim; Hermann Cron, *Die Organisation des deutschen Heeres im Weltkrieg*, Forschungen und Darstellungen aus dem Reichsarchiv, 5 (Berlin, 1923), 112; Albert Praun, *Soldat in der Telegraphen- und Nachrichtentruppe* (Wurzburg, [c. 1965]), 18–20, 26; Maximilian Ronge, "Der Telephon-Abhorchdienst," 670–729, and Beilagen, Nachlass B/126: F.2, Kriegsarchiv, Vienna.

21. R. E. Priestley, *The Signal Service in the European War of 1914 to 1918 (France)* ([London?], 1921), 106.

22. Sir Alfred Ewing, "Some Special War Work," in R. V. Jones, "Alfred Ewing and 'Room 40,'" *Notes and Records of the Royal Society of London*, 34 (July 1979), 65–90; Winston S. Churchill, *The World Crisis* (New York, 1923), 1:503–4; Admiral Sir William

James, *The Eyes of the Navy: A Biographical Study of Admiral Sir William Hall* (London, 1956), passim; Patrick Beesly, *Room 40: British Naval Intelligence 1914–18* (London, 1982).

23. Barbara Tuchman, *The Zimmermann Telegram* (New York, 1958); William F. Friedman and Charles J. Mendelsohn, *The Zimmermann Telegram of January 16, 1917 and Its Cryptographic Background* (1938, reprinted Laguna Hills, Calif., 1977); Kahn, 282–97.

24. David Kahn, *Hitler's Spies: German Military Intelligence in World War II* (New York, 1978), 185, 190–91, 214; F. H. Hinsley with E. E. Thomas, C. F. G. Ransom and R. C. Knight, *British Intelligence in the Second World War: Its Influence on Strategy and Operations* (London, 1979–), 1:20; Christopher Andrew, "The British Secret Service and Anglo-Soviet Relations in the 1920s. Part I: From the Trade Negotiations to the Zinoviev letter," *Historical Journal*, 20 (1977), 673–706 at 680; Herbert O. Yardley, *The American Black Chamber* (Indianapolis, 1931), 239–40.

25. Kahn, 394–426.

26. U.S. Patent 1,657,411; Siegfried Türkel, *Chiffrieren mit Geräten und Maschinen* (Graz, 1927), 71–94 and plates M–P; *Handbuch der Deutschen Aktien-Gesellschaften* (Berlin, 1935), 5:6610.

27. [Marian Rejewski], "Enigma, 1930–1940; Metodi i historia rozwiazania niemieckiego szyfru maszynowego (w zarysie)" (unpublished; in private collection), §1; Jürgen Rohwer, *The Critical Convoy Battles of March 1943: The Battle for HX. 229/SC122*, trans. Derek Masters (London, 1977), 231.

28. Kahn, 426–7; memorandum, Y7858/437/G/39, signed E.N.T. (Edward N. Travis), 21 July 1939, FO 850/4/X?J3968, Public Record Office, London, mentions the Royal Air Force's Typex machine. Louis Kruh and C. A. Deavours, "The Typex Cryptograph," *Cryptologia*, 7 (April 1983), 146–165.

29. Memorandum of 29 November 1937 in OKW: Wi/IF 5.2150, Bundesarchiv/Militärarchiv, Freiburg-im-Breisgau; Thomas H. Dyer (U.S. Navy cryptanalyst), interview, 12 December 1963.

30. Willi Jensen, "Hilfsgeräte der Kryptographie," Dissertation (withdrawn), Flensburg, 1955; Brian Randall, *The Colossus*, Technical Report Series, No. 90, Computing Laboratory, University of Newcastle-upon-Tyne (Newcastle, 1976); Brian Johnson, *The Secret War* (London, 1978), 327–49.

31. Among the better known are those recounted in Yardley, 289–317, and Richard H. Ullman, *The Anglo-Soviet Accord* (Princeton, 1973), 267–310.

32. Hinsley et al., *British Intelligence*, 2:65, tells of the acquisitions of Enigma machines by the Soviet Union but states that during the war Britain remained "uncertain of the extent of their SIGINT [signal intelligence] achievements" and could not determine "whether and, if so, from what dates they succeeded in reading Enigma keys."

33. Shiro Takagi, "Nippon No Black Chamber," *All Yomimono* (Showa 27, Juichigatsu (November 1952)), 157–75 (unpublished translation, "The Black Chamber of Japan," by Flo Morikami); Interrogation of Lt.-Gen. Seizo Arisue (chief of Army intelligence), United States Strategic Bombing Survey, interrogation No. 238, 10, Record Group 43, National Archives, Washington.

34. Kurt Vetterlein (engineer in charge of the intercept post), interview, 1 September 1967; transcripts of intercepts in Inland II geheim, Vol. 477 f, Politisches Archiv, Auswärtiges Amt, Bonn; Germany, Oberkommando der Wehrmacht, Wehrmachtführungsstab, *Kriegstagebuch . . . 1940–1945*, ed. Percy Ernst Schramm (Frankfurt, 1961–9), 3:854; Walter Schellenberg, *The Labyrinth: Memoirs of Walter Schellenberg*, trans. Louis Hagen (New York, 1956), 366.

35. [Kunibert] Randewig, "Taktische Funkpeilung," *Wehrtechnische Hefte*, 52 (1955), 104–10; Randewig, "Verfahren der Funkaufklärung-Empfangs- und Peildienst-Auswertung," in Albert Praun (ed.), "Eine Untersuchung über den Funkdienst des russischen, britischen und amerikanischen Heeres im zweiten Weltkrieg vom deutschen Standpunkt aus, unter besonderer Berücksichtigung ihrer Sicherheit," 18 February 1950 (unpublished; in private collection); reports of radio reconnaissance units in Heeresgruppe Nord, 74130/28, Bundes-

archiv/Militärarchiv; Herbert Schmidt (radio direction finder), interview, 30 January 1970; Fritz Neeb (operating head of Army Group Center radio intelligence), interview, 30 December 1972.

36. Report of 14 March 1942, Armeeoberkommando 11, 22279/3, Bundesarchiv/Militärarchiv; report of 19 January 1942, 24. Infanterie Division, 22006/11, Bundesarchiv/Militärarchiv; report of 25 February 1944, 3. Panzer Korps, 53975/5, Bundesarchiv/Militärarchiv.

37. Report of 1 March 1944, at 9, Heeresgruppe Nord, 75130/31, Bundesarchiv/Militärarchiv.

38. Reports at 107 and 110, Heeresgruppe D, 85459, Bundesarchiv/Militärarchiv; United States, War Department, Military Intelligence Division, *German Operational Intelligence: A Study of German Operational Intelligence,* produced at German Military Documents Section by a combined British, Canadian, and U.S. Staff, (n.p., April, 1946), 8–9, 24.

39. Kahn, 472, errs in saying that the Germans obtained the code from the Italians, who had stolen it from the American embassy in Rome and were reading Feller's messages themselves (General Cesare Amè, *Guerra segreta in Italia 1940–43* [Rome, 1954], 96–8). The Germans solved it themselves.

40. Wilhelm F. Flicke, *War Secrets in the Ether,* trans. Ray W. Pettengill (Washington, 1953, reprinted with emendations, Laguna Hills, Calif., 1977), 2:192–8; Herbert Schaedel (archivist for the Chiffrierabteilung of the Oberkommando der Wehrmacht), interview, 29 July 1969; Anton Staubwasser (British specialist in the German army high command's Foreign Armies West), interview, 9 March 1970.

41. Hans-Otto Behrendt (assistant intelligence officer to Rommel at the time), interview, 18 November 1978; Hans-Otto Behrendt, *Rommels Kenntnis vom Feind im Afrikafeldzug: Ein Bericht über die Feindnachrichtenarbeit, insbesondere die Funkaufklärung* (Freiburg, 1980), 175–8, 188–204.

42. [Adolf Hitler], *Hitlers Tischgespräche im Führerhauptquartier 1941–1942,* ed. Henry Picker, new ed. Percy Ernst Schramm (Stuttgart, 1963), transcript for 29. Juni 1942 abends.

43. Flicke, 197.

44. Ulrich Liss, "Der entscheidende Wert richtiger Feindbeurteilung—I: Beispiele aus der neueren Kriegsgeschichte," *Wehrkunde,* 8 (November 1959), 584–92 at 585.

45. Reinhard Gehlen et al., "The German G-2 Service in the Russian Campaign (Ic-Dienst Ost)," 1st Special Intelligence Interrogation Report, Interrogation Center, United States Forces European Theater (22 July 1945), 16.

46. Karl Dönitz, letter, 27 January 1970.

47. Heinz Bonatz, *Die deutsche Marine-Funkaufklärung 1914–1945* (Beiträge zur Wehrforschung, 20/21 (Darmstadt, 1970), 138; Jürgen Rohwer, "La Radiotelegraphie: Auxiliare du commandement dans la guerre sous-marin," *Revue d'histoire de la deuxième guerre mondiale,* 18 (January 1968), 41–66 at 52.

48. B-Dienst war diary, p. 78, III M 1006/6, Bundesarchiv/Militärarchiv; Wilhelm Tranow (technical head of the B-Dienst), interview, 1 July 1970.

49. Rohwer, *The Critical Convoy Battles of March 1943,* 240, 51, 61.

50. B-Dienst war diary, p. 169, III M 1006/6, Bundesarchiv/Militärarchiv.

51. Walther Seifert (head of evaluation for the Forschungsamt, Göring's codebreaking and wiretapping agency), interview, 19 August 1970; "Die Vernehmung von Generaloberst Jodl durch die Sowjets," trans. Wilhelm Arenz, *Wehrwissenschaftliche Rundschau,* 11 (September 1961), 534–42 at 539; Hinsley et al., *British intelligence,* 2:640, 641, 642.

52. Report of 10 October 1944, p. 1, in Heeresgruppe C, 75138/31, Bundesarchiv/Militärarchiv.

53. Dyer interview; Wesley A. Wright (navy cryptanalyst in Pearl Harbor), interview, 12 December 1963. Additional first-person material in W. J. Holmes, *Double-Edged Secrets: U.S. Naval Intelligence Operations in the Pacific during World War II* (Annapolis, 1979), and Edward Van Der Rhoer, *Deadly Magic: A Personal Account of Communications Intelligence in World War II in the Pacific* (New York, 1978).

54. Dyer interview.

55. Chester W. Nimitz and E. B. Potter (eds.), *The Great Sea War: The Story of Naval Action in World War II* (Englewood Cliffs, N.J., 1960), 245.

56. Letter to presidential candidate Thomas E. Dewey, 27 September 1944, in United States, Congress, Joint Committee on the Investigation of the Pearl Harbor Attack, *Pearl Harbor Attack*, Hearings, 79th Congress, 1st and 2nd Sessions (Washington, 1946), 3:1132–3 at 1132.

57. Charles A. Lockwood (commander of U.S. submarines in the Pacific), letter, 25 November 1964. See also United States, Navy, Chief of Naval Operations, OP-20-G-7, "The role of communications intelligence in submarine warfare in the Pacific (January 1943–October 1943)," 19 November 1945, SRH-011, Record Group 457, National Archives, and Clay Blair, Jr., *Silent Victory: The U.S. Submarine War Against Japan* (Philadelphia, 1975).

58. Cited in Nimitz and Potter, 422–3.

59. Burke Davis, *Get Yamamoto* (New York, 1969); Holmes, 135–6.

60. Various sources. Kahn, 19, errs in implying that the PURPLE machine used rotors. The suggestion that PURPLE was similar cryptographically to the Enigma and thus owed its solution to the Enigma solution has been educed from this Kahn error and is itself false. The solutions were entirely independent of one another.

61. *Pearl Harbor Attack*, 36:312, 34:84.

62. United States, War Department, Office of Assistant Chief of Staff, G-2, "MAGIC Summaries," 20 March to 31 December 1942, NC3-457-78-4, and "MAGIC Diplomatic Summaries," 1943, NC3-457-78-7, both Record Group 457, National Archives; Ronald Lewin, *The American Magic: Codes, Ciphers and the Defeat of Japan* (New York, 1982), ch. 11.

63. "MAGIC Summary," No. 562 of 9 October 1943 in "MAGIC Diplomatic Summaries."

64. "MAGIC Summary" of 17 December 1943, in "MAGIC Diplomatic Summaries."

65. *Pearl Harbor Attack*, 3:1132.

66. Johnson, 310; Stefan Korbonski, "The True Story of Enigma—the German Code Machine in World War II," *East European Quarterly*, 11 (Summer 1977), 227–34 at 228.

67. [Rejewski], "Enigma 1920–1930," §1.

68. Gustave Bertrand, *Enigma: ou le plus grand énigme de la guerre 1939–1945* (Paris, 1973), 29. For additional details, see article on the spy in this volume.

69. [Rejewski], "Enigma 1920–1930," §22; Wladyslaw Kozaczuk, *W Kregu Enigmy* (Warsaw, 1979), Chs. 1–6; Tadeusz Lisicki, "Die Leistung des polnischen Entzifferungdienstes bei der Lösung des Verfahrens der deutschen 'Enigma'-Funkschlüsselmaschine," in Jürgen Rohwer and Eberhard Jäckel, eds., *Die Funkaufklärung und ihre Rolle im Zweiten Weltkrieg* (Stuttgart, 1979), 66–86; Marian Rejewski, "Mathematical Solution of the Enigma Cipher," *Cryptologia*, 6 (January 1982), 1–18. For the effect of the documents, see article on the spy in this volume.

70. Bertrand, 59–60.

71. Penelope Fitzgerald, *The Knox Brothers* (New York, 1977), passim.

72. Ronald Lewin, *Ultra Goes to War* (New York, 1978), 112–13; Gordon Welchman, *The Hut Six Story: Breaking the Enigma Codes* (New York, 1982), 77–81, 295–307; Peter Calvocoressi, *Top Secret Ultra* (London, 1980), 10–13; I. J. Good, "Early work on computers at Bletchley," *Cryptologia*, 3 (April 1979), 65–77.

73. Hinsley et al., *British Intelligence*, 1:178–9.

74. Ibid, 528–48; N. E. Evans, "Air Intelligence and the Coventry Raid," *Royal United Services Institution Journal* (September 1976), 66–73.

75. H. R. Trevor-Roper (a solver with E. W. B. Gill of the hand ciphers), interview, 1972; Werner Trautman (head of Abwehr radio station in Hamburg), interview, 20 August 1970; Kim Philby, *My Private Year* (New York, 1968), 65; Hinsley et al., 1:120.

76. John Masterman, *The Double-Cross System in the War of 1939 to 1945* (New Haven, 1972), passim; Kahn, *Hitler's Spies*, ch. 26.

77. Rohwer, *The Critical Convoy Battles of March 1943*, 238; Patrick Beesly, *Very Special Intelligence* (London, 1977), 70–1; Hinsley et al., *British Intelligence*, 1:336–7.

78. Hinsley et al., *British Intelligence*, 2:229, 667. The original version of this paper followed Beesly, *Very Special Intelligence*, 110–111, in saying that the change to the four-rotor Enigma took place on 8 March 1943 and that Bletchley solved it in a few days. This is wrong. Beesly was apparently thinking of a new U-boat code for short-signal weather reports put into use on 10 March 1943 that Bletchley at first feared would be "fatal" to its work but that it in fact recovered in nine days (Hinsley et al., *British Intelligence*, 2:750).

79. Beesly, *Very Special Intelligence*, 64–5; Jürgen Rohwer, diagram "Development of German Cipher-Circles for Funkschlüssel M (naval Enigma)," in *Newsletter of the American Committee on the History of the Second World War*, No. 17 (May 1977), 5.

80. Hinsley et al., 2:229–30, 547–67, 747–52.

81. *Ibid.*, 572; Beesly, *Very Special Intelligence*, 200–1; Jürgen Rohwer, "Der Einfluss der alliierten Funkaufklärung auf den Verlauf des Zweiten Weltkrieges," *Vierteljahrshefte für Zeitgeschichte*, 27 (1979), 325–69 at 356–62; Günter Böddeker, *Die Boote im Netz* (Bergische Gladbach, 1981), passim; Alberto Santoni, *Il vero traditore: Il ruolo documentato di ULTRA nella guerra del Mediterraneo* (Milano, 1981).

82. United States Army, 6824 Detailed Interrogation Center, (MIS)M. 1121, "Information on German Secret Teletypewriters," Record Group 165, National Archives; U.S. Patent No. 1,912,983; Hans Rohrbach, "Chiffrierverfahren der neuesten Zeit," *Archiv der elektrischen Übertragung*, 2 (December 1948), 362–9 at §13, Donald W. Davies, "The Early Models of the Siemens and Halske T52 Cipher Machine," *Cryptologia* 7 ( July 1983), 235–253.

83. Randall, *The Colossus.*

84. Lewin, 325–6; [United States, Army], Memorandum for Colonel [Telford] Taylor, "Ultra and the U.S. Seventh Army," 12 May 1945, SRH-022, Record Group 457, National Archives. See also U.S. Army Air Force, *Ultra and the History of the United States Strategic Air Force in Europe vs. the German Air Force* (1945, published Frederick, Maryland, 1980), and Ernest L. Bell, ed., *An Initial View of Ultra as an American Weapon* (Keene, New Hampshire, 1977).

85. Memorandum for Colonel Taylor, "Ultra and the U.S. Seventh Army," 2. See also Hinsley et al., 2:ch. 19.

86. Lewin, 336–40; Ralph Bennett, *Ultra in the West* (London, 1979) 112–24.

87. According to records in the Berlin Document Center, the technical heads of the OKW Chiffrierabteilung (Wilhelm Fenner) and of the B-Dienst (Wilhelm Tranow) were not party members; Tranow wrested this post from an old party member (Lothar Franke, membership No. 19,852). The Foreign Office codebreaking unit's administrative head (Kurt Selchow) joined after the start of the war (1 January 1940, membership No. 7,910,928); of his three main assistants, two were party members, one early (Adolf Paschke, 1 May 1933, 2,649,870), and one late (Rudolf Schauffler, 1 January 1942, 8,743,951), and one was not (Werner Kunze). The leading officials of the Forschungsamt, Göring's wiretapping and codebreaking agency, were all Nazis.

88. Seifert, interview.

89. Leo Hepp, "Das Grösste Geheimnis des Zweiten Weltkrieges?," *Wehrkunde* (1976), 86–9 at 88–9; Dr. Erich Hüttenhain (in charge of German cipher systems in OKW Chiffrierabteilung), letter, 15 February 1979.

90. This section, especially the part dealing with the technical reasons, owes a great deal to Dr. C. A. Deavours, professor of mathematics at Kean College of New Jersey, who has thoroughly investigated the cryptology of the Enigma. I am deeply grateful to him for his help. The section has also benefited from the following people, who read it in draft and commented upon it: Dr. I. J. Good, one of the team who worked with Newman at Bletchley on the electronic cryptanalytical machines and is now University

Distinguished Professor of Statistics at the Virginia Polytechnic Institute and State University; Dr. Karl-Heinz Ludwig, professor at the University of Bremen and author of *Technik und Ingenieure im Dritten Reich* (Düsseldorf, 1974); Dr. Henry A. Turner, professor of history at Yale University specializing in 20th-century German economics; Dr. Andreas Hillgruber, professor of history at Cologne University and a leading World War II historian; Heinz Bonatz, retired Kapitän zur See, head of the B-Dienst from 1934 to 1936 and from 1942 to 1944; Dr. Erich Hüttenhain; and Dr. Alan Beyerchen, professor of history at the Ohio State University and author of *Scientists under Hitler: Politics and the Physics Community in the Third Reich* (New Haven, 1977).

91. Hinsley et al., 2:631, 639. Alan S. Milward, *War, Economy and Society 1939-45* (Berkeley, 1977), 169-193, discusses similar problems in a broader context.

92. Tadeusz Lisicki, "Die Leistung des polnischen Entzifferungsdienstes," 71-5.

93. Another general reason might seem to be that the Allies' larger population would have given them more, and probably better, people for codebreaking. But it is not known how many of the approximately 10,000 people at Bletchley were solving ciphers other than German at any particular time or how many in the German agencies were solving Soviet, Italian, Japanese, Turkish, Swedish, and other non-U.S. and non-U.K. systems at the same time. Moreover, the contributions of other governments—Canadian, Free French, Dutch, Italian, Japanese, Hungarian—to their respective allies cannot readily be measured in terms of manpower. Finally, the number of persons in field units, both Allied and German, is not known with precision. I myself have the feeling that more people in the West attacked German ciphers than worked in Germany on Allied ciphers and so I think that greater Allied population probably did contribute to greater success. But, lacking the figures that would prove or disprove this conjecture, I do not advance it. A corollary to this would be that the Allies' greater industrial capacity enabled them to help both their codebreakers and their codemakers more. But this help would have been so small in relation to either the Allied or the Axis war effort as to be insignificant. So this cannot be adduced as a factor, either.

94. Kahn, *Hitler's Spies*, 172-222, esp. 176.

95. Ibid., 534-6.

96. This is developed in more detail in ibid., 528-31.

97. Carl von Clausewitz, *On War*, trans. and ed. Michael Howard and Peter Paret (Princeton, 1976), bk. vi, ch. 1.

98. Ibid., bk. vii, ch. 2.

99. Georges Castellan, *Le Réarmament clandestin du Reich, 1930-1935, vu par le 2ᵉ Bureau de l'État-major français* (Paris, 1954); Bonatz, 93.

100. Hinsley et al., 1:12-13, 36-43; Kahn, *Hitler's Spies*, 54, 387-8, 393-8.

101. Solomon Kullback, telephone interview, 2 October 1978.

102. Tranow, interviews. The book was Roger Baudouin's *Eléments de cryptographie* (Paris, 1939).

103. W. Preston Corderman (a first student in this school, later wartime head of the U.S. Army codebreaking agency), interview, 2 November 1976; W. F. Friedman, *Military Cryptanalysis* (Washington, 1938-42).

104. United States, War Department, Technical Manual 11-380, *Converter M-209* (27 April 1942), §5b.

105. See, for example, Germany, Oberkommando der Wehrmacht, Heeresdienstvorschrift geheim 7 (also Marinedienstvorschrift 534, Luftwaffedienstvorschrift geheim 7), *Allgemeine Schlüsselregeln für die Wehrmacht*, 1 April 1944, and Germany, [Reichswehrministerium], Heeresdienstvorschrift geheim 13 (also Luftwaffedienstvorschrift geheim 13), *Gebrauchsanleitung für die Chiffriermaschine Enigma*, 12 January 1937.

106. Beyerchen, letter, 13 April 1979, says that urgency stimulated the Allies to break down the barrier between theoretical and applied mathematicians and scientists and that the lack of urgency in Germany "left their peacetime barrier intact."

107. T. H. Flowers, letter, 13 February 1979. I am deeply grateful to Mr. Flowers for this letter and one of 18 April 1979, which explain how the British advanced from electromechanical to electronic machines.

108. I. G. Good, "Early Work on Computers at Bletchley," *Cryptologia*, 3 (April 1979), 65–77 at 73.

109. Konrad Zuse (German computer pioneer), letters, 22 November 1976 and 5 January 1977.

110. Bonatz, interview, 15 November 1978.

111. See, for example, Max Pinl and Lux Furtmuller, "Mathematicians under Hitler," Leo Baeck Institute, *Year Book XVIII* (London, 1973), 129–82.

112. An attempt to trace the roots of German arrogance in Kahn, *Hitler's Spies*, 525–8.

113. Beesly, *Very Special Intelligence*, 57–8; Kahn, *Hitler's Spies*, 533.

114. Kullback, interview.

115. Kahn, 613. Rohwer, "Der Einfluss der alliierten Funkaufklärung auf den Verlauf des zweiten Weltkrieges," 361.

116. Corderman, interview.

117. Harold Deutsch, talk at colloquium on "What role did radio intelligence play in the course of the Second World War?," Stuttgart, 17 November 1978.

118. See also David Kahn, "The Ultra conference," reprinted as preceding article in this volume.

119. Preface to Praun, "Eine Untersuchung . . ."

120. Eisenhower to Menzies, 12 July 1945, Eisenhower Library, Abilene, Kansas.

121. *Pearl Harbor Attack*, 3:1133.

# Plaintext in the New Unabridged

1. Joos died 6 May 1978.

2. This and other quotations from Joos come from letters to the reviewer, dated January 4 and January 18, 1962.

3. This and other quotations from Gove come from letters to the reviewer, dated January 10 and January 23, 1962.

4. Though Joos does not say so explicitly here, these definitions embody the meanings in which the words have actually been used. They state what the word has meant to all those who have used it, as far as the definer can determine this from the citations. The definitions are emphatically not meanings that Joos or anyone else thinks the words ought to have. As the dictionary's own preface puts it: "Learned and industrial organizations have created numerous committees of nomenclature to collect, define, and standardize the terminology in their fields. . . . Nevertheless, prescriptive and canonical definitions have not been taken over nor have recommendations been followed unless confirmed by independent investigation of usage borne out by genuine citations." This guiding principle of the dictionary—description, not prescription—has come under heavy fire, on the grounds that its consequent permissiveness renders the language less precise and so less effective as an instrument of communication. But the principle has also been warmly defended as the only scientific one proper to a dictionary, whose task is to record the ever-changing facts of a language without judging them by an arbitrary standard of correctness, which can be determined only by usage. (For criticisms, see Dwight Macdonald, "The String Untuned," *The New Yorker*, 38 [March 10, 1962], 130–160, and Wilson Follett, "Sabotage in Springfield," *The Atlantic Monthly*, 209 [January 1962], 73–77; for defenses, see Bergen Evans, "But What's a Dictionary For?" *The Atlantic Monthly*, 209 [May 1962],

57-72, and "Webster's 3d Edition Defended at Meeting of English Teachers," *The New York Times* [November 24, 1962], 47.) Cryptological terms, being relatively technical, have escaped this battle.

5. The dictionary also includes the terms *albam, athbash, steganogram,* and *steganography,* which Joos did not define.

6. See Appendix III, *"Origins of Cryptology, Cryptography and Cryptanalysis."*

7. As is clearly shown in a distinction made in 1945 by a committee of Congress: "Broadly, 'cryptographic' means the use of codes and ciphers of our own, and 'cryptanalytic' means obtaining information from the cryptographic communications of other nations." *Safeguarding Military Information,* House of Representatives Report No. 1032 (to accompany S. 805), 79th Congress, 1st Session, September 27, 1945.

8. All citations of this edition refer to the 1960 printing—its last.

9. The colon (in boldface in the dictionary) introduces a definition and may be read as "is being defined as."

10. In his article on "Cryptology" in the *Encyclopaedia Britannica* (14th edition), William F. Friedman included other areas of secret communications within his definition of *cryptology:* physical security, transmission security (including such techniques as invisible inks and microdots), interception, traffic analysis, electronic intelligence, and electronic countermeasures. But this seems more the way Friedman thinks the term should be used than the way most people really use it.

11. Etienne Bazeries, *Les Chiffres Secrets Dévoilés,* (Paris, 1901), 119.

12. As in the title of War Department Technical Manual 11-380: *Converter M-209, M-209-A, M-209-B (cipher)* (Washington, 1944).

13. Later editions have deleted the "electrical" in the main portion of the definition, which now reads: "*e(1)* a cipher machine; *esp:* an electric one adaptable to automatic operation."

14. For a full and explicit statement, see William F. and Elizebeth S. Friedman, *The Shakespearean Ciphers Examined* (Cambridge, 1957), 18. See also Friedman, "Cryptology," 807A; Helen F. Gaines, *Elementary Cryptanalysis* (Boston, 1939; reprinted as *Cryptanalysis* [New York, 1956]), 169; Lambros D. Callimahos, "Cryptography," *Collier's Encyclopedia* (1962), 7:519.

15. Bazeries, 208.

16. John Holt Schooling. "Secrets in Cipher: IV," *Pall Mall Magazine,* 8 (April 1896), 616-617; Gaines, 164-165; J. M. Wolfe, *A First Course in Cryptanalysis* (Brooklyn, 1943), 2:ch. viii.

17. Wolfe, 2:ch. x, 3-8; Gaines, 12.

18. See U.S. Patents 1,460,438; 2,777,897; 2,932,693; 2,948,779; 2,987,614, etc.

19. Interestingly, this point is made in the oldest separate treatise on cryptology in the world, that of Léon Battista Alberti (c. 1466), who says, "I make two circles out of copper plates. One, the larger, is called stationary, the smaller is called movable." Translation by Charles J. Mendelsohn quoted in William F. Friedman, "Edgar Allan Poe, Cryptographer—Addendum," *Signal Corps Bulletin,* No. 98 (October–December 1937), 62. See also Donald D. Millikan, *Elementary Cryptography and Cryptanalysis* (New York, 1943), 91.

20. Joos said of this: "We had a hard struggle with this; let me now add that we were not content with the result, but had to give up."

21. For instance, *indirect symmetry of position* "is esoteric—to be found only in books by people like Fletcher Pratt and in the journals of the cryptographers' societies. Mathematically, it is a bad term; we never used it. How could it get into a novel? Oh, yes, it could; but then deliberately treated as a mysterious jargon-word." This is precisely the point this reviewer makes. Furthermore, it bars on an apparent whim a term which Joos admitted is in common use—the inference being that less common terms that Joos liked better have been granted entrance to the select circle. This is hardly right. Again, on the Hill system: "There is, for intrinsic reasons, absolutely no chance that it will

ever be in practical use; hence it can never get into a novel." If novelists used only practical systems in their books, cryptologic fiction would be a good deal poorer than it is today. Furthermore, the Hill system has recently given rise to articles in mathematical journals, indicating that interest in it is spreading beyond the strictly cryptologic. Reasons given by Joos for the elimination of other terms are as follows: *"book breaking* (self-explanatory), *bust* (military security), *cardan* (esoteric), *cardboard cipher* (nonce-term for grille), *cell* (no separate crypt. def. needed), *checkword* (I know nothing of this except that it is on my list), *chiffre quarre* (of historical interest only), *cifan/ciphan* (cifan jargon), *cryptoquote* (private invention: The Saturday Review), *bilateral* (a misprint that got quoted: a ghostword)."

22. See also his letter headed "New Dictionary" in *The New York Times Book Review* (March 25, 1962), 38, in reply to J. Donald Adams' discussion in "Speaking of Books" (February 11, 1962), 2.

23. Examples of specialized glossaries include the Army Security Agency's glossary or David Shulman's *Glossary of Cryptography* (New York: Crypto Press, 1961). Admittedly, the definitions in works like these are based not on citations but on the impressions of the compilers, who, furthermore, frequently taint their definitions with what they think the words should mean. This negates their value as guides to how common words like *code* and *decipher* are being used. But since highly technical terms have so specific and widely agreed-upon meanings, and are used in contexts that further restrict their meanings, the departure from the ideal lexicographical procedure does not affect them much. A term like *component* has only one meaning. Hence the glossaries, despite the informality of their methods, adequately fill the need for definitions of highly technical terms.

24. In United States, Congress, Joint Committee on the Investigation of the Pearl Harbor Attack, *Pearl Harbor Attack*, Hearings, 79th Congress, 1st and 2nd Sessions (Washington, 1946), 9:4333, 4673, 4714, etc.; Friedman, "Cryptology," 807D.

25. In "Countermeasures," *Time* (December 9, 1957), 65; Martin Mann, "Our Secret Radar War with Russia," *Popular Science* (January 1961), 226; "Aerospace Electronics," *Space/ Aeronautics* (reprint from April 1960, issue), 1, 2, 3, 4, etc.

26. In "Text of Statements Read in Moscow by Former U.S. Security Agency Workers," *The New York Times* (September 7, 1960), 10; Leo Rosen, "Rotor," U.S. Patent 2,402,182 (June 18, 1946), cols 3, 4, etc.

27. In Harry Schwartz, "Still the 'Riddle Wrapped in a Mystery,' " *The New York Times Magazine* (March 15, 1953), 62; Commonwealth of Australia, *Report of the Royal Commission on Espionage* (Sydney, 1955), 86; David Kahn, *Two Soviet Spy Ciphers* (Great Neck, N.Y., 1960), 12, 13, 15; "Britain Says Messages to Red Were Cooked Up in Spy Kitchen," *New York Daily News* (March 16, 1961), 4.

28. "One-time pad" is now included in the Addenda with the following definition: "[prob. fr. its original form's being a pad of keys whose sheets were torn off and discarded after a single use]: a random-number additive or mixed keying sequence to be used for a single coded message and then destroyed." No doubt the definer meant "ciphered" instead of "coded." The other terms are still not included.

29. Volume 1 of the new *A Supplement to the Oxford English Dictionary*, ed. R. W. Burchfield (Oxford, 1972), includes good definitions of *cipher officer, cipherer, code* (as verb), *code-book, cryptanalysis* ("The art of deciphering a cryptogram or cryptograms by analysis"), *cryptograph, cryptographer* (with newer examples), and *cryptography* (adds to definition: "Also, the art of writing or solving cipher"), all with useful quotations. *Cryptology* adds new citations. *Decipher* is not included here.

30. The 4th edition (1977) is improved but not ideal. Category 612 is now 614; its Section 6 now lists these nouns: "cryptography, cryptoanalysis, cryptoanalytics; code, cipher; secret or invisible or sympathetic ink; cryptographer." Still lacking are *cryptology* and *cipher machine;* the useful *steganography* and *steganogram* have been deleted, and *cryptoanalysis* and *cryptoanalytics*, in addition to being incorrect, really do not belong. Section

10 now includes *encipher* and *encode* and omits *codify*. The polysyllabic monstrosities have been banished; Section 16 includes as adjectives "coded, encoded; ciphered, enciphered; cryptographic(al)"—but still not *cryptological*. Category 486 is now 487; it still lacks *cryptanalysis* and *cryptanalyze*.

# Two Soviet Spy Ciphers

The author wishes to acknowledge with sincerest thanks his indebtedness to Howard T. Oakley, a close friend and a fine amateur cryptographer, whose thoughtful comments on the manuscript and whose original contributions have added substantially to the value of this report. Thanks are also due to James B. Donovan, Esq., Abel's attorney, to Mrs. Minnie E. McInturff, Mr. Donovan's secretary, and to Miss Jenny Hauck, who helped turn the manuscript into a booklet.

Details of the VIC and Abel ciphers come from testimony in the case of United States of America vs. Rudolf Ivanovich Abel, Case No. 45094, United States District Court for the Eastern District of New York. The transcript of the case is on file in the clerk's office at the court house, 271 Washington Street, Brooklyn, New York. Hayhanen's testimony on the operation of his cipher is on pages 342–386. Other information about his cryptographic training, transmission frequency, etc., is found *passim* in his testimony. Leonard's testimony is on page 588, Webb's on pages 724–726. The VIC cipher message (Fig. 1) is Government Exhibit 62. Figs. 2, 3, 4, and 5 were used by Maroney in explaining Hayhanen's cipher to the jury. The Abel cipher message found in his apartment (Fig. 6) is Item 16 in Exhibit C, annexed to Abel's affidavit of September 13, 1957. The two-page Abel cipher message is Exhibit 90. The one-time pad keybook is Exhibit 88.

Evaluations and comments on the systems come from general knowledge of cryptography. Information about the advanced techniques required may be obtained from Helen F. Gaines, *Cryptanalysis: A Study of Ciphers and Their Solution* (New York: Dover Publications, 1956), a reprint of a 1939 volume (a copy of the Dover edition was found in Abel's room); Luigi Sacco, *Manuele di crittografia* (Roma, 1947), translated into French by J. Brès as *Manuel de cryptographie* (Paris, 1951); and Charles Eyraud, *Précis de cryptographie moderne* (Paris, 1953).

Russian frequency tables may be found in Sacco and Eyraud. The plaintext of the nickel message contains 580 letters, 47 signs, and 8 numbers, for a total of 635 units.

Descriptions of the ADFGVX system and of its solution may be found in Sacco, §§ 38 and 102, and in Eyraud, pages 215–219.

The comments about the unbreakable cipher can stand by themselves on the basis of logic. For those who demand the backing of authority, however, William F. Friedman, who solved the Japanese PURPLE diplomatic machine cipher before Pearl Harbor and who is probably the world's leading professional cryptanalyst, writes in his *Encylopaedia Britannica* article on "Codes and Ciphers" (14th edition): "Isolated short cryptograms prepared by certain methods may resist solution indefinitely; and a letter-for-letter cipher system which employs, once and only once, a keying sequence composed of characters or elements in a random and entirely unpredictable sequence may be considered holocryptic, that is, messages in such a system cannot be read by indirect processses involving cryptanalysis, but only by direct processes involving possession of the key or keys, obtained either legitimately, by virtue of being among the intended communicators, or by stealth."

Howard Oakley suggests that the abbreviations in the checkerboard might stand for the following Russian phrases: 22 (II B T)—*povtoryat*, "repeat"; 18 (H/II)—*nacheku tsifrovoe*, "attention! numbers"; 28 (H/T)—*nacheku teksta*, "attention! test."

In an article entitled "Intimate Portrait of a Russian Master Spy" in *Life*, 43 (November

11, 1957), 122–128, Frank Gibney states that Abel used a cipher that used calculus for its operation. No evidence for such a cipher was found in the testimony.

1. Abel was exchanged on 10 February 1962 in Berlin for Francis Gary Powers, the pilot of the American U-2 spy airplane downed over the Soviet Union on 1 May 1960.

2. The gammas apparently mean the one-time pads. "Gammas" is a technical term in photography in Russian and the tiny pads may well have been reproduced photographically.

3. This may refer to a technique of Soviet espionage used by Vladimir Petrov, a spy in Australia, and perhaps to be used by Hayhanen as well, for long letters to be sent by diplomatic pouch. The spy drafts them using the jargon of espionage as one level of cover and codenames for individuals as another. Then other sensitive terms are replaced by "No. 1," "No. 2," and so on. The letter is retyped with these replacements, photographed, and sent in the diplomatic pouch with the film undeveloped so that any unauthorized person opening it would ruin it. The terms themselves are enciphered in a one-time pad and this ciphertext sent with the film in the pouch. Their replacements— "No. 1," and so on—might well be referred to as "insertions."

4. Upon reflection, I believe that I was wrong in saying this system was easy to remember. Perhaps a lot of practice would facilitate remembering it, but I now think that it is easier to forget than to recall.

5. Foote described his system in his *Handbook for Spies* (Garden City, N.Y. 1949), 250–256. Sorge's is described, on the basis of the Japanese police records, in David Kahn, *The Codebreakers* (New York, 1967), 650–652.

# Cryptology Goes Public

1. The nations of the world have paid lip service to Stimson's principle by incorporating in Article 27, Section 2, of the Vienna Convention on Diplomatic Relations the rule that "the official correspondence of the mission shall be inviolable." *United Nations Treaty Series*, 500 (New York, 1965), 110. Probably only the nations that cannot violate other countries' correspondence abide by the provision. The United States has in effect nullified its adherence by including in a 1978 law setting up procedures for electronic surveillance within the United States (including messages of foreign powers) the phrase "Notwithstanding any other law," which, under the Constitution, includes treaties. 92 *U.S. Statutes* 1786.

2. Article XV, Second Common Understanding.

3. *Public Papers of the Presidents of the United States: Jimmy Carter, 1977* (Washington, 1978), 2:1234.

4. Mitre Corporation, McLean, Virginia, *Study of Vulnerability of Electronics Communication Systems to Electronic Interception,* prepared for the Office of Telecommunications Policy, January 1977 (Department of Commerce: National Technical Information Service, PB 264447 and PB 264448), 1:17.

5. There have never been any reports of Soviet or other attempts to "tap" the transatlantic telephone cables. A submarine could lay a length of wire alongside a cable and pick up the signals by induction. But demultiplexing the numerous interleaved conversations would require considerable complicated equipment, probably too bulky for a submarine to carry. The Roosevelt-Churchill conversations that the Germans intercepted during World War II were sent by radiotelephone, since no telephone cables then existed. The Germans never attempted to tap the transatlantic telegraph cables.

6. It might seem that this decline would reduce the scale or status of the codebreaking agencies. But the need to process much more traffic to approach the quality of cryptanalyzed intelligence means having to add more men and/or machines. Thus the cryptanalytic

loss, far from being an organizational disaster, may be a bureaucratic godsend. Though the present NSA director [Inman] says that this analysis does not fit the facts, several non-NSA intelligence specialists say it is true.

7. *Public Papers of the Presidents of the United States: Jimmy Carter, 1977* (Washington, 1978), 2:1234.

8. The work of the Special Project Office may be summarized as follows: As a consequence of its program, many of the telecommunications carriers now offer bulk encryption of messages to their customers. The office surveyed the telecommunications-security procedures of more than twenty government agencies and suggested ways of improving them. It showed them how to identify categories of sensitive information. It held seminars and training programs at these agencies' offices around the country that raised management's awareness of the problem. Nearly all of these agencies tightened their telecommunications security, one spending $21 million to protect its voice and record transmissions. The office encouraged training programs to maintain a high level of consciousness of the problem. To the nation's larger corporations—as those in oil, steel, and food—though it did not analyze their problems, the Special Project Office did point out the need for telecommunications protection. In addition, it produced and distributed thousands of copies of a guide to telecommunications-security equipment. With its work largely completed, the Special Projects Office closed down on September 30, 1982, and the one man winding up its work ended that duty a year later.

9. Any jurisdictional disputes seem to have been settled at a lower level than the N.S.C. subcommittee.

10. Jansky offered this prediction when many people were expecting an explosion of sales of cryptography devices. That explosion did not take place; the growth has been much slower and more evolutionary than expected, ans so the costs have not reached the billions.

11. See "Tapping Computers," in this volume; "Report of the Workshop on Estimation of Significant Advances in Computer Technology," Paul Meissner, ed., NBSIR 76–1189, National Bureau of Standards (Washington, 1976); and "Report of the Workshop on Cryptography in Support of Computer Security," Dennis Branstad, Jason Gait, and Stuart Katzke, eds., NBSIR 77–1291, National Bureau of Standards (Washington, 1977).

12. Department of Commerce, National Bureau of Standards, *Data Encryption Standard,* Federal Information Processing Standards Publication 46 (Department of Commerce: National Technical Information Service, January 15, 1977).

13. United States Congress, Senate, Select Committee on Intelligence, *Unclassified Summary: Involvement of NSA in the Development of the Data Encryption Standard,* Staff Report, 95th Congress, 2d Session, April 1978 (Washington, 1978).

14. The firms that are manufacturing D.E.S. chips are doing so at a very low rate, and none of them now see any profit in them.

15. For an excellent discussion of the idea by its inventors, in the context of the best current survey of modern cryptography, with extensive bibliography, see the study by the Stanford scientists, Whitfield Diffie and Martin E. Hellman, "Privacy and Authentication: An Introduction to Cryptography," *Proceedings of the IEEE* (Institute of Electrical and Electronics Engineers), 67 (March 1979), 397–427. The most workable realization of public key cryptography is by Ronald L. Rivest, Adi Shamir, and Leonard Adelman, "On Digital Signatures and Public Key Cryptosystems," *Communications of the ACM* (Association for Computing Machinery), 22 (February 1978), 120–26.

16. *Code of Federal Regulations,* Title 22, Chapter 1, Subchapter M.

17. Inman moved from the N.S.A. to the C.I.A. in 1981. No bill to place all information on cryptology under government control was ever introduced in Congress. But as a consequence of an N.S.A. initiative, a Public Cryptography Study Group, consisting of representatives of learned and professional societies whose interests might involve cryptology, was organized under the auspices of the American Council on Education. On February

7, 1981, it recommended a voluntary system of censorship for cryptography articles that the societies' journals might publish. More than two years later, however, none of the societies have accepted this recommendation. On the other hand, many researchers in cryptology are voluntarily and individually submitting their papers to N.S.A. to see whether they might harm national security. N.S.A. has found no such harm in most of the papers submitted to it; nearly all the authors of those it found possibly dangerous have either eliminated the allegedly harmful portions or have not sought to publish their paper.

18. This bill died.

19. See Department of Commerce, Office of Telecommunications (now the National Telecommunications and Information Administration), *Selected Foreign Data Protection Laws and Bills,* Special Publication 78–19 (Washington, 1978).

20. This is permitted by Articles 35 and 41 of the International Telecommunications Convention of November 12, 1965. *United States Treaties and Other Informational Agreements* (Washington, 1968), 18:620, 622.

## The Ultra Secret

1. Subsequent research showed that this is not quite true. Radar was more important at first, though ULTRA later contributed much.

2. The fact is that Rejewski had made some progress, which cannot fairly be called "a partial solution," in an office in Warsaw, not in the forest of Pyry.

3. One machine was given to the French and one to the English.

## The Defense of Osuga, 1942

1. Albert Seaton. *The Russo-German War, 1941–45* (New York, 1971), 302; Werner Haupt, *Heeresgruppe Mitte* (Dorheim, 1968), 132–140.

2. Earl F. Ziemke, *Stalingrad to Berlin: The German Defeat in the East* (Army Historical Series), United States Army: Office of the Chief of Military History (Washington, 1968), 47.

3. Oberkommando des Heeres, Fremde Heere Ost, H3/199, Kurze Beurteilung der Feindlage vom 26.8.1942–31.12.1942, document 19, page 3. Henceforth, cited as OKH:H3/199 followed by document and page numbers.

4. Ziemke, 48.

5. OKH:H3/199:23:3.

6. Ibid.:28:3.

7. Franz Halder, *Kriegstagebuch,* ed. Hans-Adolf Jacobsen (Stuttgart, 1962–1964), 3:527.

8. Ibid.

9. OKH:H3/199:31:2.

10. Halder, 3:530.

11. Germany, Oberkommando der Wehrmacht, Wehrmachtführungsstab, *Kriegstagebuch . . .* , ed. Percy Ernst Schramm (Frankfurt am Main, 1961–1965), 2:782. Henceforth cited as OKW, *KTB.*

12. Ibid., 793, 800–801, 805; Gerhard Engel, *Heeresadjutant bei Hitler, 1938–1943: Aufzeichnungen des Majors Engel,* Schriftenreihe der Vierteljahrshefte für Zeitgeschichte, 27 (Stuttgart, 1947), 130.

13. OKH:H3/51:2.

14. Paul Carell [Paul Schmidt], *Hitler Moves East, 1941–43* (Boston, 1965), 367–368, 371; Ziemke, 138.

15. Germany, Oberkommando des Heeres, HDv. 92 g., *Handbuch für den Generalstabsdienst im Kriege* (1939).

16. [United States, War Department, Military Intelligence Division], *The German General Staff Corps: A Study of the Organization of the German General Staff*, produced at German Military Documents Section by a combined British, Canadian, and U.S. Staff (April 1946), 40, 32.

17. Germany, Oberkommando des Heeres, HDv. 89 g, *Feindnachrichtendienst* (1.3.1941), § 16.

18. Georg Buntrock, interview, 19 September 1973.

19. Georg Buntrock, "Mein Lebenslauf" [unpublished memoirs] (1947–1948), 59.

20. Ibid., 57.

21. Ibid., 59.

22. Ibid., 65–66.

23. Armeeoberkommando 9, 29234/11, Beilage zum Kriegstagebuch, Ia, Nr. 6, Anlagen zum Tätigkeitsbericht der Abteilung IIa/b, Berichtszeit, 1.10.1942–31.12.1942, document Stellenbesetzung am 15. November 1942. Henceforth cited as AOK 9:29234/11 followed by page or document number or title. Buntrock, 60.

24. Armeeoberkommando 9, 27970/1, Beilage zum Kriegstagebuch, Tätigkeitsbericht der Abt. Ic/AO, Berichtszeit 1.7.–31.12.42, document I, page 1. Henceforth cited as AOK 9:27970/1 followed by document and page numbers.

25. Armeeoberkommando 9, 27970/2, Beilage zum Kriegstagebuch, Anlage 1 zum Tätigkeitsbericht der Abteilung Ic/AO, Berichtszeit 1.7.–31.12.42, document dated 29.10.1942 and timed 19.30. Henceforth cited as AOK 9:27970/2 followed by date and time of document.

26. Armeeoberkommando 9, 32878/7, Beilage zum Kriegstagebuch, Anlage 5 zum Tätigkeitsbericht der Abt. Ic/AO, Berichtszeit 1.1.–25.3.43, document dated 17. January 1943, page 3. Henceforth cited as AOK 9:32878/7 followed by date of document and page number. Buntrock, 61.

27. AOK 9:27970/2:29.10.1942:19.30.

28. Ibid., 29.10.1942:19.30.

29. Haupt, 136. This corps had been commanded by General Rudolf Schmidt, brother of Hans-Thilo Schmidt.

30. AOK 9:27970/2:31.10.1942:6.15.

31. Ibid., 1.11.1942:07.10.

32. Ibid., 31.10.1942:10.00.

33. Ibid., 3.11.1942:18.20.

34. Rudolf Hagemann (O3, or adjutant to Ia, in 102nd Infantry Divison), interview, 7 October 1973.

35. AOK 9:32878/7:17. January 1943:8.

36. Armeeoberkommando 9, 26791/9, Anlage zum Kriegstagebuch, Ia, IV, Armeebefehle und Verfügungen, Berichtszeit 8.10.42–25.11.42, Band 8, document Gefechtsstärken: Stand vom 22.11.1942.

37. 102. Infanterie Division, 26562/1, Kreigstagebuch Nr. 9, Führungsabteilung vom 1.11. bis 31.12.42, documents 4a, 6, unnumbered Anlage. Henceforth cited as 102.I.D.: 26562/1 followed by number or date of document.

38. Hagemann, interview.

39. Hans Joachim Froben, *Aufklärende Artillerie: Geschichte der Beobachtungsabteilungen und selbständigen Beobachtungsbatterien bis 1945* (Munich, 1972), 574.

40. 102. Infanterie Division, 26562/4, Ic, Tätigkeitsbericht, Abt. Ic für die Zeit vom 1.11.1942–31.12.1942, document dated 5.11.42. Henceforth cited as 102.I.D.:26562/4 followed by date of document.

41. Froben, 574.

42. AOK 9:27970/2:5.11.1942:20.30.

43. OKH:H3/199:72:2–3.

44. AOK 9:27970/2:6.11.1942:07.30; Ibid., 19.15; 102I.D.:26562/4:6.11.1942.

45. 102.I.D.:26562/4:6.11.1942.

46. AOK 9:27970/2:7.11.1942:06.55.

47. 102.I.D.:26562/4:7.11.1942.

48. 102.I.D.:26562/4:7.11.1942:Anlage 5.

49. Ibid., 8.11.1942.

50. Berlin Document Center, File of Wilhelm Höttl (NSDAP Membership No. 6,309,616, SS No. 309,510), page 159.

51. Franz Seubert (espionage chief in the Abwehr post in Sofia), letters of 3 February and 12 August 1974; Otto Wagner (head of the Abwehr post in Sofia), memorandum, 16 May 1974.

52. Otto Wagner, interview, 27 June 1974.

53. Paul Leverkuehn, *German Military Intelligence*, trans. R. H. Stevens and Constantine FitzGibbon (London, 1954), 172–175; Herbert Rittlinger, *Geheimdienst mit beschränkter Haftung: Bericht vom Bosporus* (Stuttgart, 1973), 66, 224–230.

54. Seubert, letters; B. Orekhoff (head of a White Russian émigré group), letter, 22.12.74.

55. Rudolf-Christian Freiherr von Gersdorff (Ic of Army Group Center), interview, 11 March 1970; Max Bitterl von Tessenburg (liaison of radio intelligence to Foreign Armies East), interview, 10 September 1973; OKH:H3/199:passim.

56. OKH:H3/199:73:Anlage.

57. OKW, *KTB*, 2:1305–6.

58. Carl von Clausewitz, *On War*, trans. and ed. Michael Howard and Peter Paret (Princeton, 1976), Book iii, Chapter 10.

59. My analysis of the Ic reports.

60. Seaton, 190.

61. OKW, *KTB*, 2:818, 821, 823.

62. Ibid., 836.

63. Ibid., 855, 914, 921.

64. Ibid., 899.

65. Oberkommando des Heeres, Fremde Heere Ost, H3/198, Kurze Beurteilung der Feindlage, 4. April–15. September 1942, document of 13.11.1942, page 4.

66. Ibid.; AOK 9:32878/7:17. Januar 1943:2.

67. AOK 9:32878/7:17. Januar 1943:2–3.

68. OKH:H3/199:77:Anlage 1.

69. Ibid., 79:3.

70. 102.I.D.:26562/4:11.11.1942.

71. AOK 9:32878/7:17. Januar 1943:2.

72. Armeeoberkommando 9, 32151/16, Beilage zum Kriegstagebuch, Anlagenband IX zum Tätigkeitsbericht der Armee-Nachr.-Führer, Berichtszeit 1.–15.11.42, report of 9. November 1942; Armeeoberkommando 9, 32151/17, Beilage zum Kriegstagebuch, Anlagenband zum Tätigkeitsbericht der Armee-Nachr.-Führer, Berichtszeit 15.11.–30.11.42, report of 16. November 1942.

73. Fritz Neeb (operating head of Army Group Center radio intelligence unit), interview, 30 December 1972.

74. Bitterl, interview; Kurt Andrae (head of army's Main Intercept Post), interview, 26 April 1970.

75. Heeresgruppe D, 75144/33, Ic, Anlagenband II zum Kriegstagebuch, 1.–31. Juli 1944, page 4/6; Ulrich Liss, "Der entscheidende Wert richtiger Feindbeurteilung," *Wehrkunde*, 8 (November 1959), 584–592 at 585.

76. OKH:H3/199:82:2.

77. Ibid., 83:2.

78. Ibid., 84:2.

79. 102.I.D.:26562/4:13. November 1942.

80. OKH:H3/199:77:2 and Anlage 1, 78:2.

81. Ibid., 82:2, 83:2.

82. AOK 9:27970/2:20.11.1942:19.20.
83. My observations from 9th Army Ic reports.
84. 102.I.D.:26562/1:6.–16. November 1942. Temperature is in degrees Fahrenheit.
85. Paul Hilbert, *The Destruction of the European Jews* (London, 1961), 629.
86. OKH:H3/199:79:1–2.
87. OKW, *KTB* 2:882.
88. Ibid., 916.
89. Adolf Hitler, *Reden und Proklamationen*, ed. Max Domarus (Wiesbaden, 1973), 2:1940.
90. 102.I.D.:26562/1:17. November 1942.
91. 102.I.D.:26562/4:18. November 1942.
92. OKH:H3/199:86:Anlage 1.
93. OKH:H3/199:86:2.
94. OKW, *KTB*, 2:988.
95. OKH:H3/199:85:1.
96. 102.I.D.:26562/4:20.11.1942.
97. Armeeoberkommando 9, 31624/3, Kriegstagebuch (Führungsabteilung), Berichts-zeit 1.7.–31.12.1942, Band 3:24.10.–31.12.1942, entry of 20.11.1942. Henceforth cited as AOK 9:31624/3 followed by date of entry. Rudolf Langhaeuser, "Studie über die Beschaffung von Feindnachrichten im deutschen Heer während des 2. Weltkrieges an der Ostfront," United States, Army, Historical Division, Foreign Military Studies, D-407 (10 September 1952), 77.
98. 102.I.D.:26562/4:20.11.1942.
99. AOK 9:27970/2:22.11.1942:06.50.
100. 102.I.D.:26562/4:21.11.1942.
101. AOK 9:27970/2:21.11.1942:18.30.
102. OKH:H3/199:89:3.
103. 102.I.D.:26562/4:21.11.1942.
104. AOK 9:27970/2:21.11.1942:18.30.
105. AOK 9:31624/3:22.11.1942.
106. Buntrock, interview, and photograph in his possession.
107. AOK 9:27970/2:21.11.1942:untimed morning report.
108. AOK 9:27970/2:22.11.1942:06.50, 23.11.1942:untimed intermediate report.
109. XXXIX. Panzer Korps, 26522/18, Kriegstagebuch, Band 18, Ia, 6.11.42–24.11.42 mit Anlagen, document dated 23.11 [1942] and timed 10.45. Henceforth cited as XXXIX.Pz.K.:26522/18 followed by date and, if necessary, title or number of document.
110. AOK 9:31624/3:23.11.1942.
111. AOK 9:27970/2:24.11.1942:07.35.
112. 102.I.D.:26562/4:24.11.1942.
113. AOK 9:27970/2:24.11.1942:18.45.
114. XXXIX. Panzer Korps, 26522/33, Tätigkeitsbericht Abt. Ic [21.2.1942–31.12.1942], doc-ument dated 24.11.1942; XXXIX.Pz.K.:26552/18:24.11.1942:Artillerie-Kommandeur 34:Abend-meldung.
115. AOK 9:27970/2:24.11.1942:07.25.
116. AOK 9:31624/3:24.11.1942.
117. XXXIX.Pz.K.:26522/18:24.11.1942.
118. Ibid., 20:55.
119. XXXIX.Pz.K.:26522/18:24.11.1942:3679/42g.
120. AOK 9:27970/2:25.11.1942:6.50.
121. 102.I.D.:26562/4:25.11.1942; AOK 9:31624/3:25.11.1942.
122. AOK 9:32878/7:17. Januar 1943:4.
123. Armeeoberkommando 9, 28878/7, Beilage zum Kriegstagebuch, Tätigkeitsbericht der Abt. Armee-Nachr.-Führer, Berichtszeit 1.7.–31.12.1942, page 4.
124. 102.I.D.:26562/4:25.11.42.

125. Ziemke, 106–107.

126. Ibid., 115–116.

127. This was expressed in Gehlen's situation reports of 12 November, repeated on the 13th, 14th, and 15th, and of 18 November, both cited above. Three days after the Stalingrad attack Gehlen said that its success had been "doubtlessly surprising" for the Russians (OKH:H3/199:89:1); a prisoner-of-war statement supports this (OKW, *KTB*, 2:1026). Gehlen held to his view that the principal attack was that against Army Group Center until 9 December, when he finally stated that the Russians had shifted their main effort to Stalingrad; up to his death he maintained that the principal effort was originally directed against Army Group Center (Manfred Kehrig, *Stalingrad: Analyse und Dokumentation einer Schlacht*, Beiträge zur Militär- und Kriegsgechichte, 15 [Stuttgart, 1974], 118.). The Russians say, on the other hand, that they had always intended the main effort at Stalingrad, and they, too, cite documents that support this contention (Boris Semjonowitsch Telpuchowski, *Die Sowjetische Geschichte des Grossen Vaterländischen Krieges 1941–1945*, ed. Andreas Hillgruber and Hans-Adolf Jacobsen (Frankfurt am Main, 1961), 176, 178–179). The Soviet chief of military history, General P. Zhilin, did not respond specifically to this matter in his reply to my letter asking him about it. I agree with Kehrig, 119, that this question cannot be resolved with certainty until the Soviet archives are opened. But I also agree with Field Marshal Wilhelm Keitel, chief of the Oberkommando der Wehrmacht, and General Alfred Jodl, chief of the OKW operations staff, that Gehlen failed to give sufficient warning of the scope and power of the Soviet attack at Stalingrad ("Die Vernehmung von Generalfeldmarschall Keitel durch die Sowjets," trans. Wilhelm Arenz, *Wehrwissenschaftliche Rundschau*, 11 [November 1961], 651–662 at 659 and "Die Vernehmung von Generaloberst Jodl durch die Sowjets," trans. Wilhelm Arenz, Ibid. [September 1961], 534–542 at 539).

## Potential Enemies

1. George H. Gallup, *The Gallup Poll* (New York, 1972), 1:197.

2. National Archives, Record Group 165, War Department General Staff, War Plans Division, index cards for "Russia, General" from 1921 to 1941. I am grateful to William H. Cunliffe of the National Archives for this reference, and to Edward S. Miller of Stamford, Connecticut, for his penetrating comments on this subject. Of the studies of prewar U.S.-U.S.S.R. relations, only one suggests that the two nations were "nearly full-fledged enemies between 1939 and 1941" (Walter LaFeber, *America, Russia and the Cold War: 1945–1975*, 3rd ed. [New York, 1976], 7). Others say that relations were cool and mention a generalized Soviet aggressiveness or suspiciousness, but do not suggest that the United States regarded the Soviet Union as a potential enemy (William Hardy McNeill, *America, Britain and Russia: Their Cooperation and Conflict, 1941–1946*, Royal Institute of International Affairs [London, 1953], 20; Daniel Yergin, *Shattered Peace: The Origins of the Cold War and the National Security State* [Boston, 1977], 35–37; George F. Kennan, *Russia and the West Under Lenin and Stalin* [Boston, 1960], 312). Louis Fischer explains the situation best: "The alternative of joining capitalist Nazi Germany to destroy communism was never considered, much less adopted by anticommunist America or anticommunist Britain. Those two 'citadels of capitalism' put national interest above class and ideology" (*The Road to Yalta: Soviet Foreign Relations, 1941–1945* [New York, 1972], 4).

3. Henry L. Stimson, Diary, 30:154 (9/11/40), 202 (9/27/40), in Yale University Library.

4. Gallup, 1:128–29, 133–34, 288–89.

5. *The Public Papers and Addresses of Franklin D. Roosevelt*, ed. Samuel I. Rosenman (New York, 1969), 10:185. Henceforth cited as *PPA*. See also Stetson Conn and Byron Fairchild, *The Framework of Hemisphere Defense*, Department of the Army (Washington, 1960), 68–129.

6. *PPA.* 10:183.

7. United States, Department of Commerce, Bureau of the Census, *Historical Statistics of the United States: Colonial Times to 1970* (Washington, 1975). Series U-324, U-329, U-342, U-347 for 1936, 1937, 1938.

8. W. S. Waytinsky and E. S. Waytinsky, *World Population and Production: Trends and Outlooks* (New York, 1953), 44, 1000.

9. Robert J. C. Butow, *Tojo and the Coming of the War* (Princeton, 1961), 360–61, 320, 347, 267.

10. Robert Jervis, *Perception and Misperception in International Politics* (Princeton, 1976), 112–113, demonstrates the pointlessness of thinking one's way into other people's minds. Richard K. Betts, "Analysis, War, and Decisions: Why Intelligence Failures are Inevitable," *World Politics,* 31 (October 1978), 61–89 demonstrates, at 83–91, the problems of becoming a devil's advocate.

11. Howard V. Young, Jr., "Racial Attitudes of United States Navy Officers as a Factor in American Unpreparedness for War with Japan," Paper delivered at the Naval History Symposium, U.S. Naval Academy, Annapolis, 2 October 1981. This is a remarkable and eye-opening study.

12. *Sea Power and Today's War* (New York, 1939), 175–79.

13. Ibid., 175–78, passim.

14. (New Haven, 1941), 226.

15. Young, passim.

16. Louis Morton, "Germany First," in Kent Roberts Greenfield, ed., *Command Decisions,* prepared by the Office of the Chief of Military History, Department of the Army (New York, 1959), 3–38.

17. National Archives, Record Group 165, War Department General Staff, War Plans Division, Folder 4175-15, Memorandum for the Chief of Staff, November 17, 1940. These War Plans Division records are henceforth cited as WPD plus the folder number.

18. United States, Congress, Joint Committee on the Investigation of the Pearl Harbor Attack, *Pearl Harbor Attack,* Hearings, 79th Congress (Washington, 1946), 14:1062. These hearings are henceforth cited as *PHA.*

19. *PHA,* 33:958

20. WPD 4250-3, Op-12B-McC, 26 June 1940.

21. WPD 4175-18, Gerow to Assistant Chief of Staff G-2, 14 December 1940.

22. WPD 4175-15. Marshall to Stark, 2 December 1940.

23. WPD 4494, War Department Strategic Estimate . . . October, 1941.

24. *PHA,* 2:785; United States, Congress, House of Representatives, Committee on Government Operations and the Permanent Select Committee on Intelligence, *National Security Act of 1947,* Hearings before the Committee on Expenditures in the Executive Departments on H.R. 2319, 80th Congress, 1st Session (Washington, 1982), 53; Anthony Cave Brown, *Wild Bill Donovan: The Last Hero* (New York, 1982), 176–77; Thomas F. Troy, *Donovan and the CIA: A History of the Establishment of the Central Intelligence Agency* (Frederick, Maryland, 1981), 105–107; A German intelligence questionnaire asking about army bases and airfields on Oahu and Pearl Harbor defenses, passed to the Federal Bureau of Investigation by a double agent, the Yugoslav Dusko Popov, was never given to other intelligence agencies by F.B.I. Director J. Edgar Hoover, probably because of rivalry with them (John F. Bratzel and Leslie B. Rout, Jr., "Pearl Harbor, Microdots, and J. Edgar Hoover," *The American Historical Review,* 87 (December 1982), 1342–1351.

25. *PHA,* 2:899; Dwight D. Eisenhower, *Crusade in Europe* (London, 1948), 37.

26. Joseph G. Grew, *Ten Years in Japan: A Contemporary Record Drawn from the Diaries and Private and Official Papers of Joseph C. Grew* (New York, 1944), colophon and passim.

27. Robert Dallek, *Franklin D. Roosevelt and American Foreign Policy, 1932–1945* (New York, 1979), 33.

28. Ibid., 67.

29. Anne Morrow Lindbergh, *The Flower and the Nettle: Diaries and Letters of Anne Morrow Lindbergh, 1936–1939* (New York, 1976), 428; Hugh R. Wilson, *Diplomat between Wars* (New York, 1941), 91, 103, 106.

30. A. M. Lindbergh, 358–59; United States, National Archives, Franklin D. Roosevelt Library, President's Secretary's File 44, Germany, 19 June 1940 and October 1940. Henceforth cited as FDR Library, PSF plus item number.

31. Jozef Garlinski, *The Enigma War* (New York, 1980), 12–37, and article in this volume.

32. Georges Castellan, *Le Réarmemant clandestin du Reich, 1930–1935, vu par le 2e Bureau de l'État-major français* (Paris, 1954), and Robert J. Young, "French Military Intelligence and Nazi Germany, 1938–1939," paper presented at the Harvard conference.

33. Examples of the American diplomats' reports on Axis matters in United States, Department of State, *Foreign Relations of the United States: Diplomatic Papers, 1939* (Washington), 1 (1959):49, 170, 178–9, 192, 195, 422; *1940*, 1 (1959):39, 50, 228, 230. Henceforth this series is cited as *FRUS* plus date. See also National Archives, Record Group 59, Purport Book for Department of State Decimal File 852.00. On Bullitt, see introduction by George F. Kennan to Orville C. Bullitt, ed., *For the President: Personal and Secret: Correspondence between Franklin D. Roosevelt and William C. Bullitt,* (Boston, 1972), v–viii. Michael Beschloss, *Roosevelt and Kennedy: The Uneasy Alliance* (New York, 1980), cites no instances of Kennedy's mentioning German strength, but he does give numerous examples of Kennedy's expressing belief that Britain would not survive (195, 197, 203, 206, 208 and 212), which may be regarded as a negative reference to German power.

34. An instance in *FRUS, 1939*, 1:224–25.

35. WPD 4175-18. Miles to Chief of Staff, 11 February 1941.

36. *Roosevelt and Churchill: Their Secret Wartime Correspondence*, Francis L. Loewenheim, Harold D. Langley, and Manfred Jones, eds. (New York, 1975). 105, 126, 129, 130. Joseph P. Lash, *Roosevelt and Churchill, 1939–1941: The Partnership That Saved the West* (New York, 1976), gives excellent background on the Roosevelt-Churchill relationship.

37. WPD 4402-62.

38. Marc B. Powe, "The Emergence of the War Department Intelligence Agency, 1885–1918," Master's Thesis (Department of History, Kansas State University, 1974), 17; Jeffrey M. Dorwart, *The Office of Naval Intelligence: The Birth of America's First Intelligence Agency, 1865–1918* (Annapolis, 1979), 17.

39. National Archives, Record Group 165, War Department General Staff, Military Intelligence Division, Folder 2023-948, passim. These Military Intelligence Division records are cited henceforth as MID plus the folder number or name.

40. MID 2023–948, Report No. 8958, p. 4.

41. MID 2023–948, Report No. 9210, p. 2.

42. Ibid., 80, 82.

43. MID 2023–948, Report No. 8267.

44. MID 2023–948, Report No. 9210, p. 2.

45. MID 2023–1011, Report No. 10,099, p. 6.

46. Ibid.

47. MID 2023–962, Report No. 7765, p. 32.

48. Ibid., p. 33.

49. Examination of MID, Japan: Dispatch Books and Cross-Reference.

50. Ibid., p. 300–301.

51. Examination of MID, Germany: Dispatch Books and Cross-Reference.

52. National Archives, Record Group 38, Secret Naval Attachés' Reports, Vol. 1, Document 24. Henceforth cited as Secret Naval Attachés' Reports, followed by volume and document number.

53. For the techniques of radio intelligence and the organization of the American agencies engaged in it, see David Kahn, *The Codebreakers: The Story of Secret Writing* (New York, 1967), esp. ch. 1, on the events preceding Pearl Harbor.

54. *PHA*, 15:1882. 1883.

55. Ibid., 17:2629.

56. Ibid., 18:3335, 10:4673; Kahn, 47.

57. *PHA*, 35:106

58. Abraham Sinkov, telephone interview, 12 May 1980, and Solomon Kullback, interview, 27 October 1979, and telephone interview, 4 July 1980.

59. Kullback, interview.

60. Contrary to the speculations in Kahn, 18–19, the PURPLE machine was not a descendant of the German Enigma machine, even though the Japanese had purchased an Enigma. The two utilized entirely different cryptographic principles. As a consequence, the statement in several books that the American solution of PURPLE was merely an offshoot of the Polish-British solution of Enigma is erroneous. The two solutions were entirely independent.

61. Kahn, 30–31.

62. William L. Shirer via Mrs. Mary Thomas, telephone interview, 7 July 1980; Joy Schaleben, "Louis P. Lochner: Getting the Story Out of Nazi Germany, 1933–1941," Master's Thesis (University of Wisconsin, 1942).

63. Martha Dodd, *Through Embassy Eyes* (New York, 1939), 96, 98, 99.

64. Ernest R. May, "U.S. Press Coverage of Japan, 1931–1941," in *Pearl Harbor as History: Japanese-American Relations 1931–1941*, ed. Dorothy Borg and Shumpei Okamato (New York, 1973), 511–32.

65. For example, "Schacht's Diatribe Bares Basic Clash," *The New York Times* (25 August 1935), IV:5:1; "Reich Split Widens in Army-Nazi Row; Blomberg Has Quit," *Ibid.* (3 February 1938), 1:5.

66. May, 524, 526–529; John Hohenberg, *Foreign Correspondence: The Great Reporters and Their Times* (New York, 1964), 287–294, 321–330, 333–346, adds little.

67. MID, Folder 2023-949, January 4 and 29, 1935.

68. [William E. Dodd], *Ambassador Dodd's Diary, 1933–1938*, eds. William E. Dodd, Jr., and Martha Dodd (New York, 1941), 292.

69. Powe, 15; *PHA*, 2:777; Harold C. Relyea, "The Evolution and Organization of the Federal Intelligence Function: A Brief Overview," in United States, Congress, Senate, Select Committee to Study Government Operations with Respect to Intelligence Activities, *Final Report: Supplementary Reports on Intelligence Activities*, Book VI, Report No. 94-755, 94th Congress, 2nd Session (Washington, 1976), at 185; "General Miles, Intelligence Aide," *The New York Times* (October 8, 1966), 31:1.

70. Dorwart, 16; *PHA*, 4:1727, 1724; United States, Navy, Public Information Office, official biography of Theodore Stark Wilkinson.

71. *PHA*, 14:1419, 2:829, 15:1864, 4:1726.

72. Ibid., 34:139; Roberta Wohlstetter, *Pearl Harbor: Warning and Decision* (Stanford, 1962), 314.

73. Wohlstetter, 300.

74. *PHA*, 2:785; Patrick Beesly, *Very Special Admiral: The Life of Admiral J. H. Godfrey, CB* (London, 1980), 180.

75. WPD 4584-3, Memorandum from Marshall, October 20, 1941; WPD 4584-6, Minutes of the First Formal Meeting . . . , December 3, 1946.

76. Relyea, 140; Cave Brown, passim.

77. A. M. Lindbergh, 84, 187; my conclusions from C. L. Lindbergh's reports.

78. *FRUS, 1938*, 1 (1955):716–20; MID, folder 2016–1297, Report No. 17,128 (March 1, 1940), 16.

79. Wilhelm Deist, "Die Deutsche Aufrüstung in amerikanischer Sicht: Berichte des US-Militärattachés in Berlin aus den Jahren 1933–1939," in *Russland-Deutschland-Amerika: Festschrift für Fritz T. Epstein zum 80. Geburtstag*, eds. Alexander Fischer et al., Frankfurter Historischer Abhandlungen, Band 17 (Wiesbaden, 1978), 279–95 at 284.

80. Ibid.

81. *FRUS, 1938*, 1:716.

82. *The New York Times Index* for 1935, 1936, 1937, 1938, 1939.

83. Deist, 282.

84. Walter S. Ross, *The Last Hero: Charles A. Lindbergh* (New York, 1968), 264–265.

85. Ibid., 268–270, 273–274, See also Wayne S. Cole, *Charles A. Lindbergh and the Battle against American Intervention in World War II* (New York, 1974), 31–40.

86. Ross, 274–76.

87. FDR Library, PSF 87, Folder "Navy 1938—Jan.–Feb."

88. [Charles A. Lindbergh], *The Wartime Journals of Charles A. Lindbergh* (New York, 1970), 183–84, 185, 186.

89. Ibid., 82–84.

90. "Testifies on Base for Nazi Attack," *The New York Times* (22 February 1939), 3:5.

91. Dallek, 172, 213.

92. Ross, 275.

93. *FRUS, 1940*, 1 (1959):50.

94. Secret Naval Attachés Reports, No. 69 of 18 December 1940.

95. Ibid., Estimate of Potential Military Strength Summaries, 17 February 1940.

96. Cajus Bekker, *The Luftwaffe War Diaries*, trans. and ed. Frank Ziegler (New York, 1968), 377.

97. Bullitt, 419 and note at 421.

98. *PHA*, 14:1336.

99. WPD 4498, I.B. 122, "Brief Periodic Estimate of the Situation," 5 September 1941, Tab A.

100. "Die Stärke der deutschen Luftwaffe am 5.7.1941, 3.1.1942, und 31.5.1943," *Wehrwissenschaftliche Rundschau*, 11 (November 1961), 641–44.

101. FDR Library, PSF, Box 4, Folder Germany—Coordinator of Information, *The German Military and Economic Position: Summary and Conclusions*, Monograph No. 3, December 12, 1941, p. 1. The figure of 29,000 airplanes is derived by beginning with the figure given of 24,000 at the start of the Russian war, subtracting the estimated losses of 4,500 and adding the estimated monthly production of 1,960 for five months.

102. Franz Halder, *Kriegstagebuch* (Stuttgart, 1962–64), 3:341.

103. *The German Military and Economic Position*, 1.

104. Burkhart Müller-Hillebrand, *Das Heer 1933–1945* (Frankfurt, 1954–69), 2:106.

105. *The German Military and Economic Position*, 1; Mueller-Hillebrand, 2:107. The Coordinator was not the only one to err. When the Wehrmacht armaments office set a monthly production goal of 800 to 1,200 tanks and assault guns for the panzer army of 1944, an official in a rival office calculated that it would take the whole machine-tool industry two years to produce the necessary tools—provided that, in the first place, 100,000 specialists had been recalled from the army to do the work. (Alan S. Milward, *The German Economy at War* [London, 1965], 26.)

106. The question arises why, if Americans overestimated German air production at least in part because of racism, the French and the British also overestimated it (Hinsley, 75, 228–29, 299–300, 308–309; Young). Did a sense of German superiority play a role in their overestimations as well? I think it is not improbable—a belief in German efficiency may well have colored their views. I concede I know of no evidence for or against this possibility, but on the other hand none of the reasons adduced for the British and French overestimations provide satisfactory explanations. The reasons I know of are: "the tight [German] security screen and the pace with which the industry was expanding" (Young), the sparseness of "first-class intelligence material," exaggerations of the Luftwaffe's front-line strength, an assumption that the Germans had gone from one to two shifts in aircraft factories, an abandonment of the Royal Air Force expansion rate as a basis for figuring the Luftwaffe's (all Hinsley, 228–229, 299), the German failure to fulfill their own production

plans—plans that seem to have been reflected in at least some French and British estimates (R. J. Overy, "The German Pre-War Aircraft Production Plans: November 1936–April 1939," *English Historical Review*, 90 [October 1975], 778–97, comparing, for example, the French estimate at the time of Munich of a normal monthly production of 600 airplanes [Young], with the German plan then in effect to produce 585 airplanes in September 1938 [Overy, 781]), a widespread preconception "that German air power was enormous and was increasing" (Overy, 794), a British superstition about Germany's technological superiority (Donald Detweiler, personal communication), the ideological predilection of such French conservatives as army officers for the Germans (Detweiler) though this contradicts a blinding chauvinism perceived among French generals (Young), and deliberate deception by the Nazis (Central Intelligence Agency, Office of Research and Development, and Mathtech, Inc., *Covert Rearmament in Germany, 1919–1939: Deception and Misperception*, Deception Research Program [Washington, D.C., and Princeton, N.J.: 1979]). Since none of these reasons is convincing, racism may be the missing factor. If so, it would strengthen the view that racism significantly distorted American intelligence.

107. *The German Military and Economic Position*, 1.

108. Müller-Hillebrand, 1:102.

109. *PHA*, 14:1336.

110. Germany, Oberkommando der Wehrmacht, Wehrmachtführungsstab, *Kreigstagebuch, 1940–1945* (Frankfurt, 1961–69), 1:1125–38. Henceforth: OKW, *Kriegstagebuch*.

111. *PHA*, 15:1785.

112. OKW, *Kriegstagebuch*, 2:1356–57.

113. WPD 4494–21, undated memorandum signed ACW [Albert Coady Wedemeyer].

114. Müller-Hillebrand, 2:182.

115. Survey of Secret Naval Attachés Reports and of Summary of Military Attaché Reports.

116. Survey of relevant volumes of *FRUS* and of Department of State Decimal File Purport Sheets for Germany.

117. Examination of WPD 4402–65.

118. Robert Sherwood, *Roosevelt and Hopkins: An Intimate History* (New York, 1948), 304.

119. WPD 4494–17, I.B. 122, "Brief Periodic Estimate of the Situation," 5 September 1941, 1.

120. Holger H. Herwig, *Politics of Frustration: The United States in German Naval Planning* (Boston, 1976), 216–34.

121. Dallek, 287.

122. Herwig, 231.

123. Dallek, 287, 291–92.

124. Ibid., 233–35; Herwig, 187.

125. *New York Times* (June 30, 1941), 1:1.

126. WPD 4494, I.B. 122, Tab A, p. 3.

127. Ibid., pp. 1–2.

128. WPD 4494, Strategic Estimate, pp. 7–8.

129. Walter Warlimont, *Inside Hitler's Headquarters 1939–45*, trans. R. H. Barry (London, 1964), 208.

130. The best summary of Hitler's decision to declare war on the United States is Andreas Hillgruber's "Der Faktor Amerika in Hitlers Strategie," *Aus Politik und Zeitgeschichte*, B19/65 (11 May 1966).

131. *PHA*, 12:253.

132. The best study of Japan's decision is Butow. Also helpful are John Toland, *The Rising Sun* (New York, 1972), and some of the analyses in Dorothy Borg and Shumpei Okamato, eds., *Pearl Harbor as History* (New York, 1973).

133. These options as seen by Americans are most clearly set out in Miles to War Plans Division, 2 November 1941, *PHA*, 14:1363.

134. Pratt, 236, 182.

135. Puleston, 259, 116–17, and Young, citing Sutherland Denlinger and Charles B. Gary, *War in the Pacific: A Study of Navies, Peoples and Battle Problems* (New York, 1936), 277, and George Fielding Eliot, "The Impossible War With Japan," *The American Mercury*, 45 (September 1938), at 19.

136. *PHA*, 14:1380.

137. Japan, Defense Agency, Office of Military History, *Riku-kaigun Nenpyu* (Tokyo, Showa 55 [1980], vol. 102. I am grateful to Dr. Alvin Coox for this reference and for translating the relevant data.

138. Wohlstetter, 337.

139. Kahn, 8–9, 39.

140. *PHA*, 14:1059.

141. United States, Department of Defense, *The "MAGIC" Background to Pearl Harbor* (Washington, 1978), 1A:81, 3:132, 4:165.

142. *PHA*, 12:254–316.

143. Ibid., 12:165, 204.

144. Ibid., 12:137, 208–209, 215–216, 231, 236, 237, 249; 35:472, 679.

145. Ibid., 10:4659–65, 4662–63.

146. The G-2 Regional File has nothing of value about Japanese war plans at this time. NA, RG 165, G-2 Regional File, Box 2362.

147. *PHA*, 14:1363, 1372. Tab A to the 5 December report contains the astonishing statement that Japan's leaders "want to avoid a general war in the Pacific." (Ibid., 14:1381). But this was probably written by a junior officer who did not have access to MAGIC and its warnings, and it seems to have been overlooked or ignored by everybody.

148. Roberta Wohlstetter maintains an opposing view, arguing (387) that "We failed to anticipate Pearl Harbor not for want of the relevant materials, but because of a plethora of irrelevant ones. . . ." But while she is certainly right in noting that many data suggested other courses of Japanese action than an attack on Pearl Harbor, she is certainly wrong in saying that the information in American hands sufficed to foretell the attack. I believe that my exposition of what was available and what was not demonstrates this; in any event, Mrs. Wohlstetter nowhere supports her argument by listing the "relevant materials." If blame must be fixed for the Pearl Harbor disaster, I believe it must fall on the shoulders of the two commanders there, General Walter Short and Admiral Husband Kimmel, whose job it was to guard the fleet against an enemy attack, whether surprise or expected. This is also the view of the greatest scholar of Pearl Harbor, Gordon Prange, in his massive study *At Dawn We Slept* (New York, 1981). He sums it up in one lapidary comment (729): "Had U.S. forces discovered and beaten off [Admiral Chuichi] Nagumo's task force or made the attackers suffer unacceptable losses over the target, Kimmel and Short would have received the credit. By the same token, they cannot escape the onus of surprise and defeat." For a view of the psychology of Kimmel's rejections of the warnings of danger, see Irving L. Janis and Leon Mann, *Decision Making: A Psychological Analysis of Conflict, Choice and Commitment* (New York, 1977), 120–38. Richard K. Betts, *Surprise Attack: Lessons for Defense Planning* (Washington, 1982), follows Wohlstetter in her error.

149. Neither raised nor answered here is the question of whether, in the military sphere, extra money would have been better spent on intelligence than on battleships, or, in the national economy as a whole, whether it would have been better spent on military matters than on education or welfare. The question goes beyond the scope of this paper. But it was answered in the negative by the United States in the 1920s and 1930s.

150. Eisenhower, 37.

151. Ibid.

152. For an analysis of the same situation in the German Army, where it was even more pronounced, see David Kahn, *Hitler's Spies: German Military Intelligence in World War II* (New York, 1978), 531–34.

Addendum: None of the books on Pearl Harbor that have been published since this paper was delivered have added anything significant to the information in it nor have they caused me to modify the views set forth in it. For a critical analysis of the new "information" in the most sensational of these books, John Toland's *Infamy: Pearl Harbor and Its Aftermath* (New York, 1982), see my review in *The New York Review of Books* (May 27, 1982), 36–40.

## Opportunities in Cryptology for Historians

1. For an orientation, see Conyers Read, *Mr. Secretary Walsingham and the Policy of Queen Elizabeth* (Cambridge, 1925); for some documents, see Great Britain, Public Records Office, *Calendars of State Papers, Scotland*. Others, not published, are in the Public Records Office.

2. One is Ms. e Mus. 203, "A Collection of Letters and other Papers, which were at several times intercepted, written in Cipher," 1653. The two newly acquired ones are: Ms. Eng. misc. c. 475, essentially a copy of Ms. e Mus. 203, and Ms. Eng. misc. c. 382, a 323-folio volume of Wallis's own copies of his solutions of political intercepts, nearly all French, from 1689 to 1703.

3. The papers of the Decypherers are in the British Museum, Additional Manuscripts 32258–32303 and 45518–45523. For background on this subject, see Kenneth Ellis, *The Post Office in the Eighteenth Century: A Study in Administrative History* (London, 1958); James Walker, "The Secret Service Under Charles II and James II," *Transactions of the Royal Historical Society*, 15 (1932), 226–35; F. B. Smith, "British Post Office Espionage, 1844," *Historical Studies*, 14 (April 1970), 189–203, and Phyllis S. Lachs, *The Diplomatic Corps under Charles II and James II* (New Brunswick, N.J., 1965), at 37–41, 172–73.

4. Several mentioning Rossignol are cited in *The Codebreakers* (New York, 1967), 1003–4.

5. (Paris, 1950).

6. See Josef Karl Mayr, *Metternichs Geheimer Briefdienst: Postlogen und Postkurse*, Inventare Österreichischer Staatlicher Archive, V, Inventare des Wiener Haus-, Hof- und Staatsarchiv, 3 (Vienna, 1935); Franz Stix, "Zur Geschichte und Organisation der Wiener Geheimen Ziffernkanzlei," *Mitteilungen des Österreichischen Instituts für Geschichtsforschung*, LI (1937), 133–60; and Maurice-Henri Weil, *Les Dessous du Congrès de Vienne* (Paris, 1917), which published many of the *Intercepta*. In addition: Harald Hubatschke, "Ferdinand Prantner (Pseudonym Leo Wolfram) 1817–1871: Die Anfänge des politischen Romans sowie die Geschichte der Briefspionage und des geheimen Chiffrendienstes in Österreich," Dissertation . . . an der . . . Universität Wien (Wien, 1975), 1572 pp.; Harald Hubatschke, "Die amtliche Organisation der geheimen Briefüberwachung und des diplomatischen Chiffrendienstes in Österreich," *Mitteilungen des Instituts für Österreichische Geschichtsforschung*, 83 (1975), 352–413; Donald E. Emerson, *Metternich and the Political Police: Security and Subversion in the Hapsburg Monarchy (1815–1830)* (The Hague, 1968); Richard Blaas, "Mazzini-Korrespondenz in den Interzepten der Staatskanzlei," *Veröffentlichungen des Instituts des Österreichischen Geschichtsforschung*, 20 (1974), 329–44.

7. Some useful leads may be found in Joh. Ludw. Klüber, *Kryptographik* (Tübingen, 1809), 39–47, and in Emil Koenig, *Schwarze Kabinette* (Braunschweig, 1875), 12.

8. Ellis, 66. Some traces of Hanover's black chamber activity may remain in her

archives although its archive catalogue, edited by Max Baer in 1900, cites only what seems to be the peripheral matters of "Chiffres," "Censuren," "Correspondenzen," and "Depeschensachen" under the Ministry of Foreign Affairs. Some information about a particular case is cited in S. P. Oakley, "The Interception of Posts in Celle, 1694–1700," in *William III and Louis XIV: Essays 1680–1700 by and for Mark A. Thompson,* ed. Ragnhild Hatton and J. S. Bromley (Liverpool, 1960), 95–116.

9. Koenig, 48–53.

10. Many of the Swedish ciphers are preserved in the Riksarchiv, Chifferklaver. A few are reproduced in H. Stålhane, *Hemlig Skrift* (Stockholm, 1934), 150–75.

11. The best starting point is still Aloys Meister, *Die Anfänge der modernen diplomatischen Geheimschrift* (Paderborn, 1902).

12. S. Maiskii, "Chernyi Kabinet," *Byloe* (January 1918), 185–97. P. E. Shchogolev, ed., *Padenie Tsarkojo Rezhima* (Leningrad, 1925–27), 3:264, 269, 5:134–36, and perhaps elsewhere; Mikhail N. Pokrowski, ed., *Die Internationale Beziehungen im Zeitalter des Imperialismus: Dokumente aus den Archiven der Zaristischen und der provisorischen Regierung 1878–1917,* German ed., Otto Hoetsch (Berlin, 1931–1936) and (Berlin, 1939–1942), passim, for intercepted foreign dispatches; Richard J. Johnson, "Dagranichnaia Agentura: The Tsarist Political Police in Europe," *Journal of Contemporary History,* 7 (January–April 1972), 221–42 at 233, 234; Wolfgang Geierhos, "Zu bisher ungenützten Aufzeichnungen der französischen Geheimpolizei über die Tätigkeit russischer Revolutionäre 1890–1917," *Jahrbücher für Geschichte Osteuropas,* 19 (December 1971), 532–37.

13. The two discussions of cryptanalysis, both short manuscripts, are reprinted in Joaquín García Carmona, *Tratado de Criptografía* (Madrid, 1894), 200–2.

14. C. E. Bosworth, "The Section on Codes and their Decipherment in Qalqashandi's *Subh al-a 'sha,*" *Journal of Semitic Studies,* 7 (Spring 1963), 17–33.

15. Peter Olbricht, *Das Postwesen in China unter der Mongolenherrschaft im 13. und 14. Jahrhundert* (Wiesbaden, 1954), 81–90.

16. For example, see France's Ministry of Foreign Affairs archives, Mémoires et Documents: Fonds France, 1890, and Fonds Bourbon, 607.

17. Ellis, 66–7.

18. Koenig, 20; and Herbert O. Yardley, *The American Black Chamber* (Indianapolis, 1931), 86–8; Hubatschke, "Prantner," 1276–80.

19. Richard Wilmer Rowan, *The Story of Secret Service* (Garden City, N.Y., 1931), 731.

20. One series of codes that extends through the transition period and should therefore show the evolution exists in France's Archives Nationales, F⁹⁰ 11660–93. These include codes from the time of the July Monarchy, the Second Empire, the War of 1870 and the Third Republic.

21. Recently, however, new material has become available on Britain's Typex cipher machine; Louis Kruh and C. A. Deavours, "The Typex Cryptograph," *Cryptologia,* 7 (April 1983), 145–65.

22. Ladislas Farago, *The Broken Seal* (New York, 1967).

# Signals Intelligence in the 1980s

1. *Public Papers of the Presidents of the United States: Jimmy Carter, 1978* (Washington, D.C., 1979), 2102–2103.

2. Daniel O. Graham.

3. Immanuel Kant, *Zum ewigen Frieden* (1797), § I, 6.

# Acknowledgments

The author acknowledges with thanks the permission of the following organizations and publications to reprint herein articles that they first published:

"Conversations with Cryptologists"—*The Cryptogram,* official organ of the American Cryptogram Association.

"Interviews with Cryptologists"—*Cryptologia* magazine.

"How *The Codebreakers* Was Written"—*The Bucknell Alumnus,* where the article was entitled "How One Bucknellian Wrote His Book."

"Lgcn Otuu Wllwgh Wl Etfown"—*The New York Times Magazine,* © 1960 by The New York Times Company. Reprinted by permission.

"The Code Battle"—Originally appeared in *Playboy* magazine. Copyright © 1975 by Playboy.

"The Grand Lines of Cryptology's Development"—*Computers and Security,* published by North-Holland Publishing Company, a branch of Elsevier Science Publishers B.V.

"On the Origin of Polyalphabetic Substitution"—*Isis: Official Journal of the History of Science Society.*

"Herbert O. Yardley: A Biographical Sketch"—the introduction to the paperback reprint by Ballantine Books, a division of Random House, Inc., of Herbert O. Yardley's *The American Black Chamber,* © 1931, 1981 by Herbert O. Yardley, introduction © 1981 by David Kahn.

"Yardley's 'Lost' Manuscript"—*Cryptologia* magazine.

"The ULTRA Conference"—*Cryptologia* magazine.

"Codebreaking in World Wars I and II"—*The Historical Journal.*

"Plaintext in the New Unabridged"—Crypto Press.

"The Ché Guevara Cipher"—Copyright © 1969 by Daniel James. From the book *Ché Guevara: A Biography.* Reprinted with permission of Stein and Day Publishers.

"American Codes and the Pentagon Papers"—*Newsday.*

"Tapping Computers"—*The New York Times* Op-Ed Page, © 1976 by The New York Times Company. Reprinted by permission.

"Big Ear or Big Brother?"—*The New York Times Magazine,* © 1976 by The New York Times Company. Reprinted by permission.

"Cryptology Goes Public"—Reprinted by permission of *Foreign Affairs,* Fall 1979. Copyright 1979 by the Council on Foreign Relations, Inc.

Review of *The Ultra Secret*—*The New York Times Book Review,* © 1974 by The New York Times Company. Reprinted by permission.

Review of *The Man Who Broke Purple*—*Army* magazine of the Association of the United States Army.

Review of *Ultra Goes to War* and *Piercing the Reich*—*The New Republic.*

Review of *The American Magic*—The *Chicago Sun-Times,* © Chicago Sun-Times 1982. Article by David Kahn, reprinted with permission.

"The Defense of Osuga, 1942"—Reprint from *Aerospace Historian,* December 1981, with permission. Copyright 1981 by the Air Force Historical Foundation. No additional copies may be made without the express permission of the author and of the editor of *Aerospace Historian.*

"Potential Enemies"—Copyright 1983 by Princeton University Press, which has scheduled for publication an abbreviated version in a volume entitled *Knowing One's Enemies: Intelligence Assessment Before the Two World Wars,* edited by Ernest R. May. Reprinted by permission of Princeton University Press.

"Opportunities in Cryptology for Historians"—Kahn, David. "Cryptology and History: Secret Writings for Historians," *The Maryland Historian,* vol. 3, no. 2 (Fall 1972): 157–162. Reprinted by permission of the publisher.

"Signals Intelligence in the 1980s"—*Intelligence Requirements for the 1980's: Clandestine Collection,* edited by Roy Godson and published by the National Strategy Information Center.

"Two Soviet Spy Ciphers" was originally published privately by David Kahn. "The Spy Who Most Affected World War II" was written for this book.

# Index

Abel, Rudolf Ivanovich (MARK), 31, 146, 148, 161, 162, 164
Abel cipher, 31, 146, 148, 161–164
Abwehr, 238, 239, 244
ADFGVX cipher, 11, 28, 159, 215, 287
aerial reconnaissance, 234, 235, 236, 237, 241–242, 245, 277, 293, 294
Alberti, Leon Battista, 54, 56, 57–58, 60, 61
Alexander, C. H. O'D., 36
Allen, Lew, Jr., 174, 176, 178, 185
Alphabetical Typewriter '97, 108
Amè, Cesare, 19
American Banking Association, 197
American Black Chamber, The (Yardley), 21, 62–63, 65, 72, 75
American College Dictionary, 121
American Cryptogram Association (A.C.A.), 3, 18
American Historical Review, 20
American Magic, The (Lewin), 221–223
Ampex, 35
Armed Forces of the Pacific, The (Puleston), 254
Armed Forces Security Agency (A.F.S.A.), 34, 176
Army and Navy Basic War Plan Rainbow, 5, 255
Arnim, Hans-Jürgen von, 235
Arnold, Benedict, 41–42
Arnold, H. H. ("Hap"), 268
Ars inventiva veritatis (Lull), 59
Art of Love (Ovid), 51
ASCHE (Hans-Thilo Schmidt), 79, 80–83, 85, 86, 87, 88, 213
A.T.&T. (American Telephone and Telegraph), 206
Atlantic, Battle of the, 45, 119, 186, 212, 220
Atlantic Conference (1941), 258, 270
Atlantic Wall defenses, 109, 290
Atomic Energy Act, 207
attachés, military and naval, 258–259
"Au Service du Chiffre: 18 ans de souvenirs, 1907–1925" (Givierge), 287

backroom boys, 36, 89
Baltic states, 250
bank transactions, 197, 205, 206
Bartlett, Fred, 69
Bazeries, Etienne, 125
"Bazeries cylinder," 126
Bazna, Elyesa (CICERO), 29, 44, 76, 88
Beesly, Patrick, 91, 93, 97, 286
Bennett, Ralph, 288
Beobachtungs-Dienst, 15, 16, 105–106, 111, 116, 117
Bertrand, Gustave, 76–77, 79, 81, 82, 85, 86, 213
binary digits (bits), 38, 171
bisected plaintexts, 151, 159
Biuro Szyfrów, 84, 213
black chambers, 41, 64, 187, 281, 283, 284
BLACK code, 39, 83
Blackstone, William, 42
Blair, Clay, 289
Bletchley Park, England, intelligence center at, 33, 90, 91, 92, 93, 95, 110–111, 112, 115, 116, 117, 213, 218, 288
Blonde Countess, The (Yardley), 66
Bobbs-Merrill Company, 72, 73
Bodyguard of Lies (Brown), 290
bomba machine, 110, 111
Bonatz, Heinz, 97, 98
book code, 41–42
Booth, Merritt B., 258
Bozart, James, 147
Bradley, Omar, 33, 113
breeder keys, 154, 158
"Brief Periodic Estimate for the World Situation" (1941), 270
Britain, Battle of, 45, 92, 110, 211, 212, 220
British Intelligence in the Second World War (Hinsley), 288, 290
Bronshtain, David, 36
Brown, Anthony Cave, 290
Browne, Thomas, 138

Buck, F. J., 55
Bulge, Battle of the, 218
Bullitt, William C., 257, 268
Buntrock, Georg, 233, 234, 235, 237, 243, 246, 247
Bussey, Donald, 92, 93
Bye, George T., 70, 74
Byers, Mortimer W., 148

*Cabinet noir, Le* (Vaillé), 282
Caesar, Gaius Julius, 40–41
Calvocoressi, Peter, 90, 92, 93, 95, 97
Canada, military intelligence in, 69–70
Canaris, Wilhelm, 238
Cape Matapan, Battle of, 211
Carter, Jimmy, 184, 188, 190, 194, 208, 293
Castro, Fidel, 139, 143, 144
CATO, 76
Central Intelligence Agency (C.I.A.), 34, 38, 47, 281
  national security and, 176–177, 178, 182, 183, 185, 190, 193
chain addition, 154, 157, 158
Champollion, Jean François, 20
Ché Guevara Cipher, 139–145
Chiang Kai-Shek, 67, 272
*Chiffer* (Sandler), 5
Chiffrierabteilung, 105, 115
Chiffrierstelle, 80
Childs, J. Rives, 22
China, military intelligence in, 67–68, 251, 252, 259, 272, 284
Church, Frank, 176, 178
Churchill, Sir Winston:
  Roosevelt and, 37, 104, 109, 258, 270
  ULTRA as important to, 91, 92, 96, 110–111, 112, 211, 212, 218, 220
CICERO (Elyesa Bazna), 29, 44, 76, 88
Ciezki, Maksymilian, 85
"cipher," 123, 124
"cipher brains," 36, 38
Cipher Bureau, 63, 64–65, 71, 73, 74, 187
Cipher Center, 12
cipher clerks, 4, 28, 47, 103, 116
cipher machines:
  history of, 26, 51–52, 55, 57–61, 127
  recent developments in, 168, 177, 190, 192, 196, 200, 209, 293, 295
  in World War II, 34, 35, 40, 47, 103, 113–114, 117, 182
  *See also specific machines*
ciphers. *See individual ciphers*
"ciphony," 129
citizen's band radios, 199
Clark, Mark, 33
Clark, Ronald, 214–215
Clausewitz, Karl von, 116, 222
"clear language" messages, 26, 36
Cochran, Alexander S., 289
"code," 123, 124
*Codebreakers, The* (Kahn), 10, 11, 204, 282, 284, 288
codebreaking. *See cryptology*
COLOSSUS computer, 37, 52, 112, 117, 213
columnar transpositions, 151, 158
COMINT (communications intelligence), 180, 190, 216, 292, 293, 294

*Commentaries on the Laws of England* (Blackstone), 42
complexity theory, 201
computers:
  COLOSSUS as prototype of, 37, 52, 112, 117, 213
  in cryptology, 35, 37, 40, 53, 55, 110, 148, 160, 168, 169, 213, 294
  national security and, 170–172, 182, 190, 191, 197, 208, 209
Comte, Auguste, 53
*Contribution of the Cryptographic Bureaus in the World War, The* (Gylden), 5, 10
"converter," 125–126
*Corpus Juris Secundum*, 136
*Correspondance Politique*, 283
*Cours de cryptographie* (Givierge), 9
Crankshaw, Edward, 95
Creasy, Edward S., 99
*Crows Are Black Everywhere* (Yardley and Grabo), 70
"cryptanalysis," 122, 123, 134, 138, 190
Crypto AG, 285
*Cryptogram, The* (Kahn), 10
"cryptograph," 135
"cryptographia," 137
"cryptography," 122, 123, 138, 189, 205
"cryptologia," 137, 138
cryptologists, conversations and interviews with, 3–17
cryptology, 123, 134, 138, 205
  aerial reconnaissance vs., 234, 235, 236, 237, 241–242, 245, 277, 293, 294
  computers used in, 35, 37, 40, 53, 55, 110, 148, 160, 168, 169, 213, 294
  espionage vs., 28–29, 40, 114, 146–164, 178–179, 216–218, 219, 227, 234, 238–239, 256, 284, 293
  historical development of, 20–21, 27, 51–55, 281–291
  national security and, 47–48, 167–169, 175, 189, 197, 198–200, 202, 205, 207, 209
  public debate on, 186–203, 205
  radio intelligence vs., 7, 11, 52, 90, 96, 97, 99, 104, 176, 181, 190–192, 229, 234, 242, 243, 246, 256, 260, 274, 293
  in Renaissance, 8, 27, 41, 52, 53, 54, 56, 57–61, 187–188, 198, 283, 284
  terminology of, 120–138
  in World War I, 92, 96, 97, 101–104, 216, 260, 284, 285–288
  in World War II, 18, 29, 32–34, 37, 39, 44–46, 89–98, 104–119, 260–264, 288–291
"cryptomenses," 137
*Cryptomenytices et cryptographiae* (Selenus), 137
Cuban missile crisis (1962), 168
cyclometer, 110
Czajaner (Polish cryptologist), 78, 79

Damm, Arvid, 5, 285
Damm, Ivar, 5
Data Encryption Standard (D.E.S.), 52, 170–172, 196–198, 209
Davida, George I., 199, 201, 202
D-Day invasion, 33, 45, 111, 219
Dechiffrierdienst, 100
"De cifris" (Alberti), 57
"decipher," 123

"decipherment," 123, 124
De natura rerum (Isidore), 60
Denning, Norman, 91, 212
Deutsch, Harold, 91
Dewey, Thomas E., 73
diagonal board, 110
Dictionary of United States Army Terms, 135
Diffie, Whitfield, 171, 172
diplomatic dispatches, 256–258
direction-finding, radio, 260, 292, 295
disks, cipher, 57–61, 127
disruption (D) areas, 151, 159
Dodd, Martha, 263
Dodd, William E., 257, 264, 265
Dönitz, Karl, 93, 105, 187
Donovan, William J., 70, 266
double transpositions, 159
Douglas, Alec, 97
Dreyfus, Alfred, 28
DUPONT mission, 216–217

ECM (electric code machine), 114
economic data intelligence, 295–296
Education of a Poker Player, The (Yardley), 71
Eisenhower, Dwight D., 119, 277, 278, 290, 293
electronic funds transfers, 197
Electronic Secure Voice Network, 194–195
Elements of Cryptanalysis (Friedman), 138
ELINT, 180, 292
embassies, intelligence gathering by, 31, 52, 54, 179–
    180, 193–194, 256–258, 275
Enigma cipher machine, 16, 52, 56, 187, 262, 285
    German use of, 36, 37, 40, 45, 103, 108, 113, 114–
        115, 118
    Polish solution of, 76–88, 90, 109–110, 213, 220, 257
    ULTRA intercepts of, 87, 89–98, 110–111, 112, 117, 119,
        211–213, 288, 289, 292
espionage, cryptology vs., 28–29, 40, 114, 146–164,
    178–179, 216–218, 219, 227, 234, 238–239, 256, 284,
    293
"Étude Historique sur la Section du Chiffre" (Gi-
    vierge), 286–287
Eyraud, Charles, 8–9, 10, 19

Fabyan, George, 138
Familiar Letters (Howell), 138
Federal Bureau of Investigation (F.B.I.), 147–148,
    160, 182, 262
Fellers, Bonner, 105
"ferrets," 180
FIAT Review of German Science, 6
field telephone conversations, 101–102, 104
Fifteen Decisive Battles of the World, The (Creasy),
    99
Figl, Andreas, 17
fingerprinting, radio, 260
Finland, Soviet conflict with, 250
Fleisher, Wilfred, 263
"Fleissner grille," 129
Flesch, Herbert, 11
Flowers, Thomas H., 112
Focke-Wulf FW-189 aircraft, 241
Foote, Alexander, 163
Ford, Gerald R., 46, 179, 184
Foreign Intelligence Surveillance Act (1978), 184

Forschungsamt, 11, 12, 80, 83, 115
France:
    in Enigma solution, 76–77, 79, 80–83
    military intelligence in, 9, 10, 28, 101, 103, 110,
        116, 117, 213, 257, 268, 285, 286–287
Franco, Francisco, 250
FRANKFURT cipher, 16
frequency distributions, 55, 160, 162, 215
Friedman, William F., 55, 69, 71, 121, 122, 138
    PURPLE machine solved by, 108, 214–215, 261, 289
Funk & Wagnalls New Standard Dictionary, 134, 135

G-2 division, 278
Gaffarel, Jacques, 138
Galland, Joseph S., 138
Galton, Francis, 54
G. & C. Merriam Company, 120, 121, 128
Garden of Cyrus (Browne), 138
Gardner, Erle Stanley, 63
Gato submarine, 180
Geheimschreiber cipher machine, 52, 111, 114
Gehlen, Reinhard, 14, 105
    in Osuga defense, 230, 237, 238, 239, 240, 244, 245
"general system," 126
German military units:
    9th Army, 232, 234, 235, 236, 240, 241, 242, 243, 246,
        248
    XXXIXth Panzer Corps, 235, 237, 243, 245, 246,
        247
    102nd Infantry Division, 235, 236, 237, 241, 242,
        243, 244, 245, 246, 247, 248
    Army Group B, 231, 239, 245
    Army Group Center, 230, 231, 232, 234, 236, 237,
        238, 239, 240, 241, 242, 245, 247, 248
    Foreign Armies East, 230, 231, 232, 233, 234, 237,
        238, 239, 242, 244, 248
Germany, Imperial, military intelligence in, 26,
    27, 39, 42, 96, 283
Germany, Nazi:
    Enigma machine used by, 36, 37, 40, 45, 103, 108,
        113, 114–115, 118
    military intelligence in, 6, 11–16, 21, 27, 37, 44,
        46, 56, 80–83, 87–98, 104–106, 111–112, 186, 198, 208,
        290
    as potential enemy of U.S., 249–250, 251–252, 254,
        255, 257, 259, 262, 263, 264–265, 266–271, 275
    Soviet Union attacked by, 227–248, 270, 271, 272,
        277
Givierge, Marcel, 9, 286–287
Glossary of Soviet Military Terminology, 135
Godt, Eberhard, 98
Goebbels, Josef, 87
Göring, Hermann, 80, 267
Gove, Philip B., 121, 128
Government Code and Cypher School, 110
Government Communications Headquarters, 38
Grabo, Carl, 70
Graham, Daniel O., 178, 184
GRAY code, 27
Great Britain:
    Bletchley Park operation of, 33, 90, 91, 92, 93,
        95, 110–111, 112, 115, 116, 117, 213, 218, 288
    military intelligence in, 27, 36–40, 44, 101–102,
        103, 105, 106, 113, 188, 202, 257–258, 262, 282, 283,
        286, 290–291

Great Britain—*Continued*
ULTRA intercepts by, 87, 89–98, 110–111, 112, 117,
119, 186, 211–213, 288, 289, 292
*See also individual leaders*
Greater East Asian Co-Prosperity Sphere, 252
GREENUP team, 217
Grew, Joseph C., 256, 274
Guderian, Heinz, 87
Guevara, Ernesto ("Ché"), cipher used by, 139–145
Gyldén, Yves, 4–6, 10

Hackenberg, Edna Ramsaier, 68, 69, 70
Hagelin, Boris C. W., 285
Hagelin cipher machine, 8, 56, 126, 285
Hahn, Emily, 68
Halder, Franz, 119, 231, 244, 293
HAMMER group, 217
Harris, Barbara, 139, 140
Harsch, Joseph C., 263
Hay, Malcolm, 286
Hayhanen, Reino (VIC), 147, 148–149, 158, 160, 161,
164
Hebern, Edward H., 20, 208, 285
Hellman, Martin E., 171, 172, 209
Hepp, Leo, 94, 96, 98
Hermes Trismesgistus, 20–21
hieroglyphs, decipherment of, 20, 26
Hillgarth, J. N., 60
Hillgruber, Andreas, 94, 95
"Hill system," 129
Hindenberg, Paul von, 100
Hinsley, F. H., 288, 290
*Historical and Analytical Bibliography of the Litera-
ture of Cryptology, An* (Galland), 138
Hitler, Adolf, 12, 33, 44, 186, 187, 290
in defense of Osuga, 229, 232, 244
military intelligence on, 80, 87, 93, 105, 106, 108–
109, 112, 115, 117, 212, 215, 218, 219
as potential enemy of U.S., 250, 266, 267, 270,
271, 275, 276
*Hitler's Spies: German Military Intelligence in World
War II* (Kahn), 204, 288, 290
Hitt, Parker, 66
Hoffmann, Karl-Otto, 96
Hoffmann, Max, 100, 101
Hollerith, Herman, 52
Hollerith tabulators, 103, 106
HOLYSTONE program, 180
Hoover, Herbert, 65
Hopkins, Harry, 275
"horizon" astrolabe, 58
Hotsumi, Ozaki, 76, 88
Hottelet, Richard C., 263
Howard, Michael, 218, 220
Howell, James, 138
Hughes, Charles Evans, 73
Hull, Cordell, 251, 264, 274
Huston, Tom C., 175
HW-28 cipher machine, 47, 168
HYDRA cipher net, 111

IBYTA code, 77
*Index of Coincidence, The* (Friedman), 55
indicator groups, 163
Inman, Bobby, 200–201, 202, 207

Institute of Electrical and Electronics Engineers
(I.E.E.E.), 199–200
*Intercepta*, 283
International Business Machines (I.B.M.), 196, 206
International Traffic in Arms Regulations
(I.T.A.R.), 200, 201, 207
Isidore, Bishop of Seville, 60
Italy, military intelligence in, 37–38, 39, 101, 103,
104, 262, 290
*Izvestia*, 247

J-19 system, 215, 262
Jäckel, Eberhard, 91, 93
Jacobsen, Hans-Adolf, 92, 93, 96
James, Daniel, 143, 144
Jansky, Donald, 195
Japan, Imperial:
in Battle of Midway, 19, 25–26, 32, 107, 221, 223,
292
military intelligence in, 20, 27, 46, 64–68, 72, 73,
74, 106–109, 157, 198, 212–213, 221–223, 238, 290
in Pearl Harbor attack, 34, 46, 106, 107, 108, 214,
249, 255, 271, 272, 273, 275, 276, 277, 278
as potential enemy of U.S., 249–250, 251, 252–255,
257, 258–259, 261–262, 263–264, 265, 269, 271–278
PURPLE machine of, 56, 108, 114, 186–187, 214–215,
220, 222, 262, 285, 289
"Japanese Diplomatic Secrets," 65, 66
writing of, 72–75
Jefferson, Thomas, 208
Jews, in intelligence work, 117, 118
JN25b code, 106, 107, 221
Jodl, Alfred, 232
Johnson, Lyndon B., 175
Johnson, U. Alexis, 183
Joint Army-Navy Board, 266
Joint Intelligence Committee, 266
Jones, R. V., 92
Joos, Martin, cryptological terms defined by, 121,
122, 123, 125, 128–129, 130
*Journal für die reine und angewandte Mathematik*, 6
*Journal of Semitic Studies*, 21
Jukes, Geoffrey, 94–95

Käärik, Kaljo, 4, 5
kabbalah, codes in, 53, 60–61
Kant, Immanuel, 294
kata kana transpositions, 68
Katz, Amrom, 294
Kauders, Fritz (MAX), 238–239, 242
Kennedy, Joseph P., 257, 268
keys, cipher, 43, 44, 47, 55, 57, 124, 171
in Ché Guevara Cipher, 139, 141
in Enigma machine, 83, 110, 114–115
in Soviet spy messages, 149, 151, 154, 159, 162, 163
K.G.B., 148
Kirk, Alexander C., 257
Klooz, Marie Stuart, 73, 74, 75
Kluge, Günther von, 112
Knox, Dillwyn, 36, 37, 110
Koukol, Bee, 66, 67
Koukol, Clem, 66, 67
Krebs, Hans, 232, 234, 247
Kruh, Lou, 10
Kupfer, Max, 15

Kurganov (Russian deserter), 237, 241
KW-7 cipher machine, 47

Lange, Friedrich, 235, 237, 242
Langen, Henry E., 3
Langer, Gwido, 85
LDX (long-distance Xerox) room, 173
Lemoine (Richard Stallman), 81, 82, 87–88
Leonard, Michael G., 148
letter frequency, 41
Levine, Jack, 6
Lewin, Ronald, ULTRA research by, 93, 94, 96, 97, 216, 218–220, 221–223, 288
*Liberty*, U.S.S., 35, 180, 188
Lindbergh, Charles A., 264, 267–268
Lisicki, Tadeusz, 90
Liss, Ulrich, 105
Locard, Edmond, 16–17
Lochner, Louis, 263
Lodge, Henry Cabot, 45
"Lone Accordian, The," 157
LUCY Communist spy ring, 95
Ludendorff, Erich, 100
Luftwaffe, 267–269, 276
Lull, Ramon, 58–60, 61
Luttichau, Charles von, 96

Macmillan Company, 72, 73
*Maddox*, U.S.S., 188
*Magdeburg* cruiser, 39
MAGIC *Diplomatic Summaries, The* (Cochran), 289
MAGIC intercepts:
  research on, 221–223, 289, 290
  strategic importance of, 262–263, 265, 266, 271, 275
Manly, John M., 21, 65
*Manuale di Crittografia* (Sacco), 7, 17
*Manual for the Solution of Military Ciphers* (Hitt), 66
*Man Who Broke Purple, The* (Clark), 214–215
Marchant, Herbert, 91–92, 97
MARK (Rudolf Ivanovich Abel), 31, 146, 148, 161, 162, 164
Maroney, Kevin, 148
Marshall, George C., 25, 33, 96, 187, 293
  military intelligence as viewed by, 107, 109, 119, 215, 220, 254, 268, 273
Martin, William H., 25, 27, 30, 188, 198
Martini, Wolfgang, 96
Mary, Queen of Scots, 282
Mata Hari, 101
*Mathematical and Mechanical Methods in Ciphering and Deciphering* (Rohrbach), 6
Mauborgne, Joseph O., 42, 44, 69, 70
MAX (Fritz Kauders), 238–239, 242
Meckel, Hans, 97–98
Mendelsohn, Charles J., 56, 61
Menzies, Stewart, 95
*Mercury, or the Secret and Swift Messenger* (Wilkins), 137
Messerschmidt Me-109 aircraft, 267, 268
Meyer, J. A., 199
MI-8 section, 63, 64, 71
microprocessors, 201, 208, 295
microwave transmission, 191, 206
Mid-Pacific Strategic Direction-Finder Net, 261
Midway, Battle of, 19, 25–26, 32, 107, 221, 223, 292

Miles, Nelson, 265
Miles, Sherman, 265, 273, 275
Military Intelligence Division (M.I.D.), 265, 266, 269, 270, 273, 275
missile telemetry, 296
Mitchell, Bernon F., 25, 27, 30, 188, 198
Model, Walter, 232, 234, 246
modulo 10 system, 142, 157
Mondale, Walter F., 178
monoalphabetic substitution, 57, 159, 163
monome-dinome table, 141, 150, 154, 158
Montgomery, B. L., 105, 211
Mowrer, Edgar Ansel, 263
Moynihan, Daniel P., 191, 194
Müller, Helmut, 13
Munitions List, U.S., 200
Musset, Alfred de, 125
*Myth of England and Its Hieroglyphs in European Tradition, The* 20

National Bureau of Standards, 52, 170, 171, 196, 197, 209
National Foreign Intelligence Board, 177, 179
National Security Agency (N.S.A.), 29–30, 171
  national security and, 167–168, 170, 171, 172, 188, 194, 196, 197, 198, 199, 200, 202, 207, 208, 209
  operation of, 34–36, 37, 40, 45–46, 47–48, 173–185, 281, 288, 290, 293, 294, 296
National Security Council, 47
National Telecommunications Protection Policy directive, 194
*Natural Magic* (Porta), 284
naval intelligence, 16, 32, 39, 91, 105, 106–107, 117, 211, 253, 274, 276
  on U-boats, 15, 45, 93, 97, 111, 186, 212, 220, 250, 270, 286, 287
Nebel, Fritz, 11–12, 15
Neeb, Fritz, 14
*New English Dictionary on Historical Principles* (N.E.D.), 134, 137, 138
Newman, Max H. A., 112
*Newsday*, 18
newspaper correspondents, intelligence gathering by, 263–264, 267
*New Standard Dictionary of the English Language*, 134, 135
New York Public Library, 19
*New York Times, The*, 66, 120, 167, 168, 169, 266
*New York Times Book Review, The*, 62
*New York Times Index, The*, 264
*New York Times Magazine, The*, 18
Nicolai, Carl R., 199
"nihilist cipher," 126
Nimitz, Chester, 107
Nisbet, Robert, 53
Nixon, Richard M., 175
"nongovernmental cryptology," 205
*Nuit de décembre* (Musset), 125

Oakley, Howard T., 135
Office of Naval Intelligence (O.N.I.), 265, 266, 270
Office of Strategic Services (OSS), 39, 216–218, 266
one-time pads, 31, 44, 45, 47, 56, 129–130, 139, 190
  for Soviet spy messages, 161–164
OP-20-G intelligence unit, 260–261, 262, 274
Osborne, Herbert (Herbert O. Yardley), 67

Oshima, Hiroshi, 108, 109, 215
Osuga, Russia, German defense of, 227–248
OVERLORD invasion, 16
Ovid, 51
Oxford *New English Dictionary* (N.E.D.), 134, 137, 138

Painvin, Georges-Jean, 36, 287
Pale, Erkki, 95, 98
paper tape, punched, 31
Patton, George S., Jr., 33
Pearl Harbor attack, 34, 46, 106, 107, 108, 214
  military intelligence and, 249, 255, 271, 272, 273, 275, 276, 277, 278
Pearson, Karl, 54
Pearson, Lester, 69, 70
Pentagon Papers, secret codes in, 167–169
"period key," 126
perlustration, 284
*Perpetual Peace* (Kant), 294
Perrin, Robert G., 53
Persico, Joseph E., 216–218
Pers Z, 115
"phaserphone" voice scrambler, 199
Phelippes, Thomas, 282
Phillips, William, 256, 264, 265
*Piercing the Reich* (Persico), 216–218
plaintext:
  examples of, 4, 55, 56, 57, 139, 168, 169, 182, 192
  in Soviet spy messages, 151, 158, 163
Platzeck, Erhard Wolfram, 60, 61
"Playfair cipher," 127
Poe, Edgar Allan, 30, 31, 40
Pogue, Forrest, 96
Poland, ENIGMA machine solved by, 76–88, 90, 109–110, 213, 220, 257
polyalphabetic substitution, 51, 54, 77, 126, 127
  origin of, 56–61
Porta, Giovanni Battista, 284
Powers, Francis Gary, 30, 35
Pratt, Fletcher, 253–254, 273
*Précis de cryptographie* (Eyraud), 8
*Primato Italiano, Un* (Sacco), 7
Pring-Mill, Robert, 60, 61
*Progressive*, 207
public-key cryptography, 198, 200, 202, 205, 208
Pudkewitz, Boris, 237
*Pueblo*, U.S.S., 35, 181, 188
Puleston, W. D., 254, 273
punched-card collating machines, 52, 103
PURPLE cipher machine, 56, 114, 186–187, 220, 262, 285
  Friedman's solution of, 108, 214–215, 261, 289

Quinn, William, 92

radar emissions, 34, 93, 180, 211, 292
radio intelligence, cryptology vs., 7, 11, 52, 90, 96, 97, 99, 104, 176, 181, 190–192, 229, 234, 242, 243, 246, 256, 260, 274, 293
radios, 199, 260
"rail-fence cipher," 126–127
rationalization process, 53
R.C.I. (research-communications intelligence) officers, 182–183
Reagan, Ronald, 184

reconnaissance airplanes, 180
"Reconsideration of the Origins of the Conference on the Limitation of Armament, A" (Klooz), 74
Record Group 457, 288–289
*Red Sun of Nippon, The* (Yardley), 66
Rejewski, Marian, 83–87, 213
*Rendezvous*, 66
Ribbentrop, Joachim von, 275
Robinson, Gilbert, 69
Rockefeller commission (1975), 190
*Roget's International Thesaurus*, 135
Rohrbach, Hans, 6–7, 10, 18
Rohwer, Jürgen, 89, 90–91, 97
Rommel, Erwin, 105, 211, 244
Ronge, Max, 288
Room 40, 92, 102, 286
*Room 40: British Naval Intelligence 1914–18* (Beesly), 286
Roosevelt, Eleanor, 70
Roosevelt, Franklin D.:
  Churchill and, 37, 104, 109, 258, 270
  military intelligence as important to, 218, 251, 252, 255, 256, 257, 262, 263, 266, 268
Rossignol, Antoine, 282
Rössler, Rudolf, 95
Rozycki, Jerzy, 84, 213
"running key," 125
Russia, Czarist, military intelligence in, 26, 39, 42, 283

Sacco, Luigi, 7, 17, 19
Saintsbury, George, 138
Salewski, Michael, 93
SALT (Strategic Arms Limitation Talks), 178, 182, 183, 185
SALT II treaty, 188–189, 296
Sandler, Rickard, 5
Sartre, Jean-Paul, 8
satellites, surveillance, 35, 192, 216, 294
Satzbuch codes, 27, 82
S-boxes, 196
Schauffler, Rudolf, 19
Scherbius, Arthur, 78, 103, 285
Schlesinger, James R., 175, 179
Schmidt, Hans-Thilo (ASCHE), 79, 80–83, 85, 86, 87, 88, 213
Schmidt, Rudolf, 79–80, 83, 87
Schröder, Georg, 13, 113
Scowcraft, Brent, 46
scramblers, telephone, 37, 52, 104, 127, 194–195, 199
*Sea Power and Today's War* (Pratt), 253–254
Sebree, E. M., 264
secrecy orders, 199, 205, 206
Section D (Décryptements et Interceptions), 77, 79, 286–287
*Sefer Yezirah*, 60–61
Segerdahl, Carl-Otto, 19
Seifert, Walter, 12–13, 16
Selenus, Gustavus, 137
"semaeologia," 137
sequential numbers, 154, 158
Service de Renseignements, 77, 79, 81, 82
Sevastopol, Battle of, 104
SHAMROCK operation, 175
Shannon, Claude, 208–209

Shirer, William L., 263
Sicherheitsdienst (SD), 115
SIGABA cipher machine, 114, 118, 126
SIGINT (signal intelligence), 101, 119, 177, 189, 190
  recent developments in, 292–296
Signal Corps, 71
Signal Intelligence Service (S.I.S.), 261, 262
signal security, 189–190
Six-Day War, 35, 180, 188
Slessor, John, 212
Smith, Truman, 266–267, 268
Sorge, Richard, 44, 76, 88, 163
Soro, Giovanni, 283
Soviet Union, 26, 39, 42, 283
  German offensives against, 227–248, 270, 271, 272, 277
  military intelligence in, 14, 30, 31, 32, 36, 44, 46, 95, 96, 104, 173, 178–183, 188, 190–193, 205, 296
  spy ciphers used by, 146–164
  U.S. relations with, 146, 148, 250–251
Special Project Office, 195
"specific key," 126
"spoof," 180, 292
Stalin, Josef, 239, 245
"Stalin organ," 236
Stallman, Richard (Lemoine), 81, 82, 87–88
Stark, Harold L., 254, 255, 268
Statistisches Jahrbuch für das Deutsche Reich, 163
stereotyped messages, 115
Stimson, Henry L., 65, 187, 251, 270
"stradding," 159
STRETCH computer, 38
Struggle for Europe, The (Wilmot), 218
substitution ciphers, 26, 56, 57, 77–78, 109, 215
  in Soviet spy messages, 149, 151, 158
Systeme des Chiffrierens (Figl), 17

Tai Li, 67, 68
Tannenberg, Battle of, 26, 101
TATE, 88
Taylor, John, 216, 217
technical data, restricted, 200, 207
telegraph, 285
telephone eavesdropping, 190–195
Third World countries, cipher machines in, 209, 295
Thomas, Edward, 92, 93, 94, 95–96, 97
Thorndike, Lynn, 59
TICOM reports, 290
Time, 124, 128
Tojo, Hideki, 108, 252, 253
Tolischus, Otto, 263
traffic analysis, 260, 292, 295
Tranow, Wilhelm, 15–16
transposition ciphers, 26, 29, 56, 69, 77, 84, 109
  in Soviet spy messages, 149, 151, 154–159
Trithemius, Johannes, 53–54
TRITON cipher net, 111
Truman, Harry S., 176, 178, 185
Tuchman, Barbara, 22
Turing, Alan, 37, 110, 117
Typex cipher machine, 114

U-2 plane incident, 30, 35
U-boat intelligence, 15, 45, 220, 250, 270, 286, 287
  ULTRA intercepts of, 93, 97, 111, 186, 212

Ultra Goes to War (Lewin), 216, 218–220, 221, 288
ULTRA intercepts:
  conference on, 89–98, 186
  strategic importance of, 87, 110–111, 112, 117, 119, 186, 211–213, 288, 289, 292
Ultra in the West (Bennett), 288
Ultra Secret, The (Winterbotham), 89, 211–213, 218
unbreakable cipher, 42–44
United States:
  in Battle of Midway, 19, 25–26, 32, 107, 221, 223, 292
  MAGIC intercepts by, 221–223, 262–263, 265, 266, 271, 275, 289, 290
  military intelligence in, 26, 29–30, 34–36, 37, 38, 41–48, 63–65, 71–74, 103, 105–107, 116, 118, 255–266
  in Pearl Harbor attack, 34, 46, 106, 107, 108, 214, 249, 255, 271, 272, 273, 275, 276, 277, 278
  PURPLE intercepts by, 56, 108, 114, 186–187, 214–215, 220, 222, 261, 262, 285, 289
  Soviet relations with, 146, 148, 250–251
United States Air Force Dictionary, The, 135
United States Intelligence Board, 177, 179
Universalschlüssel cipher, 77
Urn-Burial (Browne), 138

Vaillé, Eugène, 282, 283
VIC (Reino Hayhanen), 147, 148–149, 158, 160, 161, 164
VIC cipher, 146–161, 164
Viète, François, 27, 283–284
Vigenère, Blaise de, 61
"Vigenère cipher," 127
Voltaire, 27
volvelles, 60
V-weapons, 186

Wallis, John, 282, 283
Walsingham, Francis, 282
"War Department Strategic Estimate" (1941), 271
Washington Disarmament Conference (1921–1922), 64, 72, 73, 74, 75
Washington Post, 167
watch lists, 174, 175
Webb, Frederick E., 161
Weber, Max, 53
Webster's Second International, cryptological terms in, 120, 122, 123, 124
Webster's Third International, cryptological terms in, 120–133, 134
Weinberg, Gerhard, 94
Welchman, Gordon, 110, 117
Welles, Sumner, 269
Werther, Waldemar, 95, 96
"Wheatstone cipher," 129
White, Theodore H., 68
Wiegand, Karl von, 263
Wilkins, John, 137
Wilkinson, Theodore S., 265
Wilmot, Chester, 218
Wilson, Hugh, 257
Wilson, Woodrow, 26
"window of accessibility," 295
Winterbotham, Frederick W., ULTRA research by, 89, 93, 211–213, 218, 219, 220, 292

*Words and Phrases*, 136
World War I:
  codes used in, 22, 26, 27, 39, 42, 102, 107
  cryptology in, 92, 96, 97, 101–104, 216, 260, 284,
    285–288
World War II:
  cipher machines in, 34, 35, 40, 47, 103, 113–114,
    117, 182
  codes used in, 32–34, 37, 39, 44–46, 198
  cryptology in, 18, 29, 32–34, 37, 39, 44–46, 89–98,
    104–119, 260–264, 288–291
  as viewed by cryptologists, 6, 9, 10, 11–16
Wright, Wesley A., 19
Wynn-Williams, C. E., 117

Yamamoto, Isoroku, assassination of, 32–33, 106, 107,
  108, 215, 221, 223, 292
Yardley, Herbert O., 3, 21, 29
  biographical sketch of, 62–71
  "lost" manuscript of, 72–75
*Yardleygrams* (Yardley), 66
Yom Kippur War, 183

Zeitzler, Kurt, 244
Zhukov, Georgi K., 245
Ziemke, Earl F., 227
Zimmermann, Arthur, 102
Zimmermann telegram, 22, 26, 102, 107
*Zimmermann Telegram, The* (Tuchman), 22
Zygalski, Henryk, 84, 213

# Note About the Author

David Kahn was born on February 7, 1930, in New York City and was raised in its suburb of Great Neck, New York. Codes and ciphers have been his hobby since, at thirteen, he read Fletcher Pratt's *Secret and Urgent*, a history of cryptology. Mr. Kahn joined the American Cryptogram Association and later the New York Cipher Society, eventually becoming president of both. He received a B.A. in social science from Bucknell University in 1951. From 1955, he worked as a reporter for *Newsday*, the Long Island daily. In 1960, upon the defection of two Americans from the National Security Agency, the United States cryptologic unit, he wrote an article on cryptology for *The New York Times Magazine* that led to an invitation to write a book on the subject. Mr. Kahn quit *Newsday* in 1963 to work full-time on the book and, in 1965, with it almost completed, moved to Paris, where he worked on the *New York Herald Tribune* (Paris edition). In 1967 he returned to New York for the publication of *The Codebreakers: The Story of Secret Writing*. The following year he began research for a book on German military intelligence in World War II, learning German to do this properly. He lived for a year in Freiburg-im-Breisgau, reading documents in the military archives there and traveling about Germany to interview former producers and users of military intelligence. After two years in New York, he moved in 1972 to England, where, two years later, he earned a doctorate of philosophy in modern history from Oxford University. *Hitler's Spies: German Military Intelligence in World War II* was published in 1978. From 1975 to 1979 Mr. Kahn taught journalism at New York University, after which he returned to *Newsday* as an editor. He has continued to write articles on cryptology for a great variety of publications and is a founder and co-editor of the scholarly quarterly in the field, *Cryptologia*. Mr. Kahn married the former Susanne Fiedler of Vienna, Austria, in 1969; they live with their sons, Oliver and Michael, in Great Neck.